Natural Law and Domestic Government in the Early Modern Period

# Legal History Library



VOLUME 80

The titles published in this series are listed at *brill.com/lhl*

# Natural Law and Domestic Government in the Early Modern Period

*Edited by*

Wouter Druwé, Randall Lesaffer and Geert Sluijs

BRILL | NIJHOFF

LEIDEN | BOSTON

Cover illustration: Theodoor van Thulden, *Allegory of Justice and Peace*, date unknown. Available in the public domain.

Library of Congress Cataloging-in-Publication Data

Names: Druwé, Wouter editor | Lesaffer, Randall editor | Sluijs, Geert editor
Title: Natural law and domestic government in the early modern period / edited by Wouter Druwé, Randall Lesaffer, and Geert Sluijs.
Description: Leiden ; Boston : Brill Academic Publishers, Inc, 2026. | Series: Legal History Library ; volume 80 | Includes bibliographical references and index.
Identifiers: LCCN 2025038217 | ISBN 9789004748705 hardback | ISBN 9789004748712 epub
Subjects: LCSH: Natural law--History | Natural law--Early works to 1800 | Natural law--Philosophy | LCGFT: Law materials
Classification: LCC K415 .N35 2026 | DDC 340/.112--dc23/eng/20250815
LC record available at https://lccn.loc.gov/2025038217

Typeface for the Latin, Greek, and Cyrillic scripts: "Brill". See and download: brill.com/brill-typeface.

ISSN 1874-1793
ISBN 978-90-04-74870-5 (hardback)
ISBN 978-90-04-74871-2 (e-book)
DOI 10.1163/9789004748712

# Contents

Notes on Contributors VII

Introduction 1
*Wouter Druwé, Randall Lesaffer and Geert Sluijs*

**PART 1**
*Sixteenth Century*

1 Bodin, Natural Law, and Statecraft in the French Renaissance Monarchy 13
*Marie Seong-Hak Kim*

2 The Mutability of Nature: Dominion, Natural Law, and the Order of Grace in Domingo de Soto's *de iustitia et iure* (1553–1554) 40
*Rafael Cronje Mateus*

3 Association and Corporation in Early Modern Jurisprudence 57
*Jeffrey Dymond*

**PART 2**
*Early Seventeenth Century*

4 *Fides* and *feudum* in the Legal Thought of Petrus Gudelinus (1550–1619): A Study on Feudal, Civil, and Natural Obligations in the Early Modern Age 83
*Pedro R.S. Santos*

5 Stewardship and Statesmanship: Justus Lipsius and Diodorus Tuldenus on the Natural Law of Government in the Early Modern Low Countries 111
*Geert Sluijs*

6 Natural Law and Governance of the State in Henning Arnisaeus 144
*Paolo Astorri and Lars Cyril Nørgaard*

7 Edward Coke's Ciceronian Common Law 161
*Rosalind Acland*

**PART 3**
*After 1650*

8 The Concept of Natural Law in Thomas Hobbes's Theory of Sovereignty 195
*Carlos Pérez-Crespo*

9 'A Title to Another's Plenty': Rights of Charity in Locke's Political Thought 217
*Signy Gutnick Allen*

10 New World, Immemorial Possession: Commons and Private *dominium* in Portuguese America (Camamu, Seventeenth to Eighteenth Centuries) 238
*Sarah Limão Papa*

Postface: When God Went AWOL – Natural Law in Early-Modern Discussions on Domestic Governance 263
*Alain Wijffels*

Index 281

# Notes on Contributors

*Wouter Druwé*
is an associate professor of Roman Law and Legal History at KU Leuven. He studied law (Ph.D. 2018), canon law (J.C.L. 2018) and theology (B.A. 2013) at the same institution. He studies the interaction between late medieval and early modern learned law (*ius commune*) and legal practice, with a particular focus on the Low Countries. Recent publications concern the literary genre of *consilia* and *decisiones*, as well as the history of the law of loans and credit, of testamentary succession, and of legal education.

*Randall Lesaffer*
(Bruges, 1968) is professor of Legal History at KU Leuven as well as Tilburg University. From 2008 to 2012, he served as dean of Tilburg Law School and is founding co-president of the Law Schools' Global League. His research focuses on the history of international law in early modern Europe. He is general editor of *The Cambridge History of International Law and the Brill/Nijhoff* and the book series Studies in the History of International Law. He is also an editor of the *Journal of the History of international Law* and the book series Global Law. He is the author of, among others, *European Legal History: A Cultural and Political Perspective* (2009) and *De rechtstaat: Een geschiedenis van het Westen* (2024).

*Geert Sluijs*
is an FWO (Research Foundation Flanders)-funded Ph.D. candidate in Legal History at KU Leuven's Faculty of Law. He holds degrees in Law and Philosophy from KU Leuven, and Political Thought and Intellectual History from the University of Cambridge. His current research interests include natural law thinking, legal methodology and public law in early modern Europe. He has published articles on the thought of the Leuven scholar Diodorus Tuldenus. He was awarded the Ius Commune Prize (2023) for his article "Jurisdiction and Its Attribution in the Works of Diodorus Tuldenus."

*Marie Seong-Hak Kim*
is a historian and jurist in Minneapolis, USA. Author of *Custom, Law, and Monarchy: A Legal History of Early Modern France* (OUP 2021), *Constitutional Transition and the Travail of Judges: The Courts of South Korea* (CUP 2019), *Law and Custom in Korea: Comparative Legal History* (CUP 2012), and *Michel de L'Hôpital: The Vision of a Reformist chancellor during the French Religious*

*Wars* (Sixteenth Century Essays and Studies 1997), and editor of *The Spirit of Korean Law: Korean Legal History in Context* (Brill 2016), she is also known for her works on Japanese colonialism and comparative law.

*Rafael Cronje Mateus*
is lawyer and researcher, holding a Master of Laws from the Federal University of Ceará (Brasil). His research explores the philosophical and theological ideas that form the intellectual foundations of legal institutions and practices, with a particular interest in the School of Salamanca and Portuguese political thought from the medieval and early modern periods. He has published articles on various topics, including the problem of the mutability of natural law, the concept of a debt of gratitude in relation to land donations and other key issues in the field of political theology.

*Jeffrey Dymond*
is a COLLEGE Lecturer at Stanford University. His research focuses on European intellectual and legal history from the medieval to the early modern periods. Articles on these subjects have appeared in the *Journal of the History of Ideas, The Historical Journal, Jus Cogens*, and several edited volumes on a range of themes in intellectual and legal history. He was previously a member of the European Research Council-funded project "The Just City," based on the University of Zürich.

*Pedro R.S. Santos*
is a doctoral researcher at KU Leuven (2020–ongoing) whose research focuses on the emergence and emancipation of public law in the Early Modern Age. His research explores this emergence from the works of the jurist Petrus Gudelinus (1550–1619) and its framing in the ius commune. He has also contributed as Latin editor to the School of Salamanca project at the Max Planck Institute for European Legal History in Frankfurt.

*Rosalind Acland*
is a Ph.D. candidate in English Legal History within the Faculty of Law at the University of Cambridge. She holds degrees in Classics (Hons) from the Universities of Newcastle and Sydney, a Juris Doctor (Distinction) from the University of New South Wales, and a Master of Law (First Class) from the University of Cambridge. She was a practicing solicitor in Australia prior to commencing her post-graduate studies. Her current research interests are early modern legal history, and the influence of classical scholarship on legal theory.

*Paolo Astorri*
(Ph.D.) is assistant professor of Legal History at the Centre for Privacy Studies, University of Copenhagen, Associate Scholar at *the Law and the Inner Self* project (University of Cork), and Co-PI of *Secrets to Patents* (University of Lund). His research explores intersections of law, religion and political thought in the early modern period. His book *Lutheran Theology and Contract Law in Early Modern Germany* (Brill) won the RefoRc Book Award (2020). His article "Can a Judge Rely on His Private Knowledge?" received the Van Caenegem Prize for best article in comparative legal history (2022).

*Lars Cyril Nørgaard*
is an associate professor at the Department of Church History, University of Copenhagen. He has been affiliated with the Center for Privacy Studies (DNRF 138) in Copenhagen and awarded with an international postdoctoral fellowship from the Independent Research Foundation Denmark. His research interests the tensions between religious seclusion and societal engagement, the relationship between manuscript, text, print, paratext and image, and the interplay between early modern theology and political thinking. He has co-edited several volumes of collected essays, most recently with Michaël Green, *Notions of Privacy in Early Modern Correspondence* (Turnhout: Brepols, 2025).

*Carlos Pérez-Crespo*
is an assistant professor at the Pontifical Catholic University of Chile. He was previously an adjunct lecturer of political theory at the University of Hamburg and a visiting doctoral student at the University of Cambridge. He won the 2023 Charles Schmitt Prize of the International Association for Intellectual History. His work examines the political and constitutional theories of France and Germany and their reception in Spain and Latin America. He is currently researching the international reception of political theorists and ideologues of autocracies, particularly the work of the German jurist Carl Schmitt.

*Signy Gutnick Allen*
is a Post-Doctoral Fellow in the ERC-funded "Just City" research project hosted by the History Department, University of Zurich, where she works on early modern debates over justice, benevolence, and the role of the state. She has further research expertise in, and has published on, the state theory of Thomas Hobbes, the history of the philosophy of punishment, and the relationship between the history of political thought and contemporary political theory.

*Sarah Limão Papa*
is a certified Brazilian lawyer (LL.B. 2018, Federal University of Ceará; LL.M. 2020) and Ph.D. candidate in Law at Goethe-Universität Frankfurt am Main. She is a researcher at the ERC-funded IberLAND project at Leibniz Universität Hannover. She specializes in 17th- and 18th-century colonial Brazilian legal history, with work on colonial governance, family law and canon law. Her current research investigates conflicts over communal access to land and natural resources in Portuguese America, analyzing the interplay between religion, customs, public and civil law in agrarian disputes and their connections to European legal traditions.

*Alain Wijffels*
(Dr.jur. Amst.; Ph.D. Cantab.; D.Litt. Cantab.) is a retired teacher of legal history and comparative law. His current research focuses on the relationship between public governance and jurisprudence in late-medieval and early modern scholarship and practice. The central theme of his work is the understanding of legal science's original vocation as a science of the art of good public governance, both domestic and foreign. Governance of foreign affairs developed in the context of international relations and contributed therefore to the development of a law of nations, and thus to attempts at establishing an international governance.

# Introduction

*Wouter Druwé, Randall Lesaffer and Geert Sluijs*

## 1 Natural Law and Domestic Government

The early modern natural law tradition as received from Antiquity and the Middle Ages was in many senses a bridging paradigm. While natural law had been a significant subject of debate among late-medieval theologians, civilians and canonists, it gained a far more central role in legal theory and scholarship from the sixteenth century onwards, in the writings of theologians, jurists and political philosophers alike. As natural law discourse developed over its early modern lifespan, it increasingly started to acquire the trappings of a legal theory – underpinning concrete legal notions and offering a paradigm which could be applied to a variety of legal domains and facts. By the early seventeenth century, it had become a major vehicle for conceptions, principles and institutions of law, relating to both private transactions and public governance.

This emergence of natural law as legal theory coincided with the emergence of one legal field to which it would be readily applied: the sphere of the state or the domain of domestic public law. In another sense, it was precisely the growing autonomy and importance of public law and the need for a legal theory underpinning it (as the classic Roman law texts provided insufficient textual support and canon law lost its universality), which fed the rise of legal natural law thinking. This intimate link between natural law and the sphere of domestic governance is made manifest especially in the first modern theories of the polity, where the articulation of the idea of a state of nature is closely tied together with the Catholic notion of natural rights. It is around this link and its two components that this book revolves.

This volume is the result of a conference on natural law and domestic government, held in Leuven in April 2023, with the support of the Research Foundation – Flanders (FWO). It contains ten contributions and a concluding '*postface*'. The chapters, which largely follow a chronological order, deal with a variety of perspectives on the relation between natural law and domestic public law in early modern Europe, and beyond. They study Roman Catholic, Lutheran and Anglican jurists, political philosophers and theologians. They contain reconsiderations of the theories of well-known figures like Jean Bodin, Domingo de Soto, Thomas Hobbes and John Locke, but also studies on some

 | DOI:10.1163/9789004748712_002

lesser known but very remarkable authors like Petrus Gudelinus, Diodorus Tuldenus or Henning Arnisaeus.

## 2 The Sixteenth Century

In the first contribution to this volume, **Marie Seong-Hak Kim** offers a historical contextualization of the political ideas on sovereignty by the French author Jean Bodin (1530–1596). Bodin's thought seemed to contain a paradox, as he was a champion of both the French king's absolute sovereignty and a free citizen's natural right to property. According to Bodin, positive law, enacted by the king, must not transgress natural law, but at the same time, paradoxically, Bodin also emphasized the absolute sovereign nature of the king's power.

One of the key issues to understand this apparent paradox is the historical interdependence of public debt and sovereignty. The sovereign French king was in dire need of credit. Taxes, however, as Bodin posited, could not be imposed without the consent of the proprietors of the taxed property. Kim argues how – in historical practice – sovereignty and respect for property rights were reconciled, at least *de iure*. When, in 1561, the king forced the clergy to contribute substantially to the state's finances, the clergy's contribution – though *de facto* forced – was formulated *de iure* in contractual terms, in the famous *Contrat de Poissy*. Thus, the king had secured himself of the consent (though forced) of the clergy.

Kim also shows how the codification campaign of customary law impacted the legal basis for the protection of property rights of individuals and privileged parties. Whereas prior to the codification and homologation of customary law, which began in the latter half of the fifteenth century, many of those rights and privileges had been grounded in centuries-old customs, they now found their origin in a royal enactment (i.e. in positive law), and – to a certain extent – in natural law. Contrary to what was the case for the old customs, however, natural law did not prescribe concrete proceedings as to how to determine whether a prince's commands were in fact contrary to natural law. This left a much greater degree of discretion for the king. Thus, in practice, Bodin's introduction of natural law reasoning in sixteenth-century French political thought, rather than substantially limiting royal power, further strengthened the legal status of the sovereign.

A more philosophical and theological approach to natural law is taken by **Rafael Cronje Mateus** in his contribution on the mutability of natural law according to the Spanish moral theologian Domingo de Soto (1494–1560). Based on the works by Aristotle and Thomas Aquinas, Soto pondered to what extent a prince could alter natural law. Mateus explains how Soto – in the Thomistic tradition – made a distinction between the 'first principles' of natural law and its operationalization in so-called 'conclusions'. Whilst the 'first principles' were unchangeable, concrete 'conclusions' did depend on the specific circumstances of place and time.

When translated into political terms, this also led to the question as to whether the precepts of the Decalogue could be dispensed from. Soto compared the position of the prince to that of God. He explained that God exercised two types of *potestates*. The first type of power (*potestas*) was based on God's position as lord (*dominus*) of all creation. A second type of power was based on God's position as a legislator and judge. As a legislator and a judge, God could dispense from those precepts of the Decalogue which didn't have in themselves justice, but which only imposed a certain way of attaining it. One could think, for instance, of the obligation to observe the Sabbath, which was not justice in itself, but a way to attain justice. As Lord of all creation, however, God could change the nature of creation, and therefore change what is just without changing the nature of justice.

Mateus explains how Soto applied these theological ideas on God's two *potestates* to political theory on the power of the sovereign. The king, like God, was a judge and legislator. In that capacity, he could dispense from natural law, but only insofar as that specific natural law precept only set a way of attaining justice, rather than containing justice in itself. As lord (*dominus*) of the land, however, a king – like God – could sometimes even change the nature of things, and thus change what would be required by natural law in a particular situation. Nonetheless, the king's power was much more limited than God's power as Lord of all creation. The king's dominion did not derive directly from God, but had been transferred to him by the people. Contrary to God, the king did therefore not have dominion over the life of his subjects. If he acted as a tyrant, he could be deposed. Thus, Mateus shows how Soto's natural law theory allowed for a large, but not unlimited power of discretion of the king, and how – contrary to Bodin's conception – Soto did propose some procedural ways to enforce natural law.

Natural law did not only define a prince's power, but was also referred to as a foundation of the early modern state as a separate legal entity, as **Jeffrey Dymond** discusses in his contribution. In the medieval *ius commune*, a distinction was made between corporations (*universitates*) and partnerships (*societates*). According to late medieval legal doctrine, a *societas* did not have any legal personality whereas this was accepted to a certain extent for a *universi-*

*tas*. This legal fiction – still according to the medieval jurists – was either attributed to the *universitas* on the basis of an explicit concession by a higher authority, or by the *ius gentium*. Even in the *ius gentium*, however, medieval jurists still considered this fiction to ultimately derive from a concession by the emperor. Dymond argues that from the sixteenth century onwards, a fundamentally different theory of legal personality would have been developed on the basis of the concept of *societas*.

Inspiration for the attribution of legal personality to a *societas* was drawn from the works of Marcus Tullius Cicero. In his *De officiis*, the latter described how a magistrate should assume the 'mask' (*persona*) of his *civitas*, how he acted on behalf of his *civitas*. These Ciceronian ideas were cited by some Renaissance humanist authors, though – as aforementioned – not by late medieval jurists such as Bartolus de Saxoferrato or Baldus de Ubaldis. It was not before the mid-sixteenth century that jurists such as François Connan (1508–1551) and Hugues Doneau (1527–1591) introduced these Ciceronian and humanist ideas into legal doctrine as well. Connan and Doneau, law professors from Bourges, were convinced that human beings were by nature social beings, and that they by nature formed a type of social group that resembled a self-constituted *societas*. Across peoples, many different groups followed this model, the family (*familia*) being a primary example. These groups consisted of individuals with mutual obligations to attain and preserve a beneficial social life. They were led by one person, who outwardly represented his group. Thus, still according to Connan and Donellus, the group gradually became an entity capable of bearing its own rights and obligations.

In the early seventeenth century, these ideas by Connan and Doneau were taken up by the natural law theorist Johannes Althusius (1557–1638), who used them to develop his political theory on state formation. Dymond explains how Althusius described a state as an association (*consociatio*) of several smaller self-constituted entities (*societates*). This association was also led by one single head, the monarch, able to enforce the mutual obligations of the separate entities within his association, and at the same time assuming the role or 'mask' (*persona*) of this durable larger entity outwardly. This happened, for instance, in the context of the developing framework of the laws of war. Thus, by taking up this position as head, the monarch granted outward existence and permanence to the state; the state became a legal entity, based on a natural law foundation.

## 3 The Early Seventeenth Century

Within the public governance of the early modern state, one of the key components of natural law was undoubtedly the concept of faith (*fides*). Keeping faith was a duty under natural law, and also for feudal relations – so crucial to the early modern world – *fides* and *fidelitas* were crucial concepts. In his contribution, **Pedro Ricardo da Silva Santos** focuses on *fides* and *feudum* in the legal thought of the Leuven law professor Petrus Gudelinus (1550–1619).

According to Gudelinus, in the 'Golden Age' of humankind, i.e. in the state of nature, faith (*fides*) was self-evidently preserved in accordance with *ius gentium primarium*, without there being any need for mechanisms of enforcement. After the introduction of *dominium* and private property, and the human vices that went along with it, however, the obligation to observe faith (*fides*) arose, based on *ius gentium secundarium*. When medieval or early modern jurists used the term *fides*, they always referred to a public type of *fides*, based on Christian theological tenets. The same term *fides* – also in a public sense – played a fundamental role in feudal law as well; Gudelinus explained how a vassal was bound to fidelity (*fidelitas*) towards his feudal lord.

There were situations, however, in which two obligations to keep faith were mutually incompatible. In those cases, a hierarchy of obligations had to be established. Through several examples, Santos shows how Gudelinus tried to strike a delicate balance. On the one hand, a natural obligation of piety towards one's parents prevailed over the feudal obligation of a vassal towards his feudal lord. On the other hand, even in those cases, breaking the obligation towards the lord, though not reprehensible *in se*, could still imply the loss of status as a vassal. Even within the realm of natural law, some obligations were more stringent than others. If one's father had betrayed homeland (*patria*) or religion (*religio*), a son's natural obligation of piety towards his father was extinguished. His natural obligation of piety towards his homeland and religion should then prevail.

Finally, Santos explains how the natural law concept of *fides* had specific and concrete consequences for how to deal with rebels. Gudelinus stressed the importance of keeping faith even with rebels; natural law demanded that peace treaties be respected. Gudelinus even went a step further: sometimes, an unavoidable bad and shameful situation (*res mala et turpis*) had to be tolerated for the sake of public peace and tranquillity. It was a message so needed in the Low Countries, a society torn apart by civil war and religious conflict.

**Geert Sluijs** devotes attention to two other crucial intellectual figures from the early modern Low Countries: the philosopher Justus Lipsius (1547–1606) and the lawyer Diodorus Tuldenus (1594–1645). Both based their theories at least partly on Stoic thought, but their conclusions on the limits to a prince's power were at times contradictory. Lipsius did not think highly of the role of the law and of its practitioners, whereas Tuldenus was an active lawyer convinced of its significance for the art of statesmanship and state-building.

According to Lipsius, the prince was in principle bound to the laws (*legibus illigandus*), although Sluijs explains we should not take this to mean he conceived of substantive limits to the prince's power. Therefore, despite this lofty principle, Lipsius left quite some room for a prince to disregard precepts of natural law. In his opinion, even some degree of injustice (*iniustitia*) was tolerable if such was necessary in order to preserve himself or the body politic. Tuldenus took up the idea that the prince was bound to the laws, but went further than Lipsius, potentially influenced by Jean Bodin. A prince's oath to respect privileges and other positive laws – for instance at the occasion of a Joyous Entry – was – so Tuldenus – binding under natural law.

Their different conceptions of the prince's power also had important consequences for the potential of participatory government. Sluijs sets out how Lipsius emphasized the centrality of the prince's will and didn't allow for any delegation to a deliberative senate. A prince could ask for the advice and help of counsellors and ministers, but he always held ultimate responsibility for his decisions; there were no formal checks and balances. Tuldenus, however, did allow for some degree of active participation in and limitation of a prince's government. Thus, he stressed the role of the Estates-General as the people's representatives. It was the Estates-General that could appoint the magistrates who were responsible for controlling the body politic's finances. It goes without saying that control over public finances formed an important limit to the prince's sovereign power.

Natural law also played an important role in the development of political theory among Lutheran intellectuals. In their contribution, **Paolo Astorri and Lars Nørgaard** focus on the treatise *De jure majestatis* (1610) by Henning Arnisaeus (d. 1636), professor of medicine at the university of Helmstedt in the duchy of Brunswick-Lüneburg, and a key exponent of Aristotelian philosophy. Among Lutheran scholars, the relation between political philosophy and theology was highly contested at the time. Contrary to other famous Lutherans such as Philipp Melanchthon (1497–1560) and David Chyträus (1531–1600), Arnisaeus was in favour of a clear distinction between politics and theology. The Republic had to take care of the Church, certainly, but it did not have any role to play in securing piety. Specific guidelines for governance could not be derived from any theological theory on divine law.

According to Arnisaeus, divine law was partly known through Revelation, and partly impressed on human hearts by God, thus granting human beings the capacity to distinguish good from evil in line with *recta ratio*. As to the specific operationalization of divine and natural law, however, Arnisaeus pleaded for a minimalist approach. He did state that political authority had divine origins, that the prince was responsible before God and that divine law required kings to be virtuous – as that was what distinguished them from tyrants, thus setting some general limits upon the exercise of the king's power (*potestas*). Nonetheless, the specific translation of this virtuous attitude into policy could not be taken from divine law. Neither did divine law imply any coercive mechanisms. Arnisaeus was, for instance, unlike Domingo de Soto, not in favour of any natural-law basis for a right of resistance. To him, divine law was merely of an exhortative nature.

In English common law, as well, references to classical natural law abounded, as **Rosalind Acland** shows in her contribution on the Ciceronian influences on the famous English jurist Sir Edward Coke (1552–1634). Marcus Tullius Cicero's definition of law as the perfection of reason permeated Coke's work, both in his *Institutes* and in his reports. He distinguished between natural and artificial reason, a distinction with very tangible consequences on English public law. Law was the perfection of artificial reason, of which Coke argued that it could only be acquired by many years of dedicated study. The king's natural reason (acquired by birth), though excellent and great, did not yet make him capable of rendering judgements in accordance with the common law, i.e. with perfect (artificial) reason. That is why common law courts sometimes were allowed to repeal royal judgements.

Coke also employed the law of nature in several specific situations, for instance pertaining to familial obligations, the prohibition against usury, or against duels. Natural law – which to Coke was immutable – was not contrary to common law. Rather, in Coke's conception, common law and natural law must align, as Acland shows through an analysis of Coke's contribution in *Calvin's Case* (1608). It could even be argued that Coke saw natural law as an inherent part of common law. In *Bonham's Case* (1610), Coke used an argument based on natural law to set limits on Acts of Parliament. If a parliamentary Act went against a natural law principle which was also recognized by common law, a common law court could adjudge this Act as void. Thus, natural law reasoning, inspired by Cicero, was used – even in the 'insular' common law – to set limits on both King and Parliament.

## 4 After 1650

In the contribution by **Carlos Pérez Crespo**, the relation between natural law and the theory on sovereignty by the famous English scholar Thomas Hobbes (1588–1679), whose *Leviathan* had been published in 1651, is approached from a historiographical perspective. This contribution starts from the paradox in Hobbes' work between an absolute conception of sovereignty and the moral-political constraints of natural law. A sovereign's commands had to be obeyed by citizens, but simultaneously Hobbes recognized an individual's rights to self-protection and self-preservation. Crespo lists and discusses the attempts by scholars since the 1930s to conceptualize natural law in Hobbes' theory of sovereignty.

Special attention is paid to the work by the Italian scholar Norberto Bobbio (1909–2004). He argued that Hobbes' theory combined a natural law perspective with a proto-positivist approach. Somewhat similar to the concept of a '*Grundnorm*' by the legal philosopher Hans Kelsen (1881–1973), in Bobbio's opinion, Hobbes used natural law as the legal basis that underpinned his theory of sovereignty. Once, however, the positive legal system had been established, all interference from natural law ended. According to this historiographical tradition, Hobbes did not recognize any enforceable right to disobey the sovereign, despite the many references to natural law throughout his work.

Another paradox is central to the contribution by **Signy Gutnick Allen** on charity and property in the political thought of John Locke (1632–1704). On the one hand, Locke framed respect for property as an issue of justice, and thus of natural law. On the other hand, he also seemed to recognize a claim of the needy to the goods of others. Gutnick Allen tries to overcome this paradox by focusing both on theory and policy advice, i.e. on Locke's famous *Two Treatises of Government* (1689) and on his essay on the topic of poor relief at the behest of the Board of Trade (1697) respectively.

According to Locke, every human being had ownership over one's own labour, which he considered a means of appropriation that increased the production of the earth. Thus, in his view, appropriation through labour did not infringe upon the rights of others, but rather left behind more for mankind than before the appropriation. Once someone had become the owner of property, that property could no longer be taken away without the owner's consent, or at least not without the consent of the majority of owners. That is why taxation too – crucial to finance domestic government – needed to be approved by a majority of those having properties, either directly or through their political representatives.

Thus, Locke pleaded for a strong protection of the right to property; how then to interpret the enforceable right for the needy to charity? Whilst this right *prima facie* seemed to open a roadway towards important limitations on the right to property, this was not the case. Locke had a very restrictive understanding of those who could be seen as truly in need. In his opinion, by far most of the poor were just idle. If they wanted, they could work and through their labour increase the production of the earth, and thus the available means. It was widespread moral depravity that kept them from work. They had no claim to charity. Truly in need were only those who were completely unable to work, even at the lowest of wages, like some of the most disabled or the most elderly. They did have a claim to charity. However, this claim to charity, even for them, was in fact only a claim to what kept them from extreme want. The living conditions that Locke proposed for them could still hardly be understood as desirable: many poor in one house, only one fire and not more than one person to look after them. Consequently, the Lockean right to property was an almost absolute one.

In this volume's final contribution by **Sarah Limão Papa**, the right to property also played a crucial role. Papa explains how in the complex and multilayered legal system of Portuguese America, several types of claims to property could be found, such as *dominium*, *possessio*, *sesmaria*, lease, emphyteusis, and servitudes, to name just a few.

These different types of claims to property collided in a case concerning the construction of a watermill for processing sugar cane in the village of Camamu in Bahia in 1779. The claim had been filed by a priest who arguably was the lord (*senhor*) and possessor (*possuidor*) of the land, and who had bought the land from the legitimate owner. Opposition came from the governor general of Brazil, who argued that the construction and operation of the watermill risked limiting the access of the local population to water, whereas the source had been in continuous possession or servitude of the local people since time immemorial, i.e. at least since the arrival of the Jesuits in the mid-sixteenth century.

In the procedure around this watermill of Camamu, access to natural resources was a crucial topic. Access of the local population to water was termed a superior right, in the public interest, that superseded any private right of possession or dominion over purchased property. Though not expressly framed in terms of expropriation, the lord (*senhor*) was not allowed to construct the watermill unless he ensured free access of the population to the water and the surrounding woods. This case study shows how – due to the scarcity of natural resources – a balance needed to be sought between all parties. It illustrates how the constraints of nature imposed limits on the individual's right of property.

## 5 Conclusion

The role of natural law for the development of domestic governance: that is the subject of this volume. Its three chronological parts offer a varied overview of themes and controversial questions that have been debated by generations of scholars, philosophers, theologians and jurists alike, in England, France, the Low Countries, the German lands, Spain and Portuguese America. Examples include the right to private property and its relation to the power of the sovereign, the right to property as opposed to claims for charity and its consequences on taxation, or the mutability of natural law depending on the circumstances of place and time. Several contributions also point at the value of a thorough historical contextualization for a better understanding of philosophical treatises and discussions on natural law. The volume ends with a 'postface' by Alain Wijffels, reflecting on all contributions and in which he adds some personal considerations on the evolving tradition of natural law from the early modern period to the present day.

## Acknowledgement

The realization of this project would have been impossible without the financial support of the Research Foundation – Flanders (FWO) for the project "Diodorus Tuldenus and the Development of Natural and Public Law in the Habsburg Low Countries" (G0C4421N). The editors also wish to thank all authors for their contribution to this volume, as well as Ms. Irene Jiang for her editorial assistance.

# PART 1

## *Sixteenth Century*

CHAPTER 1

# Bodin, Natural Law, and Statecraft in the French Renaissance Monarchy

*Marie Seong-Hak Kim*

## 1 Introduction

'Modern State' often means two things seldom found together in the Middle Ages, i.e., a state that is both 'sovereign' and 'limited.' In medieval European constitutional thought, sovereignty was the name for a collection of specific rights reserved to the crown. Jean Bodin (1530–1596) rejected this traditional view in his *Les six livres de la république*, first published in 1576 and revised multiple times before his death. Sovereignty could not be mixed or shared, he argued; it was instead the "absolute and perpetual" power in a body politic, from which all other powers and rights derived.[1] Sovereignty could reside in a collective body, as was the Venetian Senate, but in France it was vested in the king alone. Bodin defined royal authority in terms of legislative sovereignty. The king, as the author of the law, was above the law. The omnipotence of the sovereign was limited by three things only: divine and natural law which positive law must not transgress; *les lois fondamentales* of the kingdom such as *la loi salique* which prescribed the rule of succession to the throne and forbade the alienation of royal domain; and the right of ownership of the free subjects (*francs sujets*) to which corresponded the sovereign's duty to protect it.[2] According to Bodin, the royal monarch "makes himself obedient to the laws

1 *"La souveraineté est la puissance absolue & perpétuelle d'une République, que les Latins appellent maiestatem." Les six livres de la République de I. Bodin Angevin* (Paris: Iacques du Puys, 1583), Book I, Ch. 8, 122. All quotes from *Les six livres* come from this 1583 edition. Original spelling is preserved as much as possible, but some French accents have been added.

2 *"La puissance absolue des princes & seigneuries souveraines ne s'estend aucunement aux loix de Dieu & de nature,"* Book I, Ch. 8, 133; *"Quant aux loix qui concernent les lois fondamentales du royaume, & de l'establissement d'iceluy, d'autant qu'elles sont annexees & unies avec la couronne, le Prince n'y peut déroger, comme est la loy Salique,"* Book I, Ch. 8, 137; *"Si donc le Prince souverain n'a pas puissance de franchir les bornes des loix de nature, que Dieu duquel il est l'image, a posées, il ne pourra aussi prendre le bien d'autruy sans cause qui soit iuste & raisonnable,"* Book I, Ch. 8, 156–157.

 | DOI:10.1163/9789004748712_003

of nature as he desires his subjects to be toward him, rendering natural liberty and the ownership of property to each one."[3] An individual's property right is a law of nature that preserves everyone in his liberty and in the lordship of his possessions.[4]

Since authority of the sovereign rested on natural law, and since private property also rested on natural law, the king must respect the property of his subjects, whether in contracts or taxation. Bodin declared: "The prince can neither take nor dispose of another's property without the consent of its owner."[5] The king ought not to tax his subjects without consent. Bodin reiterated: "There is not a prince in all the world who has it in his power to levy taxes on subjects at his pleasure, any more than he has the power to take another's property."[6] From this he appears to say that taxation without consent is forbidden by the law of nature. Yet, one may ask, if the king cannot tax citizens without their consent, does it not negate the very definition of sovereignty to act unchecked by laws or institutions? This question has led some scholars to wonder whether Bodin's notions of natural law and the inviolability of private property were not incongruent with his doctrine of sovereignty.[7] A main difficulty in Bodin's political theory was, as Ernst Hinrichs pointed out some fifty years ago, that he placed "the right of liberty and property as legal certainty on the one hand and placed, on the other, absolute sovereign monarchy as an institution for the modernization of the legal system."[8] As scholars of Bodin

---

3 *"Le Monarque Royal est celui, qui se rend aussi obéissant aux lois de nature, comme il désire les sujets être envers lui, laissant la liberté naturelle, et la propriété des biens à chacun."* Book II, Ch. 3, 279.

4 *"Car de dire que les Princes sont seigneurs de tout, cela s'entend de la droite seigneurie, & justice souveraine, demeurant à chacun la possession et propriété de ses biens."* Book I, Ch. 8, 157. For major scholarly works on *Les six livres*, see, among others, Horst Denzer, ed., *Jean Bodin, Münchener Studien zur Politik* (Munich: Beck, 1973); Simone Goyard-Fabre, *Jean Bodin et le droit de la république* (Paris: Presses Universitaires de France, 1989); Howell A. Lloyd, *Jean Bodin: 'This Pre-Eminent Man of France': An Intellectual Biography* (Oxford: Oxford University Press, 2017); Mario Turchetti, "Jean Bodin," in *The Stanford Encyclopedia of Philosophy* (Fall 2018 Edition), ed. Edward N. Zalta https://plato.stanford.edu/archives/fall2018/entries/bodin/.

5 *"Le Prince ne peut prendre n'y donner le bien d'autruy, sans le consentement du seigneur."* Book I, Ch. 8, 157.

6 *"Il n'est en la puissance de prince du monde, de lever impôt à son plaisir sur le peuple, non plus que de prendre le bien d'autrui."* Book I, Ch. 8, 140.

7 David Parker, "Law, Society and the State in the Thought of Jean Bodin," *History of Political Thought* 2 (1981), 270.

8 Ernst Hinrichs, "Das Fürstenbild Bodins und die Krise der französischen Renaissancemonarchie," in *Jean Bodin, Münchener Studien zur Politik,* ed. Horst Denze, 291.

grappled with this seeming paradox in royal power, absolute and limited all at once, his legacy has been seen as featuring, depending on the viewer, absolutism, populism, or constitutionalism.[9] According to Hinrichs, however, this "contradiction" of Bodin's political theory was based "less on his inability to construct it consistently and more on the binding nature of his way of looking at the political, social, and economic conditions prevailing in his time."[10] In other words, Bodin's political thought had historical reasons. Cued by this insight, this chapter discusses Bodin's doctrines of sovereignty and natural law in their historical, rather than philosophical, context.

I begin by suggesting that Bodin's 'modern' theory was a response to the not-so-modern crisis of the French Renaissance monarchy, namely, wars. In the sixteenth century, France went through two major series of wars: the Wars of Italy (1494–1559) and the Wars of Religion (1562–1598). War debts left the government in dire conditions.[11] History has repeatedly shown that the costs of war were the driving force behind changes in a state's government and institutions. The troubled royal finance alarmed many contemporaries including Bodin, for whom sound and responsible fiscal policy was at the center of sovereignty. "The nerves of the Republic lie in its finances"; it was important to "find financial funds by honest means and use them for the benefit and honor of the Republic" and to "save and reserve part of them as needed," he wrote.[12]

Bodin was a keen observer of the kingdom's fiscal situation.[13] His famous debate in 1568 with Jehan de Malestroit over the causes of inflation reveals

9 John H.M. Salmon, "The Legacy of Jean Bodin: Absolutism, Populism or Constitutionalism?" *History of Political Thought* 17 (1996): 500–522.

10 Hinrichs, "Das Fürstenbild Bodins," 291–292.

11 Claude Michaud, "Finances et guerres de religion en France," *Revue d'histoire moderne et contemporaine* 28 (1981), 572.

12 *"Les nerfs de la République sont aux finances d'icelle."* Book VI, Ch. 2, 855. There are three points: *"Le premier est des moyens honnestes de faire fonds aux finances; le second est de les employer au proffit & honneur de la République; le troisième d'en espargner & réserver au besoins quelque partie."* Ibid.

13 Historians have pointed out the fiscal backwardness of France in comparison with Italy or Low Countries. For the weakness of the crown's fiscal base, see Martin Wolfe, *The Fiscal System of Renaissance France* (New Haven: Yale University Press, 1972); James B. Collins, *Fiscal Limits of Absolutism: Direct Taxation in Early Seventeenth-Century France* (Berkeley: University of California Press, 1988); Philip T. Hoffmann, *"Early Modern France: 1450–1700,"* in *Fiscal Crises, Liberty, and Representative Government 1450–1789*, eds. Philip T. Hoffman and Kathryn Norberg (Stanford: Stanford University Press, 1994), 226–252. For a comprehensive review article, see Richard Bonney, "What's New about the New French Fiscal History," *Journal of Modern History* 70 (1998): 639–667. A comparative analysis of the early modern European states is provided in James D. Tracy, "Taxation and State Debt," in *Structures and Assertions*, vol. 1 of *Handbook of European History*,

that he was well versed and closely engaged in the workings of the financial market forces.[14] Bodin's argument that the prince should avoid at all costs the temptation to debase currency, an idea he incorporated later in *Les six livres*, underscored in many aspects his theory of sovereignty. History is full of rulers succumbing to debasement and ending up destroying finance.[15] Likewise, contends Bodin, weak rulers yield to greed for the property of subjects. The ideal prince avoids devouring his own strength by tampering with private property.[16] Bodin's 'absolute' sovereign would not break contracts, not just because it would be a violation of natural law but also because it would be self-destructive, politically and financially.

It is reasonable to surmise that Bodin's firsthand observations of the royal finance critically helped shape his political thought and reform ideas. In *Les six livres*, he tried to devise a sound and stable governance in the French kingdom that was on the verge of collapse during the civil war, and, more broadly, set forth a universal order in a world that was rapidly changing during the Renaissance, in transition from the medieval to modern times. One is reminded that, in order to grasp the nature and significance of political theories, it is necessary to turn to the historical background in which they were formulated, and Bodin's case is no exception. Bodin's innovation in constitutional theory has been amply recognized and analyzed, but one may want to know the conditions to which an innovation was a response.

---

*1400–1600: Late Middle Ages, Renaissance, and Reformation*, eds. T.A. Brady, Jr., H.A. Oberman, and J.D. Tracy (Leiden: Brill, 1994), 563–588.

14 The king's currency was collapsing, causing serious inflation. Jehan Cherruyt de Malestroict, *conseiller du roi* and *maître* at the *Chambre des comptes*, published a short pamphlet, *Les Paradoxes du Seigneur de Malestroict, Conseiller du Roy, & Maistre ordinaire de ses comptes, sur le faict des Monnoyes* (1566). Shortly after, Bodin published *La Responses de Maistre Jean Bodin Advocate en la cour au paradoxe de Monsieur de Malestroict, touchant l'encherissement de toutes choses, & le moyen d'y remediers Monnoyes* (1568). Bodin's main arguments in *Responses* reappear in Book VI, Chapter 3 of *Les six livres*. Bodin published the second edition of *Responses* in 1578 by Jacques du Puys, the same publisher that published his *Les six livres*. See "Introduction" in *Response to the Paradoxes of Malestroit*, eds. Henry Tudor, Dyson, R.W. Dyson, and J.C.M. Starkey (Bristol: Thoemmes Press, 1997).

15 Jérôme Blanc, "Beyond the Quantity Theory: A Reappraisal of Jean Bodin's Monetary Ideas," in *Money and Markets: A Doctrinal Approach*, eds. Alberto Giacomin and Maria Cristina Marcuzzo (London: Routledge, 2007), 145. "Bodin's monetary thought is actually part of his theoretical construction of sovereign power," ibid., 135. See also Jérôme Blanc, "Les monnaies de la république. Un retour sur les idées monétaires de Jean Bodin," *Cahiers d'économie politique* 50 (2006): 165–189.

16 James D. Tracy, "Review of Jean Bodin: Verhandlungen der Internationalen Bodin Tagung in München, edited by Horst Denzer," *Renaissance Quarterly* 28 (1975), 247.

Liberty underpinned Bodin's assessment of property rights. The correlation of property to natural liberty is a recurring theme in *Les six livres*.[17] Since Bodin's natural law ideas resided in his belief that a sovereign king must respect his subjects' property, it is essential to examine the fiscal policies and practices of the royal monarchy, focusing on the realms of contract and taxation. The interdependence of public debt and sovereignty deserves attention. The constant need to borrow money and secure public credit led the French crown to be deeply involved in contractual relationship. The system of borrowing through pledging royal revenues was the bedrock for running the 'state as enterprise.'[18] Chief means for the kings to accrue debt were the creation of *rentes* (annuities) on municipal governments and the sale of royal offices, the two instruments Francis I (r. 1515–1547) famously institutionalized.[19] The necessary condition for this system was trust, that is, the king's assurance not to break the contracts through which he borrowed. Constituting *rentes* and selling royal offices presupposed an agreement between the ruler and subjects to keep promises and to abide by the law.

Recent scholarship tends to focus on the diffusion of power in early modern society and highlight the element of consent in an ideal government, and Bodin's dictum that 'absolute' sovereign should not tax without consent comes with a clear appeal. Yet Bodin's statements on taxes, which have been cited as the gist of his constitutionalism, require contextual considerations. When Bodin discussed natural liberty, especially securing property from arbitrary taxation, he was speaking largely in reference to the privileges and consent in a corporate society as an outgrowth of custom. Liberty in medieval and early modern Europe meant privileges; consent to taxation was not everyone's right but the privileges of the few. Financing the state was done by a tinkering of consent and coercion. While dependent on creditors, the monarchy was quite resourceful in extracting money from principal groups, through various techniques of free gifts or interest-bearing forced loans. In the 1560s, the government successfully forced the clergy to 'consent' to provide subsidies to the crown and also proceeded to the sale of church property to pay off the public debt.[20] The king argued that just as he was justified in alienating royal

17 Lloyd, *Jean Bodin*, 132.

18 Robert Descimon, "Power Elites and the Prince: The State as Enterprise," in *Power Elites and State Building*, ed. Wolfgang Reinhard (Oxford: Clarendon Press, 1996), 101–121.

19 Bernard Schnapper, *Les rentes au XVI^e^ siècle: Histoire d'un instrument de crédit* (Paris: S.E.V.P.E.N., 1957).

20 Julien Laferrière, *Le contrat de Poissy (1561)* (Paris: Sirey, 1905); A. Cauchie, "Les assemblées du clergé de France sous l'ancien régime," *Revue des sciences philosophiques et théologiques* 2 (1) (1908): 74–95.

domains in emergency so ecclesiastical temporalities and revenues could be seized in the name of the common good. But these heavy-handed measures took the form of voluntary agreements between the Crown and the Church, in full observation of legal procedures. It shows that negotiation and consent, the methods characteristic of the Renaissance monarchy, could obscure what was really going on. The contemporary notions of contract and liberty, and Bodin's usage of those terms, may have been more complex than have previously been assumed.

Bodin's *république*, which he equated with *monarchie royale*, operated on the foundation of a flow of private credit to the public chest. As he elevated respect for private property to the level of a fundamental principle of the royal monarchy, Bodin granted the prince the concept of sovereignty, an instrument that could be used against the holders of their well-acquired rights. This way, he attempted to adapt the French social and political order to the economic conditions and prevent the '*ruine des républiques*.'[21] A sovereign legislates of his own accord, no longer dependent on consent of the subjects, yet even an 'absolute' king cannot break faith with his creditors. Indeed, the early modern French crown regularly reneged on interest payments for its long-term debt, but it never repudiated the debt itself.

Bodin states that sovereignty is restrained by natural and divine law. Here resurfaces the supposed contradiction of his: the will of the sovereign is limited by divine law, yet there is nothing that can stop the sovereign prince from distancing himself from his model of divine or natural law or, quite simply, from being mistaken about it. The king is limited by natural law, but it becomes absorbed into the omnipotence of sovereignty.[22] This suggests that Bodin wished to fuse the ideals of the monarchy and good governance by resorting to natural law. He was concerned less with political philosophy or the doctrine of natural law as moral philosophy than with practical policies. Bodin's aim was not to theorize about natural freedom and property as such, but to discuss "the legal forms of communication that developed to protect them and that are understood as an element of stability of the existing state."[23]

21 Bodin listed a number of causes that could lead to the decline and ruin of the republics in Book IV, Ch. 1, 503–541 ("De la naissance, accroissement, état florissant, décadence, et ruine des Républiques").

22 Janine Chanteur, "La loi naturelle et la souveraineté chez Jean Bodin," *Théologie et droit dans la science politique de l'État moderne, Actes de la table ronde de Rome (12–14 novembre 1987), Publications de l'École française de Rome* 147 (1) (1991), 292.

23 Hinrichs, "Das Fürstenbild Bodins," 289. As one author aptly put, "Had Bodin's prime intention been a philosophical inquiry into the nature of sovereignty he would doubtless have written differently, but he wrote *de republica*, not *de majestate*. The nature of that

It was sufficient for him to show that absolute monarchy was not the antinomy of natural law and rights. One may call his natural law theory an applied natural law idea.

Some comparisons between Bodin and other theorists of natural law covered elsewhere in this volume help to put his thought in context. Francisco Suárez (1548–1617) was concerned with the relationship between positive laws of civil codes and normative natural law as the political theology of moral community.[24] Similar scholastic discussion on the nature of natural law is largely missing in *Les six livres*. Justus Lipsius (1547–1606) and Hugo Grotius (1583–1645), writers of the 'modern' school of natural law, took self-preservation of skeptics as a fundamental natural right, which would play a vital role in the construction of effective modern states.[25] Bodin, too, was deeply immersed in the idea of self-preservation. He undermined the Aristotelian concept of citizenship by saying that there was no moral distinction between a city and a family. France was not at war with Spain, unlike the Netherlands, but the French king, the father figure, needed to hold the kingdom together during the religious wars. Thomas Hobbes (1588–1679), conceiving the commonwealth as voluntary association governed by natural law, set up an absolute authority unfettered by contractual restraints.[26] As in England, France, fractured by civil war, called for an absolute prince, but for Bodin it was presumed that the king made a contract with the people to preserve the republic. It seems that he conceived and referred to the notion of natural law with the aim of justifying the legitimacy of sovereignty and positive law.

The following pages place Bodin's political and constitutional theories in their historical context. They explore the extent to which Bodin's ideas about private property and contract were influenced by his observations of the financial situation of the French kingdom. The second part of the chapter discusses the kingdom's fiscal problems. The constant need to secure public credit dictated royal policies, as the kings resorted to borrowing, creating

---

supreme power was far from being the first thing in his chain of thought." R.W.K. Hinton, "Review of Six Books of the Commonwealth by Jean Bodin and M.J. Tooley," *Cambridge Historical Journal* 12 (1956), 88.

24 See Dominique Bauer and Randall Lesaffer, eds., *History, Casuistry and Custom in the Legal Thought of Francisco Suárez (1548–1617)* (Leiden: Brill Nijhoff, 2021).

25 See Richard Tuck, *Philosophy and Government 1572–1651* (Cambridge: Cambridge University Press, 1993).

26 See Annabel S. Brett, *Changes of State: Nature and the Limits of the City in Early Modern Natural Law* (Princeton, NJ: Princeton University Press, 2011).

*rentes*, and selling public offices.[27] Bodin's assessments of the royal financial measures formed the foundation for his theories of taxation and consent, as explained in the third part of the chapter. The Contrat de Poissy in 1562, the agreement between the king and the clergy by which the latter undertook to provide subsidies to pay off the public debt, sheds light on Bodin's discussion of public and private law. The meanings of contract and consent in Bodin's treatises in the sixteenth century may not have been quite the same as what we would expect in later times. The fourth, and the last, part of the chapter explores the impact of the monarchy's efforts to streamline the sources of law on the contemporary debate of custom and natural law. The official campaigns to compile the regional and local *coutumes* placed them under royal authority and opened the path for the king to overcome serious obstacles to the exercise of his power. As custom underwent legal stipulation through codification, the ancient idea that the king could not change customary practices without consent no longer kept him in check. Natural rights, resting on the abstract notions of reason and *équité*, likewise came to pose less potent restraints on sovereignty than before.

The formulation of Bodin's theory of sovereignty was propelled by contemporary events in early modern France. When one considers that Bodin's ideas were informed by the specific political developments of his time, the supposed contradiction in his thought, that is, the postulation of sovereignty along with the inviolability of private property in natural law, fades away. Rather, it buttresses his vision of an ideal republic.

## 2 The Monarchy and Its Fiscal Problems

Bodin declared private property a natural right of individuals. Property rights, strengthened in most parts of Europe by the principles of Roman law, were taken seriously in the late medieval and early modern period. The French monarchy in the sixteenth century had plenty of problems to deal with, but one of the most pressing was the fiscal crisis. The early modern French crown possessed extensive political powers but only limited financial resources.[28] It

27 For Bodin's views on the fiscal system of the French monarchy, see Marie Seong-Hak Kim, *Custom, Law and Monarchy: A Legal History of Early Modern France* (Oxford: Oxford University Press, 2021), 199–210.

28 Roland É. Mousnier, *The Institutions of France under the Absolute Monarchy, 1598–1789*, trans. Brian Pearce and Arthur Goldhammer, 2 vols. (Chicago: University of Chicago Press, 1979 and 1984), vol. 1, 665, 740.

needed to borrow money incessantly. For Bodin, the monarch's abilities to manage fiscal policy were tightly connected with his duties to ensure the survival of the commonweal.

## 2.1 *Building Public Credit:* Rentes *and the Sale of Offices*

Francis I amassed huge debts in vain efforts to secure conquests in Italy. French kings entered the credit market later than other European princes. Until about 1520, they had eschewed borrowing from foreign bankers. But ballooning war debts led them to approach merchant syndicates (known as the *Grand Parti*) in Lyon for large loans. Lacking creditworthiness, interest rates were extremely high. Unable to raise taxation substantially or to alienate royal domain further, the government had to find other sources of credit. One of the principal devices for meeting obligations to the *Grand Parti* was the creation of *rentes*, interest-bearing bonds.

Francis I introduced in 1522 *rentes* on the Hôtel de Ville de Paris, the city government. The *rente constituée* meant that the owner mortgaged (that is, constituted a *rente* on) a portion of his property and paid interest on the capital he received. The city government of Paris had long been accustomed to selling *rentes* guaranteed by city revenues. Most *rentes* of this kind were loans by local merchants and land-owning peasants. Now the city of Paris extended the credit to the king who pledged royal revenues as security. The city sold subscribers *rentes* assigned by the king on specific income from *aides* (excise taxes) and *gabelles* (taxes on salt).[29] *Rentes* quickly became the main borrowing instrument of the crown.

Another method of raising money was selling royal offices. The sale of offices started in the fourteenth century among minor officials on a private basis. For example, a person sold his post to another or resigned in his favor for a payment. Francis I turned the practice into a matter of public policy. In 1522, he created the *Trésor des parties casuelles* to administer the sale of royal offices to the highest bidder. New loans from the financiers were used to float new bond issues which, with the proceeds from the sale of offices, were in turn used to pay old debts to the banking syndicates. Restructuring short-term debts into long-term debts, that is, "consolidating the debt into long-term loans not demandable by the creditors and granted at interest rates close to those of

29 The prohibition of usury was taken seriously in France, but canon law provisions were interpreted in a way to distinguish *rente* from usury: one cannot lend a sum of money but can donate it with the stipulation that the receiver and his successors pay an annuity on such an income-producing fund. Cauchie, "Les assemblées du clergé de France sous l'ancien régime," 81.

the money market," made perfect economic sense.[30] Salaries paid to the royal *officiers* amounted to interest payments for the loans they had extended to the king when they bought their offices. These sources of credit were tied to revenues from direct and indirect taxation and the sale of the royal domain.[31]

A broad stratum of Parisian citizens became the king's creditors by subscribing to royal loans. Étienne Pasquier testified that people flocked to the city hall to invest in *rentes*, "not shy about opening their purses."[32] Bodin expressed concerns that the popularity of the system would be detrimental to economic productivity.[33] The individuals who bought royal offices were often the same people who were the chief creditors of royal *rentes* on municipal governments. A typical pattern for aspiring wealthy urban families was to transfer capital into *rentes*, buy rural seigneuries, purchase royal office, marry into the noble family, and acquire a title. The *bourgeoisie non commerçante*, or the 'feudal bourgeoisie,' came to monopolize high positions in the king's judicial and financial bureaucracy. Their loyalty to the crown depended on whether the latter guaranteed them timely returns on their investment in royal debt.[34] The king had to play a delicate balancing game to keep the *rentiers*, *officiers*, and tax farmers content. A disruption of the public debt system would shake the credibility of the sovereign and make borrowing more difficult, and more expensive. Here was a functional limitation on the power of the sovereign prince: his creditworthiness prevented him from taking private property or failing to fulfill the contracts he entered into.

### 2.2 *Venality as Civil Law Contract*

The relationship between the crown and venal *officiers* delineated the contours of royal prerogatives, which Bodin termed "the true marks of sovereignty." Bodin was a harsh critic of the venality of offices. The sale of public

30 Robert Descimon, "Pourquoi avoir fait lire 'Colbert, la dette publique et la haute robe parisienne'?" *H-France Salon*, Vol. 14, Issue 22, No. 3. https://h-france.net/Salon/SalonVol14no22.03.Descimon.pdf.

31 The payment of interest assigned on the receipts from the *aides* and *gabelles* was secured after 1566 on the *taille* itself. J.H.M. Salmon, *Society in Crisis: France in the Sixteenth Century* (New York: St. Martin's Press, 1975). 165.

32 Étienne Pasquier, *Lettres*, in Book v, let. 4, *Les œuvres d'Estienne Pasquier, contenant ses recherches de la France* (Amsterdam, 1723), vol. 2, cols. 122. See Paul Cauwès, "Les commencements du crédit public en France: Les rentes sur l'hôtel de ville au xvi^e^ siècle," *Revue d'économie politique* 9 (2) (1895), 108.

33 Book v, Ch. 2, 710–711.

34 Hinrichs, "Das Fürstenbild Bodins," 293, note 45.

offices was "the most dangerous and pernicious plague that could be in a *république*."[35] By selling offices, the kings "sell the most sacred thing in the world, which is justice, they sell the Republic, they sell the blood of the subjects, they sell the laws, and they take away all the rewards of honor, virtue, learning, piety, and religion; they open the gates to theft, corruption, avarice, injustice, ignorance, impiety, in short, all vice and villainy."[36] Magistral offices were the property of the *république* itself, remaining within the power of those who have sovereignty.[37] Attempts by the sovereigns to alienate them risk destroying the *république*.[38] Fortunately for modern readers, Bodin's scathing denouncement of the system did not stop him from undertaking a full analysis of the legal attributes of venal offices within the framework of private law.[39] This is where his assertion that the king could not break the terms of an agreement without the consent of the other party becomes all too relevant.

Bodin conceptualized the sale of offices in terms of a civil law contract between the king and his officials. Buying and selling an office was a commercial enterprise, a financial transaction, governed by the law of obligations. It was subject to market fluctuations like any other contractual exchange of property. Bodin wrote that an office was "like a borrowed thing (*comme une chose empruntée*)."[40] This statement can be seen in dual meanings. Viewed in light of state credit, the *officier* held a portion of the public debt. In public law, the king was the owner and the official the borrower; in private law, the king was the borrower (debtor) and the official the lender (creditor). The office, akin to an object of contractual lease, served as security for the money the king had borrowed. Once the king issued an office through a *lettre de provision*, he could not demand it back arbitrarily outside the agreed terms, most importantly, not before he reimbursed the amount that had been paid into the royal

35 *"La plus dangereuse et pernicieuse peste qui soit ès République,"* Book v, Ch. 4, 742; *"De toutes les marchandises que font les Princes, il n'y en a point de plus pernicieuse ny de plus sordide, que des honneurs, offices & bénéfices,"* Book vi, Ch. 2, 874.

36 *"Ils vendent la République, ils vendent le sang des sujets, ils vendent les lois."* Book v, Ch. 4, 743.

37 "T*ous les estats, Magistrats & offices appartiennent à la République en propriété* [...] *demeurant la provision à ceux qui ont la souveraineté*." Book 3, Ch. 5, 436.

38 There was always a danger that offices would fall into the hands of the undeserved (*indignes*) or to the incompetent (*incompétents*). Book v, Ch. 4, 745.

39 Kim, *Custom, Law, and the Monarchy*, 204–206.

40 Book iii, Ch. 2, 378. See Daniel Lee, "'Office Is a Thing Borrowed': Jean Bodin on Offices and Seigneurial Government," *Political Theory* 41 (2013): 409–440.

treasury. Needless to say, the king was rarely in a position to reimburse the officials to whom he had sold the offices.[41]

Bodin famously stressed that the law should not be confused with contract. The law is a unilateral act that emanates solely from the holder of power and is binding on everyone except the lawgiver. A contract, by contrast, is a bilateral agreement in which the parties stand on equal footing.[42] While the law obliges all the subjects without obliging the Prince, the contract obliges both. Bodin elaborated: "If the prince swears unto himself that he will keep his law, he is no more bound by his law than by the oath made unto himself."[43] The king is above any limitations imposed by institutions, even the institution of oath-taking.[44] Oaths which simply invoke divine sanction for a promise do not bind if the promise does not bind.[45] On the contrary, a sovereign prince is "as bound as any individual by the just covenants and promises which he has made, whether under or not under oath."[46] How could the king, who is above the law, be bound by contract? It is because the other party has an interest in the fulfillment of the contract. The breaking of the contract by one party injures the other unjustly and is therefore contrary to natural law. Out of a desire to do justice, the sovereign respects his contracts. A breach of such kind would undermine public faith which is the foundation of the republic, whose protector is the prince.

The king regularly professed that the dire fiscal situation required him to sell offices. Bodin was not convinced: "There is no veritable excuse or real semblance to seek the ruin of the state under the pretense of poverty. And it is a ridiculous thing for a prince to pretend poverty, as he would have so many means to prevent it if he wanted to."[47] One could almost feel Bodin's frustra-

41 Bodin wrote: "in addition to the difficulty of the reimbursement which must be done, there is still more to fear that they disturb the state, who are stripped of honor, which for the ambitious means more than goods or life." Book IV, Ch. 3, 579–580.

42 *"It ne faut donc pas confondre la loy & le contract."* Book I, Ch. 8, 135. Bodin continues: "*La loy* depends on the one who has the sovereignty, which can bind all his subjects but cannot bind himself. The *convention* is mutual between the prince and his subjects, which reciprocally bind the two parties; one of the parties cannot violate it with prejudice and without the consent of the other. The prince in this case has nothing above his subject," ibid.

43 Book I, Ch. 8, 133.

44 In a monarchy the sovereign monarch "does not himself owe any oath except to God alone, […] because an oath always implies reverence toward the person to whom it is given or in whose name it is taken, which is the only reason why a lord does not take an oath to his vassal even though the obligation between them is mutual." Book I, Ch. 8, 143.

45 Julian H. Franklin, ed., *Jean Bodin, On Sovereignty: Four Chapters from The Six Books of the Commonwealth* (Cambridge: Cambridge University Press, 1992), 130.

46 Book I, Ch. 8, 133.

47 Book V, Ch. 4, 743–744.

tions, fuming over the fiscal disarray which he thought was a pitiful sign of incompetency, if not disingenuity. His irritation aside, Bodin had to admit that the sale of offices kept the monarchy afloat and that the king could not do away with it. Bodin's criticisms of the 'expedient' of the sale of offices thus centered on the fact that the king resorted to the practice so frequently and haphazardly.[48] The king could not dismiss incumbents without adequate cause – that is, without reimbursement – as it would amount to a breach of contract, quite apart from its destructive effect on the market. Opposed in principle to the venality system, Bodin could not advocate the king renouncing the contracts he had made when he sold the offices. Private property, which the offices were, could not be taken by the state except through the carefully defined legal process, with just reason, and with due compensation.

In short, the principle of the inviolability of property resided in the law of nature, yet its salient justification came from civil law (*ius civile*) and, above all, immediate political needs. The chronic deficiencies of royal finance compelled the ruler to protect the subjects' property rights and ensure legal certainty. In practical terms, the king, having entered the credit market as an interested party, had to be careful about how he treated his creditors, lest he jeopardize his credit rating, making it more expensive for the state to borrow. He thus needed to make sure that he operated within the legal boundaries, without breaching public faith. Here were the bottom-line limits to the exercise of sovereign power. The structural features of what Bodin attributed to the royal monarchy – safeguarding freedom and property, maintaining legal certainty, and cultivating trust between ruler and subjects – had a political corollary.[49] Much to his regret, however, the insolvency and financial straits of the crown during the civil wars made meaningful reforms impossible.

## 3 Taxation and Consent

Renaissance monarchs were well aware of the advantage of ruling *with* the consent of the people. History has shown that those who formalized the prin-

48 Hinrichs, "Das Fürstenbild Bodins," 296.

49 Bodin claimed "I was the very first, even in these dangerous times, unhesitatingly to refute the opinions of those who would expand the right of the treasury and the regalian prerogatives, on the grounds that they give kings unlimited power beyond the laws of God and nature." Dedicatory letter first added in the 1578 edition and preserved in subsequent editions, cited from Franklin, *Jean Bodin, On Sovereignty*, "Introduction," xxv, note 23. Bodin seemed to be referring to his debate with Malestroit.

ciple of government by consent were better able to legitimize their rule and, above all, were more successful in persuading their subjects to open their purses. There are different ways in royal control of society, either through force and the threat of punishment or through a process of negotiation. French kings – and most other late medieval and Renaissance rulers – ruled by the latter.[50] It was more effective for a king to ally with powerful subjects and use their loyalty to strengthen royal authority. Pressed by war debts and the urgent need to raise money, the French monarchy adhered to the principles of negotiation and consent. It did not mean the crown was powerless to take more heavy-handed measures, for example extracting 'forced loans'; it simply meant such measures needed to appear consensual. In this context, the monarchy's dealings with the clergy in the 1560s to pay off the public debt are of particular interest.

### 3.1 *Privileges, Liberties, and Public Good*

France was a largely decentralized state. It was a corporate society. Legal status and political influence were determined by membership in various collective bodies – communities, towns, and institutional organizations – to which substantial power and a degree of autonomy were accorded.[51] When Bodin highlighted the protection of private property and stressed trust between the ruler and the subjects as the foundational principle of the royal monarchy, he was first and foremost describing the workings of a corporate-hierarchical social order, whose scope of freedom was determined essentially by securing the acquired rights.[52] Bodin assumed that men were unequal by nature and that there "never was a commonweal where all the citizens were equal in rights and prerogatives."[53] He said that the specific and varying forms of property rights, held by the populace according to the established legal organization of the state, must be respected by the sovereign, whose duty it was to maintain the wellbeing of the *république*.

The everyday relationship between the early modern monarchy and its subjects was marked by negotiations aimed at protecting privileges. A wealth of functions had been granted by the king that formed the patrimony of their holders. A large part of the sectors that were later to be called 'public' belonged to the 'private' property of the subjects.[54] Corporate privileges

50 Tracy, "Taxation and State Debt," 563.
51 Parker, "Law, Society and the State," 272.
52 Hinrichs, "Das Fürstenbild Bodins," 301.
53 Bodin wrote: "One can say that the equality of possessions is extremely dangerous (*tres pernicieuse*) to the *républiques*." Book v, Ch. 2, 704.
54 Hinrichs, "Das Fürstenbild Bodins," 296.

were essential for the stability of the monarchy. The French king depended on the ruling classes who saw him as the guarantor of their own security through the concession of dignities and offices. Major regional and local corporate institutions included the provincial estates, the representative bodies, and the parlements, the law courts, with their own esprit de corps. The provincial estates received an increasing share of royal taxes that the crown redistributed to them, and the elites loaded off the tax burden onto the peasantry. State revenues were often mortgaged for years in advance.[55]

Bodin's prince was sovereign because he reserved the power to grant or revoke the privileges at will, as long as he abided with divine and natural law and in pursuit of common good. The law forbidding the alienation of royal domain without consent meant that an alienation by a sitting king would maintain its effect only until his death. In this regard, Bodin concurred with Chancellor Michel de L'Hôpital (1505?–1573) who refused to place the royal seal on the confirmation of privileges and exemptions from *tailles* of the Abbey of Saint-Maur-des-Fossés, even though he had been ordered to do it, because such privileges conferred a perpetual exemption. In the chancellor's opinion, which Bodin fully supported, granting a perpetual exemption from taxes was "contrary to the nature of personal privileges and diminished the power of the king's successors"; such privileges "cannot be given to corporations and guilds except for the lifetime of the prince who grants them, even if the word perpetual is used, which it never is in the *Republiques populaires & aristocratiques*."[56]

In the sixteenth century, the king worked hard to persuade the nobles, *officiers*, and financiers to accept the government plans to amortize much of royal debt. With the worsening fiscal pressure during the religious wars, he found a new target – the clergy.

---

55 The way taxes were imposed and collected in the French monarchy was quite different from what we would normally expect today. The state normally transferred the right of collection to private individuals called tax farmers, in exchange for fixed periodic payments.

56 Book I, Ch. 8, 132. For L'Hôpital's constitutional thought, see Marie Seong-Hak Kim, "Michel de L'Hôpital and Christophe de Thou: Two Perceptions of Royal Justice during the French Religious Wars," in *Suum Cuique Tribuere: Legal Contexts, Judicial Archetypes and Deep-Structures Regarding Courts of Appeal and Judiciaries from Early Modern to Late Modern Europe*, eds. Kjell A. Modeer and Matin Sunnqvist (Stockholm: Institutet för Rättshistorisk Forskning / Olin Foundation, 2018), 131–173; Seong-Hak Kim, *Michel de L'Hopital: The Vision of a Reformist Chancellor during the French Religious Wars* (Kirksville: Truman University Press, 1997).

### 3.2 *Private Contract and Public Law: Contrat de Poissy*

The royal idea of tapping into church wealth was not new. The French monarchy regularly collected the *décimes*, the clerical tenth.[57] In the 1560s, however, imminent bankruptcy compelled the government under Charles IX (r. 1560–1574) to push the clergy in an unprecedented manner. At the Estates General of Orléans in December 1560, Chancellor L'Hôpital made a shocking disclosure of the royal fiscality: the government deficit amounted to 43 million *livres*, four times the annual revenue. L'Hôpital compared the ten-year-old king to a little orphan, to whom his parents had left a terrible legacy of debts.[58] The chancellor proposed an increase of the *taille* for six years, promising no more raises in taxation. The deputies at Orléans demurred, claiming that they had no proper mandates to agree to such a proposal. When they met at Pontoise in August the following year, they again resisted the tax increase, despite that the government offered to allow the estates to oversee the tax collection process.[59]

One audacious idea floated by the chancellor and the royal council called for an annual income tax to be imposed on each ecclesiastical benefice on a graduated scale. The government justified the measure arguing that church revenues were national property; they could be appropriated, upon the consent of the people, for the needs of the realm.[60] The deputies of the second and third estates, unwilling to bear additional financial burdens themselves, eagerly responded to the plan to have the first estate redeem the royal domains as well as the *aides* and *gabelle*.[61] Outnumbered, the clergy offered to make a major sacrifice to rescue royal finances.

In 1561, the prelates agreed to pay 1.6 million *livres* annually for six years to repay the *Grand Parti* creditors and to repurchase the alienated royal domains. It also offered an additional 1.3 million per year for ten additional

57 Victor Carrière, "Les épreuves de l'Église de France au XVIe siècle," *Revue d'histoire de l'Église de France* 13 (1927): 433–465; Cauchie, "Les assemblées du clergé de France sous l'ancien régime."

58 L'Hôpital's address on December 13, 1560, in Michel de L'Hospital, *Discours pour la majorité de Charles IX et trois autres discours*, ed. Robert Descimon (Paris: Imprimerie nationale, 1993), 71. The desperate situation of royal finance was such that he "could not tell the estates about it, and to which the estates could not listen, without tears and cries." Ibid., 89.

59 Ivan Cloulas, *Catherine de Médicis* (Paris: Fayard, 1979), 157. If the chancellor's proposal to grant the assemblies the rights to control tax collection had been accepted, the Estates General would have been able to bypass the tax farmers and would almost certainly have been reborn. J. Russell Major, *Representative Government in Early Modern France* (New Haven: Yale University Press, 1980), 106–107, 161–162.

60 Cloulas, *Catherine de Médicis*, 163.

61 Kim, *Michel de L'Hôpital*, 98.

years to redeem a major part of official *rentes* on the town hall of Paris and pay the interest upon them.[62] Known as the Contrat de Poissy, this agreement between the king and the clergy, concluded in Saint-Germain-en-Laye on October 21, 1561, was an unprecedented concession made on the part of the ecclesiastical order to respond to the obligations of the kingdom. It established a new principle of the annual subsidy of the Church.

The critical issue was how to characterize this extraordinary agreement in legal terms. In the minds of many contemporaries, the contribution of the First Estate had to be of a voluntary nature, and a new way of defining the participation of the clergy in the state budget became necessary.[63] The Church was allowed to determine the form of its subsidy to the king and to handle its own payments to the treasury without interference from royal officials, thus preserving the fiction of 'free gifts.'

The clergy's contribution to the public treasury took the form of a letter of jurisdiction (*lettre de juridiction*) used in the *pays de droits coutumiers*, equivalent to a notarial act in the *pays de droit écrit* in the south. As such, it was a contract, an exchange of two promises, one by the prelates and the other by the king, with its own executory force. The credibility of the parties' intents was enhanced by the official attestation with the seal of the jurisdiction.[64] To all appearance, the contract between the king and the clergy was a purely voluntary and spontaneous agreement, concluded between two parties on a legal footing of perfect equality, the soul of all private *negotium*. But the objectives of the negotiation certainly went far beyond the usual nature of an agreement between individuals.[65] Few doubted its political nature, which was a forced financial contribution by the church to the expenses of the kingdom. But the king and the clergy deliberately chose to declare their accord in the form of private contract, because they wished to portray it as a matter of complete liberality of the clergy, granted in return for the king's firm promise to respect the absolute integrity of the property of the Church. They wanted to let it be known to the public that the deal concluded at Poissy was a voluntary act, not a royal decision or order. If it had been a result of royal command, it

62 Carrière, "Les épreuves de l'Église," 444–445; Wolfe, *Fiscal System of Renaissance France*, 121–123; Laferrière, *Le contrat de Poissy*.

63 Thierry Wanegffelen, "Comment faire payer le clergé? De l'art du compromis en France à l'aube des guerres de religion," in *Religion et impôts* (Clermont-Ferrand, 2006), https://hal.archives-ouvertes.fr/hal-00285089v2.

64 Marguerite Boulet-Sautel, "Le contrat de Poissy, acte de droit privé," in *Droit privé et Institutions régionales: Études offertes à Jean Yver* [online] (Mont-Saint-Aignan: Presses universitaires de Rouen et du Havre, 1976), http://books.openedition.org/purh/12353.

65 Ibid., para. 16 and 20.

would have been proclaimed in *lettres patentes*, stamped with the great seal of France and solemnly registered at the Parlement.

In the agreement, the clergy invoked "their privilege of paying nothing except by consent." The affirmation of "express consent," obtained through a formality of negotiation, opened the door to a compromise.[66] In return for what the prelates "promised and granted," the king "promised and granted" the exemption of the clergy from subsequent demands for subsidy and the protection of church property. Historians agree that the Contrat de Poissy marked an important juncture in the development of French public law. Transactions that were manifestations of public acts, an exercise of political power, took the form of private acts. The agreement did not mention the rights of the prince over ecclesiastical property at all. As one historian wrote, "nothing in it denoted a political subordination of one to the other; the idea of royal sovereignty was completely absent."[67] In reality, it was nothing other than the authoritative decision of the king that was thrust upon the Church.[68] Simply put, the mechanism of contract was opted to bring the prelates to an accord. The monarchy resorted to what Thierry Wanegffelen called "the art of compromise so important during the Renaissance."[69]

The solution of extracting financial contribution from the clergy under the disguise of gratuitous gifts continued until the end of the monarchy. The regularly renewed forced concessions by the Church of France dovetailed with the sacrosanct idea of taxation with consent. But historians would be missing a point if they saw these formalities as the accurate and complete institutional reality. The supposedly 'free' consent was far from free. The example of Poissy invites one to reconsider the meaning of consent in taxes, and contract in general, in the *ancien régime*. The principle of securing the agreement of the subjects could be molded to fit within the frameworks of an all-powerful state and obedience to the crown.

The Contrat de Poissy soon proved inadequate to meet the monarchy's needs. The cover of the Church's voluntary offer to pay subsidies was quickly dropped. In January 1563, the royal council authorized the confiscation of 3 million *livres* worth of church property.[70] The edict was of extraordinary

66 Wanegffelen, "Comment faire payer le clergé?"

67 Laferrière, *Le contrat de Poissy*, 147–148.

68 Boulet-Sautel, "Le contrat de Poissy, " para. 23, note 19.

69 Wanegffelen, "Comment faire payer le clergé?"

70 The size of alienation was indicated not in the amount of principal but in the value of *rentes*: the king ordered the sale of church land to create *rentes* worth 100,000 *écus* yearly, at the standard interest rate of *douze denier*, or 8.33 percent. This clearly shows that the aim of the alienation was to secure public credit. Claude Michaud, "Les Alién-

significance, not only for its material consequences but also for its constitutional implications. It was an express negation of the principle of the inalienability of ecclesiastical patrimony, which the clergy had claimed indisputable.

The edict implementing the sale of church property encountered resistance from the Parlement of Paris. The Parlement, reasserting its role as the guardian of law and the defender of the property rights of individuals against arbitrary royal power, refused to register the edict.[71] At the *lit de justice* held in May, Chancellor L'Hôpital told the *parlementaires* that royal domain, despite *loi fondamentale*, had been sold in times of war.[72] L'Hôpital convinced the Parlement that the edict was not a result of royal caprice but a measure imposed by public necessity, and therefore not a breach of property rights. More to the point, the chancellor reminded the court that the alienation of church land was proposed for the preservation of the church itself, because "it would be unreasonable to think that the church could still survive when the kingdom, of which church exists as a part and a member, was lost and ruined."[73] The king and the royal council had only reluctantly reached the decision, because "the necessity is the most strong and dominant of the reason," before which all others must yield.[74] The king was exercising his legitimate rights, inherent in the crown, for the common interest. The chancellor's address was a powerful reaffirmation of the sovereign's rights over ecclesiastical property in his state. The edict had been issued without the consent of the Church or the Pope. Rome had no choice but to accept it as a *fait accompli*, insisting that the alienated church property be used solely for suppressing heresy.

### 3.3 *Public Debt and the* République

Bodin was not oblivious to those remarkable developments unfolding at the royal court. He noted with approval that the Parlement of Paris remonstrated to the king in May 1563 that "his majesty alone could not break the contract made between him and the Clergy, without the consent of the latter, as long as

ations du temporel ecclésiastique dans la seconde moitié du XVI^e siècle. Quelques problèmes de méthode," *Revue d'histoire de l'église de France* 67 (1981), 62, note 7.

71 At the king's demand for prompt registration of the edict, the Parlement replied that it "could not and ought not to do it." Laferrière, *Le contrat de Poissy*, 239; Kim, *Michel de L'Hôpital*, 102.

72 Discourse at the Parlement de Paris, May 17, 1563. Loris Petris and David Amherdt, eds., *Michel de L'Hospital, discours et correspondance: La plume et la tribune II* (Geneva: Droz, 2013), 29.

73 Ibid., 37.

74 Ibid.

he is the debtor of justice."[75] Yet he was brought to accept L'Hôpital's exposition of the case of emergency.[76] Raising taxes could be done only "by the estates of the people, and of each province, city and community."[77] Nevertheless, declared Bodin, where there was public necessity and when the necessity was urgent the prince did not need to wait for the assembly of the estates.[78] A "just and reasonable cause" would allow the ruler to take private property or break a contract where he needed to act quickly for the "conservation of the state."[79] This is because "natural reason dictates that the public be preferred to the particular."[80] Still, the owner of the seized property must receive due compensation. It is worth quoting Bodin's words at length:

> It is a kind of legal absurdity to say that it is in the power of the prince to act dishonestly, since his power should always be measured by the standard of justice. [...] It is also a mistake to say that a sovereign prince has power to steal another's goods and to do evil, since it is rather impotence, weakness, and cowardice. If the prince, then, does not have power to overstep the bounds of natural law, which has been established by God, of whom he is the image, he will also not be able to take another's property without just and reasonable cause – as by purchase, exchange, lawful confiscation, or in negotiating terms of peace with an enemy, if it cannot otherwise be concluded than by taking the property of private individuals for the preservation of the state. Many [commentators] are not of this opinion. But natural reason would have the public [interest] preferred over the private, and have subjects not only pass over their injuries and desires for revenge, but give up their possessions also for the welfare of the commonwealth, as is ordinarily

75 Book I, Ch. 8, 152–153.

76 L'Hôpital's address to the Estates of Orléans in 1560 took place just about the time Bodin came to Paris from Toulouse in order to take up the position of *avocat* in the Parlement of Paris.

77 *"Cela ne se peut faire que par les états du peuple, et de chacune province, ville et communauté."* Book III, Ch. 7, 500.

78 It is only if *"la nécessité est urgente."* Book I, Ch. 8, 140. Whether there is urgent need is determined by the "foresight and diligence of a wise prince," on whom the people's welfare depends. Ibid. See Goyard-Fabre, *Jean Bodin*, 230.

79 "*la conservation de l'estat.*" Book I, Ch. 8, 140 and 156–157.

80 *"Mais Ia raison naturelle veut que le public soit preferé au particulier."* Book I, Ch. 8, 157. On princely obligations -- and exceptions to them -- to observe contracts concluded with natural inhabitants of the kingdom, see Eric Gojosso, "Le roi et le respect du droit naturel d'après la doctrine française (XVIe–XVIIe siècles) : l'exemple des contrats," *Slovenian Law Review* 4 (2007), 92–94.

done by one public toward another public, and by one individual toward another.[81]

A sovereign is not above contracts, but Bodin did not exclude the possibility that the king could bring his subjects to consent without violating their rights.

When considering Bodin's concept of sovereignty, one comes to a realization that whether French monarchs were allowed to deprive the subjects of their property arbitrarily may not be the most important question. The more relevant question would be to ascertain the complex nature of the notions of contract and consent. The content of consent was malleable, subject to contemporary perceptions and representations. It has been noted that the solution agreed upon at Poissy reflected the "psychological disposition of the parties, and the formula used there became customary."[82] The element of popular consent (*opinio necessitas*) in the development of customary law in the sixteenth century can be seen in a similar light. What was the relationship between the official recording of customs, taking place contemporaneous with the fiscal measures discussed above, and natural law in the French monarchy?

## 4 Custom, Natural Law, and Monarchy

In the 1560s, the campaigns to write down and reform provincial and local customs were in full swing.[83] While the Contrat de Poissy was an example of a public act conditioned by the rules of private law, the process of codifying customs showed that matters that had traditionally resided in the private realm could be brought to conform to the strict rules of public law. The codification of customs took place in the assemblies of the three estates in each locality, where members of the estates attested to what their customs were. The assemblies were presided over by royal commissioners, in most cases judges of the *parlements*, and in reality the opinions of the deputies carried little more weight than that of advice and counsel. The codification of customs was in many aspects a powerful affirmation of the legislative sovereignty of the king. The process of compiling and ratifying customs into law (called *homologation*) fell strictly under royal prerogative, but the king, committed

81 Book I, Ch. 8, 156–157. The translation is from Franklin, *Jean Bodin, On Sovereignty*, 39–40 (notes and page numbers omitted).

82 Boulet-Sautel, "Le contrat de Poissy," para. 21.

83 See Kim, *Custom, Law, and Monarchy.*

to governing with the consent of the subjects, refrained from dictating their contents.[84] With the codification of customs, much of the legal life of the subjects which had hitherto escaped the authority of the king came under his control, all this in accordance with consultative procedures involving the local estates. But such consultation was, as M.J. Tooley noted, "a matter of policy and not obligation."[85]

### 4.1 *Natural Law and French Law*

The humanist school in sixteenth-century France tended to eschew the scholastic notion of natural moral law and its abstract, rigid formulations. In comparison with the countries in central and northern Europe, there was little systematic discussion of natural law among French scholars. Natural law was not a prominent topic of academic discourse in sixteenth- and seventeenth-century France.[86] Legal humanists were preponderantly practicing jurists, and as such they focused on domestic traditions of *droit coutumier* and Roman law. Roman law was treated as one of the provincial customs, although the *Corpus juris civilis* was recognized as a representation of fundamental concepts of justice, i.e., a natural order.[87] The central ideas of natural law, deeply embedded in the compilations by Emperor Justinian, coalesced into commonly recognized principles derived from the recorded customs to give rise to the idea of 'our French law.' This convergence prompted the emergence of new legal doctrines, which approached constitutional theory through the medium of customary law and of Roman law as written reason (*ratio scripta*). The idea of drafting a well-ordered French law preoccupied many people. It has been observed that the "overstated proto-positivistic" method of early modern

84 After all, public psychology mattered. See Joseph van Kan, *Les efforts de codification en France: Étude historique et psychologique* (Paris: Rousseau & cie, 1929).

85 M.J. Tooley, "Introduction," in *Six Books of the Commonwealth by Jean Bodin (Abridged and Translated)* (Oxford: Basic Blackwell, 1955), https://www.constitution.org/2-Authors/bodin/bodin.txt.

86 See Dan Edelstein, *On the Spirit of Rights (Life of Ideas)* (Chicago: University of Chicago Press, 2019); Ivo Cerman, "On Rights without Natural Law," *Opera Historica* 21 (2020): 90–107.

87 The *droit écrit*, where it was the source of the law, was received as custom. In 1312, Philip IV (r. 1285–1314) declared that Roman law was followed in France as customary law, not written law, and this by the permission of him and his ancestors. Kim, *Custom, Law, and Monarchy*, 34. See also Marie Seong-Hak Kim, "Legal Pluralism That Wasn't: State and the Plurality of Law in Late Medieval and Early Modern Europe," *Tijdschrift voor rechtsgeschiedenis* 93 (2025): 130–167. A "classic" natural law, a product of Aristotelian philosophy, was continued into Roman law. Michel Villey, *La formation de la pensée juridique moderne, Cours du droit, 1961–1968* (Paris: Montchrestien, 1968), 58.

French humanists often obscured the jurisdictional complexity of French law at the time.[88] Bodin's discourses may have reflected the optimistic attitude of contemporary French jurists that positive law based on the reformed *coutumes*, informed by Roman law principles and systematized under the authority of the king, could serve as a just system.[89] In this program, recourse to natural law as moral philosophy remained largely a separate matter.

Just as he distinguished between law and contract, Bodin also separated custom from the law. Custom, grounded in popular consent, had binding force, but it was inferior to that of the laws enacted by the sovereign. He declared: "Custom has force only by sufferance and so long as it pleases the sovereign prince," who possessed the sole authority to make a law from it "by putting thereunto his own confirmation." Thus, "all the force of civil laws and customs lies in the power of the sovereign prince."[90] The sovereign could amend or abolish custom by a simple royal act.[91]

The inviolability of private property and the obligatory force of contracts had traditionally been grounded in custom. When customs, legal privileges once binding on royal authority, were turned into stipulated laws, the king's decisions were freed from the shackles from the past. What about the potential dangers of arbitrary and willful royal power? Since Bodin defined sovereign authority in terms of law-making power, he could place constraints on the actions of the sovereign only through non-legal means. The rights of private property appertained to the realm of natural law. Here, the novelty and profundity of Bodin's approach to 'natural law' come to the fore. In medieval and Renaissance monarchies, kings were dependent on the corporate institutions from which they drew political and financial support. Ubiquitous privileges enjoyed by the components of corporate society, legitimated by custom, imposed broad limits on royal dominion. But the codification of customs redefined the boundaries of vested rights, individual or corporate. No longer anchored in old customs, liberties and privileges now derived their justifications solely from natural law. Bodin duly placed all conceivable checks on sovereign power within the realm of natural law.

---

88 Alain Wijffels, "Ancien Régime France: Legal Particularism under the Absolute Monarchy," in *The Laws' Many Bodies: Studies in Legal Hybridity and Jurisdictional Complexity, c1600–1900*, eds. Seán Patrick Donlan and Dirk Heirbaut (Berlin: Duncker & Humblot, 2015), 99.

89 William Farr Church, *Constitutional Thought in Sixteenth-Century France: A Study in the Evolution of Ideas* (New York: Octagon Books, 1969), 80.

90 Book I, Ch. 10, 222.

91 Ibid.

Bodin's conception of natural law presumed a God-ordained, just system. The recognition that no positive law was adequate for all circumstances led to appeals to natural law. While Bodin held that sovereignty was limited by divine and natural law, however, he did not provide concrete mechanisms for determining whether a prince's commands were repugnant to natural law. The result was that the concepts of the laws of God and nature entailed only theoretical and abstract limitations, within which the king retained considerable discretion.[92] Other than the sovereign himself, no power in the state could draw the line of demarcation between the two spheres of law, that is, between civil law and natural law, and compel the ruler to adhere to the latter.[93] Put differently, whether positive law of the king was in accord with divine and natural law was subject to his own "interpretation."[94] The sovereign imposes laws by virtue of his very definition, and, insofar as the sovereign prince is the interpreter of law, it is his will that becomes the foundation of political power. This means no human agency could hold the prince accountable to divine or natural law.

In practical terms, vital changes followed when the legal basis of private property was no longer found in the customary law of the land but now found in natural law.[95] The king, constrained only by abstract natural law, could depart from the principles of the sanctity of private property, if necessary for the survival and safety of the state or the good of the commonweal. The inviolability of property rights, grounded solely in natural law, was not rigid enough to withstand the force of sovereignty, where sovereignty itself also rested on natural law. For Bodin, it was sovereignty, not natural law, that provided ultimate legitimacy of the state. He did not resort to natural law as a source of political authority or as a guide to a desirable social order.

In sum, as the binding force of custom retreated before sovereignty, so did the biting force of natural law that replaced it. Natural law became a set of principle or moral recommendations, for humane and prudent governance, and its scope within the territorial polity was where Bodin's concerns lay. What truly and effectively restrained the prince were immediate political considerations, such as how to procure public credit that he needed to operate the government and preserve the republic. Sovereign authority reinforced, not

92 Church, *Constitutional Thought*, 242.

93 Bodin states that the will of the sovereign is limited by divine law. But one may ask: "exercising in solitude, can it not be mistaken, or quite simply detach itself from its model, while keeping its attributes?" Chanteur, "La loi naturelle," 294.

94 Ibid., 291–292.

95 Church, *Constitutional Thought*, 235.

weakened royal commitment to the subjects' right to property. Bodin expected the prince to behave in faithful accordance with that fundamental constitutional principle and promise.

### 4.2 *Absolute Monarchy and Royal Justice*

The term 'absolutism' was a neologism dating from the French Revolution, but the concept of 'absolute power' was widely used in the Middle Ages and the early modern period. Medieval jurists discussed at length the Roman legal maxim *princeps legibus solutus est* — the prince is absolved, that is, freed from the laws. 'Absolute' here means 'detached from the laws,' but few claimed that the king was separate from the law. Bodin's discourse on obedience to the king postulated, in fact, the preeminence of the law. The Nominalist theology distinguished between *potentia absoluta* and *potentia ordinata*: God created the world in this way although He could have created it differently. Deviation from ordained power is possible not only for God but also for humans within the frameworks of laws given by God.[96] God Himself is bound by His own promises. As He freely limits His power, so does the king. The absolute power of a ruler in Bodin's system reaffirmed the boundaries of power, within which a king exercised sovereignty.

*Les six livres de la république* is widely viewed as a *thèse de circonstance*, a pragmatic response to the crisis of the Reformations and religious wars.[97] Bodin's theoretical ideas emanated from his crisis consciousness with certain urgency.[98] During the civil conflict, loyalty to the monarchy, the cement of the French nation and religious unity, came under threat. The Monarchomach doctrine of popular sovereignty, as espoused by figures like François Hotman (1524–1590), claimed that the public good – namely, the true religion – stood above the king, and justified the constitutional right of resistance against a tyrant-king.[99] Bodin forcefully rejected the Monarchomach theory and argued that the stability of the commonweal depended on the crown. He refined and articulated his theory of sovereignty as a viable response to the religious tensions and political chaos of his time.

---

96 See Heiko A. Oberman, *The Harvest of Medieval Theology: Gabriel Biel and Late Medieval Nominalism* (Cambridge, MA: Harvard University Press, 1963), discussed in Kim, *Custom, Law, and the Monarchy*, 12 and 18.

97 Parker, "Law, Society and the State," 269.

98 Hinrichs, "Das Fürstenbild Bodins," 281 (*"Krisenbewußtsein seiner Zeit"*).

99 The term monarchomach comes from the Greek *monarchos* and *machos*, meaning one who fights against the monarch.

The idea of the crown as the provider of justice was more urgently felt than ever during the crises of civil war. The survival of the kingdom required the reduction of the privileges and prerogatives of the principal groups in the kingdom, and for Bodin only the king possessed the authority necessary to deal with these powerful groups. But the king's objectives did not require head-on collisions; they could be better achieved through negotiations and compromise. Underlying the formalities of agreement and contract was the demand for legal certainty, which Bodin emphasized as an integral element of the king's sovereign power. Bodin's preferred model was royal monarchy which, unlike seigneurial monarchy, operated under the guarantee of the rule of law. The king ruled by constantly affirming existing laws, including royal edicts and ordinances as well as the *coutumes*, and kept his hands off private property. Bodin described how a strong monarchy in France could, and eventually did, function.

## 5 Conclusion

This chapter has discussed Bodin's political thought by focusing on the fiscal situation of the French Renaissance monarchy. There is growing recognition that state formation cannot be fully understood apart from the processes by which states raised and borrowed money, especially for war. The financial crisis during the religious wars explains in part why the sanctity of private property and contract occupied such an important place in Bodin's theory.

Counterintuitive as it may seem, the exigencies of public credit and the mobilization of the subjects' wealth and resources contributed to the emergence of a powerful *république*. The financial crisis restrained Bodin's royal monarchs, compelling them to act within the boundaries of natural law. Economic reality, far from being absolute, helped facilitate the triumph of the absolute state. Royal apologists took pains to prove that the rulers did not arbitrarily confiscate their subjects' property or take away their freedom. Bodin would simply ask: why would a reasonable king want to do that and make his job of governing more difficult?

Bodin's main concerns were not so much about formulating internally consistent theories of government as about preserving the *république* in France. The state holds the responsibility of promoting the common good, and the king must possess sufficient authority to prevent disorder and social disintegration. Bodin's absolute king seeks public good, in full compliance with natural law. If one assumes that existing social divisions are part of 'nature,' as did Bodin, then apologists for absolute monarch can claim justice is served for all.

Personal observations of the monarchy during times of crisis led Bodin to develop his theory of sovereignty and the limitations he placed on it. There were historical reasons behind his theory of sovereignty.

Finally, one may be excused for reiterating the point that discussions of law – even natural law – are historically contingent. Most existing studies of natural law in early modern Europe have focused on how medieval natural law traditions evolved into modern liberal theory. It is important, and necessary, to elucidate how changing notions of natural law informed the conception and practice of domestic governance in the early modern bureaucratic state. No less critical, however, is understanding how state governance, in turn, shaped contemporary conception of natural law. Bodin's natural law ideas serve as a valuable reminder of the interconnectedness between legal theories and institutions and of the need to study philosophy and history in tandem.

CHAPTER 2

# The Mutability of Nature: Dominion, Natural Law, and the Order of Grace in Domingo de Soto's *de iustitia et iure* (1553–1554)

*Rafael Cronje Mateus*

## 1 Introduction

The concept of dominion is central to Domingo de Soto's theory of rights, as Annabel Brett defends, for upon it he – along with the other Spanish scholastics – developed the idea of natural subjective rights.[1] It is also based on dominion that Soto investigates the problem of the mutability of natural law – a problem intimately related to another one, the question of whether God could dispense humans from obeying the ten commandments in certain circumstances.

Far from being a purely theoretical problem, the idea of natural law's mutability had practical consequences for the administration of justice during the *ancien régime*, such as what António Manuel Hespanha calls the Order of Grace[2] – the name he gives to the many powers kings, queens, and princes had, which allowed them to create political and juridical realities almost as if from the void, in a clear analogy to the divine powers.[3]

Such an analogy between divine and human power was a common way of understanding the political community. For from the perception that all things proceed from God one quickly arrives at the insight that man, nature, society, and God are part of a community of being, and that there is a struc-

1 Annabel Brett, "Scholastic political thought and the modern concept of the state," in *Rethinking the Foundations of Modern Political Thought*, eds. Annabel Brett and James Tully with Holly Hamilton-Bleakley (Cambridge: Cambridge University Press, 2006), 144.

2 António Manuel Hespanha, "Les autres raisons de la politique. L'economie de la grâce," in *Recherches sur l'histoire de l'État dans le monde ibérique (15e.–20e. Siècles)*, ed. J.-F. Schaub (Paris: Presses de l'École Normale Supérieure, 1993), 67–86; António Manuel Hespanha, *Cultura Jurídica Europeia* (Coimbra: Almedina, 2018), 164–170.

3 Hespanha, *Cultura Jurídica Europeia*, 164–166.

 | DOI:10.1163/9789004748712_004

tural identity between the human soul, the order of society, the whole of creation, and God's reason.[4] Domingo de Soto is no exception to this.[5]

While this paper focuses on the natural law's mutability as investigated by Soto, it will also provide some distinctions and categories that will be useful to better understand the Order of Grace.

## 2 Biographical and Bibliographical Notes

One cannot say anymore that Domingo de Soto's contributions to jurisprudence are unknown. In the last decades, many studies explored his actualization of Saint Thomas Aquinas' natural law theory and his reflections on moral reasoning. Some, as well, have delved into his contributions to physics, logic, and economics.[6]

Domingo de Soto is one of the first names of what came to be known as the School of Salamanca or the Second Scholastic, a group of Catholic theologians – almost all of them Dominicans or Jesuits – that recovered Saint

---

4 Aquinas' *Summa Theologiæ*, for instance, is perhaps the most complete and consolidated version of this conception. The fact that the work remained unfinished, due to practical and spiritual reasons, is a consequence of the most fundamental aspect of this view: the notion that the ultimate fulfillment of men's nature cannot be found in this life, but only in the perfect participation in divine nature – which, of course, can only be received after death. For a symbolic analysis of *Summa's* structure, see Erwin Panofsky, *Gothic Architecture and Scholasticism* (New York: New American Library, 1957). The same conception can be seen in Dom Pedro, Infante, Duke of Coimbra's work *Livro da Virtuosa Bemfeitoria*. See Infante D. Pedro, "Livro da Virtuosa Bemfeitoria," in *Obras dos Príncipes de Avis*, ed. M. Lopes Almeida (Porto: Lello & Irmão Editores, 1981), 525–764.

5 For Domingo de Soto's exposition on the matter, see the way he explains the relation between God's eternal law and creation's natural law, Fratris Dominici Soto, *De Iustitia et Iure in Libri Decem* (Excudebat Ioannes Baptista a Terranoua, 1569), 22 [B. I, Q. 3, Art. 1º]. See also Thomas Aquinas' argument in favor of the monarchy, as being the form of government that most closely resembles God's divine regimen, both in *De Regno ad Regem Cypri* (Libri I, caput 3) and in *Summa Theologiæ* (I–II, Q. 105, Art. 1º). And for broader considerations regarding the transposition of theological reasoning to political and juridical reasoning based on the similitude of circumstances, see Ernst H. Kantorowicz, *The King's Two Bodies. A Study in Medieval Political Theology* (Princeton/Oxford: Princeton University Press, 2016), 16–21.

6 See the bibliography cited in Benjamin Hill, "Domingo de Soto," in *Encyclopedia of Medieval Philosophy, Philosophy Between 500 and 1500*, ed. Henrik Lagerlund (Dordrecht: Springer, 2020), 462–466, and in Benjamin Hill, "Domingo de Soto," in *Great Christian Jurists in Spanish History*, eds. Rafael Domingo and Javier Martínez-Torrón (Cambridge: Cambridge University Press, 2018), 134–156.

Thomas Aquinas' work to reformulate Catholic theology during the Protestant Reformation.[7]

The role of Soto in the School is of such importance that Merio Scattola, for instance, considers him as one of its founders – if not its true founder – along with Francisco de Vitória.[8]

It would be a mistake, however, to think that Soto's role in the School comprised exclusively intellectual affairs. He, like many other theologians,[9] was deeply involved in the political conflicts of both the Catholic Church and the Empire, having served as the emperor's theologian at the Council of Trent and as confessor and political advisor to Charles V.[10]

Those biographical notes show that he was conscious of the potential political and spiritual impact of his intellectual work and the content of the dedication he wrote in *De Iustitia et Iure* confirms it.[11] When reading *De Iustitia et Iure*, therefore, one must try to understand its political, juridical, and theological implications, even when, on the surface, these aspects don't stand out.

The version utilized of *De Iustitia et Iure* was the second edition, from 1556 to 1557, for, according to Wim Decock, some relevant changes were made since the first edition.[12] D. Jaime Torrubiano Ripoll's Spanish translation was also consulted.[13] And a special mention goes to the digitalized and transcribed

7 Carlo Giacon, *La seconda scolastica. I problemi giuridico-politici. Suárez, Bellarmino*, Mariana (Ed. F.lli Bocca: Milano, 1950) *apud* Merio Scattola, "Domingo de Soto e la fondazione della Scuola di Salamanca," *Veritas* 54, no. 3 (2009): 53.

8 Scattola, "Domingo De Soto," 54.

9 Scatolla paints a rich image that illustrates how the roles of theologian, philosopher and jurist were almost indistinguishable in de Soto's circle: *"Se vogliamo descrivere il pensiero politico spagnolo del quindicesimo secolo, possiamo dire che si trattava di una dottrina e di una prassi politica elaborate in primo luogo da e per teologi e canonisti, la quale può bene essere simboleggiata con l'unione di cattedra, pulpito e confessionale. L'università di Salamanca era infatti il luogo di formazione dei funzionari di rango superiore, che sostenevano la monarchia nel governo dei regni iberici; essa concepiva perciò il politico fondamentalmente ed esclusivamente come il consulente, il consigliere di corte o il ministro e sviluppò una forma di pensiero politico che coincideva con questa figura e con la sua formazione."* Scattola, "Domingo De Soto," 55.

10 Vicente Beltrán de Heredia, *Domingo de Soto. Estudio biográfico documentado* (Instituto de cultura hispánica: Salamanca, 1960), 117–173, 207–237.

11 Fratris Dominici Soto, *De Iustitia et Iure in Libri Decem* (Excudebat Ioannes Baptista a Terranoua, 1569), 1–2.

12 Wim Decock, "Domingo de Soto: De iustitia et iure (1553–1554)," in *The Formation and Transmission of Western Legal Culture. 150 Books that Made the Law in the Age of Printing*, eds. S. Dauchy et al. (Dordrecht: Springer, 2016), 84–86.

13 Fray Dominici Soto, *Tratado de la Justicia y el Derecho. Tomo Primeiro*, trans. D. Jaime Torrubiano Ripoll (Editora Reus: Madrid, 1922). Fray Dominici Soto, *Tratado de la Justi-*

version of the work, provided by The School of Salamanca: A Digital Collection of Sources.[14] It proved very helpful, especially where the digital copy was blurred or illegible.

## 3 The Mutability of Lex Naturalis and Ius Naturale

The exercise of the powers of the Order of Grace depends on the possibility of change in the laws upon which the social order was constructed. For, if there is only one possible social order in accordance with the one possible determination of the natural law, then, there is simply no room for legal flexibility.

Therefore, to better understand the possibilities and the limits of royal action, a study of the problem of the mutability of *lex naturalis* and of *ius naturale* – distinctions which will be made below – is necessary.

This problem emerges in the scholastic attempts to formulate a natural law theory based on Aristotle's works, particularly the *Ethica Nicomachea*. When Soto pondered the problem, it was through the lenses of Saint Thomas, which included several differentiations and modifications, made first in his *Sentencia Libri Ethicorum*, then extended in *Summa Theologiœ*. After Aquinas' work, the Aristotelian problem was radically transformed.

Therefore, to comprehend Soto's answer in *De Iustitia et Iure*, it is necessary, first, to briefly study the changes Aquinas made. Then, Soto's particular solutions and reasonings can be presented considering the new *status quœstionis*.

In Aristotle's small fragment about the variability of right by nature – which is a part of the study about justice and its types in his *Ethica Nicomachea* (EN), *v, 1134b18–1135a5*[15] – a critical problem to any natural law theory is presented: can what is right or just according to nature change?

---

*cia y el Derecho. Tomo Segundo*, trans. D. Jaime Torrubiano Ripoll (Editora Reus: Madrid, 1926).

14 Domingo de Soto, "De Iustitia et Iure," in *The School of Salamanca. A Digital Collection of Sources*, ed. Christiane Birr (Akademie der Wissenschaften und der Literatur: Mainz, 2020 [1553]), https://id.salamanca.school/texts/W0011

15 All the citations from Aristotle's work were based on both the English and the Portuguese translations: Aristotle, "Nicomachean Ethics," trans. W.D. Ross, in *The Complete Works of Aristotle. Revised Oxford Translation. Vol. II*, ed. Jonathan Barnes (Princeton University Press: Princeton, 1995); Aristóteles, *Ethica Nicomachea v 1–15. Tratado da Justiça*, trans. Marco Zingano (Editora Odysseus: São Paulo, 2017). The Greek text is from: Aristotle, *Ethica Nicomachea*, ed. J. Bywater (Clarendon Press: Oxford, 1894), http://www.perseus.tufts.edu/hopper/collection?collection=Perseus%3Acorpus%3Aperseus%2Cwork%2CAristotle%2C%20Nicomachean%20Ethics

Aristotle's study of justice begins with a distinction between legal and natural justice, two parts of political justice (*politikon dikaion*). Then, he presents a first observation that these two parts differ based on their strength or power and their origin, and that there are some who question the existence of such thing as a natural justice, given the radical differences of opinion about what is just. Lastly, he concludes that everything that is just among men is variable (*kineton*).[16]

It is an obscure fragment, which doesn't solve any of the problems it poses and that demands a great interpretative effort to be clarified in terms of what Aristotle really meant. Some philosophers, such as Pierre Destrée, Leo Strauss, and Eric Voegelin examined the problem.[17] But their interpretation – as well as their correctness – exceeds the scope of this contribution.

Aquinas first faced the Aristotelian problem in his commentaries on Nicomachean Ethics, *Sententia Libri Ethicorum*.[18] In it, he introduced two fundamental changes which, later, provided the ground on which his more robust theory of law would be developed, in his *Summa Theologiæ*: first, he identified Aristotle's *dikaion* with the Roman *ius*; and, second, he considered the *iustum naturale*– a first translation of *physikon dikaion* – as being attached to the human mind.

He identifies *dikaion* with *ius* when, citing Saint Isidore, he affirms that *ius* is that which is said to be just.[19] To conclude, however, that the *iustum naturale* is attached to human mind, Aquinas presents more detailed arguments.[20] First, he perceives a contradiction between what Aristotle and the Roman

16 For a detailed analysis of the place this problem occupies in the Treaty of Justice, see Rafael Cronje Mateus and Gustavo César Machado Cabral, "A mutabilidade do Justo por Natureza nas Interpretações Escolásticas de Aristóteles: Tomás de Aquino, Domingo de Soto e Francisco Suarez," *História do Direito* 3, no. 4 (August 2022), 56–79.

17 See Jefferson Luiz França, "Alguns Aspectos sobre o Direito Natural na Ética a Nicômaco de Aristóteles (En, v, 10, 1134b18–1135a5)," in. *HYPNOS*, 35, 2015, 231–245; Pierre Destrée, "Aristote et la Question du Droit Naturel (Eth. Nic., v, 10, 1134b18–1135a5)," *Phronesis* 45, no. 3 (August 2000), 220–239; Leo Strauss, *Natural Law and History* (University of Chicago Press: Chicago, 1953), 156–163; Voegelin, *Anamnesis*, 140–174. For a philological commentary, see Aristóteles, *Ethica Nicomachea*, 234–246.

18 Sancti Thomæ de Aquino, *Sententia Libri Ethicorum, vol. II, libri IV–X – Indices. Opera Omnia Iussu Leonis XIII P.M. Edita. Tomus XLVII* (Ad Sanctæ Sabinæ, 1969). The English translation was used as well: Thomas Aquinas, *Commentary on the Nicomachean Ethics*, trans. C.I. Litzinger (O.P. Henry Regnery Company, 1964).

19 Aquino, *Sententia Ethic. lib. 5*, sec. 12, 1134b18, l. 17.

20 Only a brief version of his argument was presented here. For more complete exposition, see Rafael Cronje Mateus and Gustavo César Machado Cabral, "A mutabilidade do Justo por Natureza nas Interpretações Escolásticas de Aristóteles: Tomás de Aquino, Domingo de Soto e Francisco Suarez," *História do Direito* 3, no. 4 (August 2022), 56–79.

jurists mean with *iustum politicum* – *politikon dikaion*, in Greek.[21] He argues that, for Aristotle, the *politikon dikaion* is the *iustum civile* (civil law or civil justice), while for the Romans the *iustum civile* was merely a part of *iustum positivum*. This contradiction between the two opinions, he continues, has its origin in the different uses Aristotle and the jurists make of the terms *politicum* and *civile*. The philosopher speaks *ex usu*, i.e., according to the use citizens make of the *iustum politicum/civile*, and the jurists *ex causa*, i.e., according to the reason a city constituted the *iustum* for itself. This self-constituted *iustum*, to Aristotle, is the *iustum legale* or *positivum*, says Aquinas.[22]

These changes in the Aristotelian concepts are central to Aquinas' analysis. His conclusion of the two ways of observing the *iustum politicum et civile*, that is, *ex usu* and *ex causa*, are applied to the *iustum naturale* as well, which he understands as that which nature gifted the human mind or spirit.[23] Therefore, the investigation of the *iustum naturale* – and of the problem of its mutability – depends on this distinction.

*Ex usu*, Aristotle presents the *phisikon dikaion* according to the effect or the virtue it has, which is that same strength everywhere – the same virtue – to compel to the good and to keep away from the evil.[24] The identical strength – or power – everywhere exists because of human nature's persistence, which is this *iustum*'s cause, since it is the same everywhere, for there exists only one human nature – contrary to the cities or prince's *iustum*, which are many and manifest itself exclusively to its respective citizens or subjects.[25]

*Ex causa*, the specific use or perception of *iustum naturale* is indifferent, for it doesn't depend on being seen or not (*in videri vel non videri*), since it doesn't originate in the human opinion, but in nature. Its natural existence and attachment to human mind is independent of being known or manifested in positive legislation.

From that, he introduces the attachment of *iustum naturale* to human mind. An explanation of that becomes necessary at this point. Aquinas argues that this natural knowledge exists in the mode of indemonstrable principles and those that are derived or simply close to them. Those derived are formed by the principles the true study of men discovers. For example, the principle that we should avoid evil, which is evident to every man independently of being intellectually acknowledged or logically concluded. Of another kind

21 Aquino, *Sententia Ethic. lib.* 5, sec. 12, 1134b18, l. 10–9.
22 *Ibidem*, l. 24–9.
23 *Ibidem*, l. 31.
24 *Ibidem*, l. 36–40.
25 *Ibidem*, l. 42–5.

are those principles industrially devised by the visible work of men, which are called *iusta legalia*, legal justice.[26]

*Iustum naturale*, therefore, is a natural knowledge, formed by indemonstrable principles which do not demand human creation to exist and manifest themselves. It is that *iustum* to which human nature *naturally* is inclined.[27] We are, here, already at quite a distance from Aristotle's *physikon dikaion*, a notion which didn't, at first, present itself as a form of knowledge, but as one of two parts of political justice. It is after this that he arrives at the mutability problem.

In his *Summa Theologiæ*, q. 57 in IIaIIae, and qq. 94 and 97 in IaIIae, Aquinas deals with mutability in its many possibilities. First, however, he introduces a distinction which wasn't present in his previous work: that between *lex naturalis* and *ius naturale*. He does so in art. 1º, q. 57, IIaIIae. Aquinas defines *ius*[28] as that which is just (*iustum*). Therefore, the study of *ius* is part of the investigation about justice.[29] While being part of the same investigation, the objects, nevertheless, are distinct one from another, and must not be confused.

He then traces the distinction between *lex naturalis* and *ius naturale*. While *ius* is that which is just – being, therefore, different from the agent, for it is external to him – *lex* is a certain prudential rule which exists in the mind of men. *Lex* is not *ius*, for *lex* is the reason of that which is just, the *ratio iuris*.[30] *Lex naturalis* is here identified with the indemonstrable principles presented in the *Sententia* as *iustum naturale*. The distinction between *lex* and *ius* is central to the problem of the mutability.

In art. 3º, q, 57, IIaIIae, Aquinas, distinguishes the types of adjustment of *ius naturale* to the mutable human nature. The two types emerge when the question is considered in two different manners: first, by the absolute consideration of the thing, i.e., that which is natural, that which is adjusted to a certain relation with another thing (this seems to include a notion of the end, *telos*, of

26 *Ibidem*, l. 45–57.

27 *Ibidem*, l. 57–9.

28 The English translation of the word, law, brings terrible confusion, especially considering that for this particular tradition of thought the distinction between *lex* and *ius* is indispensable. In Portuguese we have specific translations for these two terms, *lei e direito*. To avoid confusion, the Latin terms will be used.

29 Tomás de Aquino, *Suma Teológica II seção da II parte, questões 57–122, vol. VI* (Edições Loyola: São Paulo, 2013), 46.

30 Aquino, *Suma*, 48.

the thing's nature); and, second, by the consideration of the consequences of the adjustment.[31]

See, for instance, the human propriety of land possession – or any possession. There seems to be no reason in the thing itself that demands an individual possession of it. Two different individuals could have the possession of one plot of land, for the land's nature is indifferent to it. Yet, if the possession's consequences are considered – how can the land be better used? Better preserved? etc. – it seems convenient that it belongs only to one man.[32] Therefore, the two types of adjustment correspond to two types of mutation of *ius naturale*: the first one to the change in a thing's nature and the second one to the changes in circumstances or opportunities, which demand different relations of justice, different adjustments of the *ius* to the thing.

In q. 94, art. 5ª, of IaIIae, Saint Thomas Aquinas presents a different account of the problem, which adds yet another layer of complexity to the Aristotelian problem: that of the divine agency. There are three modes of change in the law of nature (*lex naturæ*): change by addition, by subtraction and by an explicit divine order. The first happens when divine law or human law adds something to natural things, something that is useful to human life; the second when something that belonged to *lex naturæ* is removed from it. However, the change by subtraction is only possible in what Aquinas calls the secondary precepts, which are conclusions close to the first precepts – or first principles – of *lex naturæ* and these first principles never change.[33]

And, lastly, the third mode happens when, by divine commandment, a particular act ceases to be illicit, such as when God commanded Israel, in the Old Testament, to inflict death, some men to unite themselves with women outside the wedlock, or the appropriation of other's possessions. By human order, of course, such things couldn't cease to be illicit, but by divine, they could, as Aquinas develops in q. 100, art. 8º, of IaIIae. Therefore, both *iustum naturale* and *lex naturalis* could change according to Aquinas.

Aquinas altered the problem left by Aristotle considerably. It is almost unrecognizable. From a compact and obscure comment on the variability of *physikon dikaion*, Aquinas arrived at a complex scheme, in which God, man, nature, and society participate to constitute *ius*, with both *lex naturale* and *iustum naturale*. It is from this differentiated understanding that Domingo de Soto begins his own investigation.

31 Aquino, *Suma*, 50.

32 Aquino, *Suma*, 50–51.

33 Tomás de Aquino, *Suma Teológica I seção da II parte, questões 49–114, vol. IV* (Edições Loyola: São Paulo, 2015), 569–570.

These four additions Aquinas made to the original problem – *dikaion* as *ius*, natural law's attachment to human mind, the distinction between *lex* and *ius*, and the changes in a things' nature caused by God – were incorporated in Domingo de Soto's work. The last one, as will be seen, allows for another differentiation in the way God acts over the cosmos.

In *De Iustitia et Iure, libri I, quæstio 4, art. 4*, Domingo de Soto investigates, like Thomas Aquinas before him, if *lex naturalis* is the same to every mortal. And, again, like Aquinas he answers by recurring to the distinction between natural principles and its conclusions. *Lex naturalis,* on its principles, is the same to every mortal, affirms Soto, not only regarding the rectitude of truth, but also regarding its knowledge. It remains the same, as well, in knowing and in acting, for there is a likeness between the principles of practical reason and of speculation, all of them being true, firm, and clear considering natural reason. Therefore, every man, if he is sane of mind, can recognize truth and live in accordance with it.

However, these principles' conclusions don't have the same clarity and firmness. To correctly arrive at conclusions based on the immutable principles is a difficult process that suffers from special obstacles, and the right knowledge of them is affected by a clouded reason, which has its origin in bad habits – vices – which blind the intellectual capacities. Therefore, both the process of arriving at conclusions based on the principles and the knowledge of the principles are both deficient in men.

This deficiency affects two types of reason: the practical and the speculative. While both have the same stating point – the clear and firm principles of *lex naturæ* – they do not proceed by an identical reasoning process. Speculative reason has what is common and necessary as an object and reaches the truth in conclusions without any defect – that is, the truth this reason sees in the immutable principles of natural law. Practical reason, on the other hand, has the individual and the contingent as object and proceeds descending from the principles to the concrete things, things based on which humans act. Because of this, it will have defects. The more down to the particulars and further away from the principles it descends, the more defects it will have.

Therefore, when considering how to act, through practical reason, human beings incur many deficiencies and can easily conclude wrongly, from the principles, what is right to do. Not only that, but since the contingent reality is mutable and varied, there are many possibilities of right action, given the changes in circumstance. Different actions can, says Soto, be equally just by nature, for the *lex naturalis* is not the same to practical reason. A rightful judgment of concrete human acts, therefore, demands an analysis of the specific circumstances, which include the agent's conscience.

But what if an individual's vices affect his conscience and reason to such an extent that the principles of natural law and the intellectual process of arriving at correct speculative and practical conclusions are greatly clouded? Can the natural law be as if abolished or erased from human mind? If so, does the just also changes?

In Book 1, q. 4, art. 5°, the solution is presented. He utilizes Aquinas' distinction between the change in *lex naturæ* by addition and change by subtraction. By addition, both the principles and the conclusions of natural law can be changed by the state of an individual's conscience; and by subtraction, changes can only occur in the conclusions, both in those closer to the principles and in those more distant – i.e., more down in the hierarchy of individualization and concreteness. This means that something that exists in accordance with the first principles of natural law cannot cease to be in that way. And even the conclusions close to it can change only because of human imperfection.

Human imperfection and the practical reason's descent in the hierarchy of being, from God to temporal beings, are the cause of change in the natural law. The principle of change, therefore, is not in *lex naturæ*, but in the things themselves – and man is counted among these things. Close conclusions, in concrete and particular cases, have in themselves truths that are contrary to the general truth of principles.

In his own investigation, Soto finds the explanation for Aristotle's cryptic comment on the mutability of the *ius* called natural. The fire, being immutable, symbolizes the first principles; conclusions, on the other hand, are the part of *ius naturale* that can change – regarding man and other beings that have a mutable existence.

Lastly, on the possibility of natural law's complete abolition from human mind, Soto concludes that this cannot happen to the first principles. The second principles and the conclusions, however, can be abolished very rarely, when the human vice grows and greatly clouds conscience and reason, as seen in the lack of understanding of certain Decalogue's sins that barbarians (*barbari*) and New World's men (*Novi Orbis*) suffered from.[34]

As seen, both *ius naturale* and *lex naturalis* can change to Aquinas and Domingo de Soto. Both admit changes in nature and in circumstances, which mutate *ius*. And, with slightly different arguments, both admit addition and subtraction to the *lex naturæ*. While the changes in *ius naturale* are more detached from an individual human action which causes it, given attachment of *lex naturalis* to human mind, its mutability is closely related to changes in

34 Dominicus Soto, *De Iustitia et Iure in Libri Decem* (Ioannes Baptista a Terranoua: Salamanca, 1569), 28–31.

comprehension and perception of an individual reason. And if this individual happens to be a prince, these changes may have political consequences. Flexibility, by this account, exists in the room which nature and circumstances allow for changing. When thinking about the Order of Grace's limits, therefore, this is the most important one: the king cannot violate nature or the conscience of his subjects which demand a certain *ius*. And though he can more easily add something to the contents of *lex naturæ*, the removal can only go so far: the first principles are immutable and must be obeyed – even if they don't determine, given their generic nature, concrete human actions.

But we have not, yet, arrived at the most critical point of the investigation. At the very end of his arguments about human imperfection, Soto touches on a difficult question, that of the abolition of the secondary precepts of natural law by certain people. This becomes a grave theological problem once one remembers that God himself – apparently – commanded His own people to violate a considerable number of the Decalogue's precepts in the Old Testament. Soto faces this problem directly, and his arguments introduce a rich distinction which ultimately reveals the possibilities of action and of change in nature.

## 4 The Mutability of Nature and God's Two Powers

The problem of natural law's abolition from human mind encountered that of the Mosaic Decalogue. It may seem that Soto is confusing religious prescriptions, sentiments, or even positive divine law, with natural law. But one must remember that the Decalogue is considered as revealed natural law: its content is of *lex naturalis*, even if the specific norms were given by God. The Decalogue, even in its first tablet – which is about the relation between man and God, while the second is between men – is composed of the nature of things and abounds with them, says Soto. He develops this in Book II, q. 3, art. 8º, in which he poses the question: can the following of the Decalogue's precepts be dispensed from?

Soto follows Aquinas, whose position he qualifies as being right in the middle between Ockham's and Duns Scotus'. For Aquinas, it is not admissible to dispense from neither the Decalogue's precepts, nor its conclusions, be they of first, second, or even third degree. Aquinas arrives at his conclusion comparing what would normally happen in a human case of *dispensatio legis*. Given that, sometimes, the respect for a certain legal precept, on a concrete situation, would go against the spirit of its legislator, in that case, to dispense from precept would be just and lawful. But, since God is the perfect legislator, his precepts, contained in the Decalogue, can never go against His own will, which renders the *dispensatio* impossible.

He also argues that the Decalogue's precepts prohibit intrinsically bad actions to men that are intrinsically rational, and since it is impossible to man to be irrational, no precept can be dispensed from without a reason founded in justice and goodness, which makes it impossible to allow, through *dispensatio*, actions which are rationally bad in themselves. However, he adds, the precepts of the Decalogue that don't have in themselves the justice and the good – such as *Shabat* – but that ordain a way of attaining them, can be an object of *dispensatio* and exclusively when obeying them goes against the common good on a specific case.[35]

Such a conclusion puts Aquinas and Soto in a terrible position, for, as seen, God himself, in the Old Testament, commanded the people of Israel to kill, expropriate land, exterminate entire populations, etc. If the Decalogue's precepts cannot be dispensed from, how could God order acts which are intrinsically evil? Soto is conscious of the problem, and his solution proves his argumentative genius. His answer is founded on two distinctions: between human and divine legislation and between God's two types of power, His two powers.

First, the distinction between human and divine legislation must be considered. *Dispensatio* from human positive laws, he says, happens because they aren't inherently just, which is why, sometimes, a concrete application of it deviates from common good, as was said above. Divine laws, however, are inherently just by their own nature and their concrete application can never go against common good. Because of this, if they are dispensed, common good itself is lost. But just as human law has some contents of natural law, divine law has its positive part: the ceremonial and judicial legislation of the Old Testament, and the Sacraments in the New. Its natural part, of course, cannot be dispensed from, for if God goes against *lex naturalis*, He goes against justice, and since He himself is justice, He cannot do so; but its positive part can.[36] This is the explanation made in accordance with the first distinction. It demonstrates how, for instance, Christ could cure in the *Shabat*, and David could command his army to eat the temple's food.

The second distinction is what explains how God could order acts ordinarily considered unjust in themselves to Israel. Soto argues that God has two *potestates* over the universe (*Deus in quam duas habet potestates universum orbem*): the first one, that of *dominus*, his lordship, which He has because of being the creator of everything; and the second one, that of *legislator et iudex*

35 Soto, *De Iustitia et Iure*, 105–106.

36 Soto, *De Iustitia et Iure*, 106–107

over every man and creature. Since He has *dominium* over creation, He can give to one man what belongs to another, even if the actual possessor disagrees. This *traditio* is not the same as a *dispensatio*, for it has nothing to do with divine legislation. It is an exercise of the first *potestas*, not of the second. It is, for example, as a father that gives to a friend the clothes of one of his sons against the little son's will. One cannot say the father, or the receiver, is dispensed to uphold the seventh precept of the Decalogue, for the father is the true *dominus* of the thing, and he is not stealing from his own son. He can give it to whomever he wants.[37]

Therefore, whenever God commanded what seemed a violation of the Decalogue in the Old Testament, He was, in fact, exerting his *dominium* over creation. It wasn't that a *dispensatio* of natural law occurred; what really happened was a change in the nature of the things themselves: a land that belonged to one people was transferred to another; a man that lived was condemned to die, and his executor acted as God's hand; a woman impure was made pure; and a bastard was changed into a rightful heir. God changed the nature of things with his first *potestas*, and this caused the immutable law to be applied differently while remaining the same.[38] As Soto puts it in another passage,[39] the change in the nature of things caused a mutation in what is just in a concrete case.

When the problem of the variability of *physikon dikaion* incorporates the particular problems of Catholic theology and political theory, it is clear we are very far away from Aristotle's formulations. While justice is still a structural component of the *cosmos*, now God, as its *dominus*, can change the outcome of justice without changing justice in itself.

## 5 Natural and Divine Powers of the Order of Grace

Problems of political order, such as the origin of political community and the legitimacy of power, appear in Domingo de Soto's *De Iustitia et Iure* when he begins his investigation on commutative justice, Book 4, particularly on the problems regarding the category of dominion applied to men, in Question 4. This means that considerations about the nature of political power are to be found amid theoretical or practical problems regarding Law and justice.

37 Soto, *De Iustitia et Iure*, 107.

38 Soto, *De Iustitia et Iure*, 107–108.

39 Soto, *De Iustitia et Iure*, 178 [B. III, q. 1, art. 2°].

The investigation on Soto's opinion about the mutability of *lex naturæ* and *ius naturale* reached its most delicate point on the question about the possibility of a *dispensatio legis* of the Decalogue. By applying the distinction between God's two *potestates* to solve the problem, he demonstrated both the limits of mutability and the possibilities of acting directly upon the nature of things. Where mutability, in *dispensatio*, meets its end, *dominium* emerges as a superior faculty with deeper and more substantial effects.

If, as said in the beginning, the king occupies a similar place in the order of society than that of God in the *universum*, at least some hints of it will be found in Soto's work. If he presents a *rex* as having two *potestates* and, more importantly, as *dominus* over his kingdom – or at least over parts of it – then an application of his conclusions to the powers of the Order of Grace is a possible interpretation, according to what Soto presents.

The work's dedication to Charles, son of Philip II of Spain, illuminates some aspects of his position. Here, Soto explicitly indicates that the king is *iudex* and *legislator* over his kingdom. Charles, who is yet a prince, must know form his early years the number of nations over which he will be *iudex*.[40] Also, he must know the difference between the tyrant and a king. The first directs all public things to his own pleasure; the second, however, aims only at the common good, and for its sake only he establishes laws (*leges condat*), creates magistrates, demands tributes, gives prizes, decides on penalties, starts wars, and accords peace.[41] It is in order that kings pursue justice that God elevates them over their kingdoms, and for that they must live in full submission to reason and, specially, to God's eternal laws.[42]

Again, the king as *legislator* appears when, in Book 1, q. 1º, art. 3º, he questions whether the reason of any man can produce law. The answer is that the power to produce law belongs only to the Republic and to the one that represents and takes care of her. And since the king is the Republic's representative and caretaker, to him belongs the power to produce laws. But, to Soto, the king's powers come directly from the people, for they create the king and transfer their *imperium* and *potestas*. God gives the power to the people to constitute their republics – or nations – but they must create and transfer their powers to the king.[43]

As *iudex*, the king appears again when, in Book 1, q. 2º, art. 2º, he concludes that only the prince has the power to punish, for the punishment carries the

---

40 Soto, *De Iustitia et Iure*, VIII.

41 Soto, *De Iustitia et Iure*, VIII–IX.

42 Soto, *De Iustitia et Iure*, IX.

43 Soto, *De Iustitia et Iure*, 8.

coactive force of the law, which belongs to the republic and the king only.[44] And, later, in Book 4, q. 5°, art. 1°, the king is the guardian of the republic and the judge of justice (*custos est rei publicæ, tum & iustitie iudex*).[45]

The king as *dominus*, as said above, appears as part of the discussion regarding commutative justice. His dominion, however, is limited. Firstly, because his power is not transmitted to him directly from God, but through the hands of the *populus*, who creates him and who can depose him if he becomes a tyrant;[46] secondly, neither him nor the republic has absolute dominion over the life of its subjects, only God has. This means that a prince cannot kill an innocent man, except if he is guilty, and if there is sufficient evidence of his crimes, for the prince is not lord over life, but judge of the evildoers.[47]

He has, nevertheless, dominion. To him were transferred, by the *ius naturæ*, the republic's *potestas, imperium and iurisdictio*. But not the republic's *facultates*, which are available to the prince only when they are necessary to protect and administer her. And when the law says everything belongs to the prince, it must be understood limitedly, containing only what the public treasury obtains through taxation.[48] The prince, therefore, was *dominus*, *legislator* and *iudex*, as is God. Though, of course, in a much more limited sense. Domingo de Soto's king is not that of the Norman Anonymous.[49]

His powers do create and revoke legislation, and to dispense with the application of this legislation on concrete cases – when directly or indirectly exerted – fall under the second *potestas*. They are all limited by nature and by *lex naturæ* and *ius naturale*. And, of course, even when *epieikeia* is applied due to a deficiency in legislation, these limitations still apply. However, when the prince changes the nature of human things or redefines what belongs to each one through mercy and grace by pardoning sentences, distributing land, gifting titles and position in the administration of the republic, allowing the son of a priest to receive inheritance, etc., he is not acting under the limits of *ius naturale*, for his actions are changing it by a change in the circumstances and, perhaps, in nature itself. In those cases, the king is *dominus* exerting his first *potestas* – which he has for the republic transferred her powers to him.

The actions based on the first *potestas* cause structural changes in the order of society, affection what is due to each one. They change justice itself. It is

44 Soto, *De Iustitia et Iure*, 16.

45 Soto, *De Iustitia et Iure*, 284.

46 Soto, *De Iustitia et Iure*, 279 [B. 4, q. 4°, art. 1°].

47 Soto, *De Iustitia et Iure*, 269 [B. 4, q. 2°, art. 3°].

48 Soto, *De Iustitia et Iure*, 278 [B. 4, q. 4°, art. 1°].

49 Kantorowicz, *The King's Two Bodies*, 42–61.

possible to go further and investigate which types of justice are affected. Hespanha, for instance, identifies grace with distributive justice.[50] But such a development goes beyond the purposes of the present investigation.

## 6 Preliminary Conclusion

The parallel between the content of Soto's considerations about God's two *potestates* – including His capacity to change the nature of creatures – and the powers princes had, called by Hespanha powers of the Order of Grace, is not new. Hespanha both reaffirms it and finds it in many works of the Modern Era in Portugal and Spain – one of the first dating back to the late 15th century.

With Domingo de Soto's fine reasoning, a distinction could be made between two types of powers corresponding to the two *potestates*, which exist not only in God, but in human reality as well. It was necessary to distinguish between powers that derived from the role of *lex naturæ* in the constitution of political order and those which existed analogically to divine *potestas* of dominion.

From the answers to the mutability of natural law's problem emerges a criterion for the distinction. Human powers of changing *lex naturalis* and *ius naturale* derive from three sources: the change in the nature of things, the change in concrete circumstances – which may or may not have change in nature as a cause – and by a different understanding of what belongs to the first principles.

Human powers, therefore, exist inside the reality already created and founded on natural law. Divine powers, however, derive from God's place as the creator of the *universum*. His powers, therefore, create new realities. They are, of course, in harmony with *lex naturæ*. But they alter the things *lex naturæ* commands, creating new relations of justice.

It is acting as *dominus* that indicates the specific aspect of the Order of Grace, and the juridical agents – topped by the king – could, within the confines of a juridical order, recognize and cause changes in the *lex naturæ* and in the *ius naturale*. They couldn't, however, create new realities, for only God can create *ex nihilo in universum*. While a concrete case of land concession has many layers of juridical relations, the specific aspect that allows it to be categorized as a concession of grace is the exercise of dominion, directly or not, by the prince. This is its distinctive characteristic.

50 Hespanha, *Cultura jurídica europeia*, 167, n. 269.

Lastly, what Soto implicitly points out is that the ultimate form of mutability is not that of *lex naturæ*, for it is still limited by nature. The changing of nature itself, however, is a superior power, which allows substantial changes in the constitution of society in a similar manner to the way God realize miracles, changing nature without destroying it.

CHAPTER 3

# Association and Corporation in Early Modern Jurisprudence

*Jeffrey Dymond*

## 1 Introduction

Since the emergence of what has come to be called 'corporation theory' at the hands of medieval civilians and canonists, a distinction between a corporation (*universitas*) and an association, or partnership (*societas*), has become entrenched in both political theory and modern legal systems.[1] A corporation is, by a fiction of law, its own legal person, conceptually distinct from its members. A partnership, on the other hand, is merely a contractual relationship between natural persons; it is not a legal person in its own right. Nevertheless, in the introduction to his translation of selections from Otto von Gierke's *Das deutsche Genossenschaftsrecht*, F.W. Maitland claims that, by the time we reach the highpoint of 'systems of Natural Law' in the eighteenth century, the distinction between the two types of legal groups became blurred. According to Maitland, the *universitas*, which medieval jurists did not necessarily conceive of as founded on a contractual relationship, came to be understood as one. This, Maitland believed, resulted in a loss of mystique for the concept, a process he describes as the *universitas* being "lowered to the rank of *societas*." However, as a result of what he calls "the same process," these natural law jurists admitted that the *societas* could have its own personality, with the result that it "was raised to the rank of the *universitas*."[2] My aim in this paper is to argue that even if civil legal systems today still distinguish between a corporation and a partnership,[3] this phenomenon observed by Maitland is a sign

1 The literature on this is vast. See, for example, Pierre Michaud-Quantin, *Universitas: Expressions du Mouvement Communitaire dans le Moyen-Age Latin* (Paris: J. Vrin, 1970), 64–69; Reinhard Zimmermann, *The Law of Obligations: Roman Foundations of the Civilian Tradition* (Cape Town: Juta & Co., 1996), 455; and Ralf Mehr, *Societas und Universitas: Römischrechtliche Institute im Unternehmensgesellchaftsrecht vor 1800* (Köln: Böhlau Verlag, 2008). The status of a *universitas* as a separate legal person was a matter of debate for centuries.

2 Otto Gierke, *Political Theories of the Middle Age*, trans. Frederic William Maitland (Boston: Beacon Press, 1959), xxiii–xxiv.

3 A notable exception is Scotland, where partnerships are considered distinct persons.

 | DOI:10.1163/9789004748712_005

of an important evolution the civil law undertook in the early modern period: that a general theory of the nature of a group as a kind of *societas* was introduced into civil law, that this general theory enabled such a group to assume on some occasions the character of a person, and that this group-person could then, in turn, be registered in the law.

In his introduction, Maitland attributes the impetus for this move to an earlier recognition on the part of both political theorists and jurists that one particular form of association, the state, sits awkwardly between these two categories. Pointing to the use of this term *societas* (or its French, Italian, English, and German cognates) in a wide range of medieval and early modern works of political theory, Maitland asks why political theory "borrowed the contract of partnership rather than the apparently far more appropriate act of incorporation." His answer is that the 'classical' doctrine of corporations, which Maitland associates with the jurist-pope Innocent IV (1195–1254), understood a corporation to be "a merely fictitious personality, created by the State and shut up within the limits of Private Law," and for which reason "was not what the philosopher wanted when he went about to construct the State itself."[4] The difficulty inherent in the idea of the corporation as developed by medieval canonists and civilians, in other words, is that the status of an entity as a *universitas* ultimately depends on an act of concession from a higher authority, which poses a problem for understanding the nature of the entity that is supposed to be that higher authority. Maitland's discussion alludes to Gierke's treatment of this very problem, where he likens some medieval accounts of state formation rooted in a contract to "the self-constitution of a corporation."[5] For Gierke, this move was incoherent; he could not find in his sources a legal concept explaining how a contract of partnership could somehow produce a corporation.

The alleged incoherence to which Gierke refers is a consequence of his belief that a corporation can only come into being through an act of concession. But his account of the medieval corporation as purely a product of concession has been disputed by other scholars. In so doing, they have suggested that a self-constituting corporation does not pose the kind of conceptual problem Gierke believes it does. The solution they propose relies on the notoriously difficult – especially with respect to the medieval Glossators and Commentators – concept of the *ius gentium*, or the common law of all peoples. One

4 Gierke, *Political Theories of the Middle Age*, xxiii. Innocent's doctrinal innovations were originally devised for religious institutions such as monasteries, but they were soon adopted by the civilian Commentators and applied to other, non-ecclesiastical, bodies.

5 Gierke, *Political Theories of the Middle Age*, 89.

such critic of Gierke, Joseph Canning, cites Baldus' commentary on *Digest* 1.1.9 to make this point. Baldus admits that a *collegium* of artisans or scholars is an artificial creation, and therefore a product of concession from a higher authority. But, as Canning reads Baldus, the entity he calls the *populus*, and which he identifies with the city-states of medieval Italy whose *de facto* independence from the Holy Roman Empire he, like his teacher Bartolus, defended, is most certainly not. Not only is the *populus*' existence a product of the *ius gentium*, Baldus claims, but also its inherent capacity to govern itself as a corporate entity: "peoples (*populi*) are from the *ius gentium*, and therefore the government of peoples is from the *ius gentium* [...] by virtue of the fact that a people's (*populus*) existence necessarily presumes that it has a government, just as every animal is governed by its own spirit and mind."[6]

On this point Canning is joined by Antony Black, who cites the example of the Neapolitan canonist Niccolò Tedeschi, otherwise known as Panormitanus.[7] In his commentary on the fourth and fifth books of Gratian's *Decretum*, Tedeschi endorses the view that "all colleges are illicit," "except those approved by the *ius gentium*, or by positive law."[8] This time with reference to *Digest* 1.1.5, he claims that those corporate entities sanctioned by the *ius gentium* are "the college of the *civitas*, camps (*castri*), as well as cities (*villes*)," because "since many men must act for the support and utility of the *civitas*, it is necessary that many come together at the same time."[9] Among those congregations approved by positive law are various different colleges "of various artisans [...] and professions," such as "scholars."[10] With this evidence from Tedeschi, as well as

6 J.P. Canning, "The Corporation in the Political Thought of the Italian Jurists of the Thirteenth and Fourteenth Centuries," *History of Political Thought* 1 (1980), 22. The original Latin, translated by me from Canning's citation: "*Populi sunt de iure gentium ergo regimen populi est de iure gentium* [...] *Eo ipso quod populus habet esse habet per consequens regimen in suo esse, sicut omne animal regitur a suo spiritu proprio et anima.*" Canning's account of a *ius gentium* personality for "peoples" has been influential: see Kajo Kubala, "Hobbes, *ius gentium*, and the corporation," *History of European Ideas* 49.6 (2023): 942–958.

7 Antony Black, *Guilds and Civil Society in European Political Thought from the Twelfth Century to the Present* (Ithaca, NY: Cornell University Press, 1984), 19–21.

8 "[...] *homines non debent facere ista conventicula, seu congregationes, cum ex eis timeat conspiratio* [...] *nisi approbent a iure gentium, vel a iure positivo*," Niccolò Tedeschi, *Commentaria primae partis in primum Decretalium librum*, vol. 7 (Venice, 1591), 185v.

9 "*A iure gentium approbant collegium civitatis, castri, vel ville* [...] *nam debent homines multa agere in favorem et commodum civitatis, ideo oportet quod plures insimul conveniant,*" Tedeschi, *Commentaria primae partis*, vol. 7, 185v.

10 "*A iure positivo approbantur collegia ipsoum, quae sunt alicuius artis* [...] *vel alicuius professiones, ut sunt scholares,*" Tedeschi, *Commentaria primae partis*, vol. 7, 185v.

other jurists, Black concludes that Gierke's account of incorporation as solely the product of concession is wrong; the *ius gentium* alternative remains.[11]

These criticisms of Gierke provide much needed nuance to his claims about the character of the canonist and civilian corporation, as they suggest that some bodies could claim corporate status without necessarily having a charter from the higher authority. But this does not mean that this alleged *ius gentium* right to corporate status does not itself ultimately derive from concession. For even though Canning gives us good reason to think that Baldus believed the *populi* mentioned in *D* 1.1.9 correspond to a naturalistic, Aristotelian political community, and not an artificial creation of a higher authority, it does not necessarily follow that any legal status for this entity derives from something intrinsic to it.[12] Indeed, the dominant view on the juridical status of kingdoms and cities among jurists up until at least the fifteenth century was similar to that originally held by Accursius in the gloss: that the 'peoples' of *D* 1.1.9 were all subjects of the emperor and that any rights which they may have to govern themselves therefore depended on the emperor's concession.[13] Moreover, the distinctive identity of these 'peoples' would often be traced back by jurists to the demarcation of Roman provinces. 'Peoples' were therefore not thought of as self-constituting entities, but instead as the creatures of the Roman Empire, with the result that any ability to bear collective rights and obligations follows ultimately from an act of concession.[14] We should bear this in mind when we interpret Baldus' comments, considering that he, while certainly attached to the idea that a people's *de facto* exercise of sovereignty was legitimate, also held that ultimate authority nevertheless still remained *de iure* in the hands of the emperor.

As a result, this supposed *ius gentium* theory of corporate personality does not fully account for the phenomenon of fully self-constituting group persons observed by Gierke and Maitland in the work of early modern natural lawyers. But, as I will argue below, this phenomenon can be explained once we register the significance of the integration of a particular social ontology, derived from

11 Black, *Guilds and Civil Society*, 19–21.

12 For Canning's argument on Baldus' alleged Aristotelian naturalism, see Canning, "Political Thought of the Italian Jurists," 20.

13 Magnus Ryan, "Political Thought," in *Cambridge Companion to Roman Law*, ed. David Johnston (Cambridge: Cambridge University Press, 2015), 439–440. For further examples, see Dante Fedele, *The Medieval Foundations of International Law: Baldus de Ubaldis (1327–1400), Doctrine, and Practice of the* Ius Gentium (Leiden: Brill, 2021), ch. 2.

14 Magnus Ryan, "Historicity and Universality in Roman Law before 1600," in *Time, History, and Political Thought*, ed. John Robertson (Cambridge: Cambridge University Press, 2023), 54–66.

Cicero, into the interpretation of the civil law. This Ciceronian social ontology began to appear in the sixteenth century, when it was incorporated into civil law commentaries by a group of French Renaissance jurists affiliated with the University of Bourges, especially François Connan (1508–1551) and Hugo Donellus (1527–1591), as part of their effort to systematize Roman law in a way compatible with nature.[15] In the first section of the paper, I will reconstruct this social ontology as it is elaborated by Connan and Donellus. For these jurists, I will argue, human nature leads people into a number of associations bound by mutual obligations and in pursuit of mutual benefit, with the state, or *civitas*, being one such association. A combination of factors, in other words, contribute to the natural formation of various associations that assume the shape of *societas*. In sections two and three, I will demonstrate that they also endorse a Ciceronian theory of personality that enables these associations to assume the character of persons. Finally, in the fourth and final section, I will provide evidence suggesting that this Ciceronian social theory served as the foundation in nature upon which at least one early modern natural law system was constructed. The debt of natural law thinking to Roman law and medieval Romanist jurisprudence has recently come under re-examination;[16] my concluding discussion will suggest that the Renaissance re-orientation of Roman law scholarship around this set of beliefs about the nature of human sociability, taken from Cicero, was a key event that would go on to provide the organizing structure for early natural law reasoning.

## 2 Self-Constituting Communities

It is well-known that by the end of the fifteenth century, the texts of Roman law had begun to evolve from being treated as the law of a universal Roman

15 For the methods and aims of these jurists, see Peter Stein, *Roman Law and European History* (Cambridge: Cambridge University Press, 2004), 76–82 and James Gordley, *The Jurists: A Critical History* (Oxford: Oxford University Press, 2013), ch. 4. For their use of Cicero in pursuit of these aims, see Jean-Louis Thireau, "Ciceron et le droit naturel au XVIe siècle," *Revue d'histoire des Facultés de droit et de la science juridique*, 4 (1987), 55–85; Gaëlle Demelemestre, "La systématization du droit et la théorie du ius gentium comme droit du genre humain chez François Connan," *Revue historique de droit français et étranger*, 94 (2016), 413–438; and Jeffrey Dymond, "Ciceronian Jurisprudence and the Law of Nations," *The Historical Journal* 67 (2024): 1–20.

16 For example, Benjamin Straumman, *Roman Law in the State of Nature: The Classical Foundations of Hugo Grotius' Natural Law* (Cambridge: Cambridge University Press, 2015) and Daniel Lee, *Popular Sovereignty in Early Modern Constitutional Thought* (Oxford: Oxford University Press, 2016).

Empire, and its continuation in the form of the Holy Roman Empire, to a source of universally applicable legal political concepts.[17] As a consequence of this process, several fragments of the *Corpus iuris civilis* acquired a particularly prominent position in elaborating a set of universal legal norms. Among the most important of these fragments was *Digest* 1.1.5, or *lex Ex hoc iure*.[18] In this fragment, Hermogenianus enumerates the institutions which he claims are the products of the *ius gentium*, a list that includes wars, nations (*gentes*), kingdoms, property rights, and various obligations. As we have seen, this passage, alongside *Digest* 1.1.9, is cited by proponents of the idea that the *ius gentium* enables the self-constitution of corporate entities; an idea which, once properly contextualized, appears not as opposed to the concession theory of corporate personality as some have taken it to be. There were, however, a small group of late thirteenth and early fourteenth century jurists from the kingdom of Naples who employed this passage to support their claims for the independence of that kingdom from the emperor, on the grounds that *ius gentium* institutions embody a kind of natural state of things that had been undermined by Roman imperialism. Their accounts offer no elaboration, however, on how these natural kingdoms are established and why the *ius gentium* sanctions their autonomy.[19] I will argue in this section that the later Bourges jurists were able to offer such an account by employing the Ciceronian idea that there is a certain form of naturally occurring social life that resembles a *societas*, or partnership, and that many different groups follow this model, from the family (in some instances) to the state.

The Bourges jurists likewise develop their accounts of the *ius gentium* as a body of universal legal norms in the early chapters of their commentaries on the *Corpus iuris civilis*. They do so, also like their Commentator predecessors, by defining the relationship between *ius gentium* and natural law. Connan does this by deploying a highly developed account of the state of the nature,

17 Ryan, "Political Thought"; Ryan, "Historicity and Universality" and Lee, *Popular Sovereignty*.

18 J.P. Canning, "Law, Sovereignty and Corporation Theory, 1300–1450," in *Cambridge History of Medieval Political Thought, c. 350 – c. 1450*, ed. J.H. Burns (Cambridge: Cambridge University Press, 1988), 464–469; Ryan, "Political Thought," 433–437. For this process in an earlier period, see Martti Koskenniemi, *To the Uttermost Parts of the Earth: Legal Imagination and International Power, 1300–1870* (Cambridge: Cambridge University Press, 2021), ch. 1.

19 Ryan, "Political Thought," 437. Koskenniemi offers an account for how French jurists beginning in the thirteenth century conceptualized the process of polity formation. However, these arguments remained under the shadow of the *de iure* supremacy of the emperor. See Koskenniemi, *To the Uttermost Parts of the Earth*, ch. 1, especially 51–52.

and the transition from it to a state of society. Natural law, he argues, is the law that obtains within this state of nature: "the first men, simple and rustic," he says, "lacking desire and competition, and not seeking for themselves the protection of relatives and neighbors, but dispersed in mountains and forests, seem to have used natural law."[20] Natural law, then, is not suitable for life in society, limited "to solitary man, living life in the field with a wife and children."[21] Similarly, the jurist Hugo Donellus explains that the natural law applies to human beings outside society, regulating merely "the joining of a man and woman for the purposes of procreation, the procreation and education of children, defense, and liberty."[22]

The *ius gentium*, on the other hand, is law created specifically for social life.[23] Both authors argue that the impetus to transition into social life comes through the application of an innate natural reason. It is through natural reason, Connan argues, that human beings, "dispersed in mountains and forests," come to know natural law, and it is on account of this same natural reason that they decide to leave it. "But since [a man] is led by nature to associations (*societates*) and unions (*coetus*) of men," he says, "he gradually moved outwards, first to an association (*societas*) with kin, then to one with extended family, then to friends, later to neighbors, and finally, through commerce, to an association that encompasses the whole of humanity."[24] Connan attributes the cause of this outward movement to an aspiration to "live a more commodious life," with the resulting implication that these *societates* and *coetus*

20 *"Iure naturali videntur usi primi homines rudes illi quidem & agrestes, caeterum expertes cupiditatis & aemulationis, qui nullum adhuc cognatorum aut vicinorum praesidium sibi quaesiverant, sed in montibus & sylvis dissipati,"* François Connan, *Commentaria iuris civilis libri X* (Paris, 1553), I, 11r.

21 *"Ius itaque naturale proprium est hominis solitarii, vitam agentis in agro cum uxore & liberis,"* Connan, *Commentaria iuris civilis*, I, 13v.

22 "[…] *coniunctio maris et feominae procreandi caussa; liberorum procreatio, et educatio: defensio sui, et libertas,*" Hugo Donellus, *Commentariorum de iure civili* (Florence, 1840), I, 49. An interesting difference between Connan and Donellus is that the former's use of the language of 'wife' suggests that a relationship resembling marriage may obtain in the state of nature, whereas the latter's language of 'joining' does not. While I have not seen Connan, unlike Bodin, describe *patria potestas* as natural, Anna Becker has found that Connan was taken to be saying this by some contemporaries and criticized for it. See Anna Becker, *Gendering the Renaissance Commonwealth* (Cambridge: Cambridge University Press, 2019), 120–123.

23 For this process, see Dymond, "Ciceronian Jurisprudence."

24 *"Sed cum ad hominum societates & coetus suapte natura ferretur, paulatim exiit foras, cognationibus primum, tum affinitatibus, deinde amicitiis, postea vicinitatibus, & tandem commerciorum usu totum genus hominum societate complexus est,"* Connan, *Commentaria iuris civilis*, I, 13v.

assume a particular form: they are defined by "the exchange of duties and commercial matters."[25] Led by natural reason, in other words, individual human beings enter into different groups, beginning with the closest – the family – and extending outwards to eventually encompass the whole world, in which they pursue mutual benefit and are bound by a sense of mutual obligation. The content of the *ius gentium*, he eventually concludes, are the obligations and institutions necessary to maintain these groups: the law "which all men use who [...] are joined into association (*societas*)."[26]

Later on in the chapter, Connan makes this same point again, but this time far more abstractly. He refers to the beginning of a just "golden age," which he claims began with the intervention of a lawgiver. This lawgiver, he says, "brought together men dispersed in fields and joined them [...] he transformed them from wild and unruly beings, into peaceful (*mites*) and tame (*mansuetos*), with the result that now they administer all things more through the judgement of the mind (*animus*) than through physical strength."[27] Moreover, they now "have a method in all things concerning divine religion, human duties, and impartial justice," which enables them to "give and receive benefits from one to the other, taking nothing from another's due, only each person thinking one and the same thing, namely the utility of the whole."[28] On the surface, there is some tension between this mythological account and the historical one given earlier, but what they share in common, and what is really the point Connan wishes to emphasize, is the centrality of mutual obligation to a beneficial social life, and that the source of these obligations lies in natural reason. Social life – or at least those forms of social life in which justice is a concern – whether it is natural, or whether it is instituted through the intervention of a lawgiver, assumes this particular form, and this applies across the spectrum of groups, from the family to the state.

In addition to illustrating the same point about the nature of a certain kind of natural social body and how this serves as the foundation of law, both arguments Connan employs to make it draw explicitly from Cicero. The fable of

25 "[...] *rerum commerciis utilitates sibi quaesiverunt ad vitam commodius degendam* [...]" Connan, *Commentaria iuris civilis*, I, 13v–14r.

26 "*Nominatur autem ius gentium, quo deo utantur omnes homines qui in gentem aliquam sunt, societatemque congregati,*" Connan, *Commentaria iuris civilis*, I, 14r.

27 "[...] *qui dissipatos in agris homines conciliavit inter se, & coniunxit* [...] *Hic homines ex feris & immanibus mites reddidit & mansuetos, ut iam animi iudicio potius quam viribus corporis omnia administrarent* [...]" Connan, *Commentaria iuris civilis*, I, 14v.

28 "[...] *eneficia ultro citroque darent & acciperent, nihil detraherent de alieno sui emolumenti gratia, sed eandem putarent uniuscuiusque, quae & universorum, utilitatem* [...]" *Connan, Commentaria iuris civilis*, I, 14v.

the lawgiver is cited almost word-for-word from the introductory chapters of Cicero's rhetorical treatise *De inventione*, a text that, while widely read by rhetoricians and humanists since at least the twelfth century, had only recently begun to appear in the work of jurists.[29] Connan's other, more historical argument, comes from Book 1 of Cicero's *De officiis*. There Cicero claims that natural reason incentivizes human beings to enter into social relations by making them aware of the benefits they bring. "As the Stoics believe," he says, "everything produced on earth is created for the use of mankind, and men are born for the sake of men, so that they may be able to assist one another." "Consequently," each person should "follow nature as [their] leader" and "contribute to the common stock things that benefit everyone together." These relationships are preserved, he says, "by the exchange of dutiful services," and "by giving and receiving expertise and effort and means."[30] He then proceeds to attribute the emergence and growth of human social life to the unfolding of this particular natural inclination toward collaboration and cooperation, an account which Connan likewise cites nearly verbatim:

> There are indeed several degrees of fellowship (*societas*) among men [...] the first fellowship (*societas*) exists within marriage itself, and the next with one's children. Then, there is the one house in which everything is shared. Indeed, that is the seed-bed, as it were, of a political community (*res publica*). Next there follow bonds between brothers, and then between first cousins and second cousins, who cannot be contained in one house and go to other houses, as if to colonies. Finally, there follow marriages and those connection of marriage from which even more relations arise. In such propagation and increase, political communities have their origin.[31]

Albeit with fewer explicit references to Cicero, Donellus also employs a similar account of the nature and origins of social relations that become the object of

---

29 Cicero, *De inventione* 1.1–2. An early example is Connan's teacher Alciato, in Andrea Alciato, "Oratio in laudem iuris civilis principio studii habita cum Avenione profiteretur," in *Opera Omnia* (Basel, 1582), IV, 1025–1026. For the earlier history of *De inventione*'s reception, see Cary J. Nederman, "The Union of Wisdom and Eloquence before the Renaissance: The Ciceronian Orator in Medieval Thought," *Journal of Medieval History* 18 (1992), 75–95, and Nederman, "Nature, Sin and the Origins of Society: The Ciceronian Tradition in Medieval Political Thought," *Journal of the History of Ideas* 49 (1995), 3–26.

30 Cicero, *De officiis* 1.23. Translation from Cicero, *On Duties*, trans. M.T. Griffin and E.M. Atkins (Cambridge: Cambridge University Press, 2021), 10.

31 Cicero, *De officiis* 1.54. Translation from Cicero, *On Duties*, 23.

law. He begins by going back to "the beginnings of the world," during which a small population emerging from "the first two men" lived in relative abundance, and there was no "injury"; an idea not that different from Connan's "golden age."[32] As the population increased over time, however, scarcity became a problem. Applying "right reason" (*recta ratio*), they recognized that this "scarcity of things necessary for life" would generate multiple problems, and so, in response, they developed a principle of private property to prevent this from happening:[33] whatever a person "cultivated or procured by their labor" became theirs, and theirs alone, by right.[34]

With this institution of property – which Donellus calls the "first law (*lex*) among human beings"[35] – what had previously been a dispersed group of individuals now came to constitute one body, bound by mutual obligation to respect each other's property rights. This larger body would eventually be called the state. But the nature of the law that established this body also generated an explosive growth in forms of social interaction that assumed the same shape. For now with distinct properties, they also now ran the risk of "indigence," and, to avoid this, trading relationships (*commutationes*), which "we call exchanges (*commercia*) and contracts (*contractus*)" were established.[36] Like the larger community, the individual participants within these smaller relationships were also perceived to be bound by mutual obligation. Indeed, it was with a view toward preserving these obligations that the members of the larger community later agreed to bind themselves to follow a number of other laws: "buying, selling, tenancy, hiring, partnership, commission, trust, loans, and others of that sort."[37]

---

32 "[…] *in initiis huius mundi tempus* […] *cum enim duo homines primo conditi essent* […] *singuli homines de communi sumere possent, quantum vellent, sine alterius iniuria, aut offensione,"* Donellus, *Commentariorum de iure civili*, I, 51.

33 "[…] *recta ratio usu* […] *Illinic enim inopia rerum ad vitam necessariarum: hinc dissidia, et turbae* […]" Donellus, *Commentariorum de iure civili*, I, 52.

34 "[…] *quod (ut dixi) ut suo labore quisque coleret, ac procuraret: ita caveret sibi, ne in id alius quisquam posset invadere sine iniuria,"* Donellus, *Commentariorum de iure civili*, I, 52.

35 "[…] *hoc primum rectae rationis, et iudicii opus, et lex inter homines* […]*"* Donellus, *Commentariorum de iure civili*, I, 52.

36 *"Nam cum, dominiis distinctis, coepisset alius habere, quo ego indigerem: eo autem frui, invito domino, non possem* […] *induci eas commutations, quae commercia, et contractus appellamus,"* Donellus, *Commentariorum de iure civili*, I, 52.

37 *"Hinc ergo contractus recepti, emptio, venditio, locatio, conductio, societas, mandatum, depositum, commodatum, et similes. Ex his obligationes* […]*"* Donellus, *Commentariorum de iure civili*, I, 52.

Donellus' account clearly varies in many ways from that of Connan, but it nevertheless still shares many of the same characteristics. Above all, it describes the natural origin and existence of a certain form of social relationship, of which the political community is the most prominent example, that follows the same Ciceronian model of *societas*, in which natural reason leads individuals into groups instituted for mutual benefit and whose members are bound by mutual obligation.

## 3 The Personality of Associations

That Connan and Donellus draw on Cicero to elaborate their social theory is important for another reason: for the works of Cicero also contain an account for how a group can assume the character of a person. In this section and the next, I will turn to this account, first to explain it, and then to demonstrate that it proved integral to Connan and Donellus' jurisprudence. It is by exploiting this account of group personality that these jurists could attribute the standing of distinct persons to the *societates* that human nature leads people to form.

Across the vast body of his work inherited from the post-classical world, Cicero describes a number of phenomena, ranging from groups to abstract concepts, as *personae* capable of being represented. *Persona* was the term given to masks worn by actors in the Roman theater; and for an actor to assume a *persona* is for them to take on the recognized social role of a character by embodying its distinctive animating traits, or, as we might say, its personality. Crucial to this act of representation is that the audience recognizes the embodied actions and agrees that they can be attributed to the person (or object) the actor seeks to portray. Once an actor convincingly embodies these characteristics, then it is as if that character, previously absent, acts in the world as if it were a natural person. On this account, then, even an abstract idea can assume the role of a person, so long as its definitive characteristics are broadly recognized and someone is able to embody them accurately.[38]

By far the most famous example in Cicero's work of a non-human being with a *persona* capable of representation by an actor is the *civitas*, or state. Although this idea appears in a number of his works, it is in the *De officiis* that this idea receives its most detailed elaboration.[39] In a passage from Book 1,

---

38 Quentin Skinner, *From Humanism to Hobbes: Studies in Rhetoric and Politics* (Cambridge: Cambridge University Press, 2018), 12–19.

39 Although he also claims in *De inventione* 1.100 that, alongside the *civitas*, the laws or any place can be so represented.

Cicero argues that a magistrate must understand that it is his responsibility to "realize that he assumes the role of the *civitas*."[40] To do this, the passage continues, the magistrate "ought to sustain its standing and its seemliness, to preserve the laws, to administer justice, and to be mindful of things that have been entrusted to his good faith."[41] If assuming the *persona* of the *civitas* means acting to enforce the laws and to administer justice, then this must be because the laws are recognized by others as being constitutive of the *civitas* itself.

This interpretation derives support from Cicero's famous definition of the *civitas* as the "councils and assemblies of men associated through law (*concilia coetusque hominum iure sociati*)," found in Book 6 of his *De re publica*, and preserved for the medieval and early modern world in Macrobius' *Somnium scipionis*.[42] But it also derives support from an immensely important description of the *civitas* he gives in his oration *Pro Cluentio*:

> For the law is the bond (*vinculum*) which secures these our privileges in the commonwealth (*res publica*), the foundation of our liberty, the fountain-head of justice. Within the law are reposed the mind (*mens*) and heart (*animus*), the judgement and conviction, of the state (*civitas*). The state (*civitas*) without law would be like the human body without mind (*mens*) – unable to employ the parts which are to it as sinews, blood and limbs. The magistrates would administer the law, the jurors who interpret it – all of us in short – obey the law to the end that we may be free.[43]

The *civitas*, on this account, is a kind of body composed of different members united together by their obedience to this law, which he analogizes to a chain (*vinculum*) without which the *civitas* "cannot endure." Held together by mutual obligations between the different parts, this description conforms to Cicero's earlier inclusion of the *civitas* under the *genus* concept of *societas* we have seen he believes human nature leads people to establish.

---

40 Cicero, *De officiis* 1.124; Cicero, *On Duties*, 48.

41 Cicero, *De officiis* 1.124; Cicero, *On Duties*, 48.

42 For the reception of Cicero's definition of the *civitas* as a *societas* with its own *persona*, see Peter Stacey, *The State in Machiavelli* (Cambridge: Cambridge University Press, forthcoming 2025). For an abridged version of the argument, see Peter Stacey, "Liberty and the Rule of Law," in *A Cultural History of Democracy in the Renaissance*, eds. Virginia Cox and Joanne Paul (London: Bloomsbury, 2021), 55–57. The definition can be found in Cicero, *On the Commonwealth and On the Laws*, trans. James E.G. Zetzel (Cambridge: Cambridge University Press, 2017), 97–98.

43 Cicero, *Pro Cluentio*, 146.

Yet in this depiction of the *societas* of the *civitas*, we also see that these mutual obligations expressed in law do far more than hold the body together; they are also what give it motion. The law is the body's animating spirit (*animus*) and mind (*mens*), its judgement and its wisdom, without which "the *civitas* cannot use its parts." This claim – that the law both unites and moves the different parts of the body – recalls a way of thinking about personality ultimately indebted to Stoicism, according to which the source of a person's unique personality is their "spirit" or "soul," since this is what unites their different parts and enables them to act with one singular purpose.[44] As the thing which unites and directs the *civitas*' different parts, the law can therefore be said to be the source of its distinctive personality; and when this law is declared and enforced through the actions of an actor (or magistrate), that magistrate may be said to have assumed its *persona*, and the *civitas* brought to life. Indeed, Cicero makes just this claim in Book 3 of *De legibus*, where he states that "a magistrate is a law that speaks, and a law is a silent magistrate,"[45] as if to say that the law is the *persona* of the *civitas* that needs to be worn by an actor, and that 'magistrate' is the name of the actor whose actions are recognized by others as compatible with those of the *civitas* itself. For what the citizens of the *civitas* recognize when they see a magistrate follow the law and distribute justice equitably, are the unique set of mutual obligations that united them into the *societas* of the *civitas*, and, by extension, the group of contracted individuals who make up the body of the *civitas* itself.

## 4 Associations as Legal Persons

We are now just beginning to acknowledge the immense reach of this Ciceronian idea of the *civitas* in the history of medieval and early modern political thought. But a feature of its reception that has now become apparent is how particularly widespread it was among Renaissance humanist authors.[46] Cicero's definition of the *civitas* as a *societas*, and that this *societas* was held to possess its own *persona*, was very much at the heart of *quattrocento* humanist political thought.[47] The ubiquity of Cicero's definition of the *civitas* among

44 Annabel Brett, *Changes of State: Nature and the Limits of the City in Early Modern Natural Law* (Princeton: Princeton University Press, 2011), 130.

45 Cicero, *On the Commonwealth*, 159.

46 Skinner, *From Humanism to Hobbes*, ch. 1; Stacey, "Liberty and the Rule of Law," 41–62; Stacey, *The State in Machiavelli*.

47 Stacey, "Liberty and the Rule of Law"; Stacey, *The State in Machiavelli*.

Renaissance humanists, and their nearly unanimous use of it, stands in contrast with medieval jurists, in whose work featured a number of rival, and very different, definitions.[48] By the time of Connan and Donellus, however, this language started to become more prominent in jurisprudence, as well. And we can see them employ it in their work to explain how the *societates* nature both enables and inclines human beings to form, can also be themselves distinct persons.

A clear example of this can be seen in Connan and Donellus' treatment of the further development of *ius gentium* institutions. As we have already seen, both argue that the first laws that come to be regarded as part of the *ius gentium* have as their aim the preservation of human life in *societas*. These laws, designed to ensure that the obligations incurred in other social relations are followed, are themselves the obligations by which a group of individuals are united into the *societas* that both Connan and Donellus identify with the state. Following Hermogenianus' list of these institutions in *D* 1.1.5, both Connan and Donellus then proceed to explain the founding of kingdoms, or states, and the origin of the laws of war, and in that order.[49] A consequence of this chronology – and one to which they both draw attention – is that it explains how states themselves can be subjects of the laws of war. This process thus also offers us a chance to observe how a group comes to acquire, without concession from a higher authority, the status of a distinctive person, and for that personality to be integrated into law.

Both Connan and Donellus portray the impetus for the founding of kingdoms in similar terms. For Connan, after a period of time in which the laws intended to maintain social relations were largely observed, it came about that increasing material wealth (possibly a product of people living harmoniously) led to "luxury," and an eventual transformation of the moral landscape in such a way as to place a premium on having more than others. The consequence of this was a dramatic de-stabilization of society. "Having moved away from the road of nature," he says, many now began to think that "nothing is worthier of esteem than excelling in wealth and power."[50] Yet this decay lay on a spectrum, and luxury had not corrupted the group to such an extent that it was incapable of re-organizing itself. In response to this turmoil, the mem-

48 Julius Kirshner, "*Civitas Sibi Faciat Civem*: Bartolus of Sassoferrato's Doctrine on the Making of a Citizen," *Speculum* 48 (1973), 700 n. 23.

49 This is noted by Connan in *Commentaria iuris civilis*, I, 16v.

50 *"Sic tandem deflexit de via naturae, paulatimque eo deducta est humana ambitio, nihil ut haberetur praeclarius, quam divitiis & potentia excellere,"* Connan, *Commentaria iuris civilis*, I, 16r.

bers of this jural community "created kings," who ensured that the poor "would not be oppressed by those who had more."[51] They instituted political authority, in other words, to guarantee that everybody, rich or poor, satisfied the obligations that bind them into a distinctive community, so as to preserve that community.

Donellus makes a similar argument. Over time, it became apparent that a self-regulating people could not preserve itself intact. On account of "a natural proclivity towards disagreement," "government according to the varied judgements of men" would "forcibly separate" the group in conflicting directions. As a result, the group reasoned that they would be "better protected," "better off," and "more certain" with government concentrated in a king.[52]

From their accounts of the historical development of these institutions, it is clear that for both authors political authority is an institution adopted because it was considered necessary to preserve this larger *societas*, and by extension the various *societates* organized within it. When we turn to other sections in their commentaries, we can see that they also conceptualized this political authority on Ciceronian terms as a representative of the state itself. In a chapter addressing the meaning of law, Connan praises the law as a source "of great benefit in human affairs," for which he cites the aforementioned passage from *Pro Cluentio* as evidence.[53] Included in the citation, after "we obey the law so that we may be free," are the following words, which are absent from the *Pro Cluentio*, but which Connan nevertheless attributes to the work: "for [the laws] having been suppressed or neglected, there will be nothing that someone can claim to be their own, nothing certain to have, and nothing he can hope to leave to his children."[54] It is this concern to ensure the durability of the *civitas* in light of evolving conditions that structures his later comments on the role of the magistrate. Magistrates were created, he says, because "a law that speaks generally, neither can clearly comprehend all things in their specificity, nor

51 "[…] *sunt reges creati a populis* […] *& qui inter ipsos essent inopes, ut ne opprimerentur ab iis, qui maiores opes habebant,*" Connan, *Commentaria iuris civilis*, I, 16r. Note that this account of the creation of kings appears to come from Cicero, *De officiis* 2.41.

52 "[…] *in plurium autem administratione propter varia hominum iudicia, et naturalem ad dissentiendum proclivitatem, facile eveniret, ut distraherentur animi in diversas sententias,*" Donellus, *Commentariorum de iure civili*, I, 53.

53 "[…] *legibus vivamus, tantam attulit utilitatem rebus humanis* […]" Connan, *Commentaria iuris civilis*, I, 28r.

54 "[…] *inquit Tullius* […] *legum denique servi omnes sumus, ut liberi esse possimus. Nam his aut oppressis aut neglectis, nihil erit quod suum quisque possit dicere, nihil certum habere, nihil quod liberis suis se relicturum sperare possit,*" Connan, *Commentaria iuris civilis*, I, 28r. Connan's additions to the *Pro Cluentio* appear to come from Cicero, *Pro Caecina* 70 and 74, respectively, in which a similar argument is made.

bring equity to all things," and, as a result, "a moderator and administrator of the law was established, who would interpret the law according to his prudence, and adapt it to similar matters."[55] It is for this reason – the need to give a dynamic and living quality to the otherwise abstract law – that "Cicero, in *De legibus*, calls the magistrate speaking law, and the law a mute magistrate," and that "Martianus says that the praetor's edict (*ius hoc honorarium*) is, as it were, the living voice of civil law."[56] We may say, then, that Connan envisages the magistrate and the *civitas* itself to be in a mutually dependent relationship. The recognized role of the magistrate presumes the existence of the *civitas*, to whose laws he gives voice, while the existence of the *civitas* is itself dependent on the magistrate, whose ability to adapt to changing circumstances is necessary to maintain it. The two are, in other words, mutually constitutive.

Donellus adapts the same idea in his commentary. After enumerating a number of areas in which the public must care for its citizens, including looking after the needy and the elderly, Donellus proceeds to argue that "if the *civitas* itself could provide and administer these things on its own, then we would not need to proceed further."[57] However, he says, "the person who can bear these matters is not the *persona* of the *civitas*."[58] "The aid of another person is necessary," who, among other things, will "guard the public peace, keep citizens in their duties, punish wrong doing, and restore rights to the citizens."[59] On the other hand, without these other people acting as "defenders and administrators of the republic," there will be "no well-being (*salus*) and safety (*incolumitas*) of the citizens," and, as a result, "no republic."[60] There is,

55 "[...] *eadem causa fuit magistratuum creandorum, ut quando lex quae generaliter loquitur, neque distincte omnia potest et speciatim comprehendere, neque una omnibus rebus aequaliter convenire, legis moderator quidam et administrator constitueretur, qui pro sua prudentia eam interpretaretur, et ad similia negotia accommodaret,"* Connan, *Commentaria iuris civilis*, I, 64v.

56 *"Itaque Tullius in legibus, magistratum legem loquentem appellat: legem autem, mutum magistratum, quod Martianus dicit in ius hoc honorarium quasi vivam esse vocem iuris civilis,"* Connan, *Commentaria iuris civilis*, I, 64v.

57 *"Haec ipsa si per se procurare, et administrare posset civitas, non progrederemur longius,"* Donellus, *Commentariorum de iure civili*, I, 229–230.

58 *"Nunc autem civitatis non ea persona est, quae quidquam gerere possit in rebus,"* Donellus, *Commentariorum de iure civili*, I, 230.

59 *"Alienis auxiliis ad eam rem opus est* [...] *qui pacem publicam tueri, civies in officio continere, maleficia pro imperio coercere, civibus iura reddere, ad munera capessenda cogere invitos possint,"* Donellus, *Commentariorum de iure civili*, I, 229–230.

60 *"Ad superiors res recte administrandas defensoribus, ac reipublicae curatoribus opus est* [...] *inquibus duobus consistit salus, et incolumnitas civitatum: eoque nulla est respublica, quae his duobus careat,"* Donellus, *Commentariorum de iure civili*, I, 230.

then, a *persona civitatis*, which Donellus identifies with the laws that bind its members into a distinct group; but it is a *persona* in the sense of being merely a mask, unable to act on its own, and thus unable truly to be present. But when "the care" of this person "has been entrusted" to one or two magistrates, and institutions established to act on its behalf, then those laws can truly be made present, and the *civitas* can have an existence in the world as an entity in its own right.[61]

As they proceed with their historical account of the *ius gentium*, it becomes apparent that both Connan and Donellus treat this act of finding someone to speak on behalf of the *civitas* as enabling, in turn, the attribution of distinctive rights and obligations under the *ius gentium* to the *civitates* these magistrates represent. Indeed, the next *ius gentium* institution they address after the founding of kingdoms is the law of war, which both jurists stress came after the creation of magistrates.[62] The laws of war emerged, according to Donellus, so that "states and kingdoms themselves could be maintained."[63] This, in turn, meant "repelling enemies" and "justly reclaiming things from them."[64] For Connan, it means ensuring that the "whole body of their subjects would not be oppressed by enemies."[65] The implication, then, is the magistrate is under obligation to protect citizens from these external enemies, and, concerned as it is with preserving justice internally and therefore keeping the state alive, that this follows from their role as representative of the state they had previously assumed. With the emergence of a new body of law that specifically regulates the relations between states, it appears that, after the elevation of magistrates, a state is no longer merely a body of mutually obligated citizens, but now an entity capable itself of bearing its own rights and obligations.

Taking from Cicero both an account of the nature of social bodies and an account of how non-human entities can be considered persons, we have seen how Connan and Donellus have developed an explanation for how the state came to be recognized as a person in its own right, capable of bearing its own rights and obligations under the *ius gentium*. I would like to conclude this section with an example (in this case, from Connan) that shows how this

61 "[...] *magistratus, et praeficti, quibus reipubliae cura in aliqua parte commissa est,"* Donellus, *Commentariorum de iure civili*, I, 230.

62 Connan, *Commentaria iuris civilis*, I, 16r; Donellus, *Commentarium de iure civili*, I, 53.

63 *"Civitatibus et regnis conditis, bella introducta, nempe ad illa ipsa tuenda,"* Donellus, *Commentariorum de iure civili*, I, 53.

64 "[...] *cum bellis utamur aut ad propulsandos hostes aut res ab hostibus juste repetendas,"* Donellus, *Commentariorum de iure civili*, I, 53.

65 "[...] *ut ne ab hostibus externis universi* [...] *opprimerentur* [...]" Connan, *Commentaria iuris civilis*, I, 16r.

same mechanism explaining how associations can become legal persons is also at work with social bodies other than states.

The example appears in Connan's discussion of the ability of states, colleges and other bodies to establish their own customs. It is no wonder, he says, that colleges can have laws of their own, when "the laws of a single family (*gentis*) or agnatic line can be their own, such as, for example, when children are heirs to a greater or less extent than the law of the state commands."[66] "For this does not bring harm to the other citizens, but is a certain family right, proper to members of the agnatic line."[67] Indeed, it is this way "among our noble families" in France, "who have established their own right of succession."[68] Suggestive here is the analogy between, on the one hand, a college and a state, and, on the other, a family. For it implies that, despite not having a *legal* personality, unlike a college or a state, a family is nevertheless still understood to possess the characteristics of one. What appears to make this analogy possible is that all these bodies share certain fundamental characteristics, namely that they are gatherings of individuals held to be bound by principles of mutual obligation, and that they are organized collectively in some way in order to maintain themselves united. This aspect becomes especially clear when we consider Connan's claim that these entities – colleges, states, and families – each possess a right to punish, which he explains is an implication of these entities' fundamental characteristics as a group bound by mutual obligation. Of course, he clarifies, the extent to which these bodies, especially subsidiary bodies such as colleges, can punish is "ambiguous."[69] It is true that some penalties, while appropriate for states, are not appropriate for colleges. Yet it is nevertheless also true that they must be allowed to enact their own punishments, since "no law is sufficiently protected from wicked people, if a means of punishment is lacking,"[70] and that these internal practices indeed deserve the name of "law."[71]

---

66 *"Et quid mirandum est suas esse collegiis leges, cum et gentis unius et agnationis esse possint, puta, ut filii maiore aut minore ex parte sint haeredes, quam lex civitatis iubeat,"* Connan, *Commentaria iuris civilis*, I, 41r.

67 *"Nec enim id caeteris civibus detrimentum affert, sed est ius quoddam gentilitium, horum tantum agnatorum proprium,"* Connan, *Commentaria iuris civilis*, I, 41r.

68 *"Et sunt nonnullae apud nos familiae nobelium, quae sibi ius in suis successionibus constituerunt,"* Connan, *Commentaria iuris civilis*, I, 41r.

69 *"Sed an statutis suis poenam possint adiicere, magis est ambiguum,"* Connan, *Commentaria iuris civilis*, I, 41r.

70 "[…] *cum nulla lex per se satis munita sit adversus improbos, si desit poenae metus,"* Connan, *Commentaria iuris civilis*, I, 41r.

71 *"At vero civitates, corpora etiam et collegia civitatum, quin et eiusdem quasi gentis et agnationis populi sibi consuetudinis authores sunt, ut et fatentur: status condunt* […] *quid enim aliud est statutum quam lex?"* Connan, *Commentaria iuris civilis*, I, 41rv.

Based on these comments, it seems that, for Connan, some associations eventually develop to a point where they choose to enact collective structures for their long-term preservation. This happened with the state, but he suggests that it also takes place within other bodies such as families. And, as with the state, he appears to think that a consequence of this formal institutionalization is that these other groups, also initially abstract, will likewise have assumed a distinctive group presence, and therefore the character of a person.

## 5 Conclusion: Renaissance Jurisprudence and Early Modern Natural Law

I would like to conclude with evidence that this social theory of groups and group-persons, ultimately derived from Cicero and made integral to Roman law scholarship in the work of jurists such as Connan and Donellus, would become the foundation for at least one highly influential early modern natural law theory. My example here is Johannes Althusius' *Politica* (1604, 1610, and 1614) and his *Dicaelogicae libri tres: totum et universum ius* (1618), texts with broad ambitions to construct a universal theory of politics and jurisprudence, respectively, but which, unlike many of the other most celebrated contributions to the genre of natural law, are heavily focused on the internal government of states. In each work Althusius argues that the subject of both politics and law is "association," what he calls *consociatio*.[72] He opens the *Politica* this way: "Politics is the art of associating (*consociandi*) men for the purpose of establishing, cultivating, and conserving social life among them [...] The subject matter of politics is therefore association (*consociatio*), in which the symbiotes pledge themselves each to the other, by explicit or tacit agreement, to mutual communication of whatever is useful and necessary for the harmonious exercise of social life (*vitae socialis*)."[73] There are a number of different types of association that follow this model, ranging from the family, to the

72 Gio Maria Tessarolo has shown how this structuring concept of Althusius's thinking is indebted to the Roman law concept of *societas*. See Gio Maria Tessarolo, "The Politics of *societas* and the Early Modern State," *The Historical Journal* (2024): 1–21.

73 "*Politica est ars homines ad vitam socialem inter se constituendam, colendam & conservandam consociandi* [...] *Proposita igitur Politicae est consociatio, qua pacto expresso, vel tacito, symbiotici inter se invicem ad communicationem mutuam eorum, quae ad vitae socialis usum & consortium sunt utilia & necessaria, se obligant,*" Johannes Althusius, *Politica Methodice digesta, atque exemplis sacris et profanes illustrata* vol. 1, ed. with intro. by Corrado Malandrino (Turin: Claudiana, 2009), 220. Translation from Johannes Althusius, *Politica*, ed. and trans. Frederick S. Carney (Carmel, IN: Liberty Fund, 1994), 17.

private association (*collegium*), to the *civitas*, to "provinces," to, finally, the "universal and major public association" which he sometimes calls the *regnum* and, other times, the *res publica*. Families and private associations are *societates* composed of natural persons, while public associations, such as the *civitas* and the *res publica* or *regnum*, are constituted, in the case of the former, by a *societas* between families and *collegia*, and, in the case of the latter, of "families, cities (*civitates*) and provinces," which "existed by nature prior to [commonwealths], and gave birth to them."[74] They are constituted, in other words, by smaller *societates* that are capable of associating in the manner of individual natural persons. As he says with respect to the *civitas*: "the members of a community are private and diverse associations of families and college, not the individual members of private associations."[75]

Althusius then proceeds with an argument for why human beings are creatures prone to live in *societates*. In what appears to be a reference to Cicero's *De inventione*, he states that "the needs of body and soul, and the seeds of virtue implanted in our soul, drew dispersed men together into one place." "These causes," he continued, "have built villages, established cities, founded academic institutions, and united by civil unity and society a diversity of farmers, craftsmen, laborers, builders, soldiers, merchants, learned and unlearned men and so many members of the same body [...] called the commonwealth."[76] With a direct quotation from Cicero's *De legibus*, Althusius later tells us that these "seeds of virtue" are in fact knowledge of the laws that permeate a highly juridical image of the world: "Common law has been naturally implanted by God in all men [...] 'For there was reason derived from the nature of the universe,' Cicero says, 'urging men to do right and recalling them from wrong-doing, and this reason did not first become law at the time

74 *"Nam familiae, civitates & provinciae natura sua prius quam regna, quae ex hisce sunt orta, exstiterunt,"* Althusius, *Politica Methodice digesta* vol. 1, 508. Translation from Althusius, *Politica*, trans. Carney, 66.

75 *"Membra universitatis [Althusius uses universitas analogously with civitas] sunt privatae diversaeque consociationes conjugum, familiarum & collegiorum, non singuli cujusque consociationis privatae,"* Althusius, *Politica Methodice digesta* vol. 1, 326. Translation from Althusius, *Politica*, trans. Carney, 66.

76 *"Corporis itaque & animi necessitates atque virtutum semina animis nostris insita, homines dispersos & dissipates in unum locum contraxerunt. Hae caussae aedificarunt vicos, construxerunt civitates, fundarunt Academias, multorum agricolarum, artificum, fabrorum, architectorum, militum, mercatorum, doctorum atque indoctorum varietatem, tanquam totidem ejusdam corporis membra, unitate & societate civili copularunt* [...] *omnes pariter in publicum quoddam corpus (quam Rempublicam vocamus),"* Althusius, *Politica Methodice digesta* vol. 1, 230–232. Translation from Althusius, *Politica*, trans. Carney, 23.

it was written down, but at its origin'."[77] For Althusius, then, much like Connan and Donellus, human beings enter into organized societies due to a desire to improve their material conditions, and these societies are bound by the perception of mutual obligations, the content of which is derived from natural reason. These two attributes – mutual obligation and mutual benefit – are the two poles upon which every *societas* stands: "this mutual communication, or common enterprise," he says, "involves (1) things, (2) services, and (3) common rights (*iura*) by which the numerous and various needs of each and every symbiote are supplied, the self-sufficiency and mutuality of life and human society is achieved, and social life is established and conserved."[78] For this reason, he continues, "Cicero said, 'a political community is a gathering of men associated by a consensus as to the right and a sharing of what is useful'."[79] While Cicero in this passage refers to the *res publica*, Althusius is here talking about all forms of association, public and private, since they all follow this same model.

It is precisely because these associations are held together by mutual obligation, or law, Althusius continues, that "in every association and types of symbiosis some persons are rulers (heads, overseers, prefects) or superiors, others are subjects or inferiors."[80] For, "nothing, as Cicero affirms, 'is suited to the natural law and its requirements as *imperium*, without which neither household nor city nor nation nor the entire race of men can endure'."[81] In the family, this role of "director and governor of common affairs pertaining to this

77 *"Communis* [*law*] *est, quae natura sua omnibus hominibus a Deo est ingenerata* [...] *Cic. lib. 2. De legib. erat enim, ait, ratio profecta a rerum natura, & ad recta faciendum impellens, & a delicto revocans, quae non tunc demum incipit lex esse scripta, sed tunc cum orta est,"* Althusius, *Politica Methodice digesta* vol. 1, 910. Translation from Althusius, *Politica*, trans. Carney, 139.

78 *"Communicatio illa mutua* [...] *quam dixi, fit rebus, operis, juribus communibus, quibus indigentia varia et multiplex singulorum et universorum symbioticorum suppletur* [...] *et societatis humanae perficitur, seu vita socialis constituitur et conservatur,"* Althusius, *Politica Methodice digesta* vol. 1, 222. Translation from Althusius, *Politica*, trans. Carney, 19.

79 *"Unde Cicero dixit, populum esse coetum juris consensus et utilitatis communione consociatum,"* Althusius, *Politica Methodice digesta* vol. 1, 222. Translation from Althusius, *Politica*, trans. Carney, 19.

80 "[...] *in quavis consociatione et symbiosi specie sint quidam imperantes, praestites, praepositi, praefecti seu superiores: quidam vero obsequentes, seu inferiores,"* Althusius, *Politica Methodice digesta* vol. 1, 224. Translation from Althusius, *Politica*, trans. Carney, 20.

81 *"Et nihil, ut Cic. lib. 3. De legib. ait, tam aptum est ad jus conditionemque naturae, quam imperium, sine quo, nec domus ulla, neque civitas, neque gens, nec hominum universum genus stare* [...] *potest,"* Althusius, *Politica Methodice digesta* vol. 1, 224. Translation from Althusius, *Politica*, trans. Carney, 20. The reference is to Cicero, *De legibus* 3.1.

association is the husband,"[82] while in the college, the city, and the *res publica*, it belongs to a duly appointed rector. It is the same power in all associations, although only in the *res publica* is it called "sovereignty" (*maiestas*). This position of associational head is, according to Althusius, immensely important; without it, the body of the association will fall apart. In a passage replete with what we have seen to be this Ciceronian language of group personality, he says with respect to the *res publica* that this figure is the "the bond (*vinculum*), soul (*anima*), and vital spirit (*vitalis spiritus*) of the commonwealth," without which – emphasizing once again that the head's role is to enforce the mutual obligations that bind the association – it either "becomes a band of robbers and a gang of evil men," "or disintegrates" into its consistent parts.[83] Without the head, there is no justice, and therefore no association.

Finally, and crucially, all of these aspects of a *consociatio* – a group of individuals bound by agreement to mutual obligations for mutually beneficial ends, and made durable through subjection to a head tasked with enforcing those obligations in order to realize those ends – come together to make each association its own person. Althusius makes this claim in the *Politica*,[84] but it is put especially clearly in the *Dicaelogicae*. In a chapter that considers the juridical status of "men naturally conjoined," Althusius makes a distinction between "two different genres of association, one by nature and by the will of men."[85] But regardless of whether they are joined by nature or artifice, both types of association share the same characteristics; what it is at issue in the distinction is the end a particular association pursues and the circumstances that led to its origin, not its fundamental form. What defines these

82 *"Director et gubernator communium negotiorum ad hanc consociationem spectantium est maritus,"* Althusius, *Politica Methodice digesta* vol. 1, 260. Translation from Althusius, *Politica*, trans. Carney, 29.

83 "[…] *in hac potestate* […] *vinculum, anima & vitalis spiritus regni* […] *continetur* […] *eo vero sublato, omnis illa vita symbiotica concidit, & vel incipit esse latroncinium, malorumque hominum congregation, vel ex uno regno fiunt diversa plura alia regna, aut provinciae,"* Althusius, *Politica Methodice digesta* vol. 1, 520. Translation from Althusius, *Politica*, trans. Carney, 70.

84 "[…] *administratores et rectores, universalis consociationis corpus, seu totum et universum populum, a quo constituti sunt, repraesentant* […] *ejusque personam gerunt in iis, quae Reipublicae seu regni nomine faciunt,"* Althusius, *Politica Methodice digesta* vol. 1, 706. Translation: "The administrators and rectors of the universal symbiosis and commonwealth represent the body of the universal association, of the whole people by whom they have been constituted […] they bear its person (*gerere personam*) in those things they do in the name of the commonwealth," Althusius, *Politica*, trans. Carney, 97.

85 *"Coniuncti homines sunt duorum generum consociati, nimirum et uniti natura, vel hominum placito,"* Johannes Althusius, *Dicaelogicae Libri Tres: Totum et universum ius* (Herborn, 1649), 17.

associations – variously known as a "*societas*," "union," "*consociatio*," and "body of many men" – is "order, agreement of minds, sharing of counsel and mutual assistance, and a sharing of mutual advantage."[86] Entailed in this idea of "order" is that "the actions of the conjoined men, are accommodated and directed according to their condition and agreement."[87] Once suitably ordered, and maintained by subjection, this entity can then be considered its own person, "because a union, not of singular men in and of themselves, but a whole, a durable (*constans*) body consisting of multiple people [...] assumes the role of one person, or is held in the place of one."[88] Put otherwise, once organized under a rector who enforces obligations and secures benefits, an association acquires an a stability and permanence it may otherwise lack, with the result that we can now begin to attribute actions to it, in turn enabling us to think of it, and to treat it in law, as one person.

Althusius is traditionally not considered to fall under the same category of jurist as Connan and Donellus, even if he sometimes cites them. His use of the theory is thus good evidence for its spread and the broader transformation its introduction into civil law interpretation enabled: a transformation that helped usher in the period of natural jurisprudence and giving shape to the various early modern associations, public and private, recognized and regulated by it. While, of course, partly a product of an already emerging tendency to see the *Corpus iuris civilis* as a source for universal legal concepts, we should therefore also view the incorporation of this Ciceronian social theory into legal interpretation as an enabler of Roman law's transformation into a key source of a universal, natural, law.

## Acknowledgement

This work has received funding from the European Research Council (Erc) under the European Union's Horizon 2020 research and innovation program (grant agreement No. 864309).

86 "[...] *societas, unio, communio, consociatio, corpus hominum plurium, plures hominem in unam societas collecti* [...] *Haec hominum coniunctio consistit in ordine, consensione animorum, communicatione consilii et auxilii mutui, et commode participatione,"* Althusius, *Dicaeologicae*, 17.

87 *"Ordo est* [...] *qua actiones coniunctorum hominum, iuxta eorundum conditionem et consesum attemperantur et diriguntur,"* Althusius, *Dicaeologicae*, 17.

88 *"Propter hanc unionem sit, ut non singuli homines per se et in se, sed totum, ex personarum plurium comprehension corpus, constans, consideretur tanqaum una persona,"* Althusius, *Dicaeologicae*, 17.

# PART 2

## *Early Seventeenth Century*

CHAPTER 4

# *Fides* and *feudum* in the Legal Thought of Petrus Gudelinus (1550–1619): A Study on Feudal, Civil, and Natural Obligations in the Early Modern Age

*Pedro R.S. Santos*

## 1 Introduction

Petrus Gudelinus (1550–1619) is a particularly interesting jurist because he is proof that modern chronological divisions into *medieval/modern* can be quite useful but not absolutely accurate to study the politico-legal thought in the sixteenth and seventeenth centuries.[1] As a *professor primarius* of civil law at

1 In this article, we will not dedicate a section to the author's biography, but we leave this note about his life. Most of his biography is contained in a *Oratio funebris* given by Maximilian Wittebort in 1519 at the funeral of Gudelinus and that can be read in the first edition of the *De iure novissimo*, cf. Maximilian Wittebort, *In Authoris Obitum Funebris Oratio*, in *Commentariorum de iure novissimo libri sex, optima methodo, accurate ac erudite conscripti, additis harum vicinarumque regionum moribus, opus ut diu avideq[ue] expetitum, ita scholis foroq[ue] utilissimum, cum indicibus* (Antuerpiae: Ex officina Hieronymi Verdusi, 1620), 333–338. Valerius Andreas also wrote a section on Gudelinus' life and career in *Bibliotheca Belgica: de belgis vita scriptisq[ue] Claris* (Lovanii: Iacobi Zegers, 1643), 741–742. Despite being unknown today even to scholars, he was a relatively famous jurist in the Netherlands in both the seventeenth and eighteenth centuries, having been widely consulted by Arnoldus Vinnius, cf. passim *Commentarius Locupletissimus, academicus & forensis, in quator Institutionum Imperialium* (Lugduni Batavorum: ex officina Ioannis Majre, 1462).

Petrus Gudelinus was born in the city of Ath in 1550, one of the main cities of the County of Hainaut. In 1564, at the age of fourteen, he began studying philosophy at one of the preparatory colleges of Leuven, the College of the Falcon (*paedagogium falconis*), where the current Law Faculty of the KU Leuven is situated, and in 1568 he would begin his law studies. In 1572, after finishing his degree, he went to Mechelen to start the legal practice with his cousin Jacques Bousset, a lawyer and secretary in the Great Council of Mechelen. It is estimated that he worked in Mechelen for 3–4 years and then returned to his hometown of Ath, where he worked as a lawyer and participated in the political life of the city. He would leave Ath around 1577 to return to Leuven and start teaching. Gudelinus did well as a professor of civil law and as an official of the old University of Leuven, as he was professor regius and primarius of the *Digesta* and *Codex*, and was also elected Rector of the University twice. He died on October 1619, leaving his two older sons, Petrus-Paulus and Philippus, with the responsibility to publish his works. He taught civil law for over 30 years at Leuven and was famous in his time for his commentaries on Justinian's *Novellae*, the last legal codifica-

 | DOI:10.1163/9789004748712_006

the University of Leuven, Gudelinus became famous due to the lectures on the *Novellae* of Justinian, where he deals with the *ius publicum* as a separated subject from the *ius privatum*, foreshadowing a distinction that would dominate the academic programmes of later centuries: all of this can be interpreted into a process of emancipation of public law as a distinct legal category. However, one 'medieval' aspect dominates in Gudelinus' legal thought: the law of fiefs (*ius feudorum*).[2] This aspect was totally unexpected for the author of this article, who expected to find a description and disposition of political powers in the style of Francisco Vitoria or Jean Bodin and instead comes across a scholar to whom the law of fiefs is of primary importance to understand his legal thought.[3] After surveying the treatises *De iure feudorum*[4] and *De iure*

tion made by that Emperor, which corrected or added to earlier legislation. However, his commentaries and lectures did not focus only on the texts of the *Novellae* but also on post-Justinian legislation, mainly feudal and canonical law of the Middle Ages and the early modern period. That is why the title of his commentaries, *De iure novissimo*, should be read as "on the most recent law" or else "on the newest law".

2 As Dirk Heirbaut recently observed, feudal institutions were already operational in various regions of Europe before the *Libri feudorum* appeared, and they had an influence on the various societal spheres of the ancien régime. The Low Countries, in particular, were fertile ground for the expansion of feudal institutions and contributed to the germination of various polities (counties, duchies, margraviates, etc.). The word *feudum* was not restricted to a legal apparatus but also had religious and moral dimensions. In this sense, the word *fides* and derivatives such as *fidelis* and *fidelitas* are found in treatises on feudal law, and this is not surprising: the process of assigning and receiving a *feudum* implied *fides* between both parties. However, the debate surrounding the origin of fiefdoms led legal humanists to agree that feudal law was a post-Roman creation, which had its beginnings with the Carolingian dynasty. Vid., Dirk Heirbaut, "Feudal Law", in Heikki Pihlajamäki, Markus D. Dubber, and Mark Godfrey (eds), *The Oxford Handbook of European Legal History*, Oxford: University Press, 2018), pp. 529–548.

3 Gudelinus was aware of Jean Bodin's *De republica libri sex*. The references to it are few, but intriguing. On the one hand, an earlier preliminary study showed that references to Jean Bodin's works in Chapter IV in the first book of the *De iure novissimo* have been suppressed since their first publication in 1620. However, the 1608 manuscripts of the same commentaries written by a law student at the University of Leuven prove that Gudelinus had cited Bodin during his lectures of that year. Perhaps Gudelinus decided to suppress Bodin out of fear that he was an author found in several *Indices librorum prohibitorum*, unless it was suppressed by his sons during the editorial finishing of the work. In any case, Jean Bodin's name is cited only once explicitly in Petrus Gudelinus, *De iure novissimo*, 196, and only to disagree with Bodin on an issue concerning the relationship between feudal lords and public law. I have dealt with this question previously in a study that has not yet been published.

4 Petrus Gudelinus, *De iure feudorum commentarius: in partes VI distributus, Belgii & Franciae mores, ac illustria exempla exactissima methodo complectens* (Lovanii: ex officina Henrici Hastenii, 1624). We will refer to this work as *De iure feudorum* from now on.

*pacis*,[5] which is a continuation of the first, and analysing them in the legal and political context of the second half of the sixteenth century, we can observe that notions about the nature of the *feudum* are taken very differently from those bequeathed one century later by scholars of the French Enlightenment.[6]

Gudelinus was quite aware of the fact that fiefs and their law were a non-Roman creation. Still, such did not represent a medieval 'corruption' of Roman law to him, as many eighteenth-century intellectuals would argue. Instead, the law of fiefs (*ius feudorum*) was seen as a part of the normative existence of legal persons (*personae*) and things (*res*) in the framework of natural, divine, and positive legal orders. That is an essential aspect of his view on the political disposition of the various Christian polities back then. It also finds an ally in another concept of major importance in Western and Eastern Christianity: the concept of *fides* and its derivates, such as *fidelitas* and *fidelis*. To Gudelinus, the legal bonds established under the *ius feudorum* are defined by *fidelitas*. This becomes paramount when he deals with obligations from different branches of law that could collide.

Despite the anti-feudal and anti-medieval propaganda in the eighteenth century and all the associated prejudices still enduring today, historians have mainly rejected two narratives that have been propagated since the late eighteenth century. The first, which argues that the 'Middle Ages' is an era of backwardness and stagnation, is no longer accepted in modern historiography. Therefore, the use of certain terms such as 'Dark Ages' to designate the High Middle Ages is avoided by historians.[7] However, another narrative is more difficult to fight and still remains somewhat implicit in modern historical teaching, i.e. the narrative that associates 'feudalism' or 'feudal society'

5 Petrus Gudelinus, *De jure pacis commentarius in quo praecipuae de hoc jure quaestiones distinctis capitibus eleganter pertractantur* (Lovanii: Typis Philippi Dormalii, 1620). For a deep analysis of this treaty and its placement in the tradition of the Ius commune, vid. Randall Lesaffer, "An Early Treatise on Peace Treaties: Petrus Gudelinus between Roman Law and Modern Practice," *Journal of Legal History* 23, no. 3 (2002): 223–252.

6 On the opposition to feudal institutions in the Enlightenment, vid. J.Q.C. Mackrell, *The attack on Feudalism in eighteenth-century France* (London: Routledge and Kegan Paul, 1973), 48–76.

7 The concept of the 'Dark Ages' or *'Saeculum obscurum'* has a longer history than we can go into in this chapter. However, it's worth noting that the semantics of this concept date back to Petrarch and were widely adopted by intellectuals in the sixteenth century. One of the most famous was Caesar Baronius in his monumental work *Annales Ecclesiastici* (1588–1607), where he coined the concept of *saeculum obscurum* for the period from the end of the Carolingian Empire (ninth century) to the period of Gregory VII (eleventh century). Vid. Theodore E. Mommsen, "Petrarch's Conception of the 'Dark Age,'" *Speculum* 17, no. 2 (1942): 226–242.

exclusively to the Middle Ages, and then meets its end in the beginnings of the early modern Age.[8] Nothing could be further from reality. Despite the economic and social transformation from the early Middle Ages to the early modern age, the feudal political order dominated the European political realm until the late eighteenth century. Suppose the feudal order had disappeared by the end of the Middle Ages or at the beginning of the early modern age; then why did so many intellectuals try to fight it politically in the eighteenth century? In particular, the legally trained revolutionaries who contributed to the French Revolution, such as Maximilien de Robespierre (1758–1794), sought to eliminate feudal institutions explicitly.[9] Although the topic of this study does not revolve around eighteenth-century legal scholarship, it is nevertheless worth sharing a premise implicit in this article. In our understanding, feudal law progressively ceased to be seen as belonging to the natural order throughout the early modern age, being instead associated with customs (*consuetudines*) of human and positive origin. As we shall see, Gudelinus already made this association at the beginning of the seventeenth century in his lectures in *De iure feudorum* (1624),[10] by perceiving feudal and natural obligations as belonging to different legal orders and how the latter had pre-eminence over the former. However, he was not a revolutionary, nor was he seeking to revolutionise the legal scholarship of his time.

## 2 Feudal Historiography, a Never-Ending Debate

Feudal law is not the favourite subject of legal historians, especially when dealing with the politico-legal issues of the Christian West in the early modern

8 This topic has recently been treated by Matthew Gabriele and David M. Perry in *The Bright Ages: A New History of Medieval Europe* (New York: Harper, 2021).

9 Jonathan Israel, *Revolutionary Ideas: An Intellectual History of the French Revolution from The Rights of Man to Robespierre* (Princeton: University Press, 2014); Idem, *Radical Enlightenment Philosophy and the Making of Modernity* 1650–1750 (Oxford: University Press, 2002); on the influence of the French Revolution on the emergence of a new demarcation for property rights, which opposed the feudal rights of the ancien regime, vid. Rafe Blaufarb, *The great demarcation: the French Revolution and the invention of modern property* (Oxford: University Press, 2016).

10 This is not to say that natural law did not regulate certain feudal customs, as Ullmann and Canning have argued earlier. But as we shall observe, in the case of conflict between feudal and natural obligations, the latter were preferable. On the treatment of feudal custom as natural law, Vid. Walter Ullmann, *The individual and society in the middle ages* (London: Methuen, 1967), 83; Joseph Canning, *The political thought of Baldus de Ubaldis* (Cambridge: University Press, 1987), 82–83.

age.[11] Nonetheless, the twentieth century has seen numerous contributions that have given a new impetus to feudal studies, not only the important classics of historiography, such as Marc Bloch's classic *La société féodale* (1939),[12] which defined the concept of 'Feudal Society' in modern historiography, and the works of François Louis Ganshof who, in addition to his contributions to the study of the Carolingian period, also made diverse contributions on the study of feudal-vassalic relationships along the lines of Bloch.[13] However, both authors mostly focused on the Early and Late Middle Ages, dedicating short lines to the early modern age. Donald R. Kelley changed this by approaching it through its ideological prism and by extending its *terminus ad quem* to the early modern age with the approach of authors such as Franciscus Duarenus (1509–1559), Jacques Cujas (1522–1590), and François Hotman (1524–1590).[14]

A particular debate has marked feudal scholarship in recent decades. Two historians have challenged the concept of 'feudalism' and its application as an operative concept in historical studies, particularly when dealing with medieval charters. In 1974, Elizabeth A.R. Brown in her article "The Tyranny of a Construct: Feudalism and Historians of Medieval Europe", criticised the word 'feudalism' as a historical construct that originated in the eighteenth century.[15] However, the concept of 'Feudalism' would meet its greatest challenge twenty years later when Susan Reynolds published her polemical study *Fiefs and Vassals. The Medieval Evidence Reinterpreted.* Not only does Susan Reynolds start from the same premises as Brown, but she also deepens the problem by addressing the concept of 'Feudalism' as a *post-medieval* concept which implies a feudal framework created by sixteenth-century jurists.[16] Rey-

11 Apart from Canning and Ullmann's works, Kenneth Pennington and Magnus Ryan also made important contributions to the study of feudal law and the legal understanding surrounding oaths. Cf. Kenneth Pennington, "The formation of the jurisprudence of the feudal oath of fealty," *Rivista Internazionale di Diritto Comune* (2004), 15: 57–76; Magnus Ryan, "The oath of fealty and the lawyers," in *Politisches Denken und die Wirklichkeit der Macht im Mittelalter,* eds. J. Canning and O.G. Oexle (Göttingen: Vandenhoeck & Ruprecht, 1998), 211–228.

12 Marc Bloch, *La société féodale: la formation des liens de dépendance* (Paris: Albin Michel, 1968, 1st ed: 1939).

13 François Louis Ganshof, *Qu'est-ce que la féodalité* (Tallandier, 1982, 1st ed. 1944).

14 Donald R. Kelley, "De Origine Feudorum: The Beginnings of an Historical Problem," *Speculum* 39, no.2 (April 1964): 207–228; Idem, *The Beginning of Ideology: Consciousness and Society in the French Reformation* (Cambridge: University Press, 1981).

15 Elizabeth A.R. Brown, "The Tyranny of a Construct: Feudalism and Historians of Medieval Europe," *The American Historical Review* 79, no. 4 (October 1974): 1063–1088.

16 Susan Reynolds, *Fiefs and Vassals. The Medieval Evidence Reinterpreted* (Oxford: Clarendon Press, 1994), 1–16.

nolds' study has been widely debated and often criticised for neglecting essential sources to the understanding of the legal relations established between a lord and a vassal in the form of an oath.[17] However, the main thesis that 'feudalism' is a post-medieval concept was not challenged.[18] Indeed, no critic or review has challenged the claim of the concept of 'Feudalism' being a post-medieval construct.

In this article, we propose that an aspect of medieval and early modern political thought has been overlooked when dealing with topics connected with the feudal political order. We refer to the conventional explanation to expose the ancient feudal order departing from a geometrical framing, proper of the emerging scientifical spirit of the seventeenth and eighteenth centuries, and which is opposed to the organic perspective that previously dominated the politico-legal thought of the Latin West. Political communities and their constituent parts were described organically by words like *corpus*, *membra*, *caput*, *manus*, and others referring to other organs that had symbolic meanings, such as *mens* (mind) and *cor* (heart).[19] The political body thus had its head which commanded and the members which obeyed. Other metaphors derived from this organic premise, e.g., the relation between the secular arm and the spiritual arm. Besides corporeal metaphors, the organic perspective on politics also used metaphors associated with the family, such as *pater*, *filius*, and *frater*. Thus, we observe Petrus Gudelinus still following medieval ontological notions in describing the political community as a body. To him, feudal relations took place within that body, so they were implicitly organic.

---

17 Kenneth Pennington, in particular, criticised Reynolds for neglecting canon law sources and their importance in shaping the "secular oath of fidelity and other aspects of feudal law." Cf. Kenneth Pennington, "Feudal Oath of Fidelity and Homage," in *Essays in Honor of James A. Brundage*, eds. Kenneth Pennington and Melodie Harris Eichbauer (Ashgate, 2011), 93–115 (esp.114); another of the most criticised aspects of Reynolds' work was the radical denial of the concepts of Fief and Vassal as "too vague". Dirk Heirbaut concisely assesses this aspect in his review, cf. Dirk Heirbaut, *Tijdschrift voor Rechtsgeschiedenis*, 1998, 66 (3–4), 411–413.

18 In an article published twelve years later, Susan Reynolds admitted some mistakes of her best-selling title. Cf. Susan Reynolds, "Fiefs and Vassals after twelve years," in *Feudalism: New Landscapes of Debate*, eds. Sverre Bagge, Michael H. Gelting, and Thomas Lindkvist (Turnhout: Brepols Publishers, 2011), 15–26 (esp. 24).

19 The reference to the political community as a body has its origins in Aristotle and was adopted by medieval Western intellectuals like Aquinas. Christoph Philipp Haar has recently addressed this question. Vid. Christoph Philipp Haar, *Natural and Political Conceptions of Community: The Role of the Household Society in Early Modern Jesuit Thought, c.1590–1650* (Leiden/Boston: Brill, 2019), 1–26.

However, this perspective on the feudal past has progressively shifted since the eighteenth century. John Whitaker (1735–1808) is the first author to employ the word 'feudalism' in a historical monography.[20] Another peculiar introduction of this author was the notion of 'feudal pyramid' as a frame for the feudal political order.[21] This notion is still today a conventional perspective of framing the feudal past. However, the frame of the feudal order as a geometrical body is opposed to the vision of an organic body. In this way, part of the dynamism that comes from the organic notion of a historical society is lost when one begins to see that same society as a rigid structure.

Moreover, the top-bottom hierarchical order itself, with the king at the top, does not reflect the vision of the feudal order in the medieval past. The king was not the *caput* of the body politic but the Emperor. During the Middle Ages, European princes strengthened their power in their territories. Certainly, one cannot speak about 'states' in the same sense today, but kings, counts, and dukes became 'emperors' in their realms only gradually. However, the only legally recognised *Caesar* of the Latin West was the Emperor (*Imperator*) of the Holy Roman Empire, who was also King of Germany and Italy. The emperor's authority was always limited and contested by others, and even inside the Holy Roman Empire his power was rather limited.[22] Gudelinus states that the pre-eminence of the emperor is due to the fact he is the *antesignatus* and the first of all Christian princes.[23] This meant that he was to be

20 John Whitaker, *The History of Manchester in four books* (London: J. Murray, 1773).

21 Elizabeth A.R. Brown refers to this theme when dealing with a diagram present on the *Ius feudasticum* of Hotman as a sort of precursor of the feudal pyramid. Curious enough, Hotman's efforts to reduce the whole feudal law to some basic and overarching principles still perceive the feudal order as part of nature, Vid. François Hotman, *De feudis commentatio tripartita. Hoc est, Disputatio de iure Feudali. Commentarius in vsus Feudorum. Dictionarium verborum Feudalium* (Lugduni: Iohannem Lertotium, 1574), 62–63. Still, Brown does not seem to observe that the geometrisation of political bodies (or societies) that would dominate the late eighteenth century is ontologically opposed to the anthropocentrism that dominated the political narrative until then. Vid. Elizabeth A.R. Brown, "Reflections on Feudalism: Thomas Madox and the Origins of the Feudal System in England," in *Feud, violence and practice: essays in medieval studies in honor of Stephen D. White*, eds. Tracey L. Billado and Belle S. Tuten (eds.), Stephen D. White (honoree) (Farnham, Surrey: Ashgate, 2010), 135–149 (esp. n. 35).

22 The legal limitations of the emperor, or the prince, were explored by Kenneth Pennington, *The Prince and the Law 1200–1600* (Berkeley: University of California Press, 1993).

23 Gudelinus, *De iure feudorum*, 17–18. *Antesignatus* was used in the Roman legions to designate the soldiers that took the first line of combat. When applied to the emperor, it means that he is commanding the first line. Cf. Ratti Stéphane, "Julien soldat, antiquaire et dévot (Ammien Marcellin 23, 5, 15–24), " *Vita Latina* 163 (2001): 18–27 (19).

the leader of the Christian army, commanding kings, dukes, counts and other princes in the common fight against the enemies of the faith.

## 3 *Fides publica* and *privata*

The history of *fides* has a long course that begins in Ancient times and goes through the Middle Ages and the early modern period. Several authors argued that *feudum* derived from *fides*, usually associating the latter with another word current in feudal law treatises and charters containing feudal oaths: the concept of *fidelitas*. Recent studies have paid attention to this relationship with late-medieval authors such as Baldus de Ubaldis and early modern jurists such as Hugo Grotius and John Locke, and how it influenced their politico-legal thought.[24] Indeed, the meaning of *fides* went far beyond its legal sense in the medieval and early modern periods. *Fides* was primarily a theological concept and meant *faith in the word of God* broadly, implying its entire temporal manifestation in the community of believers, the *Ecclesia*.[25] Even during the Reformation, the various sects claimed to be the true community of believers, the successor of the early Christian Church of the apostles and martyrs.[26] The application of *fides* in other non-theological contexts, whether civil, natural, or feudal, always implied this theological origin and sanctioning, in which the *fides* rendered would receive a final judgement by God. In short: there was no secular conception of faith, and all Oaths, because they always implied the observation of *fides*, were theologically binding. In this way, we see a reconceptualisation of legal concepts such as *bona fides* and *fides publica* in comparison to their use in ancient Roman law, which was a kind of theological-civil law, where the religious ritual was indistinguishable from civic life.[27]

24 Dante Fedele, *The Medieval Foundations of International Law: Baldus de Ubaldis (1327–1400), doctrine and practice of the ius gentium* (Leiden/Boston: Brill, 2021), 168–200; Marc de Wilde, "Fides publica in Ancient Rome and its reception by Grotius and Locke," *Tijdschrift voor Rechtsgeschiedenis* 79, no. 3–4 (2011): 455–487.

25 Teresa Morgan, *Roman Faith and Christian Faith: Pistis and Fides in the Early Roman Empire and Early Churches* (Oxford: University Press, 2015).

26 A study that highlights the "Reform" as "returning to the original form" is the biography of Luther written by Schilling. Cf. Heinz Schilling, *Rebell in einer Zeit des Umbruchs* (C.H. Neck, 2012), 13–20 and 23–55.

27 John Scheid, *An Introduction to Roman Religion*, trans. Janet Lloyd (Bloomington: Indiana University Press, 2003).

After all, *Roma* was a goddess, and *Jupiter Optimus Maximus* observed from his temple on Capitoline Hill various meetings of the Senate.[28]

With the rise of Christianity, a new public realm began to manifest itself, underlining the distinction between the temporal and the spiritual.[29] Religion remained a part of public life, the soul of the public body. Roman polytheism knew no such distinction, and we can even speculate that the ideal Roman's 'afterlife' was to be remembered and celebrated in the future for past deeds (*res gestae*), always in the same worldly realm. The 'afterlife' of a Christian, by contrast, was distinguished by its emphasis on a spiritual goal and a reward in another life and realm. The reconceptualisation of terms like *verbum* or *fides* under biblical theology reveals even more about Roman legal and religious thought. If *fides* stood as a major concept to the Christian, it was also of no minor importance to the ancient Romans, who saw it as a Deity of Oaths, and betraying *publica fides* was punishable by death or exile.[30] Christianity would give a new meaning to the word *fides*. It is no longer the public faith of the Roman people, in the sense of being a people who can be trusted by others who place themselves in their trust, a *deditio in fidem*,[31] but of a people who gave their trust to the Christian God. This shift is of major importance in legal history, for it lies at the basis of a tradition of legal thought that was to flourish in the Christian West during the medieval period. The concept of *fides privata* was not important to jurists or theologians. The only possible legal *fides* was in its public dimension. Instead of the concept of *fides privata*, which is almost non-existent in the primary sources, scholars usually look to *bona fides* as one of the foundations of private contract law, implicitly or explicitly.[32] In fact, it is

---

28 Pierre Grimal, *Histoire de Rome* (s/l: Mille et une nuits, 2003), 15–20.

29 Larry Siedentop, *Inventing the Individual: The Origins of Western Liberalism* (Cambridge/ Massachussets: Harvard University Press, 2014), 126–140.

30 Even in the late Empire, Rutilius Namatianus despises anyone who betrays *fides*, cf. Toivo Viljamaa, "A Traitor to Rome (Rutilius Namatianus 2.41–60)," *Acta antiqua et archaeologica* 26 (Szeged 1994): 57–64.

31 The *deditio in fidem* occurred when a people surrendered to the sovereignty of Rome, which took possession of the citizens, gods and goods of the community. However, the community that gave itself in faith (*deditio in fidem*) did so under an agreement with the Romans, who would have to keep it.

32 Due to its importance in modern law, the concept of *Bona fides* has received a good deal of attention in recent decades. Vid. Luigi Lombardi, *Dalla "fides" alla "bona fides"* (Milano: Giuffrè, 1961); Mario Montorzi, "Nascita della fides publica," *Rechtsgeschichte – Legal History*, 2004 (Rg 05): 232–235; Laurent Waelkens, "Réflexions sur la bona fides et la mala fides dans la tradition du droit romain," *Tijdschrift voor Rechtsgeschiedenis* 86 (1) (2018): 1–12.

not even considered that an action in bad faith (*mala fide*) has any legal sanction, either under canon law or under civil law.

## 4 *Ius naturale*, *civile*, and *commune*

Of all Gudelinus' works, the *Syntagma regularum iuris* (1646) is probably the most extensive in legal theory and definitions.[33] In this work, Gudelinus proposes to deal with various points of the legal science by means of his own rules (*regulae*), discussing notions and topics that he does not deal with so extensively in other works.

The first legal distinction that interests us is between *ius civile* and *naturale*. According to Gudelinus, the question starts with the authorship of the law:

> Indeed, law is established not only by the civil community (*civitas*), the people or the prince who presides over it, but also by nature. One is called natural law, and the other civil law. The natural [law] is also called the law of nations because natural reason – that force (vis) which the author of nature, God, inscribed in the minds of men – has persuaded all nations to follow.[34]

Drawing from the legal sources of the *Corpus iuris civilis*, especially Gaius' views on natural law in *Dig. 1.1.9* and *Dig. 41.1.1*,[35] Gudelinus also quotes ancient

33 Petrus Gudelinus, *Syntagma regularum iuris utriusque, nova method &congruo ordine digestum: adiectis passim harum vicinarumque Regionum Moribus* (Antuerpiae: ex officina typographica hieronymi Verdussi, 1646). From now on, only *Syntagma*.

34 *Syntagma*, 2–3: "*Etenim ius constituit, non solum civitas, vel populus quisque, aut Princeps, qui ei praefit, verum etiam natura. Hoc ius naturale, illud civile dicitur; ac quod naturale, idem ipsum vocatur ius gentium; propterea quod ratio naturalis, id est, vis illa, quae insculpta est ab auctore naturae Deo mentibus hominum, id omnibus gentibus persuaserit.*"

35 *Dig* 1.1.9: "*Omnes populi, qui legibus et moribus reguntur, partim suo proprio, partim communi omnium hominum iure utuntur. Nam quod quisque populus ipse sibi ius constituit, id ipsius proprium civitatis est vocaturque ius civile, quasi ius proprium ipsius civitatis: quod vero naturalis ratio inter omnes homines constituit, id apud omnes peraeque custoditur vocaturque ius gentium, quasi quo iure omnes gentes utuntur*'. *Dig.* 41.1.1, pr.: "*Quarundam rerum dominium nanciscimur iure gentium, quod ratione naturali inter omnes homines peraeque servatur, quarundam iure civili, id est iure proprio civitatis nostrae. Et quia antiquius ius gentium cum ipso genere humano proditum est, opus est, ut de hoc prius referendum sit.*"

Roman authors in his legal elaborations. Cicero's authority is the first to be acknowledged:

> Not only by nature, i.e. by the law of nations, but also by the laws of peoples, by which the commonwealth is upheld in each community, has it been established in the same way that it is not allowed to harm another for the sake of one's own interest.[36]

This sentence by Cicero suggests a distinction between *civitas* and *respublica*. The first, *civitas*, corresponded to the legal community of citizens and their citizenship, *respublica*, on the other hand, corresponded to the political community (or body) common to citizens of various legal communities with their laws. One *Respublica* could contain many *civitates*, but one *civitas* did not contain several *Respublicae*. Thus *Respublica Romana* was constituted by the Roman community (*civitas*) and allies (*socii*). As these allied *civitates* were distinguished by having different laws and customs, natural law appears as a unifying and binding element of the different communities, "so that it is not allowed to harm others for the sake of one's own benefit." Thus, *Respublica* in this fragment of Cicero can have two meanings: *Respublica romana*, meaning the political community that supports the existence of various legal communities (*civitates*), or a *Respublica omnium gentium*, according to the Greek Stoic philosophical tradition that saw the cosmos as a place shared by all humanity and Gods; in this way, the extensions of the *Respublica* go beyond the political realm by entering in the natural one, as it suggests the existence of a natural commonwealth. In any case, the Stoic cosmological vision coincided with the destiny of Rome for Cicero, so it is not surprising that he saw the *Respublica Romana* as an ideal political community destined to govern the whole of mankind.[37]

Natural law had been defined by the ancient jurists as a right common to all animals. Gudelinus is aware of this, but he focuses on aspects of this legal order which concern mankind in particular, for it is a law shared by all people (*omnium gentium*):

36 *Syntagma*, 3; Cicero, *De officiis*, 3, 23: "*Neque vero hoc solum natura, id est iure gentium, sed etiam legibus populorum, quibus in singulis civitatibus res publica continetur, eodem modo constitutum est, ut non liceat sui commodi causa nocere alteri* [...]."

37 In fact, the conception of history as a succession of world empires was already present in Roman culture before the arrival of Christianity. Like Polybius, Cicero also saw Rome as the heir of the Greeks. Vid. Richard Faure, Simon-Pierre Valli and Arnaud Zucker, eds., *Conceptions of Time in Greek and Roman Antiquity* (Berlin/Boston: De Gruyter, 2022).

> Although natural law is sometimes understood as that whose certain semblances are perceived in beasts and animals. Natural law, or the law of all people, also includes Piety toward parents and homeland, Charity toward relatives, indeed toward any person, and whatever depends on these.[38]

Gudelinus also defines *Ius civile*, by arguing that "Civil law is said to be the law of each community."[39] From here, he develops the idea of community (*civitas*) and he bases his definition on a description of Julius Caesar in the first book of *De bello gallico*:

> The term "community" is not limited to the boundaries of a single city, but is used in a broader sense to encompass all those subject to the same rule (*principatus*), as Caesar stated in his Commentaries when he referred to the community of the Helvetians, where the term denotes not only the law of each municipality, but also the law of an entire kingdom or region.[40]

The peculiarity of the *Ius civile* arises from the fact that it was a law specific to a civil community, in this case to the Roman citizens, but which at the same time had been adopted by other non-Roman civil communities. According to Gudelinus, the Romans were no exception to this rule, for they had also adopted the civil laws of other *civitates*, such as Athens and Sparta, to draw up the Laws of the Twelve Tables.[41] However, the target of this fragment is not the Helvetians or the Romans but Gudelinus' contemporaries. Like the

---

38 *Syntagma*, 3: "*Licet alias naturale ius sumatur specialius, pro illo, cuius quaedam simulacra cernuntur in brutis et animantibus. Juris naturalis, seu omnium gentium, sunt Religio, Pietas erga parentes et patriam, Charitas erga propinquos, immo erga quemcumque hominem, et quaecumque ex his dependent.*"

39 *Syntagma*, 5: "*Dictum est Civile, quasi proprium cuiusque civitatis.*"

40 Ibidem: "*Civitatem non moenibus unius urbis circumscribo, sed late accipio, ut cunctos, qui eiusdem sunt Principatus comprehendam, quemadmodum Caesar in Commentariis dixit civitatem Helvetiorum, ut non solum ius municipii cuiusque, verum etiam ius Regni aut regionis alicuius integra, hoc nomine contineri intelligatur.*" Caesar on chapter 12 also tells that the *Civitas Helvetia* is divided in fous districts (*pagos*), cf. Julius Caesar, *De bello gallico*, I, 12: "[…] *nam omnis civitas Helvetia in quattuor pagos divisa est.*"

41 The Law of the Twelve Tables (*Lex Duodecim Tabularum*) was the most archaic civil legislation known and attested on Roman history. The whole text is lost, resting just some fragments concerning issues of private and procedure law. By the time of Cicero, the *lex Duodecim tabularum* was already out-to-date. Godefroy's publication of the fragments continues to be a good source to study them. Cf. Jacques Godefroy, *Fragmenta XII*.

Romans, who adopted the laws from Sparta and Athens, and the allied *Civitates,* that adopted the Roman Laws, Gudelinus sees a similar trend in his time with *ius commune,* "which we, the Franks, and many other European people use when our native laws (*patriae leges*) are insufficient, even though we are not subject to the Roman Empire."[42] Gudelinus calls to this common adoption of Roman civil law the *ius commune*:

> Hence it deserves the name of 'common law'; because in order to have force among us and others, it has been given effect by our own laws and those of each one who has received it. However, it should be noted that those who are subject to different principalities have never agreed to establish a common law for themselves; hence, it is rightly said that those who share a common legal community or authority should have a common civil law, although among others it can be equal as to the use, still its authority varies among different peoples.[43]

The *ius civile* that Gudelinus identifies as *ius commune* was distinguished from the *ius naturale* not only by its extension (natural law applied to all humans, while the former did not) but also by the common use of natural reason to all humans.[44] In addition, Gudelinus puts forward other common opinions by legal scholars: on the one hand, civil law was "partly written and unwritten,"[45] while agreeing with Cicero in *pro Milone* that the "natural law or the law of nations was inscribed and imprinted on the hearts and souls of men,"

*Tabularum, suis nunc primum tabulis restituta* (Heidelbergae: Typis Johannis Lancelloti, 1616).

42 *Syntagma*, 5: "*Ac proprium dicitur, quamvis aliæ gentes eodem utantur: immo quamvis id ab aliarum gentium institutis fuerit assumptum, quale fuit illud Romanorum, quod Decemviri ab Atheniensibus et Lacedemoniis acceptum in* XII *Tabulas retulere,et quale nunc est ius Justinianeum, quo nos, et Franci, et multi alii Europae populi, licet Imperio Romano minime subditi, ubi patriae leges deficiunt, utimur.*"

43 Ibidem: "*Unde iuris communis appellationem meruit; quoniam ut id apud nos, et alios robur habeat, propriis nostris, et singulorum qui id receperunt, legibus effectum est: numquam enim qui diversis Principatibus subiecti sunt, convenere, ut commune ius sibi statuerent. Unde recte dicitur, eiusdem civitatis seu imperii esse oportere, inter quos iuris civilis communio est: etiam si enim apud alios par usu esse potest, tamen auctoritas eius apud diversos diversa est.*"

44 Ibidem: "*In quo differt ius civile ab eo, quod vocatur ius gentium & naturale, quod commune omnium hominum ius est, & ex una eademque potestate rationis naturalis, diffusa in omnes, profectum.*"

45 Ibidem.

without possessing a written form.[46] Moreover, civil law is unstable and changeable, exposed to the contingencies of times and necessities, while natural law remained "constant and immutable as if established by divine providence."[47]

## 5 *Fides*, *Ius gentium*, and Natural Obligations

Gudelinus enumerates *fides* as an innate right within the *ius gentium primarium*. The twofold distinction of the *ius gentium* into *primarium* and *secundarium* was according to the *opinio communis* of the lawyers: the *ius primarium* was associated with the natural rights acquired by men from their origin and common to all by birth, such as the right to religion (*religio*), piety (*pietas*) and *fides*. The *secundarium* resulted from the various peoples' needs and constraints.[48] Despite the attribution of *fides* as a right to the *ius gentium primarium*, Gudelinus immediately poses a question: "Is, therefore, the natural obligation by which one is bound to observe faith attributed to the primary law of nations?" Gudelinus answers that "by no means, for it is established that obligations were instituted under that law from which distinctions of dominions, wars, captivities, and servitudes have arisen," that is, from the *ius gentium secundarium*.[49] Quoting from Ovidius' Metamorphoses, Gudelinus argues that early humans lived in a 'Golden Age' (*aurea illa aetate*) where justice and faith

46 Ibidem: "*Secunda differentia est, quod ius naturae seu gentium in nullis tabulis prescriptum extet; ac quoties dicitur scriptum, inculptum, impressum in cordibus et animis hominum, figurata locutio est.* The quote of Cicero in *Pro Milone oratio*, IV, 10: *Est igitur haec, iudices, non scripta, sed nata lex; quam non didicimus, accepimus, legimus, verum ex natura ipsa adripuimus, hausimus, expressimus; ad quam non docti sed facti, non instituti sed imbuti sumus, – ut, si vita nostra in aliquas insidias, si in vim et in tela aut latronum aut inimicorum incidisset, omnis honesta ratio esset expediendae salutis.*"

47 In this part Gudelinus is using Justinian's *Institutiones*, cf. *Inst.* 1, 2, 11: "*Sed naturalia quidem iura, quae apud omnes gentes peraeque servantur, divina quadam providentia constituta, semper firma atque immutabilia permanent: ea vero quae ipsa sibi quaeque civitas constituit, saepe mutari solent vel tacito consensu populi vel alia postea lege lata.*"

48 *Syntagma*, 110: "*Distinctio quaedam fit inter ius gentium primarium, id est, quod a primo ortu humani generis ortu fuit, et secundarium, scilicet quod postea, humanis necessitatibus ita cogentibus, adinventu est.*" For an overview on the history and development of *Ius gentium*, vid. Dante Fedele, I*us gentium: The Metamorphoses of a Legal Concept* (*Ancient Rome to Early Modern Europe*), in *Empire and Legal Thought: Ideas and Institutions from Antiquity to Modernity*, ed. Edward Cavanagh (Leiden: Brill, 2020), 213–251.

49 *Syntagma*, 111: "*Utrum igitur et obligatio naturalis, qua quis ad fidem observandam tenetur, iuri gentium primario attribuetur? Minime: nam obligationes institutas eo iure, ex quo dominiorum distinctiones, bella, captivitates et servitutes prodierunt, expressum est.*"

were observed spontaneously without constituting an enforceable obligation as opposed to a natural obligation, so their bonds were not necessary for the maintaining of society. However, when humankind was divided into various dominions, the obligation to observe faith was instituted by natural reason for the 'preservation of human society'.[50] He further adds that "The integrity of the first humans scarcely lasted, as testified by sacred history," and therefore one must judge the origin of obligations along the same lines.[51]

This fragment suggests that Gudelinus understood the relationship between the *ius gentium primarium* and *secundarium* in two ways: the *primarium* dealt with natural rights that were innate in all human beings; the *secundarium* sanctioned them to ensure that these rights were observed. Besides faith, it can also be said that '*pietas*' and '*religio*' were other obligations that had to be observed for the 'conservation of human society'. In our understanding, the idea implicit in this framework was that the *ius naturale* aimed at the conservation and integrity of the human body and, by extension, the political body. It is worth remembering that Gudelinus is not talking about subjective or private rights in the modern sense. *Fides* was always public and accessible to all and not a matter of personal decision. Moreover, a layer of historical-linguistic interpretation is also mandatory. The *ius gentium primarium* was associated with a 'Golden Age' metaphorically and poetically, an early mythological epoch where men knew no division and war among themselves. The Romans recalled a similar era during the celebrations of the Saturnalia. The *ius gentium secundarium* was instituted in a second era in which men no longer followed faith spontaneously, and so natural reason instructed men to oblige themselves to observe it by force of necessity.[52]

This understanding of the human past may imply that humanity under the *ius gentium primarium* constituted a society without a civil authority to enforce the observance of obligations. One can certainly wonder whether Gudelinus saw any role for the *ratio naturalis* in the context of humanity under the *ius gentium primarium*. Suppose natural obligations appeared with the *Ius gentium secundarium*, and such were imposed by *ratio naturalis*. In that case, one can presume that reason did not instruct humanity to ensure

50 Ibidem: "*Quia autem secundarium hoc gentium ius, quo dominia fuerunt primum distincta, etiam ex ratione naturali hoc fieri, ad societatis humanae conservationem necessarium esse suggerente, originem traxit, dictum est haud secus quam alterum, ius naturale, quin etiam cum humano ipso genere proditum, quia paulo post exortum.*"

51 Ibidem: "*Integritatem primorum hominum vix durasse historiae sacrae testantur: par iudicium esse debet de origine obligationum.*"

52 On the law of obligations on the *Ius commune*, vid. Reinhard Zimmermann, *The Law of Obligations: Roman Foundations of the Civilian Tradition* (Oxford: University Press, 1996).

its preservation during the *ius gentium primarium*, since humanity was not divided. People observed justice and faith spontaneously, which, in our opinion, implies the belief that people did not live according to reason, but according to faith. In biblical terms, this *ius gentium primarium* would then correspond to the age before the Fall, when men had not yet tasted the fruit of the Tree of Reason. Nonetheless, Gudelinus invokes the authority of Ovidius and Greco-Roman mythology to support his argument. Ironically, the work cited, Metamorphoses, corresponds to the Old Testament Genesis in terms of comparative cosmology.[53]

Thus, it is possible to observe that Gudelinus, a jurist who did not neglect civil and canonical legal matters, already shows signs of having a conception of a pre-civil human past where there was a consensus of humanity in all matters.

## 6 The Authority of Feudal Law in the *Ius commune*

In addition to natural and civil law, Gudelinus also recognises another legal category of major importance for the legal system of his day: feudal law. At first, he refers to the importance of feudal law with respect to, most of all, the property of the nobles and magnates, treating them as certain goods (*res*) "*quae mobiles non sunt*."[54] After a deeper reading, one realises that the extent of feudal law goes beyond mere rights and titles of immovable property and that Gudelinus understands it as a part of the customs and historical contingencies that Western Christendom had gone through since the Germanic invasions that brought down the Western Empire. For Gudelinus, this was obvious because there was no mention of it in the Justinian legislation: "In the entire corpus of Justinian law, there is no mention of this law. It is probable that this law was introduced after barbarian peoples sacked the Roman Empire; the employment of numerous barbarian terms in its exposition indicates this."[55]

53 For an overview of Ovidius' influence on literature and art, vid. Charles Martindale, ed., *Ovid renewed: Ovidian influences on literature and art from the Middle Ages to the twentieth century* (Cambridge: University Press, 1988).

54 *De iure feudorum*, 1.

55 *De iure feudorum*, 12–13: "*Nulla enim in toto iure lustinianaeo huius iuris mentio extat: ac probabile est, exposito iam praedae barbararum gentium Imperio Romano, hoc ius introductum; quod et barbaries plurimorum vocabulorum, quorum in hoc iure explicando usus est, arguit.*"

The *Libri feudorum* had been incorporated into the *Corpus iuris civilis* in the Middle Ages, mostly through Accursius' gloss.[56] Besides dealing with the '*Consuetudines Feudorum*', taking as their legal source the customs of the Lombards and Italian cities like Milan, the *Libri feudorum* also propose a general framework of feudal procedures for investitures and other feudal institutions that became part of medieval and early modern legal education.[57] Gudelinus argues that feudal law originated more from the customs of the Lombards than from written laws. So he asks, "whether feudal law should be considered on the same level as written and common law, and whether its authority should be followed everywhere, just like other books of civil law."[58]

Although some jurists claimed that the *Libri feudorum* should not be followed, like Charles Dumoulin,[59] the *communis opinio* of legal experts was that the *Libri feudorum* should be adopted just like the other books of the *Corpus iuris civilis*, and Gudelinus explains this by arguing that these books were taught in schools (*Gymnasiis*) and applied in trials. Such could only happen because the reception of the *Libri feudorum* in legal education and legal procedure had been "tacitly approved by the Princes."[60]

Thus, Gudelinus states that when local laws and customs are deficient in any feudal issue, it is preferable to consult the *Libri feudorum*, rather than any other civil law book.[61]

---

56 Joseph Canning, "Feudal Law," in *Encyclopedia of Medieval Philosophy*, ed. H. Lagerlund (Springer, Dordrecht: Springer, 2011), 354–356.

57 M.G. di Renzo Villata, "La formazione dei Libri feudorum," in *Il feudalesimo nell'Alto Medioevo* (*Settimane di Studio del Centro Italiano di Studi sull'Alto Medioevo* XLVII) (Spoleto: Centro italiano di studi sull'alto Medioevo, 2000), 651–721; In addition to Karl Lehmann's editions of the *libri feudorum*, Brill has just released a new edition of the *Libri feudorum* very useful. Vid. Attilio Stella, *The Libri Feudorum* (*the "Books of Fiefs"*) *An Annotated English Translation of the Vulgata recension with Latin Text* (Leiden/Boston: Brill, 2023).

58 *De iure feudorum*, 3: "*Unde quaestio est, An ius feudale pro iure scripto & communi haberi debet, eiusque authoritatem ubique sequi oporteat, perinde atque aliorum Librorum juris Civilis?*"

59 In his *Commentaria in consuetudines parisienses*, Dumoulin negates in the first title (*De matiere feodal*) the legal validity of the *libri feudorum*, going so far as to state "[…] *in hac sum sententia contra omnes, quod ille liber seu eius scriptura, non habet per se vim legis, nec consuetudinis, nec potest denominari lex, vel consuetudo* …" (I hold the opinion that this book or its writing does not have by itself the force of law or custom and cannot be called a law or custom). Cf. Carolus Molinaeus, *Commentaria in Consuetudines Parisienses* (Parisiis: Ioannes le Preux, 1572), 7–8 (n.46).

60 *De iure feudorum*, 3.

61 Ibidem.

## 7 Definition of *Feudum* and Its Obligations

Gudelinus starts to define *feudum* by following the *opinio communis* of the jurists, which equated *Feudum* as *Beneficium*.[62] A vassal could justly lose his *feudum* because of ingratitude (*ob ingratitudinem*), but when he receives a *feudum*, he would be receiving it as *beneficium*, meaning that it was due to a 'good deed'.[63] Gudelinus explores this definition through Seneca's *De beneficiis*, which defines *beneficium* as a 'benevolent action' (*benevola actio*).[64] Gudelinus points out that it is not so much the fief, as a thing (*res*), that is defined in this formula, but rather the concession of the fief (*actio*); in other words, the *Beneficium* corresponded to '*actionem feudi*', and not to the '*dationem in Feudum*'. In this way, Gudelinus understood that the *Beneficium* was an *actio*, a legal procedure of bestowing (*tribuens*) a *res non mobilis*.[65] The *beneficium* was supposed to be freely given (*gratuito*) by the lord, and received by the vassal due to friendship and honour rendered to his lord. This feudal bond implied that the vassal, or *fidelis*, should render *Fidelitas* and *Obsequium* to his lord. On a material level, this meant that the vassal would hold the *dominium utile* of a land, being able to explore it economically, while the lord maintained

62 Randall Lesaffer, *European Legal History: A Cultural and Political Perspective* (Cambridge: Univesity Press, 2019, 1st ed. 2009), 150–155. In the *libri feudorum* we find this definition: "*Huius autem generis species quaedam est beneficium illud, quod ex benevolentia alicuius ita datur, ut proprietate quidem rei immobilis beneficiatae penes dantem remanente ususfructus illius rei ita ad accipientem transeat, ut ad eum heredesque suos masculos sive feminas, si de his nominatim dictum sit, in perpetuum pertineat, ob hoc, ut ille et sui heredes fideliter domino serviant, sive servitium illud nominatim, quale esse debeat, sit expressum sive indeterminate sit promissum.*" (In the first place, you need to know that the definition of "benefice", as a general category, is as follows: a benefice is nothing but a benevolent act which gives joy to them who receive it and receives it from giving, and which in doing so is well-inclined and voluntarily prepared. Moreover, a specific type of this general category is that benefice which is given out of someone's benevolence so that, whilst the ownership of the immoveable property that is given in benefice remains with the giver, the usufruct of that property is transferred to the receiver in such a way that it should belong perpetually to him and his male heirs, or female if express mention is made of them. [And it is given] so that he and his heirs serve the lord faithfully, regardless of whether that service is expressed precisely as to what it ought to be or is promised indeterminately.) Latin text and English text apud Stella, *The libri feudorum.. opus cit.*, 2023: 122–123.

63 *De iure feudorum*, 6–7.

64 cf. Lucius Annaeus Seneca, *De beneficiis* I, 6: "*Quid est ergo beneficium? Beneuola actio tribuens gaudium capiensque tribuendo in id, quod facit, prona et sponte sua parata. Itaque non, quid fiat aut quid detur, refert, sed qua mente, quia beneficium non in eo, quod fit aut datur, consistit, sed in ipso dantis aut facientis animo.*"

65 *De iure feudorum*, 6–7.

*dominium directum* of the same land. Gudelinus' argument identifies an interesting aspect of the relationship between feudal lords and their property. His source about the state of art on the different kinds of *dominia* is Franciscus Duarenus, who refused to use the 'vulgo' *Dominium directum* and *utile* because they were inventions of *Accursiani*, not to be found in the older charters.[66] Departing from Duarenus' thesis, Gudelinus explains that the concepts of *dominium directum* and *dominum utile* did not exist at the time when Obertus wrote the *Libri feudorum*, so he used the Roman law concepts '*proprietas*' to designate what was attributed to the lord, and '*usufructus*' to explain the vassal's rights.[67]

Although Gudelinus' definition broadly corresponds to immovable property whose rights could be transferred, he explains that it is necessary to have a 'broader' definition of *res immobilis*, which incorporates not only all corporeal goods but also all 'incorporeal goods' like jurisdictional rights.[68] There was not so much that distinguished the grant of a fief from a donation. However, Gudelinus points out that the substance of the fief lies in the *Fidelitas* between lord and vassal; in this way, a vassal was also called *fidelis*. This aspect that defines the substance of feudal goods also distinguishes *res censuales* and *emphyteuticas* from feudal ones since the former are not bestowed due to fidelity.[69] Moreover, secular subjects are also distinguished from ecclesiastical ones:

> Those who wrote that all ecclesiastics or even bishops are vassals of the Supreme Pontiff have shamefully erred. To be considered a fief or vassal, it is necessary to have accepted something in exchange for fidelity. However, what the clergy receive from the goods of the Church is granted to them not for their faith but for the sake of their ecclesiastical ministry.[70]

Gudelinus also argues that the nature of *Feudum* can change according to local laws and customs. Thus, while the ancient definition of a *feudum* implied

---

66 Franciscus Duarenus, *Disputationum Anniversariarum libri duo* (Coloniae Agrippinae: Apud Ioannem Gymnicum, 1573), lib. I, c. XVII ( 36): "*Dominium vulgo partiuntur Accursiani in directum, & utile: quae verba ab ipsis conficta sunt, nec apud veteres usquam leguntur.*"

67 *De iure feudorum*, 7.

68 Idem, 7–8.

69 Idem, 8.

70 Ibidem: "*Ac turpiter errarunt, qui Ecclesiasticos omnes, vel Episcopos esse Summi Pontificis vassallos scripserunt. Ut namque sit Feudum, seu ut quis vocetur Vassallus, necesse est rem gratia fidelitatis data acceptamque esse; atqui quod accipiunt Clerici ex bonis Ecclesiae, non Fidei, sed Ministerii ecclesiastici causa ipsis tribuitur.*"

that only male children should succeed, the feudal law of Gudelinus' day also accepted that women could succeed. This is particularly true according to the customs of the various provinces of the Low Countries, as in the Kingdom of France.[71] Gudelinus sums up the definition of *feudum* as *res* in a simple formula: "A fief is an immovable property accepted for the sake of fidelity (*Feudum, est res non mobilis, accepta Fidelitatis causa*)."[72]

Although he refers to the '*natura feudi*', there is nothing to suggest that he recognised the *Ius feudorum* within the category of *Ius naturale*. In addition to the fact that he considered the *Ius feudorum* as part of civil law, in a chapter on 'The duties of vassals', Gudelinus observes that feudal obligations could even clash with natural obligations, resulting in a conflict of obligations. The question dealt with a passage on the *Libri feudorum* which is quite intriguing. Should the son of a vassal offend his father's lord, the vassal would be obliged to render service to his lord and deliver his son to the lord or even expel him from his domain. Should he refuse, he could lose his feudal title.[73] Gudelinus extends the case in order to include other family members and whether the same could happen to a vassal son whose father was threatening his lord. How should the son act, knowing that he is obliged to observe piety towards his parents and that this comes from natural law?

> Whether the vassal must serve all others in this way, and help his lord, so that neither brother, nor son, nor father is excepted in any way, can be doubted. It is stated that the vassal owes service and assistance even against those. At first sight, this seems rather harsh and contrary to the duty of piety which the law of God and natural reason prescribe, especially in regard to parents. Is this because of the oath by which the vassal has bound himself to the lord, as some have written? But no agreement or oath, indeed no constitution of the people or prince can prevail against divine and natural law. Therefore, some have understood that what is expressed means that one should also help the lord against the father if the homeland or religion is being attacked by him; in which case, so far is it from being a crime to kill one's father, that a reward is deservedly due

71 Idem, 10.

72 Idem, 11.

73 Attilio Stella, *The Libri Feudorum..opus cit.*, 2023, 188: "*Insuper si filius vasalli dominum offenderit, pater a domino requisitus deducat filium ad satisfaciendum domino, vel a se filium separet, alioquin feudo privetur. Sin autem pater vult eum deducere, ut satisfaciat, et filius contemnit, patre mortuo in feudum non succedat, nisi prius satisfecerit domino, parique modo vasallus pro omnibus suis domesticis faciat.*"

> for it, as if there were a certain natural order among these laws, and a supreme one, which protects the safety of the people and religion.[74]

Indeed, the terms *pater*, *frater* and *filius* were used in feudal contexts quasi-interchangeably in the relations between lords and vassals and *pares*. Jacques Cujas attempted to simplify this confusion by removing the word *pater*, but this did not solve the problem. As François Hotman observed, the word *filius*, to whom "mercy and charity were equally due," was still present in the feudal vocabulary.[75] In the spirit of providing an answer to a discussion involving the conflict between feudal and natural obligations, Gudelinus suggests an interpretation:

> I, having set aside the interpretations of others, have devised this understanding. I believe that this text teaches us not whom we should absolutely and primarily assist (it is certain that we should assist parents, children, and others of such kindred whom blood more closely unites to us), but rather to what cause each vassal is bound by his fief. The reason of piety advises us to assist those more closely related by blood, but feudal obligations require us to prefer our lord. However, if anyone fails to be present and to serve his lord against his proper father or son, he commits little or no wrong; but then the reason to enjoy the fief ceases, since it is proper to render this service of aid given. It is also the duty of a vassal to reconcile a son or relative who is thought to have offended his lord.[76]

---

74 *De iure feudorum*, 192–193: "*Porro an contra omnes cæteros sic servire, & Dominum adiuvare debet Vasallus, ut nec frater, nec filius, nec pater quidem excipiatur, dubitari posset. Expressum est, Vasallum debere & contra hos servire, seu auxilium praestare. Id prima facie perquam durum videtur, & adversans officio pietatis, quam Lex Dei, & ratio naturalis erga parentes in primis praescribit. Utrum hoc (ut ab aliquibus scriptum est) propter illud iurandum quo Vasallus Domino se obstrinxit? At nullum pactum vel iurisiurandum, imo nulla populi vel Principis Constitutio valere potest contra Ius divinum, & naturale. Quare illud quod expressum est, etiam contra patrem adiuvare Dominum debere, sic intellexerunt alii, si parens vel Patriam, vel Religionem oppugnet: quo caso tantum abest ut scelus sit patrem occidere, ut praemium ob id merito debeatur: nimium quasi inter Leges istas naturalis ordo sit quidam, & illa suprema, quae salutem populi, Religionemve tuetur.*"

75 Idem, 193.

76 Idem, 193–194: "*Ego sepositis aliorum interpretationibus, hanc excogitavi. Existimo isto Textu doceri, non quos absolute et praecipue adiuvare debeamus (certum est parentes, filios, et reliquos eiusmodi quos sanguis arctius nobis coniunxit), verum ad quid causa Feudi quisque teneatur. Pietatis ratio monet, ut sanguine coniunctos potius adiuvemus; caeterum ratio obligatioque Feudi illud vult, ut Dominum praeferamus; cui si contra*

Two observations should be made to this fragment: a conflict emerges between feudal and natural obligations, but the latter was preferable because they meant 'little or no wrong'; on the other hand, the obligations of one area of law did not criminalise or negate the obligations of the other. Thus, the obligation to observe piety towards one's parents did not annul the obligation to help and rescue the lord if attacked by a parent, although it was preferable. The feudal obligation to observe fidelity to the lord does not override the natural obligation to observe piety towards parents and relatives, even though it might mean losing a legal title to the usufruct of the *Feudum*.

## 8 The Obligation to Keep Faith with Rebels

After having dealt with the conflict between natural and feudal obligations, we will explore the relationship of *fides* in the relationship between vassal and lord in the work *De iure pacis commentarius* (1620).[77] The question of the 'necessity of keeping faith with rebellious subjects' leads Gudelinus to explore the topic in different lines.[78] The problem now revolved not around a conflict between feudal or natural obligations, but rather around *subditi* who were in open conflict with their lord. Assuredly, Gudelinus had the Protestant rebels of the northern provinces in mind, but the historical background he presents deals with the *Pax Constantiae* (1183), which ended the uprising of the Lombard League against Emperor Frederick I.[79] The revolt of the Lombards ended

---

*patrem, vel filium adesse servireque quis omittat, parum aut nihil delinquit; sed tamen cessare tunc videtur causa ob quam Feudo fruatur, utpote proprium id servitium auxilii dato; cum etiam officium sit Vasalli, filium, vel coniunctum, qui Dominum offendisse putatur, reconciliare."*

77 Petrus Gudelinus, *De jure pacis commentarius in quo praecipuae de hoc jure quaestiones distinctis capitibus eleganter pertractantur* (Lovanii: Typis Philippi Dormalii, 1620).

78 In 1607, the theologian Martinus Becanus addressed the similar question of "on the duty to keep faith with heretics" in the form of a *Disputatio Theologica*. Gudelinus does not approach the question in the same way and with the same sources, but from a juridical/civil perspective. The target of the enquiry is not heretics, but rebels. As we'll see below, a rebel is a civil dissident in conflict with the political leader, but that does not mean he is also a religious heretic. For example, the rebels who made up the Lombard League were at war with the Emperor, but they were not heretics. For a more in-depth reading of Martinus Becanus' work, see the recent translation of his *Disputatio theologica de fide haereticis servanda* (1607) in *On the duty to keep faith with heretics*, ed. Wim Decock, trans. Isabelle Buhre (Grand Rapids, MI: CLP Academic, 2019).

79 With the peace of Constance, the rebels saw their *regalia* and jurisdictional rights confirmed by the emperor. For an overview, vid. G. Raccagni, "The teaching of rhetoric and the Magna Carta of the Lombard cities: the Peace of Constance, the Empire and the

in a peace in which the rebellious subjects had their rights recognised back. As Randall Lesaffer considered before, this *opusculum* can be seen as more than a commentary and should be treated as a treatise.[80] This is because Gudelinus abstracts from the historical context of the *Pax Constantiae* to discuss more generally the *ius post bellum* of the peace treaties of his time.[81]

The conflict between the Habsburg Netherlands and the United Provinces formed a background to Gudelinus in writing *De iure pacis*. Perhaps that factor may have had some influence in raising the question of 'preserving faith with rebellious subjects'.[82] Unlike the vassal, the *fidelis*, who could not respond to his lord's call when there was a conflict between feudal and natural obligations, the rebels represented another problem. They were *infideles* by definition, for they had betrayed the faith of their sovereign.[83] Several authors argued that the prince was not obliged to keep faith with the rebels. Gudelinus disagrees. What was the law that bond the contract between the prince and the rebels? Vasquius thought that was "the civil law or that of the community of which the prince is the ruler, and that the subjects are bound by it."[84] However, this made no sense to Gudelinus, for the prince was above civil law, which only bound the subjects of the same *civitas*. Moreover, the obligation to preserve the faith was not a civil obligation, but a natural one; hence, not surprisingly, one observes Gudelinus ascribing the legal force of peace contracts to the natural obligation of "cultivating and keeping faith."[85]

---

Papacy in the works of Guido Faba and his leading contemporary colleagues," *Journal of Medieval History* 39 (2013): 61–79.

80 Randall Lesaffer, "An Early Treatise on Peace Treaties: Petrus Gudelinus between Roman Law and Modern Practice," *Journal of Legal History* 23, no. 3 (2002): 223–252.

81 Jens Iverson, *Jus Post Bellum: The Rediscovery, Foundations, and Future of the Law of Transforming War into Peace* (Leiden/Boston: Brill, 2021), 71–75.

82 *De iure pacis*, 1620, 56–62: Caput XI (*Utrum subditis etiam rebellibus fidem pacis seruari sit necesse*).

83 However, Gudelinus also claims that this statement is "obscure", "ambiguous", and that one should consider giving faith to rebels as a last resort (*nisi ad extremum*), cf. *De iure pacis*, 58: "*infideles vero esse illos qui suo Principi fidem prius fefelle. Equidem concedo posse hos infideles dici; versiculum autem illum aio esse ambiguum atque obscurum. Nam si hinc sibi sumunt, nullam esse fidem, quae infideli data sit, videant* (*inquit ibidem Cicero*) *ne quaeratur latebra periurio. Addo perfidiam perfidia ulcisci omnibus saeculis vituperio habitum. Ac cur versiculus ille sic commodius et verius accipi non potest, ut rebelli et perfidioso fides difficillime sit danda, ac laudandus sit qui hoc non fecerit? Quia praesumptio est eum, qui semel fuit malus, fore semel adhuc malum. Fateor hac ratione ad pactionem cum rebellibus nunquam veniendum, nisi ad extremum.*"

84 Idem, 57. Vasquius, *Illustrium Controversiarum Aliarumque Usu Frequentium Libri tres* (Lugdun.: Franc. Fabri & Iacobi Stoer, 1595), 1, 3, 2.

85 Ibidem.

However, several arguments still existed for not keeping faith with rebels. One of the issues had been raised by Cicero and revolved around the question of the equivalence of rebels to the status of pirates and thieves. Gudelinus says that may be true, but immediately fences "*Sed quid tum postea?*" (So what?), arguing:

> Is it not the case that faith should not be placed in such people, nor should there be a common oath? Even if Cicero says so, in my judgment, nothing is more false. For the law of nature and of divine origin has not established any distinction between enemies and robbers, nor between free and enslaved persons, nor between any individuals, and the prince is subject to this law no less than his subjects. So why is it that by this law, the prince is not obligated when making peace and giving assurances to his subjects, as Frederick the Emperor did in the peace of Constance?[86]

Another argument defended that the prince could act out of fear because of the treachery of his enemies, for they may not keep their part of the agreement: "Would not that be a valid excuse for the prince?" To this question, Gudelinus replies that "No, not really, even though in fear, which is impressed upon him by real enemies and indeed by law, he has rejected the distinction between private and public faith."[87] As we can see, one of the few occurrences of the expression *fides privata* appears in this *opusculum* of Gudelinus, but only to deny it convincingly. This meant that all faith given by the prince to the rebels should be public and observed by natural obligation. To break an agreement because of private fear would mean acting out of private faith. And acting on private faith perhaps meant something similar as acting on 'bad faith'.

## 9 Enduring an Evil Thing

Besides the obligation to keep faith with rebels, Gudelinus also argued that the prince should endure 'an evil thing' when he is not in power to fight it, thus having to tolerate the existence of subjects unfaithful to public religion. How-

86 *De iure pacis*, 59.

87 Idem, 61: "*An non par caufa excusationis in Principe? Minimè; quanquam in metu qui à veris hostibus atque adeò iure incutitur distinctionem reieci fidei privatae & publicae: hanc tamen hic recipio, affirmans fidem quae publicè seu à Principe rebellibus data est, ut observet, non modo magnanimitati eius convenire, verum etiam ad id astringi.*"

ever, Gudelinus does not argue in favour of freedom of religion or conscience; on the contrary, he considers it a 'terrible scourge':[88]

> It may be objected that a heretic is a bad and shameful thing, and that any agreement regarding it is of no consequence. I admit that religious freedom is a terrible scourge, but just because it is bad, it does not follow that enduring it is always bad. Prostitutes and brothels are tolerated, money-lenders are tolerated, to prevent worse things from happening. In former times, Constantine, Theodosius, and Justinian also tolerated things like divorce, usury, and concubinage (for there are many constitutions in their own Code dealing with these matters), not because they approved of them, but because these and many other practices, which had become established by the laws of the Pagans, could not be entirely abolished at that time in the Roman world. They eventually disappeared as Christianity became more widespread.[89]

Gudelinus' response of tolerance was not one of inclusion but of preserving public peace and tranquillity when necessary. According to Cicero, "The welfare of the people is the supreme law,"[90] and when a crowd could not be punished without threatening public suggestion and peace, then it was "better to tolerate than to punish" (*tolerandos esse potius quam puniendos*). However, this was done within legal formalities, with a signed agreement between the parties. If there was no shame in tolerating what could not be avoided, then the agreement born from the need to maintain public peace "contains no inherent shamefulness."[91]

Petrus Gudelinus lived in the Habsburg Netherlands, during the first phase of the Eighty Years' War and through the oppressive period of the Duke of Alba

88 *De iure pacis*, 46: *Fateor & libertatem Religionum quandam pestem esse teterrimam.*

89 Idem, 46–47: "*Obijcietur haeresim esse rem malam et turpem, pactum autem omne de re turpi nullius esse momenti. Fateor libertatem Religionum quandam pestem esse teterrimam; verum non continuo si ea mala est, toleratio eius semper quoque est mala: tolerantur meretrices et prostibula, tolerantur mensae foeneratorum, ne peiora eveniant; toleraverunt olim Constantinus, Theodosius, et Justinianus, qui toties se Christianos et sacrorum Canonum cultores, defensoresque esse, rituque Paganorum execrari profitentur, divortia, usuras, concubinatum (nam de his extant plurimae ipsorum Codice constitutiones) non quod illa approbarent, sed quod ea, multaque eiusmodi quae ex legibus Paganorum invaluerant, nondum tunc temporis in orbe Romano penitus tolli potuerint, quae tandem Religione Christiana crescente evanuerunt.*"

90 Cicero, *De legibus*, III, 3, 8: "*Salus populi suprema lex esto.*"

91 *De iure pacis*, 47: "*Si permissio haeresis, quando necessitas cogit, turpis non est, sequitur pactionem de ea permittenda, nihil quoque turpitudinis in se continere.*"

and the various counterattacks and insurgencies of Calvinists and Huguenots. The conflict even reached his home town of Ath in 1578.[92] A heretic was no less a man than a Christian in rights under natural law, and this same natural order obliged both princes and vassals to respect natural obligations mutually. In this way, an agreement with heretical rebels would be no less and no more binding than any other agreement requiring to keep faith. Perhaps that is why the importance given to 'public peace and tranquillity' assumed a pre-eminent role in Gudelinus' thought, for he treats them as if they were higher norms to follow in conflict resolution:

> Can there be any greater thing than public peace and tranquility? And should it not always be given priority over all other things? And if we allow the breaking of public faith out of fear, do we not cut off the willingness of all rebels to make peace with their Prince, even in the face of great danger? Finally, if someone argues that it is not expedient to keep faith in bad promises, I will say what I said before: an agreement to tolerate an evil thing, which cannot be resisted, is not evil in itself. Therefore, even if something has been forgiven to rebels out of necessity, which would not otherwise be forgivable, this agreement must still be honored.[93]

## 10 Conclusion

This chapter has touched on a short section of the thought of an intellectual who still has much to offer. As we mentioned in the introduction, Gudelinus has an organic understanding of law and politics, and this changes the approach one can take in legal research or study. Feudal law, *fides* as the binding norm among men and, above all, natural law were regarded by him as normative authorities, imposing their power tacitly and without coercion.

---

92 Édouard Waltre, *La histoire de la Ville d'Ath* (Tournai: Delmée, 1861), 53–59.

93 *De iure pacis*, 62: "*Potestne enim ulla res major esse quam pax et tranquillitas publica? Et an non ei semper prae cunctis aliis rebus consulendum? Et nonne si hoc admiserimus, ut ob metum fidem quoque publicam frangere liceat, praecidemus omnem rebellium pacificandi cum Principe suo, etiam in maximis periculis, voluntatem? Postremo si quis obiecerit in malis promissis fidem servari non expedire, dicam in quod superius dixi, pactionem de toleratione rei malae, cui resisti non potest, malam non esse: ut ideo quamvis quippiam rebellibus, necessitate suadente, condonatum fuerit, quod alias minime esset condonandum, pactio haec nihilominus servanda sit.*"

Nowadays, feudal law is often restricted to medieval scholarship, faith is regarded as an exclusively private and personal phenomenon and natural law no longer has a voice within the framework of legal positivity. Throughout this chapter, we have observed that *fides* holds a particular place in Gudelinus' thought, being a particular axis of the *ius gentium primarium* and a founding element of the *fidelitas* implicit in feudal obligations. From this point on, we see that feudal obligations can clash with obligations from the natural realm, and Gudelinus makes it clear that the latter are preferential to the former. But the role of natural law does not end there. When discussing the obligation to keep faith with rebels, Gudelinus also indicates that this obligation is bound by natural law, to which the sovereign was subject (unlike civil law).

Gudelinus' work and thought must be framed within the rise of legal humanism of the sixteenth and seventeenth centuries. In addition to the *Corpus iuris civilis* and classical authors such as Cicero, Gudelinus also benefited from the tradition of *via media* between *mos gallicus* and *mos italicus* cultivated at the old University of Leuven.[94] However, we end this chapter by suggesting an alternative interpretation of *via media*, and one that is more restricted to the subject dealt with on the previous pages. In our view, the response of tolerance towards rebels and heretics is in itself a *via media*, meaning a response of mediation intended to solve a given conflict. This should come as no surprise since the *ius commune* was *common* to both Catholics and Protestants. It is also possible that the solution found in France to end the wars of religion influenced Gudelinus. Although he did not leave any commentary on the Edict of Nantes (1598), which guaranteed religious tolerance to Huguenots, Gudelinus was certainly aware of this legal solution since he was interested in the legal literature of the Toulouse lawschool in particular and the law of the French kingdom in general. In any case, advancing a response of tolerance as a *via media* between Protestants and Catholics may have been one of the reasons for the additional title of the 1648 edition of the *De iure pacis*: "In which, the main and most essential questions regarding this Law [of peace] are proposed and examined, especially now, as the European Peace of Münster is being discussed."[95]

---

94 Randall Lesaffer, "An Early Treatise," 244.

95 Petrus Gudelinus, *De iure pacis commentarius: In quo præcipuæ & nunc maxime, dum de Europa Pace Monasterii agitur, necessariæ de hoc Iure quæstiones proponuntur & expenduntur* (Lugduni Batavorum: Franciscum Molaerdum, 1648).

## Acknowledgement

This article makes part of a larger doctoral thesis in the context of @AULAM project (BOF Research Fund, project number: C14/19/012) "Innovation Through Education: Pioneering Change in Law and Theology in Louvain's Golden Age" (https://www.kuleuven.be/lectio/research/aulam, last access: 26/05/2024). The aim of our doctoral project is to assess and discuss the contributions of Petrus Gudelinus to the emergence of an autonomous field of Public Law.

CHAPTER 5

# Stewardship and Statesmanship: Justus Lipsius and Diodorus Tuldenus on the Natural Law of Government in the Early Modern Low Countries

*Geert Sluijs*

## 1 Introduction

There is no doubt that in the early seventeenth-century intellectual climate of the Southern Low Countries, Justus Lipsius[1] (1547–1606), the great interpreter of Seneca and Tacitus, cast a long shadow. His political thought, clearly in the tradition of *raison d'état* and expounded mainly in his *Politica*, has always been difficult, even during his lifetime, to position in relation to the author it clearly draws upon: Machiavelli. Authors such as Robert Birely SJ[2] have put forward the suggestion that there was something essentially Catholic, anti-Machiavellian and Netherlandish about the system he set out.[3] While he was, as a high-profile humanist, subjected to the political events playing out around him, it has often been unclear how precisely they relate to his thinking.

The beginning of his intellectual career hailed by the publication of his Variae Lectiones in 1569, coincided with the start of the first stage of the Eighty Years' War. His dedication of the work to Cardinal Granvelle, chief advisor to King Philip II, clearly signalled his (then-)loyalty to the Spanish regime in the Southern Netherlands. His acceptance of a position at the Lutheran University of Jena (1572–1574) and later the new, Calvinist University of Leiden (1577–1591) marked his shifting allegiance, away from the Catholic faith and towards the emerging Northern Netherlandish state. In Leiden, he wrote his first philosophical work of international renown: *De Constantia in Publicis Malis* (1583–1584). The publication of the aforementioned *Politica* or *Six Books of Politics or*

1 For a Lipsius biography, we refer to Gerhard Oestreich's critical analysis of Lipsius' autobiography: "Justus Lipsius in sua re" in: G. Oestreich, *Geist und Gestalt des fruhmodernen Staates. Ausgewählte Aufsätze* (Berlin: Duncker and Humblot, 1969) 80–100.

2 Robert Bireley S.J., *The Counter-Reformation Prince: Anti-Machiavellianism or Catholic Statecraft in Early Modern Europe* (Chapel Hill: University of North Carolina Press, 1990), 72–100.

3 For a broader overview of the literature and a thorough evaluation of Bireley's position: Christopher Brooke, *Philosophic Pride: Stoicism and Political Thought from Lipsius to Rousseau* (Princeton: Princeton University Press, 2012), 12–36.

 | DOI:10.1163/9789004748712_007

*Civil Doctrine* in 1589 and its dedication to Stadtholder Maurice of Orange caused a wave of controversy in both Lutheran and Catholic circles.[4] It was later revised between 1593 and 1595 to prevent the work appearing on the delayed 1593 *Index Librorum Prohibitorum*.[5] Specifically his recommendations that successful political communities should permit just one faith and vigorously persecute religious dissidents to safeguard the said community were perceived as dangerous by both sides of the religious conflict. After all, they could be taken as an endorsement of the treatment of Catholics in the North of the Netherlands, or a vindication of the wars fought against Protestants in the Holy Roman Empire. The controversy was further fuelled by the sharp invectives and accusations of Machiavellism by his fellow Dutch humanist, Dirck Volckertz Coornhert.[6]

While he had been preparing to return to the South before publication of the *Politica*, the uproar likely expedited his decision, as staying in Leiden in the wake of the episode would have tied his fate firmly to the Dutch Republic. He departed Leiden in 1590 under the pretext of taking the waters at Spa and submitted himself for a high-profile reconciliation with the Catholic Church in Mainz. He returned to the South in 1591 and published an amended version of the *Politica* in 1596. Rehabilitated as a loyal Catholic subject of the Spanish Crown and sovereign Archdukes Albert and Isabella, he published a sequel to his *Politica*, the *Monita et exempla politica*, in 1605.

When he died little under a year later, his immediate legacy was that of the court theorist and intellectual of the Archdukes, a prodigal son of the South and humanist who had seen what was on offer elsewhere and decided that the Southern Netherlands should be his ultimate home. His influence outside of the South is held to be as varied as it is vast. Gerhard Oestreich famously argued that Lipsius, as the standard-bearer of the so-called Netherlands Movement, pioneered a Neostoic ethic of duty and military discipline that would form the core idea of the early modern European absolutist state.[7] Michael Stolleis, on the other hand, credits him with being the essential progenitor for the development of public law thinking as an autonomous discipline in the Holy Roman Empire and Europe at large, as well as a major influence on

---

4 For a general context of the work and introduction to Lipsius' thought, Jan Waszink's critical edition with extensive introduction is unsurpassed. Jan Waszink, *Justus Lipsius, Politica. Six Books of Politics or Political Instruction* (Assen: Van Gorcum, 2004), 3–203.

5 For the Index episode, see Ibid. 120–121 and 173–175.

6 Brooke, *Philosophic Pride*, 13.

7 Gerhard Oestreich, *Neostoicism and the early modern state*, eds. B. Oestreich and H.G. Koenigsberger (Cambridge: Cambridge University Press, 1982).

the Grotian school of natural law and the development of later mature political theory.[8]

Although not separated by many years, the circumstances in which our second Low Countries protagonist found himself during his glory days were quite different. Diodorus Tuldenus[9] (1594–1645) too experienced the start of the 'golden age' of the Archdukes, and the subsequent period of peace ushered in by the Twelve Years' Truce (1609–1621), when he studied in Leuven. A direct meeting between the young Tuldenus and the older Lipsius is unlikely, but the two are intimately connected through the Leuven humanist Erycius Puteanus (1574–1646), Lipsius' pupil and in turn Tuldenus' beloved mentor. Tuldenus' academic career as a legal writer begins with his *De principiis iurisprudentiae* (1621), quickly followed by his *De causis corruptorum iudiciorum et remediis* (1624). Both are inspired by his concern with the administration of justice and the dangers threatening the legal profession. They also provide a lens into the ideas animating his later legal works, his commentaries on the Institutes (1628) and Code (1633). Both were intended as handbooks for first-year law students when he taught the *Paratitla* of the Institutes and Code from 1620 until 1633.[10] His other published works include *De iurisprudentia extemporali* (1628–1629), a practical guide on legal interpretation, the *Initiamenta iurisprudentiae* (1633) a collection of his inaugural lectures, *De civili regimine* (written approximately 1625, published posthumously in 1702) on political theory and his course notes on the Digest (published posthumously in 1702), the course of which he taught in 1633–1645.

Where Lipsius was ever the philosopher and humanist, Tuldenus was a dyed-in-the-wool lawyer who actively sought a role in public affairs. This is attested by his practice of advising the provincial Estates and highest state councils (the Privy Council and Council of State),[11] as does his appointment to the highest judicial body in the Southern Low Countries, the Great Council

8 Michael Stolleis, "Lipsius-Rezeption in der Politisch-Juristischen Literatur des 17. Jahrhunderts in Deutschland" *Der Staat* vol. 26, 1 (1987): 1–30.

9 For a more detailed bibliography, we refer to Victor Brants, *Un juriste belge du XVIIe siècle. Diodore Tulden, Professeur à Louvain* (Brussels: Goemaere, 1915), 35 p. and Wouter Druwé and Geert Sluijs, "Reforming legal education in Leuven. The humanist ideas of Diodorus Tuldenus (1594–1645)," *Historia et Ius* vol. 20, 1 (2021): 5–8.

10 A distinctly novel approach to teaching the law: Druwé and Sluijs, "Reforming legal education," 17 *ff.*

11 There is only limited direct, textual evidence of many of these legal advices. Some are included as examples in his coursebooks and course notes, and he refers to his frequent legal advice in his letters to Erycius Puteanus. See for instance Letters of Diodorus Tuldenus to Erycius Puteanus, Royal Library of Belgium (KBR), ms. 19112, nr. 34 and 41.

of Mechlin. Tuldenus therefore presents us with an intellectual window into the Netherlandish period almost immediately following Lipsius' time. Tuldenus, after all, became a *regius* professor of the *Paratitla* of the Code and the Institutes in 1620, a mere year before hostilities between North and South resumed and the joint reign of the Archdukes ended with the expiration of the Act of Cession, which provided for a return of the sovereign Southern Netherlands to the Spanish Crown. Where Lipsius in his day could be mobilised to project the aura of a new Rome around the burgeoning Belgian state under the Archdukes, few would have disagreed with Tuldenus' characterisation of the South as a Sparta, war-torn by religious strife, in 1628.[12] But as Sarah Mortimer has remarked: "[…] it was in those areas where religious tensions ran high, and where localized political loyalties were simultaneously both entrenched and vulnerable, that some of the most innovative and influential political thinking took place."[13] Even if that were untrue and one takes the 'troubled years' of the South to be an intellectually impoverished age, Tuldenus at least offers us a way by which we can assess the great Lipsius' immediate influence in the country of his birth and earthly repose. Equally, we cannot understand Tuldenus' moves without seeing them in the Lipsian context in which they were conceived.

In this, they are both representatives of the two competing political moralities and intellectual frameworks at the turn of the seventeenth century:[14] Lipsius, to a greater or lesser degree, is aligned with the tradition of Machiavelli, the *politiques* and *raison d'état*,[15] while Tuldenus is rooted in the natural law tradition. Gauging the influence of Tuldenus and whether he could successfully establish himself as an alternative to Lipsius (which, as we will see, he seems to have intended) is then tied together with how much Lipsius truly was a thinker concerned with elaborating a constitutionalist vision of

12 Diodorus Tuldenus, *De iurisprudentia extemporali* (Leuven, 1628), p. vi.

13 Sarah Mortimer, *Reformation, Resistance, and Reason of State (1517–1625)* (Oxford: Oxford University Press, 2021), 4.

14 As famously described by Skinner, citing Pedro de Ribadeneira's anti-Machiavellian treatise *Tratado de la religion* (Madrid, 1595); Quentin Skinner, *The Foundations of Modern Political Thought. Vol 2: The Age of Reformation* (Cambridge: Cambridge University Press, 1979), 172.

15 *'Reason of state'* as a term to describe both a genre of practical statecraft literature and the political theory behind it was popularised by Giovanni Botero's *Della Ragion di Stato* (Venice, 1589), who intended to offer a vision of a moral, Christian reason of state in opposition to Machiavelli's. For a broader overview of the reason of state literature, see i.a. Noel Malcolm, *Reason of State, Propaganda, and the Thirty Years' War* (Oxford: Oxford University Press, 2007), especially 92–123, and Ethienne Thuau, *Raison d'Etat et pensée politique à l'époque de Richelieu* (Paris: Editions Albin Michel, 2000).

politics which was in opposition to Machiavelli's. We shall be taking Chris Brooke's position as a point of reference here, who has argued that, in constructing a modified Senecan (and thus properly 'Neostoic') and mirror-for-princes framework in the *Politica*, Lipsius intended to offer both a critical response as well as a partial appropriation of Machiavellian political theory.16 Crucially, in Brooke's reading, Lipsius repudiates the Machiavellian divide between prince and principality: prince and principality make up a harmonious whole, and the price should therefore strive for the *bonum publicum* and welfare of his citizens, not idle glory.[17]

While this characterisation of Lipsius absolutely has its merits, and investigating it fully is beyond the bounds of this contribution, we shall argue that it over-emphasizes the novelty of the image of a prince guided by the *bonum publicum* and under-emphasizes what Lipsius has to say (and perhaps more tellingly, what he omits) about the role of law and natural law. While there are ways – and we shall propose a novel one, looking at the Netherlandish context – in which Lipsius could be read to be a constitutionalist thinker, none of them stand up to sustained scrutiny.

Tuldenus, then, must be seen to take up the glove of some late scholastic political thinkers: all reason of state thinking is ultimately Machiavellian, and there is but one alternative framework that can mount a credible challenge: natural law. Stoic political thinking, and Seneca in particular, has been too readily appropriated by *raison d'état* thinkers and careful effort is needed to separate its true roots from what later princely flatterers have read into it.

Ideas of natural justice therefore animate Tuldenus' entire corpus and his ideas on everything from legal interpretation to the power of the prince. For Lipsius, there is a marked absence of many notions of natural law in his political works, even though in his *Constantia in publicis malis* he develops an argument from Stoic state of nature. If Lipsius – especially assuming his Neostoic ideas influenced later natural law theorists – appears to have little concern for natural law arguments, this raises the question how his ideas can be made to fit into such a project in the first place. This thorny question has so far escaped broad scrutiny, despite studies investigating the reception of Lipsian ideas by

---

16 On the intellectual origins of the mirror-for-princes genre, see Peter Stacey, *Roman Monarchy and the Renaissance Prince* (Cambridge: Cambridge University Press, 2007), especially 37 *ff.* and 173-204 and for a bibliographical overview: Ronald W. Truman, *Spanish Treatises on Government, Society, and Religion in theTime of Philipp II: The 'de regimine principum' and Associated Traditions* (Leiden: Brill, 1999).

17 Brooke, *Philosophic Pride*, 21–36.

natural-law titans such as Hugo Grotius[18] and Christopher Besoldus[19] – both eagerly read by Tuldenus.

The goal of this paper is therefore threefold. Firstly: to investigate Lipsius' position and establish that his main work could not be interpreted as offering anything resembling anti-Machiavellian constitutionalism. Secondly, to examine how natural law thinkers – such as Tuldenus, operating within the Lipsian intellectual orbit – could appropriate his ideas and idiom while still recognizing the fundamental opposition between their views. Thirdly, and most importantly, to explore what the natural law alternative looks like against the political backdrop of the Southern Netherlands, focusing in particular on the constraints envisaged by each author on princely power, and whether they allow for multiple political actors (i.e., not exclusively the prince) to share public authority. The paper concludes that positions of either author are only fully intelligible when the political situation in the Netherlands is taken into account, as both systems are undeniably shaped by pressing political realities.

## 2 Lipsius and the Limits of Government

By way of preliminary observation, it must be remarked that the *Politica* is, in a manner reminiscent of a commonplace book, mainly composed of citations of classical authors – Lipsius seldom refers to contemporary authors, with the exception of Machiavelli, whom he occasionally draws into the discussion. Yet Lipsius had a clear contemporary vision of politics in mind when writing his *Politica*, and one ought not to underestimate his agency and plan (even artifice) in making his political theory palatable to an audience by cleverly presenting and omitting.[20]

From this composition, a few themes emerge. Lipsius' work, in line with the conventions of the mirror for princes, is based on the idea of princely virtue. This builds on the Roman Stoic idea found in Seneca's *De Clementia*, the

18 See Arthur Eyffinger, "Amoena gravitate morum spectabilis. Justus Lipsius and Hugo Grotius," in *The world of Justus Lipsius: A contribution towards his intellectual biography*, Bulletin de l'institut historique belge de Rome 67 (Rome: Institut historique belge de Rome, 1998), 300; Bo Lindberg, "Stoicism in Political Humanism and Natural Law," in *(Un)masking the Realities of Power. Justus Lipsius and the Dynamics of Political Writing in Early Modern Europe*, eds. E. De Bom et al. (Leiden: Brill, 2011), 73–93; Jan Waszink, "Lipsius and Grotius: Tacitism," *History of European Ideas* vol. 39, 2 (2013): 151–168.

19 Stolleis, "Lipsius-Rezeption," 13.

20 Waszink, *Politica*, passim but esp. 202–203.

mother text for the mirror for princes genre, which was addressed to the young Emperor Nero. Lipsius' innovation, so Brooke convincingly demonstrates, was to revive the genre by incorporating some of Machiavelli's critique and teachings, while also strengthening its underpinnings by reinterpreting the Stoic idea of deterministic fate as Christian providence.[21]

Lipsius' fundamental assumption, at a first glance, seems the same as that of the Stoics: the cultivation by the prince of these virtues is ultimately what guarantees his subjects' flourishing.[22] As he describes in the 'idealist' second book of the *Politica*, the most important of these virtues (next to Clemency) is *Justitia*, "the sun" of princely virtue.[23] This Justice is "a virtue that firmly upholds law and justice in oneself and others." Lipsius continues: "I said 'in oneself', because I bind the prince himself to this, as it is good for the prince to be subject to the laws, even if (according to some): 'No one writes laws for a prince'."[24] This is followed up with a citation from Plato's *Statesman* (*Politicus*): "For a lawless reign is harmful, and difficult to submit oneself to."[25] The explanatory marginal note at this citation spells out explicitly what only seems to be hinted at: the prince is "bound by the laws" (*legibus illigandus*). A problem immediately becomes manifest: what, precisely, is Lipsius referring to with these *legibus*? Lipsius here clearly alludes to and generally seems to repudiate the Roman law adage *princeps legibus solutus* ("the prince is unbound by the laws"), which is found in D.1.31.1 and is often read together with the fragments in D.1.4.1 and C.1.14.4.[26] Oestreich was quick in stating that Lipsius "sided with the Spanish (scholastics)" against the broad application of this formula – in other words, the prince is bound by some laws.[27] Given the centrality of this adage to sixteenth and seventeenth-century constitutional thinking, however, the point bears examining a bit further. The rule allowed for granularity when read together with the tripartite division of law into

21 Brooke, *Philosophic Pride*, 12–36, especially 27–29.

22 Justus Lipsius, *Politica* (Assen: Van Gorcum, 2004), ed. J. Waszink, preface and lib. II, cap. 9.

23 Ibid. lib. II, cap. 10.

24 Lipsius, *Politica*, lib. II, cap. 10. Reference to Plinius' *Panegyric*, 65. *"Quam in hac mea re definio 'Virtutem ius et aequum in se inque aliis firmiter servantem.' In se, dixi: quia Principem ipsum huic alligo: quem legibus placet subiici, etsi (quorundam sensu) 'Principi eas nemo scripsit.'"*

25 Ibid., lib. II, cap. 10, translation of Waszink. Reference to Plato's *Politicus*, 302 e11.

26 D.1.4.1: "Quod principi placuit legis habet vigorem" and C.1.14.4: "Digna vox maiestate regnantis legibus alligatum si principem profiteri; adeo de auctoritate iuris nostra pendet auctoritas."

27 Oestreich, *Neostoicism and the early modern state*, 75.

divine law, natural law and positive law which was suggested by Thomas Aquinas[28] and seemed to be echoed in the division of law in *ius civile, ius gentium* and *ius naturale* in D.1.1. The '*legibus*' referred to in D.1.3.31 could, in that scheme, be taken to mean only the lowest part of the tripartite division: positive law. This was then read by many to mean that the prince was unbound by positive law which he himself or his predecessors had enacted, but nonetheless remained bound by the other above mentioned sources of law: natural law and divine law.[29]

One might therefore think that the most obvious reading, in line with this classic interpretation of D.1.3.31, is that the prince is indeed bound by natural law and divine law. Yet Lipsius here and elsewhere seems to keep this implicit at best, even though the point is hardly trivial, considering the amount of ink spilled by jurists and theologians alike in answering the question as to which laws, exactly, the prince could or could not deviate from or abrogate.[30] The more likely reading is that Lipsius mainly sought to stress the responsibility of the prince to act predictably, to honour agreements made in good faith, and not irresponsibly to alter or revoke laws that he had enacted, without as such recognizing concrete or binding limits on the power of the prince. The rest of his discussion of Justice in book two amounts to no more than an extolment of the virtue itself, including exhortations that adhering to justice is noble, honourable, and especially seems to bring a prince glory and – that most valuable a currency for rulers – a good reputation.[31]

These exhortations to adhere to the virtue of Justice and abide by the laws would bite if Lipsius was a Stoic political thinker in his core – if he equated what is honest (*honestum*) or worthy (*dignum*) with what is expedient

28 Thomas Aquinas, *Summa Theologiae* (Leonine ed.), Part I–II, Q. 91.

29 A comprehensive overview of the *topos* by itself is surprisingly difficult to come by, especially in early modern scholarship. We can refer to Dieter Wyduckel's (somewhat deceptively named) *Princeps Legibus Solutus. Eine Untersuchung zur frühmodernen Rechts- und Staatslehre* (Berlin: Duncker & Humblot, 1979), 48–62 and 130–137, note 176. See also Kenneth Pennington, *The Prince and the Law. Sovereignty and Rights in the Western Legal Tradition* (Berkeley: University of California Press, 1993) and the still influential Adhemar Esmein, "La maxime *princeps legibus solutus est* dans l'ancien droit public français", in *Essays in Legal History*, ed. Paul Vinogradoff (Oxford: Oxford University Press, 1913), 201–214.

30 See for a work which problematises this point well in Jean Bodin: Daniel Lee, *The Right of Sovereignty. Jean Bodin on the Sovereign State and the Law of Nations* (Oxford: Oxford University Press, 2021), 94–96.

31 See Lipsius, *Politica*, II.10 *in fine*.

(*utile*).[32] Such a reading, as Bireley is eager to demonstrate,[33] might be supported by a fragment in the later *Monita*, where Lipsius enjoins the reader not to separate the honest (*Honestum*) from the useful (*Utile*) and to avoid pretence (*fucus*) and deceit (*fraus*). The "teacher from Italy" might teach differently, but he "shapes petty tyrants, not legitimate princes and kings."[34] This position and the clear rebuke of Machiavelli therein would indeed put him convincingly in the camp of early seventeenth-century anti-Machiavellian Jesuit writers such as Giovanni Botero and Pedro de Ribadeneira, as Jan Papy *et al.* have also argued.[35]

Yet despite the clarity of Lipsius' statement in the *Monita*, it is plainly contradicted in the fourth and first of the 'realist' books of the vastly more influential *Politica*. The beginning of this book four sets the programme for what is traditionally considered the more important half of the *Politica*[36] – an inquiry into the skill or wisdom (*Prudentia*) of governing which Lipsius intends to impart to the prince. Book four deals with *Prudentia Civilis*, while five will deal with military prudence.[37] As Oestreich demonstrates, *Prudentia Civilis* denoted the technical and teachable skill of government divorced from moral considerations, which was closely related to the civic notions of 'police' and 'regiment.'[38] The term was in vogue in late sixteenth-century practical political and legal writing and coincided with the rising popularity of the reason of state literature. Though Lipsius seems anxious to present his counsel to the prince as virtue and prudence intertwined, where one cannot exist without the other,[39] it shall become clear that *Prudentia Civilis* is the defining notion for a prince, which we can translate here as 'Stewardship.'

---

32 See Brooke, *Philosophic Pride*, 19–22. Waszink, *Politica*, 202–203.

33 Bireley, *Counter-Reformation Prince*, 81. See also Bireley, *Botero, Reason of State*, xx–xxiii.

34 Justus Lipsius, *Monita et exempla politica* (Leuven: Leuven University Press 2022), ed. Jan Papy *et al.*, lib. I, cap. 7, 235: *"A good description and admonition. Be righteous and upright, and from the depths of your mind honourable and useful plans will grow. For let us not separate those: the honourable from the useful. And the teacher from Italy who leads in another direction is mistaken. He shapes petty tyrants, not legitimate kings or princes. Let him go away. You, remove pretence and fraud, which can neither be strong nor last for long. More about this will follow later."*

35 Jan Papy, Toon Van Houdt and Marijke Janssens, "Towards a Reassessment of Lipsius' Political Views" in *Justus Lipsius, Monita et exempla politica. Political Admonitions and Examples*, ed. Jan Papy *et al.* (Leuven: Leuven University Press, 2022), 48.

36 Ibid., 84.

37 Lipsius, *Politica*, IV.1–2.

38 Oestreich, *Neostoicism*, 155–165. See for an overview of *raison d'état* writers using the term Malcolm, *Reason of State*, 100, note 22.

39 Lipsius, *Politica*, I.1 and I.7. See Brooke, *Philosophic Pride*, 26.

The notion that virtue should be an overriding concern, as Lipsius implies in the *Monita*, is dispelled in the oft-cited chapters thirteen and fourteen of book four on the '*prudentia mixta*,' or '*reason of state*'[40] as Waszink translates it. Here, Lipsius considers whether a prince can debase virtue and prudence with deceit (*fraus*) and clearly states that "some Zenos" err in stating that the prince can and should only follow the path of virtue.[41] Any attempt to interpret Lipsius as having an overriding concern for the prince's virtues, therefore, does not withstand scrutiny when confronted with the structure of his work. Although the focus on a prince's virtues may be distinctly Stoic, even Lipsian, the absence of any higher reason for adhering to them makes it especially important to examine which deviations from virtue Lipsius ultimately deems acceptable, as this would reveal the precise boundaries of princely power.

Lipsius does indeed defend, as a general point, the permissibility of debasing virtue with deceit, so that the prince might be able to defend himself from others who might do the same.[42] When, in the next chapter, he discusses precisely which types and degrees of deceit are permissible, Lipsius tolerates (*tolero*) the least grave and condemns (*damno*) the gravest degree of deceit, "which retreats not only from virtue, but also from the laws."[43] The middle kind – encompassing bribery (*Corruptio*) and manipulation (*Deceptio*) – could be seen as harmless, even virtuous when one considers the *bonum publicum*, yet "just and divine law" (*rectam illam divinamque legem*) seems to contradict this, and Lipsius admits to great uneasiness.[44] Lipsius concedes that "it is difficult to resolve this either for you or myself" but in slightly sophistic fashion, he considers that there is only 'limited' guilt when 'lesser' acts of the middle degree are committed by a righteous prince against evildoers.[45]

40 Waszink, *Politica*, 48.

41 Lipsius, *Politica*, IV.13: "*Quaesitum an Prudentia mixta locum apud Principem habeat? Id est, ea in qua fraudes. Dictum, et doctum, aliquem habere. Videor liberaliter satis & pena, quod dicitur, manu, tibi prompisse e gemine Prudentiae fonte: & quidem probum ac merum. Fasne est ut leviter misceam, & iungam aliquid e fraudium faece? Ego puto, quidquid Zenones quidam mihi abnuant, quibus "unum illud ad laudem, cum virtute directum iter, probatur".*

42 Lipsius, *Politica*, IV.13.

43 Lipsius, *Politica*, IV.14. "*Quae non a virtute solum sed legibus etiam recedit.*"

44 Lipsius, *Politica*, IV.14. "*Atque haec, humanam Prudentiam si consideras, proba. Quidni? Ad Bonum enim publicum referuntur: quod insitum in iis malitiae virus facile exsugit & absorbet. Ut medicamentis venena laudabiliter miscemus, salutari illo fine* [...]. *Imo necessitatem etiiam, quod contra tot insidiantes, vix est ut se suosque aliter tueatur bonus Princeps. Quibus caussis ego quoque praedixi tolerari Medias has fraudes a me, non tolli. Quis tamen, rectam illam divinamque legem si considero? Haero valde & sudo.*"

45 Ibid.

The gravest degree of deceit consists of *Perfidia* (treachery) and *Iniustitia*, terms which must be seen to have a specific meaning: Perfidia is the breaking of (solemn) promises and agreements; Iniustitia is contempt for "the laws and justice" mentioned in book 2.[46] The latter vice occurs when interests are pursued in violation of rights and laws (*iura et leges*), with wickedness rather than cunning (*improbe potius quam callide*).[47] He discusses three examples: political murder or assassination, the revocation or infringement of subjects' privileges and laws, and finally waging an aggressive – that is, unprovoked – war of conquest. Our author here states that even though "a variety of sayings and schools of thought" might permit these, he remains unconvinced, though he is "forced to admit" that "a ruler, in very troubled and adverse circumstances 'should not follow what is appealing to say, but necessary in practice'."[48] In such circumstances, it is permitted "to lightly deviate from the laws" (*abire leviter ab legibus*), yet "only to preserve oneself, never for the sake of gaining more" (*sed non nisi sui servandi causa, augendi numquam*). After all, "necessity is a great excuse for human weakness; it breaks every law" (*omnem legem frangit*).[49] That is the final, lukewarm word on the permissibility of these severe violations of natural law, where Lipsius ultimately cannot bring himself to state outright there is a norm forbidding them, if only the need is high enough. While Lipsius has therefore waxed lyrical about the virtue of Justice and toed the constitutionalist line on the *princeps legibus*-question in his first books, it should be clear that this ultimately does not amount to a great deal. Lipsius seems aware of the tension and indeed suggests that natural law would object to anything but the mildest deceit: "just and divine law" seems to forbid bribery and manipulation, contrary to what one thinking principally of the *bonum publicum* might think. In addition, the worst deceit (or perhaps 'evil') a prince could muster is definitionally against justice itself, and while such wickedness certainly offends all rights and laws, it nonetheless seems permissible if neces-

46 We can refer here to Pedro R.S. Santos' contribution in this volume, titled "*Fides* and *Feudum* in the Legal Thought of Petrus Gudelinus (1550–1619): a Study on Feudal, Civil and Natural Obligations in the Early Modern Age" which should serve to illustrate the polysemous and technical nature of the term *fides* in the learned law, and Marie Seong-Hak Kim's "Bodin, Natural Law, and Statecraft in the French Renaissance Monarchy" which also deals with the role of promises in early modern monarchies.

47 Lipsius, *Politica*, IV.14.

48 Curtius, *Historia Alexandri Magni Macedonis*, 5.1.8.

49 Lipsius, *Politica*, IV.14 *in fine*. "*Illud saltem dederim, Principem in rebus valde afflictis et adversis, 'non speciosa dictu, sed usu necessaria sequi'. Tunc, inquam, abire leviter ab legibus; sed non nisi sui servandi causa, augendi numquam. 'Necessitas enim magnum imbecillitatis humanae patrocinium, omnem legem frangit.*" The quotation is from Seneca Senior, *Declamationes*, 9.4–5.

sary for the preservation of the state. This, at least, puts him squarely at odds with contemporary natural law thinkers in whose company he is occasionally placed. The picture which Lipsius paints perhaps appears reminiscent of certain Protestant political theories, where natural law as a category is expunged in favour of positive law and divine law, the latter of which remains as the only limiting factor on the prince's power.[50] While a Calvinist influence – owing to his time in Leiden – cannot be discounted, Lipsius does not follow a recognizably Calvinist way of thinking to arrive at similar conclusions. After all, Calvinist scholars would stress the total rupture of man and nature since the Fall and the absolute reliance on God's grace to make his laws intelligible to us. Natural law is recognized as a valid and in theory binding source of law, just not one that humans can meaningfully access.

What then ultimately separates Lipsius' thinking from the ideas of "the Florentine" and his disciples, the "old tricksters of the court" (as he refers to them)? Brooke's suggestion is that Lipsius emphasises the pursuit of the common good[51] to distinguish himself from the Machiavellian dictum for a prince to seek personal glory and use a principality as a means to an end. This is, for him, reflected in Lipsius' warning that deviating from the laws by committing grave deceit is permissible only for self-preservation, never to extend one's position.[52] That, however, assumes that Lipsius could still meaningfully set himself against Machiavelli on this point. While, indeed, Lipsius was (among) the first to consciously reclaim the Senecan mirror for a virtuous prince following Machiavelli's critique, other parts of Machiavelli's challenge did not survive nearly as long. Interpreters of Machiavelli such as Gerolamo Cardano and the later Scipione Ammirato quickly wrapped Machiavelli's insistence on princely glory in the classic Ciceronian language of *salus populi suprema lex esto*.[53] The goal of a prince and the highest reason of state should not be personal glory,

---

50 Such a similarity was already remarked upon by the prewar German historian Otto Hintze. See: Felix Gilbert ed., *The Historical Essays of Otto Hintze* (New York: Oxford University Press, 1975), pp. 88–154. See also H.J. Berman, *Law and Revolution. The Impact of the Protestant Reformations on the Western Legal Tradition* (Cambridge, MA: Harvard University Press, 2004), 71–99.

51 The "comfort, safety and welfare" of the prince's subjects, see Lipsius, *Politica*, II.6. In Cicero's words, cited by Lipsius in the same chapter, it is the "*beata civium vita*," which should always be the prince's aim.

52 Brooke, *Philosophic Pride*, 29.

53 Malcolm, *Reason of State*, 95–96, 101–102 and 117. See also the forthcoming Gábor Almási, *Science Meets Politics: Machiavelli's Influence and the Birth of Political Science* (Leiden: Brill, 2025), 115–161 and Sydney Anglo's study of Agostino Nifo's selective appropriation of Machiavelli's writings: Sydney Anglo, *Machiavelli – The First Century. Studies in Enthusiasm, Hostility and Irrelevance* (Oxford: Oxford University Press, 2005), 42–84.

but the *salus populi* – the people's welfare. This change, aside from making it appear more palatable, gave it an obvious point of attachment to the still very influential Roman legal mainstream and the *legibus solutus* question outlined above. It also insulated the 'political realist' project from a changing political awareness that increasingly saw political power being abstracted from any singular person.

In other words, there was nothing particularly new about Lipsius' departure from Machiavelli in insisting that safeguarding the common good was the highest reason of state – others in the post-Machiavellian *raison d'état* literature had made similar moves. The state of the art in the late sixteenth century meant that any anti-Machiavellian project that accepted this premise (even for rhetorical purposes) had to engage with the *raison d'état* literature on these terms, usually by stressing that for a Christian prince, abiding by God's law, Christian virtue and natural justice was always to the greater benefit of the people. In such thinking, there is and can be no opposition between the demands of the *bonum publicum* and those of natural and divine law, despite short-lived temptations to the contrary. Natural law-thinkers such as Tuldenus, however, rejected the premise outright: the *salus populi* was not, in fact, the highest law. The highest reason of state is justice; all other fruits emanate from it.[54]

Perhaps, finally, Lipsius' insistence that a principality should be conferred only "in accordance with morals and rights",[55] could be read in a way that it obliges the prince to respect many of the constitutionalist arrangements – such as conformity with the principality's fundamental laws – which some of his contemporaries considered *conditiones sine qua non* for the exercise of public power. Note that in the Netherlands the constitutional ritual of the Joyous Entry made the burden the prince undertook in maintaining the privileges, rights and promises of his predecessors a significantly heavier one than in other states, such as the Kingdom of France. Lipsius states that those who are unfit or seek the principate for the wrong ends are held back by custom (*mos*) and the law of nations (*lex gentium*) through the double barrier of either succession or election.[56] In the latter, a prince is designated by election "*cum spreto naturalium iure*" – against the right of natural successors or hereditary right.

---

54 See clearly Tuldenus, *De principiis iurisprudentiae*, II.16 *in fine*.

55 Lipsius, *Politica*, II.4.

56 Ibid. *"Itaque Principatum multi appetunt, nec boni ipsi nec bono fine. Quos repressit tamene mos sive lex genium repagulo duplici, Electiones & Successionis."*

While this passage is notable for its explicit consideration of the law of nations and the law of natural succession, the way in which it is constructed suggests that Lipsius sought mainly to prevent principalities from being usurped, not impose any substantive limits on the power of the prince once he had come into his principality. It is also unclear what exactly the consequence would be if a prince was appointed based on a contested succession or election. There is no suggestion that the law of nations remains operative after the succession or election has taken place – an intentionally minimalist understanding of the higher sources of law.

Indeed, while Brooke is right that Lipsius in the *Politica* does in general not say a great deal about the law at all,[57] what he does say is revealing and in line with the picture sketched here. That he takes a dim view of the study of the law and legal practitioners in general,[58] and is inherently suspicious of a rule by (positive) law, is apparent from fragments in book II, also under the discussion of Justice. In a scattering of fragments in 2.II, he states that laws proliferate in corrupt states and implores the prince to find a cure for 'these many laws' (in the marginalia pleading for a 'new and different Justinian'). He further repeats Cato the Elder's wish that the forum be covered in caltrops, scolds lawyers for being faithless mercenaries and condemns the art and study of litigation (*litigandi ars et studium*) as a means to profit from the commonwealth's decay. He concludes with the mildly ominous quotation that cities before were prosperous enough without lawyers, and that they will be again in the future.[59]

The *Politica* therefore offers a vision of politics where, aside from the most rudimentary limits such as the requirement of a valid succession or election, the prince is bound by little but expedience, and public or Christian morals. Those are at times in agreement; Lipsius is certainly not blind to the wisdom scripture and classical writers have to offer. Yet often they are not, and in these cases he is unambiguous: the Stoics err in only considering virtuous behaviour permissible for a prince. In such a scheme the *leges fundamentales* of a principality, the *ius gentium* and most importantly, natural law have no real purchase on a prince intent on breaking them. A prince must enjoy the maximum

57 Brooke, *Philosophic Pride*, 35.

58 This is in spite of his training as a lawyer, which in 1574 he came back out of exile in Jena from to finish in Leuven, graduating with a degree in civil law. That an individual so seemingly dedicated to obtaining a legal degree is so dismissive of that very science is another Lipsian paradox which has so far escaped broad scrutiny.

59 Lipsius, *Politica*, II.11.

possible latitude in acting for the *salus populi*, and especially not suffer the interference from meddlesome jurists and their doctrine.

Lipsius was not uninterested in natural law; it was simply excised from his political theory. That he was well-acquainted with Stoic natural law arguments and used them when it suited him can be demonstrated by looking at his famous earlier work, *De Constantia*. There, he develops an argument from the Stoic state of nature to counsel against excessive devotion to one's fatherland. He explains that excessive attachment to our fatherland rests on an attribution error. In the first stage of natural society, individuals divide goods and land between them and acquire personal ownership of goods, and they join together in protection of their private property, giving rise to a communal existence. In a later stage of community life, individuals start to consider communal goods – such as the community's rituals, laws and goods – their property, as if they have somehow acquired a personal stake in them. This error causes us to place outsized value on these goods, leading us to despair if the state we belong to perishes.[60]

Lipsius' position in the later, idealist *Monita*, holding that permitting princes to act against virtue is the purview of petty tyrants, not legitimate princes,[61] has been taken by some authors to be evidence of his underlying anti-Machiavellian and constitutionalist sensibilities. This, of course, makes abstraction of the fact that his two political works plainly contradict each other on this point. Ultimately, there is a clear hierarchy present in his works: the *Monita* was written as an addendum to the 'less important' first two idealist books of the *Politica*, when the second edition of the *Politica* was published in 1596.[62] There is no suggestion that Lipsius intended to amend his ideas – to that his refusal to make substantial changes to the *Politica* attests, even when faced with the real prospect of censorship.[63] Some contradiction is also already inherent in the *Politica* itself between the idealist and realist halves, and Lipsius is nothing if not comfortable with discrepancies between his moral and pragmatic teachings.

Therefore, while the base structure of the *Politica* and the theme of princely virtue are decidedly Stoic, the work is no kin to the anti-Machiavellian works written by contemporaries, despite arguments to the contrary. While it might have served as an important reference for natural law thinkers, it cannot in any way be considered germane to their ideas.

60 Justus Lipsius, *De constantia in publicis malis* (Leuven, 1605), lib. I, cap. 11.

61 See note 33.

62 Papy *et al.*, *Monita*, 22–31.

63 See Brooke, *Philosophic Pride*, 20 and Waszink, *Politica*, 120–121 and 173–175.

## 3 Tuldenus and Natural Justice

A first indication that Tuldenus intends to take a very different position from Lipsius is his statement in *De Principiis Iurisprudentiae*, at the start of the long chapter II.15 on "*Whether and to what extent Majesty is unbound by right and laws.*"[64] According to Tuldenus, Seneca's *De Clementia*, that foundational text for the mirror-for-princes genre, speaking in "rhetorical" superlatives about the prince's power,[65] has been taken for unadulterated truth by "certain flatterers" (*assentatores*). It is the interpreters of the law, so Tuldenus implicitly tells us, who we need to look to for an answer, even if they disagree amongst themselves. As such, one cannot expect the tradition of these flatterers to produce a refined and legally sound response to the question. Tuldenus then proceeds to infer the true meaning of what Seneca intended to say in the rest of the chapter – we shall examine an example shortly. A second indication is Tuldenus' private assertion in a letter to his mentor Puteanus, who had been Lipsius' treasured pupil and inheritor of his academic network. He minces no words when he addresses Lipsius' disdain for the study of the law and lawyers: "Lipsius has decidedly spoken with more emotion than sense on this subject, in wanting to suppress not only litigators but the study of law (*iurisprudentia*) itself".[66] In other words, Tuldenus considers the study of the law and the role of jurists in expounding natural law essential to the business of governing, and Lipsius errs in discrediting this study of the law. In this, Tuldenus notes, his mentor Puteanus "might yet exceed the great Lipsius".[67]

This private opinion gives us some suggestion as to how to read Tuldenus' references to Lipsius. For example, in chapter 3 of book 2 of *De Principiis Iurisprudentiae*, Tuldenus turns his attention to the question of what natural

64 Diodorus Tuldenus, *De Principiis Iurisprudentiae* (Leuven, 1702), lib. II cap. 15, 32. "*An & quatenus Majestas legibus & jure exsoluta sit? De potestate eius ordinaria, & extraordinaria: utraque suis & legitimis limitibus distincta.*" His expansive treatment of the question here closely mirrors that in the Commentary on the Code. Such is hardly surprising, given that he was teaching the course on the Code when he wrote the *Principiis*.

65 The reference is to (an abridged version of) Seneca's *De Clementiae*, lib. I, cap. 1. "*Ego vitae necisque; arbiter. Quidcuique mortalium fortuna datum velit, meo ore pronuntitur: nulla pars usquam, nisi volente me floret. Haec tot millia gladiorum, quae pax mea comprimit, ad nutum meum stringentur. Quas nationes funditus exscindi, quas transportari, quibus libertatem dari, quibus eripi velim, quaeruant urbes, quae oriantur, mea jurisdiction est.*"

66 Diodorus Tuldenus to Erycius Puteanus, Royal Library of Belgium (KBR), ms. 19112, nr. 29. "*Lipsius sane maiore spiritu quam peritia de his disseruit: et lites, fere cum iurisprudentia opprimi voluit.*"

67 Ibid.

law entails. To answer this question, Tuldenus relies on citations from Lipsius' *Politica* I.5, which deals with conscience, seamlessly equating the two topics. Natural law is, according to Tuldenus' interpretation of Lipsius, "*Conscience, the witness regarding right and wrong actions*" or "*The remaining spark of right reason* (recta ratio) *in man, indicator and judge of wicked and good deeds*". This right reason is "*the inborn judgement of the human soul regarding divine and human matters*" as they relate to life.[68] Tuldenus builds on this: wrong actions clearly imply there is a rule or law to be transgressed, which must have existed even before God had revealed his commandments. This law is the law of nature and transgressing it can indeed incur the most severe of punishments, to that the flood attests.[69] By presenting citations taken from Lipsius' discussion on conscience in a foundational chapter on natural law, Tuldenus seems to be doing two things. Firstly, the way Tuldenus sets up the chapter, the cursory reader might be led to believe Lipsius had natural law in mind when discussing conscience and that Tuldenus is simply a learned humanist in citing him. Secondly, Tuldenus' discussion of the existence and binding nature of natural law, following the fragments of the *Politica,* seems to strongly imply that while Lipsius might have had useful things to say regarding virtue and conscience, he should not have stopped there. The careful reader of both Tuldenus and Lipsius is guided towards the conclusion that for all Lipsius writes about virtue and is concerned with the prince's conscience, he is awfully light on the consequences of not heeding the dictates of conscience. This slight misdirection and subtle criticism seems to constitute a pattern that holds true in the other instances where Tuldenus cites Lipsius.

Similarly, in the already-mentioned chapter II.15,[70] when Tuldenus ponders the true meaning of Seneca's assertion that the prince is "*arbiter of life and death*",[71] he refers to Lipsius' final chapter 20 of book V on warfare and military prudence[72] – a perennial topic in *raison d'état* literature. Tuldenus states that the sword was indeed granted to the prince by God (*gladium ei Deus concessit*), but in a way that matches his interpretation of the '*ius gladii*'

68 Tuldenus, *De principiis iurisprudentiae,* lib. II, cap. 3, referring to Lipsius, *Politica*, lib. I, cap. 5. "*Est ipsa Conscientia; quae est testimonium de delicto & recte facto:* sive, ut definit Lipsius, *Reliqua in homine rectae rationis scintilla, bonorum malorumque facinorum index & judex:* sive, *Internum animi judicium, approbans recte facta damnans contraria.* Est autem recta ratio *ingenium animae humanae judicum de divinis & humanis*, quatenus ad vitam pertinent."

69 Ibid II.3.

70 Tuldenus, *De principiis iurisprudentiae*, II.15, 34.

71 See note 60.

72 Lipsius, *Politica*, lib. V, cap. 20.

in D.2.1.3:[73] the power to punish evildoers and protect the good also entails the most complete power to forgive, remit and exonerate. Blurring the line between the prince's power to declare war and the power to impose the death penalty, Tuldenus suggests that this power of the sword should always serve the goal of peace: this is attested by the princely power of clemency and the ability to abolish offences. *Politica* V.20, on the other hand, comes at the end of a long book on military matters and mainly consists of an exhortation for princes to – having put the teachings of the prior nineteen chapters into practice – be magnanimous, reasonable and peaceable in victory. Tuldenus' reference to this chapter can perhaps not be constructed as overt criticism, but it is certainly somewhat misleading, seeming to suggest that Lipsius concurs that the sword should only be wielded to further peace. That is a far cry from the rather short chapter in the *Politica*, seeking to convince a prince of the benefits of not being cruel to a defeated enemy, where his earlier virtue of Clemency goes unmentioned. Here too, it seems as if Tuldenus wants to nudge the attentive reader to be critical of Lipsius' influential manual of government and seriously ponder whether Lipsius does not too easily conflate 'can' and 'ought.'

A subtle jab, wholly in line with Tuldenus' comments to Puteanus, might also be found in chapter II.10, on why jurists were and are called '*prudens*' ('wise' or 'knowledgeable'). Tuldenus offers that such is the case because the study of the law, unlike mathematics, which is governed by general and unchanging rules, entails having the faculty to decide in a variety of individual cases. It is practical wisdom on how to act and is as such related to politics and ethics – referring here to Lipsius's exposition of *prudentia civilis* at the start of *Politica* book 4 – yet the science of the law (*doctrina Juris*) remains a lot more certain (*certa*) and defined (*finita*) than these.[74] This certainly matches Tuldenus' statements elsewhere, holding that the disciplines of politics and ethics are the handmaidens of the law, certainly no substitutes.[75] Again, one can consider this a straightforward assertion that Lipsius rightly and usefully described the study of politics as a kind of wisdom rather than a true science. Yet it also does not require much imagination to read in this a rebuke: the

73 Geert Sluijs, "Jurisdiction and its attribution in the works of Diodorus Tuldenus (1594–1645)" *The Legal History Review* vol. 90 (2022): 235–237.

74 Ibid. II.9. "*Id quid evenit potissimum in iis rebus, quae non in nuda cognitione, sed in actione versantur, ut iis, quae ad Politicen atque Ethicen spectant: quibus tamen doctrina Juris magis certa atque finita est, ut inconstantior atque diffusior, quam scientiae Mathematicae.*"

75 See i.a. Ibid. I.1, I.15, IV.2, IV.7–8.

great teacher of politics and practical wisdom for rulers might have benefited from building his theory on firmer grounding. The study of politics by itself, in other words, can only go so far in teaching princes and holders of public power how they ought to exercise their office.

Jurists, in other words, are instrumental in both exercising public power and in conceiving of the nature and limits of that public power. When Tuldenus distinguishes jurisprudence – the science and practice of law in its broadest sense – from litigation in his correspondence to Puteanus, he alludes to a theme which runs as a leitmotif through his many works: the study of law can be used for noble, as well as for wicked ends.[76] He admits bad lawyers (and bad jurisprudence) can cause immense damage, the likes of which Lipsius seems to be inveighing against. Tuldenus credits such faithless lawyers with endless litigation, with corruption of the forum and of public morals, and with sedition and war.[77] Any pursuit of the law therefore needs to be in accordance with timeless precepts of natural justice; adhering to them and fighting injustice is the calling of the statesman – to practice jurisprudence is to practice *Architectonica* (state-building) and *Prudentia Civilis*.[78] This *Prudentia Civilis* seems to be of a wholly different nature than Lipsius.' It is not practical statecraft or stewardship but seems rather closer to Cicero's original usage of the term: a learnedness in the matters of law, justice and equity,[79] in other words, Statesmanship. Tuldenus' usage of the term can then perhaps be seen an attempt to assert the true meaning of '*Prudentia Civilis*' in reclaiming its Ciceronian, natural-law roots.[80]

The implication of this idea and the sharp distinction between litigation and jurisprudence is that the calling of the jurist is a fundamentally civic one, and that the levers of state power should be operated by moral jurists, with a

---

76 See Diodorus Tuldenus, *Initiamenta jurisprudentiae* (Leuven, 1702) *Oratio Auspicalis* V: *De consultissima ad jurisprudentiam via*; Diodorus Tuldenus, *De causis corruptorum Iudiciorum et remediis* (Leuven, 1702), lib. I, cap. 6–7 and 8–11; Diodorus Tuldenus, *De principiis iurisprudentiae* (Leuven, 1702), 1-2; Diodorus Tuldenus, *Initiamenta Jurisprudentiae. Laudatio funebris Stephani Weymsii* (Leuven, 1702), 62, §11. See more broadly Druwé and Sluijs, *Reforming legal education*.

77 Diodorus Tuldenus, *Initiamenta Jurisprudentiae. Laudatio funebris Stephani Weymsii* (Leuven, 1702), 62, §11.

78 Tuldenus, *De principiis iurisprudentiae* (Leuven, 1702), 2.

79 See Cicero, *De Oratione*, lib. 1, XIV, 60 "Prudentia rerum civilium" and XIX, 85 "[...] quandam prudentiam, quae versaretur in perspiciendis rationibus constituendarum et regendarum rerum publicarum".

80 On Cicero and natural law, we can refer to Jeffrey Dymond's "Association and Corporation in Early Modern Jurisprudence" in this volume.

strong notion of justice.[81] States, their heads and other holders of public office are bound by the precepts of natural justice – and spurning them will see the commonwealth perish. We see this echoed in Tuldenus' account of the state of nature and how this state of nature evolved into a political community, as described in *De civili regimine* and his commentary on the Digest. Also relying on Seneca and a Stoic account of the nature of human society, Tuldenus, in short, considers that humans naturally come together to care for one another, and in doing so form natural communities, driven by mankind's innate desire for community. This desire Tuldenus identifies as *Politica*, even though it does not seem to be a full-fledged political community yet at this stage. These natural communities of mankind are quickly and inexorably corrupted by the greed and ambition of individuals, therefore this *Politica* then inspires us to found civil institutions (*instituta civilia*) to maintain our communities. These civil institutions transform natural communities into political ones.[82]

In the next chapter with the heading "*de fine Reipublicae*," the link to his broader thought becomes obvious: justice is what binds political societies together (*societatis coagulum Justitia est*). Society, in turn, is Justice's sanctuary (*asylum*) and where it can thrive.[83] This is logical; it is civil institutions which effectuate a transformation from natural to political society, which man is impelled by '*Politica*' to found. This '*Politica*,' as the inborn tendency towards protection of one's communities is the force underlying *Prudentia Civilis*: jurisprudence which conforms to justice. The practical pursuit of natural justice is what makes political communities possible and is what defends them against the forces that would seek to despoil them: sophistry, driven by greed and self-interest. Though a later transfer of power (*imperium*) to a prince is inevitable,[84] some of these original civil institutions yet persist into the societies of Tuldenus' time. The concrete object of study of this statesmanship is the law of the state (*ius publicum*), and any future *gubernator* of the state should be well-versed in public law. Hence, Tuldenus laments that the children of feudal magnates disdain the study of law, as it has the reputation of preparing future litigators, not helmsmen of the commonwealth. Here, at least, Tuldenus seems to share Lipsius' pessimistic outlook on those who would study the law, though their remedies could not be more different. After all, to those who have the diligence and disposition for it, knowledge of the *ius publicum*

81 See Tuldenus, *De civili regimine* (Leuven, 1702), lib. 1, cap. 5, 3.

82 Tuldenus, *De civili regimine*, lib. 1, cap. 5, 3–4.

83 Tuldenus, *De civili regimine*, lib. 1, cap. 6, 4-6 and *De principiis iurisprudentiae*, lib. 1, cap. 2.

84 See Tuldenus, *Commentarius in Digesta* (Leuven, 1702), at D.1.4.1*pr.*, cap. 1, 23.

offers a rarefied prize which Justinian himself promised: "the reward of governing the commonwealth" (*praemium regendae reipublicae*).[85]

The concrete constitutional consequence is that the prince is tightly constrained by the demands of natural justice: *princeps legibus illigatus*. The prince is bound by the laws, not merely morally or theologically, but also practically, in order to avoid the many evils that would befall the commonwealth should he transgress these laws (one must only recall the flood). Tuldenus discusses this *topos* at multiple points in his oeuvre, but we will mainly look to the expansive treatment of the matter in his commentary on the Code under C.1.14, where he also discusses the D.1.3.31-fragment.[86]

Tuldenus in his baseline position deviates clearly from the learned law mainstream: *princeps legibus illigatus* entails that the prince is bound by all laws – he is not categorically unbound by civil law. To arrive at this point, Tuldenus considers two types of argument. The first is pragmatic and easily summarised: a prince abrogating laws undermines the authority of the very thing by which he rules. A cavalier disrespect for the laws is therefore ultimately self-destructive.[87] By seeing to respect the laws, he fosters a sense of justice in his subjects, which makes his rule easier and causes the commonwealth the flourish. In this, he and Lipsius at least seem perfectly in unison.

The second is technical-legal and nuanced. He considers two main arguments which in his understanding support a classic reading of the *princeps legibus solutus* – adage of a prince unbound by positive law but constrained by higher sources of law, a position he will attempt to disprove.[88]

The first argument reads that the prince in his guise as legislator can plainly be seen to amend and change laws, which he could only do if he were unbound by them. After all, peers have no jurisdiction over one another (*par in parem non habet jurisdictionem*[89]), or so the adage goes, which crucially

85 Tudenus, *De causis corruptorum iudiciorum* (Leuven, 1702), lib. I, cap. 15 (b), 30–1.

86 Tuldenus, *Commentarius ad Codicem* (Leuven, 1650), at C.1.14, 26-30. See also the parallel discussions in: *De principiis iurisprudentiae* (Leuven, 1702), lib II, cap. 15, 32–6 and *De civili regimine* (Leuven, 1702), lib 1, cap. 15, 11.

87 Tuldenus, *Commentarius ad Codicem*, ad C.1.14, 29.

88 Tuldenus, *Commentarius ad Codicem*, ad C.1.14, 28–30.

89 An adage (and its variations) that seems to have had its origins in the Decretals of Gregory IX and which had, by the sixteenth century, trickled into public legal consciousness and the lexicon of the ius commune. There, it was specifically invoked in cases where a prince was tried at law by a nominal equal, e.g. Mary, Queen of Scots in 1586. It only later came to stand for the fundamental rule of state immunity in modern international law. See for a brief history and later significance: Yoram Dinstein, "Par in Parem Non Habet Imperium," Israel Law Review 1, no. 3 (July 1966): 407–410.

"seems all the more valid in the case of an inferior vis-à-vis a superior". Tuldenus' construction of this argument is interesting for multiple reasons. Firstly, while the broad outline of the argument was not new, the reference to a little-known adage (at least at that point in time), establishing a minor point in the *ius gentium*, is remarkable. More so because it is unclear – as opposed to the other two arguments – who exactly Tuldenus is claiming is making this argument. We can thus consider it Tuldenus' own understanding of his opponents' position, revealing a great deal of what he considers the legal-technical pitfalls of his own position and how to evade them. Even more significantly, but beyond the scope of this contribution to examine fully, it gives us a fundamental insight into Tuldenus' legal reasoning and how he reaches his most important conclusions.

Tuldenus in the chapter seems to allude to a common *topos* among sixteenth-century natural law authors writing on the *ius gentium*, such as Vitoria[90] and Gentili,[91] which stated that natural law operated between princes (or 'sovereign' principalities), in absence of a legislator or judge. The law and customs states recognized and generated in their interactions were therefore considered binding as they were grounded on principles of natural law, but were not enacted, and most significantly could not be enforced involuntarily. This later found its most cogent description in Hobbes (following Grotius) who stated that princes, after commonwealths have been established, are the only ones to remain in a state of nature to one another.[92] Within the state, natural law is completely subsumed and suspended in favour of positive law, but in the space between states natural law is the only operational law, including the principle of binding covenants.

The position Tuldenus constructs to argue against therefore reads as follows: if princes are free to disregard or unilaterally change rules of the *ius gentium*, based on natural law, then they are not properly speaking bound by them. And if peer princes cannot bind each other or enforce agreements or

90 Andreas Wagner, "Francisco de Vitoria and Alberico Gentili on the Legal Character of the Global Commonwealth", *Oxford Journal of Legal Studies* vol. 31, 3 (May 2011): 367–373.

91 Anthony Pagden, "Gentili, Vitoria, and the Fabrication of a 'Natural Law of Nations'" in *The Roman Foundations of the Law of Nations: Alberico Gentili and the Justice of Empire*, eds. Benedict Kingsbury and Benjamin Straumann (Oxford: Oxford University Press, 2010), 346*ff.* For Hobbes' notion of natural law, we refer to Carlos Pérez-Crespo's contribution in this volume: "The Concept of Natural Law in Thomas Hobbes' Theory of Sovereignty".

92 David Dyzenhaus, "Hobbes on the International Rule of Law", *Ethics & International Affairs* vol. 28, 1 (2014), 53–64. Hobbes, *Leviathan* (Cambridge: Cambridge University Press, 1999), ed. Richard Tuck, 1999, Ch. 13, 90 and Ch. 30 *in fine*, 244.

rules of natural law against each other – as is established by a rule of the *ius gentium* – then it is absurd to consider that they could be made to abide by the lower-tier jurisdictional order of positive law. In other words, it could be argued there exists, even in an ordinary situation, a legal hierarchy between a prince, operating exclusively on the level of natural law, and positive law.[93] Where writers of the *ius gentium* look at this hierarchy from the outside and tend to be interested in the rules that govern the conduct of princes among one another (and especially, what is to be done when princes infringe upon these rules) Tuldenus looks inwards-out at what tethers this prince, 'floating above' in the state of nature, to the positive law by which he deals with his citizens. With some charity, we might consider that Lipsius was alluding to a similar theme: there is simply no lawmaker whose authority the prince might be subject to.

For Tuldenus, however, the response and solution is twofold. Firstly, a lower-order rule, which Tuldenus admits is generally not of a jurisdictional nature to bind the prince, can be made binding if it rests on a higher-order natural law one; that is, if it is subject to the natural law rule of *pacta sunt servanda*. A reciprocal promise of a prince towards his citizens, even if it would be considered of positive law, is very much binding according to natural justice; not even the prince can exempt himself from a contract validly entered into. Hence, a solemn oath to uphold the privileges and laws of his predecessors, which in the South was formalised in the form of the Joyous Entry, was binding according to natural justice. Joyous Entries as a Low Countries political ritual had been (and is still, by the Belgian kings) routinely practiced by lords high and low since the High Middle Ages, of which the Joyous Entries by the Dukes of Burgundy into the Duchy of Brabant as the *primus inter pares* of the provinces were the most significant.[94] The Entry into Brabant of 1356 led to the signing of a charter, also called the Joyous Entry, which was formally repealed a few years later. Despite this swift repeal (much like the example of the Magna Carta) it entered public consciousness as the foundational consti-

93 Pagden, "Fabrication of a 'Natural Law of Nations", 346–353. See for a link with Lipsius and the *raison d'état literature*: Malcolm, *Reason of State*, 101–102.

94 See as a selection out of a rich body of scholarship: Margrit Thofner, "The Ideal of Sovereignty in the Joyous Entries of the Archduke Albert and the Infanta Isabella" in *Albert & Isabella, 1598-1621*, eds. Werner Thomas and Luc Duerloo (Turnhout: Brepols, 1998), 55-56; Henri Lonchay, 'Philippe II et le mariage des archiducs Albert et Isabelle', Académie royale de Belgique, *Bulletin de la Classe des Lettres et des Sciences Morales et Politiques et de la Classe des Beaux-Arts* 6 (1910), 364–388; Margrit Thofner, "'Willingly We Follow a Gentle Leader ... ': Joyous Entries into Antwerp" in *The Dynastic Centre and the Provinces*, eds. Jeroen Duindam and Sabine Dabringhaus (Leiden: Brill, 2014), 185–202.

tutional document, the *lex fundamentalis*, of the Low Countries. The various ceremonial and formal acts of swearing to uphold the privileges in every feudal polity by the Dukes of Burgundy were thus for many feudal potentates inextricably connected with the written constitutional provisions in the Brabantine Entry. This way, the political practice of the Low Countries, for Tuldenus, puts into practice one of the key ideas of early modern natural law thought: the grounding of the legal and political order on the principle of the binding nature of contracts. Such a principle, as in Hobbes, would function as an essential device in the transition from state of nature to political community.[95]

Secondly, the applicability of the adage itself is dubious: a prince being bound to his own promises does not seem to violate the '*par in parem non habet jurisdictionem*' rule, as it is not other men who have the authority to pass judgement on the prince, "as power and authority stem from God, nature and reason, which are certainly higher than the prince."[96] Yet even further and in clear contravention of the (extended) rule, Tuldenus observes that nominal inferiors can and do pass judgement on their princes. The practice of many states suggests that in a variety of areas judgements are handed down regarding the prince and the royal treasury, and judgements are per definition handed down to the unwilling.[97] Hence, much like rules of the *ius gentium* are instructive for domestic public law, domestic government practice has lessons for the theory of the *ius gentium*. The rebuttal that a prince cannot be made to forcibly comply with these judgements holds no water for Tuldenus: that is a matter of fact, not of law. Following that line of reasoning, anyone with sufficient funds and influence could be said to be 'unbound by the laws.'[98] The same applies when a government's legal act is declared null and void. As it is the prince's representatives who would have to enforce this nullity, the prince

95 After all, for Hobbes the natural law obligation to keep to one's promises (within limits) is the essential device to escape the state of nature and establish the Commonwealth. See R.A. Grover, "The Legal Origins of Thomas Hobbes' Doctrine of Contract," *Journal of the History of Philosophy* fr 18, 2 (1980): 177–194.

96 Tuldenus, *Commentarius ad Codicem*, ad C.1.14, 29. "*quia vis & auctoritas a Deo, natura, & ratione est, quae utique sunt supra Principem.*"

97 There is a certain allusion here to the concept of natural obligations, where natural justice compels the prince (or any subject) to satisfy obligations which normally cannot be enforced through civil courts, which might nonetheless deprive the obligated party of certain remedies if they voluntarily satisfy the obligation.

98 A matter which was not as theoretical as it might seem, as the members of the Burgundian Order of the Knights of the Golden Fleece enjoyed jurisdictional immunity by royal and papal prerogative.

can hardly force himself to consider his own act void: "a distinction of persons is required between the one compelling and the one being compelled."[99]

Yet even the practical fact that there is generally no power to compel the prince – and here Tuldenus assumes the mantle of a resistance theorist – ceases to be valid when the prince not only violates moderation and honesty (*moderationem & honestatem*), but justice itself.[100] Notable is Tuldenus' distinction of the various degrees of severity of infractions against natural law, which closely resembles Lipsius' categorisation of *Corruptio* and *Deceptio* as moderate deceit and *Iniustitia* as grave deceit. While, in this reading, a prince violating moderation and honesty still transgresses natural law, there is nonetheless the implication that some *raison d'état* behaviour is to be expected from a prince and that transgressions against natural law can be of variable severity.

After all, any magistrate or judge with ordinary jurisdiction is endowed with the general power to compel and take coercive action (what Tuldenus elsewhere described as *mixtum imperium*[101]). As when Nero and his ilk had turned the laws upside down and made what was unjust, just, they were rightfully rebuked by the Senate, which is the people's representative. As this should again demonstrate, "*vis coactiva juris non semper a Principibus abhorruit*"; the coercive power of the law has not always shrunk back from the prince.[102] While the theme of overthrowing a legitimate prince is not one which Tuldenus is either eager or finds necessary to explore, he imagines other pathways by which political actors (and named here are judges, magistrates and the Senate) might deploy this coercive power of the law against the prince. Significantly, natural law is not suspended or 'asleep' *pendente conditione*, resuming operation once a certain line has been transgressed. It is always operative; judges merely require a high threshold of violation before being justified in turning their public power against a sovereign prince. After all, a magistrate's ordinary jurisdiction and coercive power emerge directly from the law itself, cannot be alienated and can be disposed of as the magistrate sees fit – this is inherent in the very office they hold.[103]

---

99 Tuldenus, *Commentarius ad Codicem*, ad C.1.14, 30. "*inter cogentem & coactum requiritur distinctio personarum.*"

100 *Ibid. "Nam ea hactenus ad Principem pertinet, ut leges violando non tantum moderationem & honestatem, sed ipsam quoque justitiam violare intelligatur."*

101 Sluijs, "Jurisdiction and its attribution in the works of Diodorus Tuldenus (1594–1645)," *The Legal History Review* vol. 90 (2022): 235–237.

102 Ibid.

103 Ibid. 243–245.

Tuldenus' whole line of reasoning here is similar to the move he makes at the *ius gladii* point above: the principles of natural law at play in the law of nations fundamentally mirror those in domestic public law and vice-versa. In Tuldenus' system, this naturally follows from the fact that there is no clean break between the state of nature and the establishment of the body politic. The operation of the fundamental and universal principles of natural law might be in part mediated by the existence of the body politic (as they are by the customs of state interaction) but is in no way suspended. Looked at in this way, querying the law of nations as to the principle that also applies domestically is highly logical. Public law – the law governing the exercise of public power – is the same regardless of whether it is inter-national public law or domestic public law.

The second argument Tuldenus considers is presented as a rebuttal: the prince is the supreme guardian of the commonwealth and public welfare. In cases of dire need he must be able to disregard the laws and regular course of justice to restore order, to preserve the common good and the existence of the body politic itself – what we would now term a state of exception. Tuldenus does not fundamentally disagree but distinguishes: the prince has both an ordinary and extraordinary power. In the normal course of affairs, he is bound by much of the civil law he uses to treat with his citizens, it is only when the commonwealth itself is at stake and he uses the latter, exceptional prerogative that he operates outside of civil law – but he must still abide by justice and natural law.[104]

## 4 Participatory Government

These views on the role of natural law of course have important implications for whether there is space in either author's theory to conceive of other political actors aside from the prince to exercise political power in their own right.[105]

104 See also Tuldenus, *De principiis iurisprudentiae*, lib. II, cap. 15. The idea of a *potestas ordinaria* and *extraordinaria* of the prince is an old idea in the learned law, going back to early canon law. See Kenneth Pennington, *The Prince and the Law 1200–1600. Sovereignty and Rights in the Western Legal Tradition* (Berkeley: University of California Press, 1993), 73 and 108–112. See for a variation of the theme Rafael Cronje Mateus' work in this volume: "The Mutability of Nature: Dominion, Natural Law, and the Order of Grace in Domingo de Soto's *De Iustitia et Iure* (1553–1554)".

105 This question, of course, can be asked multiple ways and in different vocabularies. Ideas on natural justice inform most Tuldenus' thinking, and he arrives at similar political

Lipsius' ideas regarding the limits of the power of the prince are reflected in the concrete recommendations he directs at the prince as to how his government should be organised. Firstly, there is the admonition that the prince's government should in any case be *adstrictus* – limited or 'selective': "so that not only the greatest power and honor come from you, but they are also with you. Indeed, from you, so that greatest matters are either handled by you personally or are approved by you: 'and do not weaken the power of the Principate, by referring everything to the Senate'."[106] This directive seems absolute and simple; anything not directly commanded by the prince or personally affirmed by him is null. The reference to Tacitus' *Annales* is particularly revealing: delegating decisions to a deliberative Senate undermines the prince's own power. While Lipsius prefaces this with the recommendation that princes should eschew reformatory zeal and only gradually introduce changes in laws and custom, the reason for this caution leaves little room for doubt as to the inherent value of those laws: "gain power gradually, and draw the functions of the laws and magistrates into oneself."[107] There is in this scheme, of course, room for advisors – Lipsius more than recommends princes seeking advice – but all should be aware that everything depends on the prince's will.

To that end, there are only two categories of helpers (*Adiutores*) that may support the prince in his sole stewardship of the commonwealth: Counsellors (*Consiliarii*) and Ministers ([*Ad*]*ministri*).[108] Counsellors – as Lipsius sees them – are older, loyal servants of the prince, who put their expertise at their prince's disposal.[109] Yet the prince should seek advice proactively and in a timely fashion. The gravest deficit of a Polyarchy or rule-by-many is, after all, the inability to make efficient and fast decisions. When so many need to be involved in government, timely deliberations become a rarity: "Here is where

consequences with more strictly legal reasoning when he discusses the terms *jurisdiction* and *imperium* in the Corpus Iuris. For the conclusions he reaches in investigating these fragments, I refer to Sluijs, "Jurisdiction and its attribution," 222–249. The interconnectedness of these ideas with other public law *topoi* shall be discussed at length in the doctoral thesis on Tuldenus.

106 Lipsius, *Politica*, IV.11. Reference to Tacitus, *Annales*, 1.6. "[…] *ut non solum a te praecipua vis et honos, sed etiam Apud te sint. A te quidem, ut maxima rerum aut agas ipse, aut firmes: 'neu vim Principatus resolvas, cuncta ad Senatum revocando."*

107 Lipsius, *Politica*, IV.11. Reference to Tacitus, *Annales* 1.2. "*insurgere paulatim, munia legum et magistratuum in se trahere."*

108 Lipsius, *Politica*, III.3. See for the theme of counsellors in *raison d'état* literature: Malcolm, *Reason of State*, 108.

109 Lipsius, *Politica*, III.4 and *ff.*

the state of many errs."[110] The second kind – the minister or civil servant – provide their prince the use of their person to some particular end. One of the most important criteria for the selection of ministers is that they are just (*rectus*), but not lofty (*erectus*).[111] To the would-be minister, Lipsius has a few choice pieces of advice: "*obsequiosi este*" – be wary of becoming too high for yourself, never measure yourself by the lofty position of the prince, which only gives rise to jealousy. Do not seek or revel in glory, and credit your achievements to your prince.[112] To conclude Lipsius' position with a citation from *De constantia*: "One Single state, as I have said, and like a common ship, under one king and under one law."[113]

Tuldenus' frequent metaphor of jurists trained in public law being the *gubernatores* of the same seems if not an explicit challenge, then at least a notable point of departure. Building on what we have described above, Tuldenus needs a strong notion of natural law (and justice), and enforceability of that natural law to justify other political actors having their own base of power. We shall look at one such an example specifically, which Tuldenus discusses in his commentary on the Digest under the heading D.1.13, where he considers the jurisdiction of the Roman *quaestor*. The fragment reads:

> It should be noted here that even under the Kings, certain individuals who manage the public treasury have been appointed by the people. For even today, the Estates of the realm appoint treasurers to manage the public treasury for the Prince. These officials, therefore, in regard to the administration of their office, are subject to no other jurisdiction than that of the Estates.[114]

Given this, it is much clearer what Tuldenus is thinking of when he mentions civil institutes, and why he stresses this point: the Estates of the realm ('*Ordines patriae*', hence the Estates-General) as the people's representative appoint the magistrates who still control the body politic's finances. After this frag-

110 Lipsius, *Politica*, III.8. *Peccatur hic in Plurium statu. Ubi "illud ex liberate vitium, quod non simul, nec iussi conveniut"*

111 Lipsius, *Politica*, III.10.

112 Lipsius, *Politica*, III.11.

113 Lipsius, *De constantia in publicis malis* (Leuven, 1605), lib. I, cap. 11. "*Unus aliquis status, ut dixi, et communis velut navis, sub uno rege aut sub una lege.*"

114 Tuldenus, *Commentarius in Digesta*, ad D.1.13, 41. "*Notandum hic, quod etiam sub Regibus, quidam, qui publicum aerarium curent, constituti fuerint a populo. Sic enim hodieque Ordines patriae Questores constituent pecuniae Principi pensitandae. Qui proinde, quod ad officii administrationem attinet, non alii Jurisdictioni, quam Ordinum subiiciuntur.*"

ment, he mentions a brief case from the Great Council of Mechlin, which nullified fines which royal commissioners had used to pressure a treasurer of the Estates into producing his account books for examination.

This idea reflects not only the influence of Spanish scholastic thought, but is also and especially reminiscent of French, *monarchomach* political thinking, which stresses the existence of actual representatives of the people who can check the power of the prince. François Hotman (1524–1590) emphasises the role of the Estates of the realm as representative of the people, while the anonymous *Vindiciae, contra tyrannos* instead looks to the magistrates who had received their authority from the people to act like ephors unto the prince.[115]

What is more, in D.1.4.1*pr.*, when Tuldenus discusses the original transfer of public power (*imperium*) he argues that bodies, such as the Estates, that seem to exercise some part of public power are to be presumed to have always had it. In other words, the existence of a certain custom is retroactively considered to have been part of the conditions of transfer of power from the incipient political society to the prince.

## 5 Conclusion

This study has looked at two authors with two very different ways to conceive of political power and how that power is to be exercised. In the *Politica*, Lipsius draws on Stoic political thought and the idea of princely virtue, yet never fully closes the circle. Lipsius gestures towards some legal and constitutionalist topics such as the *princeps legibus solutus* question and the rules of the *ius gentium* but remains a *raison d'état* thinker foremost. His *Prudentia Civilis* is that of the steward and consists in practical statecraft or the variety of ways in which a prince might go about doing what might be unpleasant, but necessary for the public good. Tuldenus' *Prudentia Civilis* is that of the Ciceronian statesman, concerned with natural justice and upright moral judgement in public affairs.

Both Leuven humanists draw deeply from the well of classical antiquity. Though Lipsius is often considered the great reviver of Stoic thought into the European political and philosophical tradition – and the figure who made it available to later thinkers – Tuldenus himself makes plentiful use of that Stoic tradition. His dedication of his *De principiis iurisprudentiae* to Cato the Younger, avowed Stoic and staunch defender of the Roman Republic against Julius

115 X, *Vindiciae, Contra Tyrannos* (Basel, 1579), 46.

Caesar's centralisation of power – "it is his verdict whether this work should stand or fall"[116] – is but one example of how Tuldenus wants to portray his work as a more truthful interpretation of Roman Stoic political thought.

Tuldenus was certainly aware of the challenge that Lipsian *raison d'état* thinking presented to his system, and the latter's intellectual legacy was inescapable, as is well attested in his private correspondence. Tuldenus, therefore, selectively appropriates the Lipsian idiom, at times seeming to offer criticism or rebuke in insisting on the role of the law, the dictates of natural justice (such as the binding nature of contracts) binding the price and constitutionalist arrangements where judges and representatives of the Estates can check the prince if need be. The state of nature and the conditions of transfer of political power, which do not play a role in Lipsius' thinking in the *Politica*, is hence used by Tuldenus as a lever to break open the prince's monopoly of power. That is not to say Tuldenus was a republican, or sceptical towards central authority as such, or even sceptical of a powerful prince – his esteem for the role of the prince is apparent from many passages in *De Principiis Iurisprudentiae* and *De Civili Regimine*. Yet Tuldenus was a thoroughly constitutionalist thinker, endorsing a mode of governance where multiple political actors or 'civil institutions' could check one another, under the watchful eye of jurists. Such an arrangement seemed to conform best to man's natural way of organising communities.

All this, of course, was not idle theorising. Lipsius wrote his *Politica* when preparing his return to the South, and a few years after his return he accepted a position as Historiographer Royal of Philip II in 1595. Around the time his revised *Politica* went to press in 1596, he started to write a didactic appendix to the various books of the *Politica*, to furnish his political dicta with historical examples. He completed two chapters that year, but they were not published until 1605 as the *Monita*.[117] The remaining four books of the Politica went uncommented – though the Monita remains inextricably tied to its parent work, especially its idealist half. He therefore had a continued interest in the promotion of the *Politica* and the theory contained therein, which could be gainfully utilised by a powerful and dynamic prince. Albert and Isabella's reign, starting in 1596, corresponded well to that picture and Lipsius was an eager supporter of their regime.[118] Already in 1596, Lipsius wrote to Albert to

116 Diodorus Tuldenus, *De principiis iurisprudentiae* (Leuven, 1702), 2.

117 See for the *Monita's* publication history: Papy *et al.*, *Monita*, 22–31.

118 See Violet Soen, "The *Clementia Lipsiana*: Political Analysis, Autobiography and Panegyric," in *(Un)masking the Realities of Power. Justus Lipsius and the Dynamics of Political Writing in Early Modern Europe*, eds. Eric De Bom *et al.* (Leiden: Brill, 2011), 231.

inform him he would be dedicating the *Monita* to him, extolling his many virtues and dubbing him the *optimus princeps*.[119] In 1599 Lipsius firmly cemented his position as the resident court intellectual of the Archdukes when he delivered an academic lecture to the Archdukes in Leuven during their Joyous Entry, sparing no effort to advertise the episode to a broad audience after.[120]

One of the characteristics of this regime, while it enjoyed wide support in the Catholic South, was that it had inherited a distinct suspicion towards the body of the Estates-General. The power of the Estates-General to give discontent a platform, rally very disparate rebellious factions and project political might had been one of the essential accelerants of the early Dutch Revolt.[121] Hence, there is the strong suggestion that Lipsius, ultimately loyal to the country of his birth, thought it time to dispense with some of the classic constitutionalist arrangements to which his countrymen were so attached. A decisive and powerful prince might be able to force a breakthrough and achieve the lasting peace (and perhaps even reunification) that had so far proven elusive.[122]

Lipsius himself did not live to see the crowning achievement of the rule of the Archdukes, the Twelve Years' Truce in 1609. Yet even by the time that the peace and the Archdukes' joint reign had expired, Lipsius' ideas on princely rule and virtue were still highly influential. However, the situation had fundamentally changed, and the Southern Netherlands had returned to being a war-torn province governed by faraway Madrid. When Tuldenus was appointed ordinary professor of the Digest in Leuven in 1633, a tug of war was taking place between the then-in-session Estates-General of the South and Philip IV, King of Spain.[123]

Tuldenus' challenge to Lipsian *raison d'état* thinking – which he develops over his works, but is certainly still present in his teaching of the course of the

---

119 Papy *et al.*, *Monita*, 35–36. See Lipsius, *Monita*, preface.

120 Toon Van Houdt, "Justus Lipsius and the Archdukes Albert and Isabella," in *The world of Justus Lipsius: A contribution towards his intellectual biography*, ed. Marc Laureys, Bulletin de l'institut historique belge de Rome 67 (Rome: Institut historique belge de Rome, 1998) 405–432.

121 René Vermeir, "Early Seventeenth- Century Representative Institutions and Law Making in the Habsburg Netherlands," in *Early Modern Sovereignties. Theory and Practice of a Burgeoning Concept in the Netherlands*, eds. Eric De Bom et al. (Leiden: Brill, 2021), 289–290, 295; John Gilissen, "Les Etats- Généraux des Pays de Par Deça (1464–1632)," *Anciens pays et assemblées d'États* vol. 33 (1965) 294.

122 See Soen, "*Clementia Lipsiana*", 207–209.

123 René Vermeir, "Le duc d'Arschot et les conséquences de la conspiration des nobles (1632–1640)," in *Beleid en bestuur in de oude Nederlanden. Liber Amicorum Prof. Dr. M. Baelde*, eds. René Vermeir and Hugo Soly (Gent, 1993), 477–489.

Digest – is therefore linked to real political events, playing out at that very moment. From 1595 onward, when Albert was appointed Governor-General, before becoming sovereign Archduke, standing orders from Philip II, King of Spain, forbade the Governor and later nominal sovereigns from convoking the Estates-General without express permission from the king. Military defeat in 1632 prompted the various Estates of the Realm and a group of 'conspirator' nobles to organise a gathering of the Estates-General and declare themselves in session, without Madrid's consent. As the belief was still held – in North and South – that a final peace and reunification would be possible if the Estates-General of both parts of the Low Countries came together to negotiate,[124] the clandestine Estates-General could be seen as an attempt to force the peace process in absence of a personally committed sovereign.

Yet the Estates-General was also a practical body, which gathered to discuss problems of military discipline. In this context, they demanded an edict that would make the civil courts competent to judge crimes of misbehaving Spanish soldiers and mercenaries. If such an edict was not granted, the problems of military discipline (which the Estates reasoned were largely due to payment issues) would be resolved by setting off the wage costs of the Spanish regulars and mercenaries with the yearly subsidy ('*bede*') which the Estates granted by way of tax to the Spanish crown. Such a threat did not miss its purpose, as it would imply that the Estates-General would get a permanent say and veto over the Spanish budget, which would give them a formal constitutional role and would necessitate them staying in session indefinitely. The edict was granted in October 1633, and the convocation of the Estates-General was adjourned in 1634. The episode reminded Madrid once again that allowing the Estates-General free rein was an immensely dangerous proposition; it would never be convoked again during Habsburg times.

Tuldenus' positions need to be seen in this context. That Tuldenus in his course of the Digest taught that the autonomous fiscal jurisdiction of the Estates-appointed *quaestores* was autonomous and inviolable was a coded, though – when treated in context – clear endorsement of that body's right to assembly and claim to political power, at the very moment that it was in session for the last time. This is further strengthened by Tuldenus' interpretation at D.1.4.1*pr.*, which elevates a 'constitutional' custom to an established part of the country's law of government. Once the Estates-General would have leave to exercise its fiscal powers to the fullest, there would be no way back. After all,

124 Violet Soen and Bram De Ridder, "The Act of Cession, the 1598 and 1600 States General in Brussels and the Peace Negotiations during the Dutch Revolt," in *The Twelve Years' Truce (1609)*, ed. Randall Lesaffer (Leiden: Brill, 2014), 67–68.

the prince swears to formally uphold the privileges and laws of the realm at the occasion of the Joyous Entry. Not doing so is a violation of natural law, which might justify magistrates turning their coercive power on the prince. Seen in this way, Tuldenus' thought constitutes a coherent system of legal positions which presents a challenge to the prince-centric and centralistic *raison d'état* mode of governance endorsed by Lipsius.

## Acknowledgement

This contribution was made possible through the support of the Research Foundation – Flanders (FWO project nr. G0C4421N). Its findings will be part of the doctoral thesis on 'Diodorus Tuldenus (1594–1645) and the Development of Natural and Public Law in the Habsburg Low Countries', for which this research grant was awarded.

CHAPTER 6

# Natural Law and Governance of the State in Henning Arnisaeus

*Paolo Astorri and Lars Cyril Nørgaard*

## 1 Introduction

In *The Foundations of Modern Political Thought*, Quentin Skinner identified the Spanish scholastics as pioneers in the field of natural law. The Salamanca scholars laid the groundwork for a vocabulary that "Grotius, Hobbes, Pufendorf and their successors all adopted and developed in building up the classic version of the natural-law theory of the State in the course of the following century."[1] Skinner remarked that this groundwork was developed in direct opposition to assumptions associated with the Lutheran faith. All differences aside, the Jesuits and Dominicans in Spain agreed that the Lutherans had severed the bond between the conduct of politics and theories of natural law.[2] Of course, Skinner does not infer from this that Lutherans took little or no interest in natural law during the sixteenth century. They most certainly did take such an interest. Indeed, earlier Protestants had recognized the need for natural-law theory.[3] Between 1521 and 1525, Philipp Melanchthon (1497–1560) began addressing the issue. During the 1530s, Melanchthon worked on Aristotle's *Ethics* and *Politics*, viewing *politica* as an *ars* that concerned itself

1 Quentin Skinner, *The Foundations of Modern Political Thought*, 2 vols. (Cambridge: Cambridge University Press, 1978) vol. 1, 184.

2 Skinner, *The Foundations of Modern Political Thought*, vol. 1, 138–140.

3 See Merio Scattola, *Das Naturrecht vor dem Naturrecht: zur Geschichte des 'ius naturae' im 16. Jahrhundert* (Tübingen: Niemeyer, 1999); J. Witte, Jr., *Law and Protestantism: The Legal Teachings of the Lutheran Reformation* (Cambridge: Cambridge University Press, 2002); H.J. Berman, *Law and Revolution, II: The Impact of the Protestant Reformations on the Western Legal Tradition* (Cambridge: Cambridge University Press, 2003); M. Schmoeckel, *Das Recht der Reformation, Die epistemologische Revolution der Wissenschaft und die Spaltung der Rechtsordnung in der Frühen Neuzeit* (Tübingen: Mohr Siebeck 2014); Martin Heckel, *Martin Luthers Reformation und das Recht: Die Entwicklung der Theologie Luthers und ihre Auswirkung auf das Recht unter den Rahmenbedingungen der Reichsreform und der Territorialstaatsbildung im Kampf mit Rom und den 'Schwärmern'* (Tübingen: Mohr Siebeck, 2016).

 | DOI:10.1163/9789004748712_008

with the *ordinatio civitatis*.[4] This concern for the order of society related to private property, the status of the ruler, the legitimacy of laws, contracts, sanctions, and the obligations of citizens.[5] While the societal order was instituted and conserved by God, Melanchthon viewed natural law as something that moral philosophy could elucidate,[6] because it concerned external actions.[7] Famously, Melanchthon viewed the magistrate as the guardian of both tables of the Decalogue. The magistrate was called upon to enforce laws that complied with natural law, and human laws were to specify circumstances not defined by natural law but nonetheless in compliance with its precepts.[8]

Melanchthon's approach to natural law and moral philosophy was further developed by David Chyträus (1531–1600). Together with Martin Chemnitz (1522–1586) and Timotheus Kirchner (1533–1587), Chyträus was commissioned by Duke Julius of Brunswick-Lüneburg (1528–1589) to write the statutes for the University of Helmstedt. Chyträus proposed to establish Aristotle as a point of reference for scientific method, and Melanchthon's former student, Owen Günther (1532–1615), was appointed as professor of philosophy.[9] In 1589, Günther was joined at Helmstedt by Johannes Caselius (1533–1613). While Günther had studied under Melanchthon, his new colleague, while recognizing Melanchthon's important contribution, seems to have wanted something more. As professor of Greek and philosophy, Caselius proposed a program of moral

4 The turn to Aristotle has been interpreted as a theological appropriation of philosophy. On this interpretation, natural-law theory becomes a stage in Melanchthon development of a theological system, see Günter Frank, *Die theologische Philosophie Philipp Melanchthons (1497–1560)* (Leipzig: Benno, 1995); Merio Scattola, "*Notitia naturalis de Deo et morum gubernatione:* Die Naturrechtslehre Philipp Melanchthons und ihre Wirkung im 16. Jahrhundert," in *Melanchthon und die Marburger Professoren (1527–1627)*, ed. B. Bauer (Marburg: Universitätsbibliothek Marburg, 1999) vol. 1, 865–882; Christoph Strohm, "Zugänge zum Naturrecht bei Melanchthon," in *Der Theologe Melanchthon,* ed. G. Frank (Stuttgart: Jan Thorbecke Verlag, 2000), 339–356; Antti Raunio, "Divine and Natural law in Luther and Melanchthon," in *Lutheran Reformation and the Law,* ed. V. Mäkinen (Leiden: Brill, 2006), 21–62. For a different approach to Melanchthon's understanding of philosophy as powerful tool that can clarify theological concepts and political conflicts, see Nicole Kuropka, *Philipp Melanchthon. Wissenschaft und Gesellschaft: ein Gelehrter im Dienst der Kirche (1526–1532)* (Tübingen: Mohr Siebeck, 2002); Nicole Kuropka, "Philip Melanchthon and Aristotle," in *Philip Melanchthon: Theologian in Classroom, Confession, and Controversy,* eds. I. Dingel, R. Kolb, N. Kuropka and T.J. Wengert (Göttingen: Vandenhoeck & Ruprecht, 2012), 19–28.

5 Philipp Melanchthon, *Commentarii in aliquot Politicos libros Aristotelis*, in CR XVI, 418.

6 Philip Melanchthon, *Ethicae doctrinae elementorum libri duo*, in CR XVI, 167.

7 Philip Melanchthon, *Philosophiae moralis epitomes libri duo*, in CR XVI, 22.

8 Melanchthon, *Ethicae doctrinae elementorum libri duo*, in CR XVI, 229.

9 Owen Günther, *Aristotelis Stageritae. Ethicorum ad Nicomachum Libri X* (Helmstedt: Jakob Lucius, 1585).

philosophy that returned to Aristotle as the original framework for thinking about morals.[10] The following year, Cornelius Martini (1568–1621) found employment at the Academia Julia as professor of logic. He had studied in Rostock under Caselius, and his brand of Aristotelianism included novel ideas about metaphysics. While Günther had introduced metaphysics as an ideal, Martini's lectures on Aristotelian metaphysics, running from November 1597 until October 1599, marked an important turning point in scholasticism as it could be envisioned at a Lutheran university.[11]

In this paper, we shall consider one of Martini's most famous students and collaborators. Henning Arnisaeus (†1636) was a key exponent of Aristotelian philosophy as it developed at Protestant universities during the first decades of the seventeenth century.[12] Our focus is on Arnisaeus's understanding of natural law as it can be gleaned from the pages of *De jure majestatis* (1610).[13] This work is part of the emerging discourse on political theory; however, and according to Arnisaeus, it also presupposes a broader framework of the sciences and their foundations. Our paper seeks to trace the historical background of this 'holistic' approach, which distanced itself from a theological framework while simultaneously laying claim to a Melanchthonian legacy. The paper is divided into two parts. First, we outline the intense intellectual climate in which Arnisaeus's understanding of natural law and human nature took shape. Second, we examine *De jure majestatis* and analyze the 'minimal' theory of natural law that Arnisaeus presents in this work. This dual approach aligns with a historical narrative in which Arnisaeus and his contemporaries contributed to the foundation of a concept of the state based on a secular theory of natural law. In retrospect, *De jure majestatis* represents a key piece

---

10 Johannes Caselius, *In Aristotelis de vita et moribus librorum interpretationem, programma* (Helmstedt: Jacob Lucius, 1593).

11 "*Tu enim primus in Germaniae Academiis Metaphysicae veram faciem reddidisti, quae ab aliis prorsus abolita, a nonnullis futilibus nugis deturpata, ab omnibus certe neglectim habita erat*," Henning Arnisaeus, *De Constitutionen et partibus Metaphysicae* (Frankfurt an der Oder: Johann Thieme, 1606), Unpag. [1]. This statement comes from the prefatory dedication dated to 20 April 1603 and addressed to Martini. To this assessment, see Peter Petersen, *Geschichte der aristotelischen Philosophie im protestantischen Deutschland* (Leipzig: Felix Meiner, 1921), 123; Ernst Lewalter, *Spanish-Jesuitische und Deutsch-Lutherische Metaphysik des 17. Jahrhunderts* (Hamburg: Ibero-Amerikanisches Institut Hamburg, 1935), 48ff.

12 Our contribution builds on the seminal study by Horst Dreitzel, *Protestantischer Aristotelismus und absoluter Staat. Die "Politica" des Henning Arnisaeus (c. 1575–1636)* (Wiesbaden: Franz Steiner, 1970).

13 Henning Arnisaeus, *De iure maiestatis libri tres* (Frankfurt an der Oder: Johann Thiemen, 1610).

in this larger puzzle.[14] While natural law cannot account for the emergence of the state or grant coercive force to civil laws, it can place some general limits upon the exercise of *potestas*. It is the natural foundations of these general limits that we shall attempt to elucidate.

## 2 Arnisaeus and Aristotle

Arnisaeus viewed his disputations on Aristotle's *Politics* as part of an overall engagement with philosophy.[15] These disputations were compiled into a stand-alone work,[16] and this work laid the grounds for his later writings on politics, where he incorporated legal terminology, although he had no formal training as a jurist. We also find biblical references, although he surely was no theologian. Arnisaeus had obtained dual degrees in medicine and philosophy from the University of Helmstedt. During his formative years, he was also enrolled at the University of Frankfurt an der Oder, where he studied from 1602 until 1605. Next, he traveled in Europe, becoming professor *extraordinarius* at Frankfurt upon his return in 1608. Here, he taught medicine and moral philosophy. Two years later, in 1610, he defended his thesis in medicine at the University of Helmstedt.[17] In 1612, he was promoted to a full professorship in Frankfurt, only to leave the following year when he became professor of medicine at Helmstedt. Thereafter, Arnisaeus dedicated most of his scholarly attention to medical issues. Thus, his thinking developed in two phases. The first phase began around 1600, when he completed his philosophical training in Helmstedt, and ended in 1613: this period centers on different topics within Aristotelian philosophy and politics,[18] and its primary output was disputations edited and compiled into epitomes or developed into stand-alone

14 See Annabel Brett, *Changes of State. Nature and the Limits of the City in Early Modern Natural Law* (Princeton University Press: Princeton and Oxford, 2011), 62–89.

15 Henning Arnisaeus, *Disputationum politicarum in Academia Iulia propositarum*, I–XIII (Helmstedt: Jacob Lucius, 1605).

16 Henning Arnisaeus, *Doctrina politica in genuinam methodum Aristotelis reducta* (Frankfurt a.M.: Johannes Thiemen, 1606).

17 Henning Arnisaeus, *De calcvlo renvm et vesicae dignoscendo et cvrando* (Helmstedt: Jakob Lucius, 1610).

18 Of course, there are exceptions to this general rule. During 1610 and 1611, around the time when Arnisaeus defended his thesis in medicine, he also completed several disputations within the same field. See Henning Arnisaeus, *Disputatio medica de apoplexia et epilepsia cognoscendis et curandis* (Frankfurt an der Oder: Johann Eichorn, 1610); Henning Arnisaeus, *Observationes aliquot anatomicae: ex quibus controversiae multae medicae & physicae breviter deciduntur* (Frankfurt an der Oder: Johann Eichorn, 1610); Henning Arni-

works. The second phase began in 1613 and lasted until 1636, when Arnisaeus died in Hillerød, just outside of Copenhagen: his intellectual output during these years dealt almost exclusively with medical issues.[19]

Arnisaeus's brand of Aristotelianism must be seen within the context of the Faculty of Philosophy at the University of Helmstedt. In this environment, he offered disputations on ethics,[20] psychology,[21] and physics.[22] These disputa-

saeus, *Disputatio medica de lue venerea cognoscenda et curanda* (Frankfurt an der Oder: Andreas Eichorn, 1610); Henning Arnisaeus, *Disputatio medica therapeutica. De praeservatione a peste* (Frankfurt an der Oder: Friedrich Hartman, 1611); Henning Arnisaeus, *Disputatio therapeutica de venae sectione seu de legitimis sanguinis ex vena mittendi scopis* (Frankfurt an der Oder: Nikolaus Voltz, 1611).

19 The focus on medicine was supported by Arnisaeus's acceptance of the position of royal physician to the Danish king Christian IV. He formally accepted the position in 1619 and arrived in Copenhagen the following year. We do not know much about his time in Copenhagen, but he collaborated with scholars such as Thomas Fincke (1561–1656), Jacob Fabricius (1576–1652), and Ole Worm (1588–1654). According to Thomas Bartholin (1614–1680), Arnisaeus donated a human skeleton to the university that would later become part of the anatomical theater in Copenhagen. See Thomas Bartholin, *Domus anatomica* (Copenhagen: Henrik Gøde, 1662), 48–49. His name also appears in official statements issued by the faculty of medicine in relation to a particular case where a miscarriage might have been an abortion and thereby constituted infanticide. Thomas Bartholin, *Cista medica hafniensis* (Copenhagen: Henrik Gøde, 1662), 318–331. The issues at stake in cases of abortion had already been discussed in three disputations at Helmstedt; Henning Arnisaeus, *De partus humani legitimis terminis* (Helmstedt: Jakob Lucius, 1618); *De partus humani legitimis terminis, resp. Hermann Willerdingius* (Helmstedt: Jakob Lucius, 1618); *De partus humani legitimis terminis* (Helmstedt: Jakob Lucius, 1618).

20 Henning Arnisaeus, *De summo bono quod nobis in humana societate obtingere natum est: diuinam Aristotelis doctrinam, in 1. Eth. ad Nicomachum explicatam* (Helmstedt: Jacob Lucius, 1600); Henning Arnisaeus, *De voluptate et summo bono: ex 10. ethicorum nicomachicorum desumta* (Helmstedt: Jacob Lucius, 1600); Henning Arnisaeus, *De principiis virtutum moralium ex Aristotelis tertio Eth. ad Nicom. fideliter desumta* (Helmstedt: Jacob Lucius, 1600).

21 Henning Arnisaeus, *De anima rationali siue mente humana, auream Aristotelis doctrinam* (Helmstedt: Jacob Lucius, 1600).

22 Henning Arnisaeus, *Disputatio physica de principiis rerum naturalium* (Helmstedt: Jacob Lucius, 1600). This disputation belongs to a series of disputations on Aristotle's *Physics*, see Henning Arnisaeus, *Disputatio Physica. Ex secundo Aristotelis de anima libro. De sensibus exterioribus* (Helmstedt: Jacob Lucius, 1600); Henning Arnisaeus, *Disputatio physica de anima in genere. Ad cuius positiones praeuio Deo sapientißimo duce Aristotele* (Helmstedt: Jacob Lucius, 1600), cf. Henning Arnisaeus, *Epitome doctrinae physicae, continens brevem et dilucidam explicationem fundamentorum Aristotelicorum: adiecto succincto examine et amp; decisione plerarumq[ue] quaestionum, qua circa doctrinam Aristotelis et veritatis fundamenta excitari solent* (Frankfurt an der Oder: Johann Thieme, 1607).

tions played into a heated debate on the status of philosophy that had escalated in 1598 but had been brewing at the university since its foundation. Duke Julius had initially been a strong supporter of the efforts to establish common ground among the Lutheran factions. The Academia Julia was intended to play an important role in this consolidation of Lutheranism. More specifically, the duke had envisioned that Chyträus should hold a prominent position within the Faculty of Theology. This commission proved impossible to realize. Positions could also not be secured for the theologians who had overseen the implementation of Lutheranism in Braunschweig-Wolfenbüttel. For different reasons, Martin Chemnitz, Peter Ulner (1523–1595), Jacob Andreae (1528–1590), and Nicolaus Selnecker (1530–1592) did not find employment at the new institution. In their place, other theologians were commissioned to uphold the purity of Lutheran doctrine. Among them, Tilemann Hesenhus (1527–1588) defended the position of the so-called Gnesio-Lutherans, which manifested itself in a skeptical attitude toward philosophy.[23] Hesenhus openly affirmed his reservations towards Melanchthon, and his position therefore seems to have been at odds with Chyträus's original vision for the institution. Still, Hesenhus had supporters in Helmstedt, including not at least the powerful Basilius Sattler (1549–1624) who shared Hesenhus's reservations towards philosophy and, especially, its use within theology.[24] Accordingly, the intellectual environment where Arnisaeus developed his understanding of natural law was characterized by a conflict between the spirit of Melanchthonian humanism and dreams of Lutheran orthodoxy.

This conflict was further intensified by Duke Julius's decision to retract his signature from the Formula of Concord. After the 1580 retraction, the confessional status of the duchy remained Lutheran, but the door was left open for more diverse opinions. During the reign of Julius's successor, Heinrich Julius, the orthodox theologians felt marginalized. The new duke was more inclined towards humanism than devout piety. At the turn of the century, when Arni-

23 "*Ratio enim nihil eorum percipit, quae sunt Spiritus. Non igitur Philosophia miscenda est cum Theologia. Neque articuli fidei ex Philosophia expunendi sunt,*" Tilemann Heshusius, *Explicatio prioris Epist. Pauli ad Corinthios* (Jena: Ernst von Gera, 1573), 46.

24 Sattler had studied theology in Tübingen and he arrived in Braunschweig-Wolfenbüttel in 1569. Three years later, he became pastor at the prestigious Beatae Mariae Virginis, and a few years later he was awarded with a seat in Julius's consistory. In 1586, Sattler became court preacher, and from 1589 until 1624 he also served as general superintendent to Duke Henrich Julius (1564–1613), see Wolfgang Sommer, *Gottesfurcht und Fürstenherrschaft. Studien zum Obrigkeitsverständnis Johann Arndts und lutherischer Hofprediger zur Zeit der altprotestantischen Orthodoxie* (Göttingen: Vandenhoeck & Ruprecht, 1988), 225–254.

saeus was completing his studies at Helmstedt, the rapport between philosophers and theologians went from bad to worse.[25] As mentioned above, Martini began lecturing on Aristotelian metaphysics in late 1597: he seems to have expanded upon Melanchthon's understanding of dialectics by using Aristotelian logic.[26] Manuscript copies of Martini's lectures soon circulated a Protestant universities.[27] In their natural state, humans, according to Martini, have the capacity to understand about their world that God exists. Humans can also infer certain aspects about God's mode of being. For instance, God is one. This natural capacity does not allow human beings to make further inferences about the divine. Articles of faith like the trinity, the incarnation, justification by faith alone, the resurrection of the dead, and the last judgement remain beyond the limits of the human *mens*.[28] Thus, Martini clearly distinguished *articuli mixti* from *articuli meri*, where the latter kind of articles of faith can only be known from revelation, while the first kind can also be known by natural reasoning.[29] In different ways, he attempted to convince his opponents that Melanchthon had shared his understanding of philosophy and the role it had to play within the education system.[30] While Martini failed in this regard, there is no reason to doubt his conviction.

---

25 To the following, see Inge Mager, "Lutherische Theologie und aristotelische Philosophie an der Universität Helmstedt im 16. Jahrhundert: Zur Vorgeschichte des Hofmannschen Streites im Jahre 1598," *Jahrbuch der Gesellschaft für niedersächsische Kirchengeschichte* 73 (1975), 83-98; Markus Friedrich, *Die Grenzen der Vernunft. Theologie, Philosophie und gelehrte Konflikte am Beispiel des Helmstedter Hofmannsstreit und seiner Wirkungen auf das Luthertum um 1600* (Göttingen: Vandenhoeck & Ruprecht, 2004).

26 Cornelius Martini, *Metaphysica. Commentatio compendiose, succincte, et perspicue comprehendens universam Metaphysices doctrinam* (Strassburg: Carolus, 1605).

27 One of these manuscript copies was received by Johann Gerhard (1582–1637), while he was enrolled at the University of Wittenberg; see Mager, "Lutherische Theologie und aristotelische Philosophie an der Universität Helmstedt im 16. Jahrhundert," 87.

28 Cornelius Martini, *Theologiae compendium quod ab interitu vindieavit Heinricus-Iulius Scheurl moralium, civiliumque professor pubheus et suam naturalem theologiam adecit* (Wolfenbüttel: Buno, 1650), 27.

29 In a later metaphysical disputation, Arnisaeus repeats Martini's stance, excluding the trinity and the mystery of the incarnation from what can be inferred by natural reasoning; see Henning Arnisaeus, *Disputatio Metaphisica de Deo continens naturalem Dei cognitionem* (Frankfurt an der Oder: F. Hartmann, 1604) n. 74–6; 84. Like Martini, he also affords human beings with the capability to know God's existence and some general aspects about his mode of being, see Arnisaeus, *Disputatio Metaphisica de Deo*, n. 7–8, cf. Martini, *Theologiae compendium*, 63.

30 See, e.g., Martini's dedication in his edition of Philipp Melanchthon, *Oratio de philosophia studiosos theologiae necessaria* (Helmstedt: Jakob Lucius, 1600).

Despite Martini's relatively moderate claims and his clear support of theology as the science of revelation, Daniel Hofmann (1538–1611) launched a violent attack against him and the other members of the Faculty of Philosophy. Until 1579, Hofmann had been affiliated with this same faculty, and his philosophical propositions from 1575 develop a picture of natural reason that comes very close to Martini's. A few years later, he came under the influence of Hesenhus, and this influence radically changed his outlook. In 1597, he attacked the Wittenberg theologian Ägidius Hunnius (1550–1603), because his teachings on divine ubiquity afforded human will with certain liberties. Hunnius's *Articulus de libero arbitrio* from 1597 maintained against his controversial colleague Samuel Huber (1547–1624) that some human beings would be damned. Huber's radical idea of the universality of Christ's atonement had to be rebutted, but such a rebuttal entailed a problem of its own. Later codified by the Dutch Reformed Church at the Synod of Dordrecht (1618–1619), a notion of double predestination makes God responsible not only for the salvation of humankind but also for the damnation of some humans. Hunnius found the latter idea problematic, and therefore he proposed that, while humans could not decide to believe – humans cannot save themselves – they could, however, influence their own constitution: Hunnius did not base this kind of *facilitas* in a natural constitution but rather in the attitudes and character of believers, which could be transformed through discipline; the willingness to make such transformation does not justify humans in the eyes of God but it is nevertheless indispensable in the preparation for justification. Hereby, the Wittenberg professor attempted to secure a position, according to which God cannot be held responsible for damnation, although it is entirely his decision. Human nature can and must show itself willing to be saved from its sinfulness. Hofmann viewed this as a compromise that allowed human nature, despite its sinfulness, to cooperate with and thereby encroach on the atonement of Christ's sacrifice.

The following year, Hofmann and Caspar Pfaffrad (1562–1622) proposed a set of propositions in Helmstedt, where they sharply criticized philosophy and its metaphysical claims about God.[31] In these propositions and in a 1600 disputation,[32] Hofmann stressed the fundamental difference between claims for-

31 Daniel Hofmann and Caspar Pfaffrad, *Propositiones de Deo et Christi tum persona tum officio. Asserentes puriorem confessionem D. Lutheri, feces scholasticas expurgantis, oppositae Pontificiis et omnibus cauponantibus verbum Dei* (Helmstedt: Jacob Lucius, 1598).

32 Daniel Hofmann, *Pro duplici veritate Lutheri a philosophis impugnata, & ad pudendorum locum ablegata* (Magdeburg: Dunckerus, 1600), cf. Hofmann and Pfaffrad, *Propositiones de Deo*, xv–xx, 4–5. To the double-truth theory and its Lutheran interpretation, see K. Heim, "Zur Geschichte des Satzes von der doppelten Wahrheit," in *Studien zur systematischen Theologie*, ed. F. Traub (Tübingen: Mohr-Siebeck, 1918), 1–16; L. Bianchi, *Pour*

mulated within theology and claims formulated within philosophy. By insisting upon the incommensurability of such claims, Hofmann reserved truth for theology and concluded that philosophy had no role to play in Lutheran education. Only the *gratia Dei* makes it possible to formulate a *veritas spiritualis*, and, while he allowed for a plurality of truths within the different scientific disciplines, Hofmann reserves objective truth to the domain of theology.

In response to this attack, the above-mentioned Owen Günther argued in favor of a commonality between philosophical and theological truth-claims. He made this case with reference to an anthropology where God-given reason and sinful affects existed within humans, where they remain in constant conflict, but the natural state of human beings remains intact.[33] For Günther, natural law served the function of controlling sinful inclinations, but it also explained how philosophy and theology could use different names for the same thing. As we have seen, Martini held a slightly different opinion. Within his metaphysical system, theology should attend to the articles of faith that Scripture reveals. Philosophy, in her turn, could formulate claims about the divine that are equally true but independent from theology. Metaphysical statements about God are true on their own terms. Thus, Martini advocated a pluralization of the truth.[34]

---

*une histoire de la double vérité* (Paris: Vrin, 2008); B. Hägglund, *Theologie und Philosophie bei Luther und in der occamistischen Tradition. Luthers Stellung zur Theorie von der doppelten Wahrheit* (Lund: Gleerup, 1955); S. Streiff, *"Novis linguis loqui". Martin Luthers Disputation über Joh 1,14 „verbum caro factum est" aus dem Jahr 1539* (Göttingen: Vandenhoeck & Ruprecht, 1993); G. White, *Luther as Nominalist: a Study of the Logical Methods Used in Martin Luther's Disputations in the Light of Their Medieval Background* (Helsinki: Luther-Agricola-Society, 1994), 124–180.

33 Günther Owen, *Theologiae et philosophiae mutua amicitia ostensa* (Lemgo: Konrad Grothe, 1600).

34 It is a common feature within the research on the Helmstedt Aristotelianism that it had a secularizing effect on politics, see Dreitzel, *Protestantischer Aristotelismus und absoluter staat*, 192–193; Robert von Friedeburg and Michael J. Seidler, "The Holy Roman Empire of the German Nation," in *European Political Thought 1450–1700. Religion, Law and Philosophy*, eds. H.A. Lloyd, G. Burgess, and S. Hodson (Yale University Press: New Haven, 2007), 156–162; Ian Hunter, *Rival Enlightenments: Civil and Metaphysical Philosophy in Early Modern Germany* (Cambridge: Cambridge University Press, 2001), 68; 77–81. We might here note about the *De jure majestatis* that this book is not a closed system that excludes references, arguments, and topics, because they belong to the religious domain, cf. Brett, *Changes of State*, 65. Another student of Martini's, Georg Calixt (1586–1656), explicitly entertained supra-confessional dreams, and he outlined a program for The Faculty of Theology in Helmstedt that he anchored in Melanchthonian humanism, see Johannes Wallmann, "Zwischen Reformation und Humanismus: Eigenart und Wirkung Helmsteder Theologie unter besonderer Berücksichtigung Georg Calixtus," *Zeitschrift für Theologie und Kirche* 74 (1977), 344–370. It would obviously be wrong to interpret Calixt's

## 3 Natural Law and Governance

Jurists during the Middle Ages imposed certain limitations upon the government of state and church. Natural law offered a vocabulary to deliberate these limitations. The aim of such deliberation was to secure that government within the political and ecclesiastical domains was not simply subject to the whims of whoever was appointed ruler. A theory of natural law afforded rules with a foundation that was unchangeable.[35] In the early modern period, Jean Bodin (1530–1596) became what Daniel Lee calls "perhaps the most important and technically sophisticated early modern theorist of popular sovereignty."[36] Bodin posited that *majestas* endowed the prince with the power to change, abrogate, or derogate positive laws: sovereignty entailed a type of absolutism where rulers were not bound by the laws they themselves made, or by the laws their predecessors had made. However, there was an important exception. The ruler was not exempt from past laws if those laws involved an oath. A small constitutionalist idea seems to complicate the picture of Bodin as a theorist of absolute monarchy. Sovereignty was bound by oaths, and in broader terms by the binding force of contracts, because divine law and natural law constrained the *imperium* of the ruler.

Arnisaeus' approach to the theory of natural law is clearly indebted to Bodin, although it also involves important innovations. While he maintained that the aim of the republic was the glory of God, Arnisaeus stressed that politics must be distinguished from theology. Theology determined true or false religion and, as such, it deliberated over how believers can go to heaven. Furthermore, the republic is charged by Arnisaeus to care for the church, but it has no role in securing piety. Paradoxically, the aim of politics can be defined with biblical reference: politics, as distinct from theology, exists so that "we may lead a quiet and peaceful life in all godliness and dignity" (1 Tim 2,2). Its

ideas about the science of theology as secular, but we might view his 'natural' theology as part of a process of secularization.

35 Dieter Wyduckel, *Princeps Legibus Solutus. Eine Untersuchung zur frühmodernen Rechts- und Staatslehre* (Berlin: Duncker & Humblot, 1979); Kenneth Pennington, *The Prince and the Law, 1200–1600. Sovereignty and Rights in the Western Legal Tradition* (Berkeley: University of California Press, 1993), 278–279.

36 Daniel Lee, *Popular Sovereignty in Early Modern Constitutional Thought* (Oxford: Oxford University Press, 2012), 187–188. See also for a detailed examination of the debate on the medieval roots of Bodin's thought, Merio Scattola, "Diritto medioevale e scienza politica moderna nella dottrina della sovranità di Jean Bodin," *Jus commune* 26 (1999), 165–209.

aim is to secure, with reference to Aristotle, the common good.[37] We might here recall how Bodin repeatedly criticized Aristotle for entertaining an exclusive concept of citizenship. Instead, the pursuit of the common good should take every free member of society into account, and Bodin's idea of *majestas* rests on the ideal of establishing mutual obligations between sovereign and citizen.[38] This ideal seemed too ambitious for Arnisaeus. He defines *majestas* as the highest, most absolute and perpetual mode of power that can be ascribed to a juridical person.[39] From this perspective, sovereignty is subordinated only to God: nothing can be recognized as beyond the power of the sovereign except for the divine.[40]

This exception does not signify that God's glory can be defined by politics or should guide its enterprise: the aim of society and the reason behind its organization are questions that should be answered politically. Therefore, divine law contains eternal precepts that are partially impressed on human hearts during creation and partially expressed through sacred revelation. We can recognize the influence of Martini: these precepts constitute *articuli mixti* and presuppose the rational structures of the human mind that do not change over time but remain the same.[41] Importantly, Arnisaeus makes no references to biblical passages that could support this understanding. We might have expected the Melanchthonian division between the two tables, but, when discussing issues of natural law, Arnisaeus seems to have been more concerned with the obvious fact that divine law refers to divine power. For this reason, precepts can be altered by neither popes, emperors, nor princes.

The almost formal structure of divine law in Arnisaeus becomes clear, if we compare his understanding to the work of Lutheran theologians like Christian Matthiae (1584–1655), who received his doctorate at Giessen and then became professor of theology at Altdorf. For Matthiae, the notion of *majestas* connects to a divine and a societal aim. First, *majestas* is ascribed to a person so that the church can be protected: this divine aim is to secure the propagation of true religion. Second, *majestas* serves the end of conserving morality and protecting civil life from deteriorating into complete sinfulness.[42] Like Melanchthon,

37 Henning Arnisaeus, *De republica seu relectionis politicae libri II* (Frankfurt am Main: Johann Thieme, 1615), 54–55.

38 Anna Becker, *Gendering the Renaissance Commonwealth* (Cambridge: Cambridge University Press, 2020), 168–174.

39 Arnisaeus, *De jure majestatis*, 12–13.

40 Arnisaeus, *De jure majestatis*, 43.

41 Arnisaeus, *De jure majestatis*, 263.

42 Christian Matthiae, *Systema politicum in tres libros distributum* (Gießen: Kaspar Chemlius, 1618), 303.

Matthiae presents the magistrate as the guardian of both tables.[43] This Lutheran commonplace is nowhere to be found in Arnisaeus's works. However, we need to stress that Arnisaeus, despite his minimalistic approach to divine law, insists that *potestas* is granted by God, and he refers to 1 Sam 8 as the biblical commonplace for this picture of political power.[44]

Accordingly, the prince is responsible only in front of God, and Arnisaeus cites Gratian's *De poenitentia* (*Totam*, D 3 c 24 de poen.), where princes are held accountable for their sins only before God. Moreover he extends *Aliorum* (C. 9 q.3 c.14) that described the pope as responsible to God alone; this description holds true for the prince.[45] By this extension, the prince becomes bound by the *honestum*, that is, a moral framework centered on compliance with the virtues and distinguishable from civil law, because the latter does not punish all forms of illicit behavior; civil law tolerates certain vices that a prince, however, cannot commit. This commitment to virtuous behavior distinguishes kings from tyrants. The latter does not comply with the *honestum* but instead abused their power. This line of thought, which connected political governance to the virtues, had also been pursued by Caselius,[46] and this seems to have been the clear source of inspiration for Arnisaeus.

As we have seen, divine law remains central to Arnisaeus's construction, because it offers him with a template for reflecting on the origins of political authority. However, this type of law supplies him with no rules for governance.[47] The consequence of this framework for governance is that the ruler becomes entirely unbound by positive laws.[48] Within this framework, Arni-

43 Matthiae, *Systema politicum*, 310–311

44 Arnisaeus, *De jure majestatis*, 214–223, cf. Annette Weber-Möckl, *"Das Recht des Königs, der über euch herrschen soll." Studien zu 1 Sam 8, 11ff. in der Literatur der frühen Neuzeit* (Duncker & Humblot: Berlin, 1986).

45 Arnisaeus, *De jure majestatis*, 52. For Gratian's De poenitentia see Atria A. Larson, ed., *Gratian's Tractatus de Penitentia* (Catholic University of America Press: Washington, 2016), 174–175. This approach is an adaptation of Bodin's position, see Wyduckel, *Princeps Legibus*, 152–155.

46 Merio Scattola, *Dalla virtù alla scienza. La Fondazione e la trasformazione della disciplina politica in età moderna* (Franco Angeli: Milano, 2003), 203–210.

47 Arnisaeus, *De jure majestatis*, 69–70. Here, Arnisaeus refers us to the Lutheran theologian Johannes Brenz (1499–1570), who also insisted that the exercise of *potestas* was divinely ordained, and princely violations of divine law, natural law, or *jus gentium* should therefore constitute a sin and invoke God's vengeance. From Brenz, Arnisaeus relays his readers with examples of such vengeance, cf. Johannes Brenz, *Opera omnia*, 8 vols. (Tübingen: Georg Gruppenbach, 1576–1590) vol. 2 (1576), 366–375.

48 Arnisaeus, *De jure majestatis*, 53. Arnisaeus equates *jus gentium* with natural law, see Dreizel, *Protestantischer Aristotelismus*, 202–203.

saeus nevertheless speaks of natural law as a divine spark in the human mind. Such a claim about the human mind as divine implies that human nature has remained somewhat intact after the Fall. This relative intactness allows human beings to make rudimentary distinctions between good and evil. Again, Arnisaeus separates theological reasoning from philosophical anthropology. Referring to the *locus classicus* where Paul states that natural law is imprinted in the human heart (Rom 2,15), Arnisaeus interprets this biblical statement with reference to Cicero and the idea that human nature possesses a *ratio* that commands what is to be done and what must be avoided.[49] In this sense, natural law "*nihil aliud est, quam recta ratio et fundamentum virtutum*,"[50] and this *ratio* hinges upon a picture of human nature according to which its *intellectus* in its natural state is a *potentia pura*. Put differently, this faculty of the mind is like a surface upon which nothing has been imprinted; it is like a *tabula rasa* that can receive everything. Arnisaeus further remarks that no complete propositions are ingrained in the mind in its natural state.[51] Thus, the knowing capability is in a state of absolute potentiality with respect to objects of knowledge. Following Aristotle's account in the opening chapter of the third book in *De Anima*,[52] which deals with the animal mind and the transformation of raw sense data into perception, Arnisaeus describes how the eyes have a *vis* that allows sight to see colors and to distinguish between them. The four remaining senses accomplish similar tasks in the animal mind, and such distinct perceptions are linked together and categorized into a "common perception." Arnisaeus extends this natural faculty in the animal mind to a human capability of discerning good from evil or honest from shameful. From this natural lawfulness there is not dispensation: this capability constitutes natural law in all people; this is the *recta ratio* and the immutable condition of sociability.[53] Here, natural law does not account for the emergence of the state. It is rather a capability to make a certain type of judgements that is limited to rational beings, although Arnisaeus draws an analogy to the animal mind. The second table of the decalogue becomes the *tabula rasa* of the human mind.

Let us briefly return to the above-mentioned Matthiae, who understands the *majestas* as unconstrained by divine law, natural law, the *leges fundamentales*, and even civil laws. Adopting the distinction between *vis directiva* and

49 Arnisaeus, *De jure majestatis*, 76.
50 Arnisaeus, *De jure majestatis*, 280.
51 Arnisaeus, *De jure majestatis*, 279.
52 Aristotle, *De Anima* (Indianapolis: Hackett Publishing Company, 2017), Book III/1, 45–46.
53 Arnisaeus, *De jure majestatis*, 279.

*vis coactiva* from Aquinas,[54] Matthiae can posit about the prince that he should be guided by the laws in his political exercise of *potestas*. However, he cannot be compelled to abide by them. Civil law, in Matthiae, reflects natural law and as such it has a kind of directive force that should guide how society is governed.[55] Like Melanchthon, Matthiae views civil law as a specification of circumstances not described in the general precepts that constitute natural law.[56] Many of the Spanish scholastics proposed a similar interpretation, while others blurred the lines between the directive force and the coercive force of civil laws. This holds true for Juan de Mariana (1536–1624) and Francisco Suárez (1548–1617), who ascribed the directive quality of civil laws with a coercive quality: the ruler should act in such way that he appears to be guided by the laws; such appearances were a matter of political prudence and princely instruction.[57] In the works of the German Jesuit Adam Contzen (1571–1635), we find another version of this conflation. According to Contzen, the ruler is bound by the positive laws that he himself authors: God is the true author of princely power, and therefore the prince, as his instrument, must be guided by laws that ensure the common good of the republic.[58] Natural law affords civil laws with a coercive force that also binds the prince.[59] Like the laws, the prince himself becomes an instrument for securing that his subjects live virtuous lives.[60] Princes, like doctors, has to care for their people and prevent them from sinning.[61]

Arnisaeus rejects this picture of a coercive force. Instead, he draws a distinction between virtues and laws. Referring to Seneca, Cicero, and Plato, a virtue is defined as something that exhorts us to follow what is *honestum*, while laws are purely coercive. The coercive force takes you by the hand and guides you along, while virtues require discursive deliberation: convincing is something fundamentally different from coercion, because it involves the *intellectus*. Thus, Arnisaeus explicitly rejects the opinions of Gabriel Vásquez (1549–1604) and Diego de Covarrubias y Leyva (1512–1577), according to whom

54 ST 1a 2ae, QU 96, 5.

55 Matthiae, *Systema politicum*, 317–319

56 Matthiae, *Systema politicum*, 363.

57 See Harald E. Braun, *Juan de Mariana and Early Modern Spanish Political Thought* (Aldershot: Ashgate, 2007). For a recent account of the Spanish Scholastics' thought, see the essays included in Harald E. Braun, Erik De Bom, and Paolo Astorri, eds., *A Companion to the Spanish Scholastics* (Leiden: Brill, 2022).

58 Adam Contzen, *Politicorum libri decem* (Cologne: Balthasar Lipp, 1621), 305.

59 Contzen, *Politicorum libri decem*, 305.

60 Contzen, *Politicorum libri decem*, 280.

61 Contzen, *Politicorum libri decem*, 281.

the prince was only bound by the *vis directiva* and not by the *vis coactiva*.[62] He also positions himself against the Monarchomachs, who viewed any exception from the laws as a gateway to tyrannicide.[63] Between these alternatives, Arnisaeus distinguished between the legislator or magistrate, who are *privati*, and the *majestas*, who is not. The magistrates can issue laws, but the force of the law emerges with the *majestas*.[64] Importantly, the prince remains obliged by natural law understood as the *recta ratio*, and in this sense natural law can impose certain limits. Natural law as an immutable capacity in the human mind cannot offer specific guidelines for how society is to be governed. However, this governance must fit with the *ratio* that is natural to human beings. The coercive force of laws does not refer to laws that are natural, but to the *honestum* that all humans, naturally, have the capacity to understand and to deliberate about.[65]

## 4 Conclusion

In his *Regales disputationes*, the reformed Italian jurist Alberico Gentili (1552–1608) claimed that structures of political governance should be less restrictive than those imagined by Arnisaeus. According to Gentili, *potestas* should be ordinary – its exercise should be subject to law – and not extraordinary, that is, an exercise completely unbound by law.[66] As we have argued above, for Arnisaeus *potestas* was not entirely extraordinary. Natural law circumscribes the *majestas*, and the *recta ratio* offers limits to the exercise of *potestas*. These limitations manifest themselves in civic life and target marriage, wills, property, and currency. Arnisaeus observes that it is unnatural, if the ruler forces someone to marry.[67] Similarly, it goes against nature to revoke the last will of a subject.[68] A prince cannot breach contracts, since these are based on *ius gentium* that coincides with natural law.[69] Personal property cannot be appropri-

62 Arnisaeus, *De jure majestatis*, 54.

63 For a recent studies of the Monarchomachs, see David P. Henreckson, *The Immortal Commonwealth. Covenant, Community, and Political Resistance in Early Reformed Thought* (Cambridge: Cambridge University Press, 2019); Sarah Mortimer, *Reformation, Resistance and Reason of State (1517–1625)* (Oxford: Oxford University Press, 2021).

64 Arnisaeus, *De jure majestatis*, 56.

65 Arnisaeus, *De jure majestatis*, 59.

66 Alberico Gentili, *Regales disputationes tres* (London: W. Antonius, 1605), 10–1.

67 Arnisaeus, *De jure majestatis*, 453–455.

68 Arnisaeus, *De jure majestatis*, 282–283.

69 Arnisaeus, *De jure majestatis*, 283–284.

ated by rulers, because such an appropriation goes against natural law and *jus gentium*,[70] unless the prince, e.g. in times of war, is acting for the common good.[71] Although the ruler has the power to change currency, such a change conflicts with natural law, if it damages the people living within the commonwealth.[72]

In these instances of civic life, natural-law theory formulates limits for the exercise of *potestas*. It expresses, negatively, what the ruler cannot do, while it presupposes a universal capacity to infer the value of something and to contextualize this inference with regard to the common good. What natural law does not supply is a coercive force that can bind the ruler to follow civil laws. It also cannot support the right of resistance.[73] Unlike many of his contemporaries, Arnisaeus understood *majestas* as completely removed from the arena of political interests and deliberations. The source of this interpretation is philosophical. Indeed, Arnisaeus can elsewhere speak of *potestas* as form imposed upon matter, that is, a heap of people assembled in cities and sharing a basic understanding of the common good.[74] For the emergence of a genuine structure of political governance – a *res publica* – something more is required, and

---

70 Arnisaeus, *De jure majestatis*, 455.

71 Arnisaeus, *De jure majestatis*, 477–478.

72 Arnisaeus, *De jure majestatis*, 432–433. In Arnisaeus, there are certain exceptions to such natural limits. Following a scholastic paradigm, hunting is presented as a natural *dominium* but also as a shared *dominium*. God has created all humans as ruling over all animals, and the hunting of animals therefore belongs to *ius gentium*, where the animal constitutes *res nullius*: they do not belong to anybody but to everybody. Hence, the prince can impose limits or entirely forbid the right to hunt without compromising the right to property and thereby coming into conflict with natural law; see Arnisaeus, *De jure majestatis*, 525–527. Another exception is slavery. Arnisaeus observes that this institution clearly conflicts with human nature but nevertheless it is regulated by *ius gentium*, see Arnisaeus, *De republica*, 61. His solution to this issue involves a Thomist layering of natural law, see Dreitzel, *Protestantischer Aristotelismus und absoluter Staat*, 198.

73 On this vast topic, see Merio Scattola, "Controversia de vi in principem: Vertrag, Tyrannis und Widerstand in der Auseinandersetzung zwischen Johannes Althusius und Henning Arnisaeus," in *Wissen, Gewissen und Wissenschaft im Widerstandsrecht* (*16.–18. Jh.*), ed. Angela De Benedictis and Karl Heinz Lingens (Frankfurt am Main: Klostermann, 2003), 175–249. On Lutheran hesitation towards Arnisaeus's understanding of resistance theory, see Paolo Astorri and Lars Cyril Nørgaard, "Publicus–Privatus. The Divine Foundations of Authority in Dietrich Reinking," *Journal of Early Modern Christianity* 9 (2022/1), 111–117.

74 Arnisaeus, *Doctrina politica*, I, VI, 125. Following a basic Aristotelian suggestion in the *Metaphysics*, Arnisaeus posits that the commonwealth relates to the city as a whole (ὅλον / το πᾶν) relates to a heap of things (σωρός): the first contains something more than its elements (στοιχεῖα) or its matter (ὕλη); a whole has a form (εἶδος), and this component, missing in heaps of things, accounts for why unity exists in wholes; see H. Arnisaeus, *Epitome Metaphysices*, 91-119. On Aristotelian mereology, see also H. Arnisaeus, *Disputa-*

this excessive feature is the *majestas*. Legislators and magistrates enforce laws but they cannot secure the force of laws. As such, they are *privati* and remain on the level of negotiating and mediating between different interests. Arnisaeus uses a mélange of sources to argue that the *majestas* remains absolved from the political domain itself. These sources include biblical passages such as 1 Sam 8, but the divine foundation of political authority remains purely theoretical. Divine law offers no precepts on how to govern. Likewise, natural law is tied to a minimal account of the intellectual capability that characterizes human beings: it cannot offer us with anything more than the coordinates of civic life. This minimal account might leave us wanting more or it might make us think of Hugo Grotius (1583–1645) and his strong separation of natural law from any natural state.

## Acknowledgement

This research has been funded by the Danish National Research Foundation (DNRF138). The authors contributed equally to the writing of this article.

---

*tionum metaphysicarum tertia de uno continens doctrinam unius et multi, totius et partium* (Frankfurt an der Oder: Hartmann, 1605).

CHAPTER 7

# Edward Coke's Ciceronian Common Law

*Rosalind Acland*

## 1 Introduction

Sir Edward Coke (1552–1634) is arguably the single most influential figure of seventeenth century English common law. His writings have been considered as having "had more influence upon the law than those of any other law writer – certainly in England – who ever lived".[1] He has been described as the embodiment of the 'common law mind'.[2] However, he has also been described as 'insular',[3] in the sense of having his "back [...] ever turned against learning outside the common law".[4] In this paper, I propose that far from being 'insular', Coke was directly influenced in his conception of law by classical sources, and in particular by the works of the ancient Roman statesman, advocate, and orator Marcus Tullius Cicero. I argue that Coke's jurisprudence is distinctly (although of course not solely) Ciceronian,[5] and that Coke's Ciceronian natural law jurisprudence directly influenced the evolution of seventeenth century English common law through his seminal judgments in *Calvin's Case* and *Bonham's Case*. Although several scholars have noted that certain aspects of Coke's definition of law are drawn from Cicero,[6] this has not been analysed in detail, and the implications of this for Coke's jurisprudence, and for early modern English common law jurisprudence more widely, have not been examined.

1 John Marshall Gest, "The Writings of Sir Edward Coke," *Yale Law Journal* 18, no. 7 (1908): 505.

2 J.G.A. Pocock, *The Ancient Constitution and the Feudal Law: A Study of English Historical Thought in the Seventeenth Century: A Reissue with a Retrospect* (Cambridge: Cambridge University Press, 1987), 56.

3 Pocock, 56.

4 W.O. Hassall, ed., *A Catalogue of the Library of Sir Edward Coke*, Yale Law Library Publications; No. 12 (New Haven, Conn; London: Yale University Press; Oxford University Press, 1950), iv, discussing critics of Coke.

5 Coke's writing also displays influences from Aristotle, Aquinas and St German, for example.

6 See, e.g., Allen D. Boyer, "Sir Edward Coke, Ciceronianus: Classical Rhetoric and the Common Law Tradition," *International Journal for the Semiotics of Law* 10, no. 1 (1 February 1997): 3–36; David Chan Smith, *Sir Edward Coke and the Reformation of the Laws: Religion, Politics and Jurisprudence, 1578–1616*, Cambridge Studies in English Legal History (Cambridge, United Kingdom: Cambridge University Press, 2014).

 | DOI:10.1163/9789004748712_009

In Section 2 of this paper, I examine Coke's writing and propose that significant aspects of his theory of law are derived from several of Cicero's works. I analyse these aspects of Coke's legal theory and their Ciceronian origins. In Section 3, I examine Coke's understanding and use of natural law principles in his theoretical and judicial writing, and undertake studies of his judgments in *Calvin's Case* and *Bonham's Case*. I argue that this use, which introduced natural law principles as authority for novel issues of law, is in part a direct consequence of Cicero's influence.[7]

## 2 A Ciceronian Jurisprudence

### 2.1 *The Common Law as the Artificial Perfection of Reason of Learned Men*

Perhaps the most well-known articulation of Coke's conception of law is the following, written in the First Volume of his *Institutes* and published in 1628. It is useful to extract this in full:[8]

> *Nihil quod est contra rationem est licitum.* For reason is the life of the Law, nay the common Law it selfe is nothing else but reason, which is to be understood of an artificiall perfection of reason, gotten by long study, observation, and experience, and not of every man's naturall reason, for, *Nemo nascitur artifex.* This legall reason, *est summa ratio.* And therefore if all the reason that is dispersed into so many severall heads were united into one, yet could he not make such a law as the Law of England is, because by many succession of ages it hath beene fined and refined by an infinite number of grave and learned men, and by long experience growne to such a perfection, for the gouvernment of this Realme, as the old rule may be justly verified of it, *Neminem oportet esse sapientiorem legibus*: No man (out of his owne private reason) ought to be wiser than the Law, which is the perfection of reason.

Coke here refers to law as being the 'artificial perfection of reason'. He also refers to the law as being the culmination of the reasoning of generations of learned lawmen, refined over many years. The notion of the law as reason is an ancient concept central to a number of jurisprudential traditions. I am not suggesting that Coke's definition of law simply as 'reason' originates from Cic-

7 Translations are my own unless otherwise noted.
8 Co. Litt. 97 b.

ero. Rather, in this section, I propose that Coke's notions of the perfection and artificiality of the law's reason, and the central place of wise and learned lawmen in its practice, are Ciceronian. I examine each of these three ideas separately, and suggest that Coke adapted and expanded them for the purposes of not only expounding his belief in the unparalleled excellence of the common law, but also to guard against its corruption, and the ensuing undesirable uncertainty and conflict, by those he considered unworthy to construe it and apply its principles.

### 2.1.1 Law as the Perfection of Reason Which Commands and Prohibits

As we have seen in the extract of the *Institutes* above, Coke describes law as the "perfection of reason."[9] He often links law as the perfection of reason with its functions of commanding right action and prohibiting the contrary. Coke's most famous formulation of this definition is also found in the First Volume of his *Institutes*, as follows: "*Lex est ratio summa, quae iubet quae sunt utilia & necessaria, & contraria prohibet*; and arguments drawne from hence are forcible in Law."[10]

In the early nineteenth century work *A Systematic Arrangement of Lord Coke's First Institute on the Laws of England*, Thomas extracts this formulation of Coke's, and adds the following footnote:[11]

> Of the several definitions of law, which have been given by various writers, it has been justly observed, that this definition by Lord Coke is one of the most successful. Cicero defines law thus: *Lex est justorum, injustorumque distinctio, quiddam aeternum in mente Dei existent; recta ratio summi Jovis* – Cicer. de Legibus lib. 1 & 2.

Thomas then lists a number of similar definitions from Aristotle, Gerson, Grotius, Sanderson, Pufendorf, Hooker, Suarez, *Bracton*, and Aquinas.[12] Following

9 Coke "adhered firmly to the Ciceronian interpretation of law as reason": Paul Raffield, "Contract, Classicism, and the Common-Weal: Coke's Reports and the Foundations of the Modern English Constitution," *Law and Literature* 17, no. 1 (2005): 71.

10 Co. Litt. 319 b, emphasis added. The Latin adjective '*summa*' is more often translated as 'highest' or 'greatest'. I suggest, however, that Coke's English formulation of law as the 'perfection' of reason is his translation of this term. See also Chan Smith, *Sir Edward Coke and the Reformation of the Laws*, 154–155. Lewis and Short's *A Latin Dictionary* lists 'perfection' as a translation of the related noun '*summa*'.

11 J.H. Thomas, ed., *A Systematic Arrangement of Lord Coke's First Institute of the Laws of England*, vol. 1 (S. Brooke, 1818), 15–16.

12 This is the order in which Thomas lists these authors.

these, he states: "But the negative part is omitted by all these writers, except the two last."[13] By "the negative part", Thomas is referring to the law's prohibition of contrary actions. Two points should be noted here. Firstly, the Ciceronian quote to which Thomas refers is not the correct source of Coke's definition, which is, in fact, a close paraphrasing of Cicero's statement in *De Legibus* that "*lex est ratio summa insita in natura, quae iubet ea, quae facienda sunt, prohibetque contraria.*"[14] Secondly, of 'the two last' definitions quoted by Thomas, which do include the 'negative' aspect (those of *Bracton* and Aquinas), that attributed to *Bracton* ("*Lex est sanctio justa jubens honesta, et prohibens contraria*")[15] most closely approximates Coke's.

*Bracton's* precise formulation is taken directly from the *Summa Institutionum* of the twelfth to thirteenth century civilian glossator Azo, which work is itself a commentary on the sixth century *Institutes* of the Roman Emperor Justinian. Azo is here discussing the wide and narrow definitions of '*lex*' as found in Justinian's *Institutes*. In relation to its narrower definition, he states that *lex "specialiter significat sanctionem iustam, iubentem honesta, prohibentem contraria."*[16] *Bracton* copies this verbatim.[17]

Fortescue then adopts this formulation, modifying the case of the Latin to the nominative and replacing '*iusta*' with '*sancta*', in ch. III of his *De Laudibus Legum Angliae*. He states: "*Lex est sanctio sancta iubens honesta et prohibens contraria.*"[18] Coke employs Azo and *Bracton's* '*iusta*', but retains Fortescue's use of the nominative case, in the Second Volume of his *Institutes*, in the context of commenting on the statute *De Asportatis Religiosorum*. He states:

---

13 Thomas, *A Systematic Arrangement of Lord Coke's First Institute of the Laws of England*, 16.

14 Cicero, *On the Laws*, trans. Clinton W. Keyes. Loeb Classical Library 213 (Cambridge, MA: Harvard University Press, 1928); 1.18. John Underwood Lewis, "Sir Edward Coke (1552–1688): His Theory of Artificial Reason as a Context for Modern Basic Legal Theory," *Law Quarterly Review* 84, no. 3 (1968): 334, states that Coke's definition here 'parallels' those set down by these authors on the basis of Thomas' commentary. This in my view does not go far enough. Chan Smith has identified that Coke's definition originates in this statement of Cicero's: Chan Smith, *Sir Edward Coke and the Reformation of the Laws*, 154–155.

15 Thomas, *A Systematic Arrangement of Lord Coke's First Institute of the Laws of England*, 16.

16 Azo's commentary on Justinian's *Institutes* 1.1, in Frederic William Maitland, ed., *Select Passages from the Works of Bracton and Azo*, Publications of the Selden Society 8 (London: Quaritch, 1895), 24.

17 *Bracton*, 1.3.1, in Maitland, *Select Passages from the Works of Bracton and Azo*, 19.

18 John Fortescue, *De Laudibus Legum Anglie*, ed. S.B. Chrimes. Cambridge Studies in English Legal History (Cambridge: Cambridge University Press, 1949), ch. III, 6, 8.

"Bracton saith, that *Lex est sanctio justa, jubens honesta, & prohibens contraria.*"[19] A marginal note attributes this to 'Bract.lib.I.cap.' As may be seen above, this is the formulation that Thomas also attributes directly to *Bracton*. It should be observed that Coke expressly acknowledges the source of this definition of law, in contrast to the Ciceronian definition which he employs in the First Volume of his *Institutes*, extracted above. I suggest that this is a further indication of the importance he attached to Cicero's own formulations: while he is content to attribute definitions of law to their English sources in his theoretical works, he appears to subsume Cicero's definition into his own legal theory entirely.

Further, on the title page of the first (and subsequent) edition of the First Volume of Coke's *Reports*, published in 1600, is the following quote: "*Lex est certa ratio e mente divina manans, quae recta suadet, prohibetque contraria.*" Coke attributes this expressly to Cicero. I have been unable to find the direct source of this quote as formulated by Coke in Cicero's works.[20] It is possible that he synthesised the quote from multiple Ciceronian sources to create a pithier articulation of the relevant concepts. As we shall see, it appears that he did this on more than one occasion. In this instance, it is possible that he extracted and combined aspects of Cicero's definitions of law from his *11th Philippic*, and parts of *De Legibus*. In the former work, Cicero states: "*Est enim lex nihil aliud nisi recta et*[*iam*] *a numine deorum tracta ratio, imperans honesta, prohibens contraria.*"[21] Cicero states in the latter work: "*est enim unum ius, quo devincta est hominum societas, et quod lex constituit una; quae lex est recta ratio imperandi atque prohibendi.*"[22] He also states: "*neque enim esse mens divina sine ratione potest, nec ratio divina non hanc vim in rectis pravisque sanciendis habet.*"[23] Coke's quote appears to be an amalgamation and condensation of these statements. The placement of this quote alone on the title page of Coke's first published work goes some way towards indicating the impor-

19 Co. Inst. 2, 588.

20 It does not appear to be included in contemporary compilations of ancient sources either, such as the *Polyanthea Nova*. Raffield notes that Dugdale cites Coke's quoting of Cicero here, but does not provide any information on the quote's origin: Raffield, "Contract, Classicism, and the Common-Weal," 71, citing William Dugdale, *Origines Juridiciales* (London: Printed by F. and T. Warren for the author, 1666).

21 Cicero, "Philippic 11," in *Philippics 7–14*, ed. and trans. D.R. Shackleton Bailey, rev. John T. Ramsey, Gesine Manuwald. Loeb Classical Library 507 (Cambridge, MA: Harvard University Press, 2010), 28.

22 Cicero, *On the Laws*, I.42.

23 *Ibidem*, II.10.

tance he attached to Cicero's thought, and the centrality of this definition of law to Coke's own jurisprudence.[24]

There are also several external materials which link this aspect of Coke's conception of law explicitly to Cicero. For example, Moore's report of the case *Davenant v Hurdis* attributes the following statement to Coke (who, as Attorney General in 1599, was acting for the complainant): "*Tully escria en ses offices Natura, vi rationis, hominem conciliat homini ad vitae societatem, & daver reward & davoider punishment est vis rationis naturalis.*"[25]

The examples in this section demonstrate that Coke was thoroughly familiar with Cicero's writings, and that he was aware of, and consciously adopted, the Ciceronian understandings of law as 'the perfection of reason' and as a 'just' or 'sacred' sanction commanding right action and prohibiting the contrary.

### 2.1.2 Law as Artificial Reason

Coke's notion of the law as artificial reason has close ties to a long tradition of classical rhetorical principles, understood primarily through Cicero's writings.[26] The study of rhetoric, in Elizabethan England, included not only the oratorical craft, but also reasoning and the composition of legal judgments. Ciceronian rhetoric overlapped methodologically with logic, and a study of Coke's writing reveals "a lawyer steeped in such Ciceronian rhetoric."[27] He expressly emphasises the importance of a classical rhetorical education to the student of law in the First Volume of his *Institutes*,[28] and his trial rhetoric was on occasion taken directly from Cicero.[29]

This ancient rhetorical tradition emphasised a distinction between the natural and the artificial, particularly in the areas of logic and memory. I

24 See also Coke's Preface in Edward Coke, *Le quart part des reportes del Edward Coke* (London: In ædibus Thomæ Wight, 1604), unpaginated.

25 (1599) 72 Eng. Rep. 769, 774; Moore 576, 584.

26 See Alessandro Giuliani, "The Influence of Rhetoric on the Law of Evidence and Pleading," *Juridical Review* 7 (1962): 216–251; R.J. Schoeck, "Rhetoric and Law in Sixteenth-Century England," *Studies in Philology* 50, no. 2 (1953): 110–127; J.W. Tubbs, *The Common Law Mind: Medieval and Early Modern Conceptions* (Baltimore, Md.: Johns Hopkins University Press, 2000); Ian Williams, "English Legal Reasoning and Legal Culture, c.1528–c.1642" (Ph.D. thesis, University of Cambridge, 2008). Glenn Burgess, *The Politics of the Ancient Constitution: An Introduction to English Political Thought, 1603–1642* (Basingstoke: Macmillan, 1992), 42 appears to assume that Coke and Dodderidge developed this notion spontaneously.

27 Boyer, "Sir Edward Coke, Ciceronianus," 4.

28 Co. Litt. 235 b.

29 Boyer, "Sir Edward Coke, Ciceronianus," 9.

suggest that Coke has transposed this distinction onto the reason of the law, conceiving of its artificial reason as an independent entity created from the combined knowledge of generations of learned men, which must be brought to one's natural reason and, over many years of study, received and adopted as one's own. Only then is the practitioner able to correctly construe and apply the law.[30]

It is useful to further sub-divide this aspect of Coke's conception of law into two separate notions: law as an independent entity composed of 'right reason'; and the artificiality of this legal reason. Both of these ideas may be linked closely to Cicero. Regarding the former, Cicero refers to humans' possession of 'right reason' (*recta ratio*) as proof of humanity's possession of law (which is itself 'right reason' commanding and prohibiting) in several places in *De Legibus*. For example, he states:[31]

> Because nothing is better than reason and this is both in man and in god, the principal trait shared by man with god is the fellowship of reason; while reason is common among them, among the same furthermore right reason is common; since this right reason is law, through law likewise we must suppose that men are associated with the gods.

Coke also describes law as possessing its own 'right reason' on several occasions. For example:[32]

> The reason of the Law is the life of the law, for though a man can tell the law, yet if he know not the reason thereof, he shall soone forget his superficiall knowledge: but when hee findeth the right reason of the law, and so bringeth it to his natural reason, that he comprehendeth it as his own, this will not onely serve him for the understanding of that particular case, but of many other. For *Cognitio legis est copulata & complicata*: And this knowledge will long remaine with him.

30 Chan Smith, *Sir Edward Coke and the Reformation of the Laws*, 154–155, conceptualises this similarly. See also Charles M. Gray, "Reason, Authority and Imagination in the Jurisprudence of Edward Coke," in *Culture and Politics from Puritanism to the Enlightenment*, ed. Perez Zagorin, Publications from the Clark Library Professorship, UCLA 5 (Berkeley: University of California Press, 1980), 31–32.

31 Cicero, *On the Laws*, 1.23. The Latin is: "*quoniam nihil est ratione melius eaque est et in homine et in deo, prima homini cum deo rationis societas; inter quos autem ratio, inter eosdem etiam recta ratio communis est; quae cum sit lex, lege quoque consociati homines cum dis putandi sumus.*" See also *ibidem*, 1.33.

32 Co. Litt. 183 b. See also Co. Litt. 394 b.

This understanding of the law's right reason as something independent and obtainable is also seen in Coke's Latin, although, interestingly, not in his English, formulation of a statement in the Preface to his First Volume of *Reports*. He justifies the publication of his *Reports* by emphasising the importance of accurate reporting to the correct understanding and application of the law. He states that other law reports often record the reasoning of cases inaccurately. In the English, he simply asserts that in these reports, "most commonly the right reason and rule of the Judges [is] utterly mistaken."[33] However, in the Latin, he portrays this 'right reason' as an entity which 'moves' the judges: "*recta vero ratio & regula quae movebat Iudices semper aut penitus neglecta aut non animadversa fuerit.*"[34] The Prefaces in each first edition of Coke's *Reports* appeared in both Latin and English. As far as I have been able to discover, it is not known as a certainty whether Coke composed his Prefaces in both languages, or just one or the other. Given his mastery of each, and his professed hope that as many people as possible would read and absorb the information in his *Reports*,[35] it is, in my view, likely that he wrote and supplied the Prefaces in both languages.[36] This, of course, leaves the question of why he would make only the Latin statement so precise. Perhaps he considered that the possessive in the English provided sufficient clarity, or assumed that the more learned of his readers would refer to the Latin in any event. However, although the English presents the law's reason as something belonging to the judges, it does not specify that it is separable from them. The precision of Coke's Latin is therefore particularly useful in analysing his theory in this regard.

It is likely that the latter idea, of law as artificial reason, originates in the classical rhetorical distinction between the natural and the artificial.[37] The source of the term '*ratio artificialis*' would appear to be a passage in the *Insti-*

33 Coke's Preface in Edward Coke, *Les reports de Edvvard Coke* (London: In ædibus Thomæ Wight, 1600), unpaginated.

34 *Ibidem*, unpaginated.

35 See, e.g., *ibidem*, unpaginated.

36 Baker has noted that no trace appears to remain of the manuscript versions of Coke's prefaces: J.H. Baker, "Coke's Note-Books and the Sources of His Reports," *The Cambridge Law Journal* 30, no. 1 (1972): 74. Garnett has posited that Coke wrote the English first, and then translated it into Latin, citing Baker's inference of this on the basis of the Prefaces' 'pithiness': George Garnett, "The Ould Fields: Law and History in the Prefaces to Sir Edward Coke's Reports," *Journal of Legal History* 34, no. 3 (2013): 247, citing J.H. Baker, "The Three Languages of the Common Law," in *Collected Papers on English Legal History*, ed. John Baker, vol. 2 (Cambridge: Cambridge University Press, 2013), 515–536.

37 See Gerald J. Postema, "Classical Common Law Jurisprudence (Part II)," *Oxford University Commonwealth Law Journal* 3, no. 1 (2003): 10–11; J.W. Tubbs, "Custom, Time and

*tutio Oratoria* of the Ancient Roman rhetorician Quintilian,[38] and it is used as a technical term of art in the context of a discussion of rhetorical skills, specifically altercation, which is the art of attack and rebuttal in rhetorical argument. The distinction between the natural and the artificial, however, is articulated and explained most clearly and comprehensively by Cicero. In *De Oratore,*[39] Cicero analyses memory as a sub-discipline of classical rhetorical training. Memory was concerned with learning speeches, and was subdivided into natural and artificial.[40] Natural memory was inherent in the mind of an individual and required no training to cultivate, whereas artificial memory "was understood to be neither innate nor involuntary," but was a mnemonic technique composed of a set of rules describing how to effectively memorise specific information.[41] Cicero explains that although nature is the primary source of memory, the function of artificial memory is to strengthen natural memory.[42]

The classical rhetorical notions of natural and artificial memory may be seen in early modern English legal theory. The personal memory of the trained legal practitioner was viewed as distinct from the customary memory of the layman, and a reliable memory was essential to the law student. Discussions of memory were included in contemporary legal treatises, for example, in John Dodderidge's *The English Lawyer*.[43] Chan Smith asserts that "[t]he idea of artificial reason encapsulated Coke's understanding of the problem of reason and its recovery from memory. He related the functioning of artificial reason to the reason of the common law."[44] Coke himself articulates the connection between memory and reason, stating that a particular testator[45]

> was not of sane and perfect memory [...] for by law it is not sufficient that the testator be of memory when he makes his will, to answer familiar and

Reason: Early Seventeenth-Century Conceptions of the Common Law," *History of Political Thought* 19, no. 3 (1998): 394; Tubbs, *The Common Law Mind*, 167.

38 Quintilian, *The Orator's Education, Volume III: Books 6–8*, ed. and trans. Donald A. Russell. Loeb Classical Library 126 (Cambridge, MA: Harvard University Press, 2002), VI.4.4.

39 See Joe Grimwade, "Memory in Roman Oratory: Theory and Practice" (Ph.D. thesis, University of Cambridge, 2021).

40 Cicero, *On the Orator: Books 1–2*, trans. E.W. Sutton and H. Rackham. Loeb Classical Library 348. (Cambridge, MA: Harvard University Press, 1942). See Grimwade, "Memory in Roman Oratory," 11.

41 Grimwade, "Memory in Roman Oratory," 20.

42 Cicero, *On the Orator*, II.356–357. See Grimwade, "Memory in Roman Oratory," 22.

43 See Chan Smith, *Sir Edward Coke and the Reformation of the Laws*, 147.

44 *Ibidem*, 153.

45 Pawlet Marquess of Winchester's Case (1599) 77 Eng. Rep. 287, 288; 6 Co. Rep. 23 a, 23 a. See Chan Smith, *Sir Edward Coke and the Reformation of the Laws*, 147.

> usual questions, but he ought to have a disposing memory, so that he is able to make a disposition of his lands with understanding and reason [...] and that is such a memory which the law calls sane and perfect memory.

A similar distinction between the natural and the artificial is apparent in theories of classical logic. The 'artificial logic' distinguishing rhetoricians' discourse from that of uneducated laymen is 'closely and obviously' related to Coke's artificial reason,[46] the clearest parallel being the belief that training and practice can improve upon innate talent.[47] In my view, Coke has amalgamated a Ciceronian conception of law as 'right reason' able to be cultivated by humanity with the classical rhetorical distinction between the natural (something inherent in humanity) and the artificial (something external which is able to be obtained and developed through learning and experience) to arrive at his understanding of law as artificial reason.

#### 2.1.3 Law as the Reason of Learned Men

Coke states repeatedly that many years of dedicated study and experience are necessary to acquire and retain this perfect and artificial legal reason. For example:[48]

> *Ratio est Radius divini Luminis.* And by reasoning and debating of grave learned men the darknesse of ignorance is expelled, and by the light of legall Reason the Right is discerned, and thereupon Judgment given according to law, which is the perfection of Reason. This is of Littleton here called *legitima ratio*, whereunto no man can attaine but by long studie, often conference, long experience, and continuall observation.

Coke's statements are once again highly reminiscent of Cicero's. For example, Cicero states: "Therefore, just as that divine mind is perfect law, so, when [reason] is perfected in man, [that is Law; truly this perfected reason is] in the mind of the wise man."[49]

---

46 Boyer, "Sir Edward Coke, Ciceronianus," 32.

47 *Ibidem*, 33.

48 Co. Litt. 232 b. See also Edward Coke, "A Treatise of Bail and Mainprize," in *Three Law Tracts*, ed. William Hawkins (London: Printed by his Majesty's law-printer; for J. Worrall, at the Dove, in Bell-Yard, near Lincoln's Inn, 1764), 302.

49 Cicero, *On the Laws*, II.11. The square brackets refer to interpolations of missing Latin text as suggested by Vahlen. See also *ibidem*, I.18; Chan Smith, *Sir Edward Coke and the Reformation of the Laws*, 154.

Coke is clear in his writings that it is not flaws in the law itself, as the 'artificial perfection of reason', which lead to litigation. Rather, imperfect learning and poor construction or application of the law are the sources of uncertainty and disagreement. Coke was of the view that the best way to safeguard the common law against such evils was to ensure that its practitioners accumulated and absorbed legal knowledge over many years of dedicated study. Although, of course, this sentiment cannot be identified as uniquely Ciceronian, Coke's statements on this issue are remarkably similar to those of Cicero in his discussions on the same topic. For example, in the course of praising the common law and its learned practitioners, Coke states that if there is diversity of opinion, it arises from the vice of man, not the legal profession. In fact, the greatest questions of law arise not from rules of the common law, but from imperfect instruments and statutes. If men were truly learned in the law and drafted their instruments correctly according to it, there would be little need or cause for legal dispute.[50] Cicero expresses the same view, much more succinctly: "*ac potius ignoratio iuris litigiosa est quam scientia.*"[51]

Coke's articulations of the common law as the artificial perfection of reason of learned men are not limited to his theoretical writing. One of the instances in which Coke's Ciceronian jurisprudence had a direct influence on public law principles of the English common law was the *Case of Prohibitions Del Roy* in 1608.[52] In his report of the case, he explains the circumstances of the decision as follows: "A controversy of land between parties was heard by the king, and sentence given, which was repealed, for this, it did belong to the common law."[53] Coke records that his determinations in the case as Chief Justice of the Common Pleas included that "The King in his own person cannot adjudge any case, either criminall [...] or betwixt party and party [...] but this ought to be determined and adjudged in some Court of Justice, according to the Law

50 Coke's Preface in Edward Coke, *Le second part des reportes del Edvvard Coke* (London: In ædibus Thomæ Wight, 1602), unpaginated.

51 Cicero, *On the Laws*, 1.18. See also Coke's Preface in Edward Coke, *La neufme part des reports de Sr. Edvv. Coke* (London: Printed for the Societie of Stationers, 1613), unpaginated. Cf. Cicero, *On Duties*, trans. Walter Miller. Loeb Classical Library 30 (Cambridge, MA: Harvard University Press, 1913), 1.33.

52 (1608) 77 Eng. Rep. 1342; 12 Co. Rep. 63. Boyer, "Sir Edward Coke, Ciceronianus," 6, describes Coke's artificial reason as "a marvellously effective weapon for striking down anything found 'unreasonable'."

53 *Ibidem*, 64.

and Custom of England."[54] James I was predictably upset at this pronouncement. Coke reports that in response:[55]

> the King said, that he thought the Law was founded upon reason, and that he and others had reason, as well as the Judges: To which it was answered by me, that true it was, that God had endowed his Majesty with excellent Science and great endowments of nature, but his Majesty was not learned in the Lawes of his Realm of England, and causes which concern the life, or inheritance, or goods, or fortunes of his Subjects; they are not to be decided by naturall reason, but by the artificial reason and judgment of Law, which Law is an act which requires long study and experience, before that a man can attain to the cognizance of it.

Here we see Coke employing his Ciceronian conception of law as the perfected artificial reason of learned men to thwart the king's perceived overreach and interference with common law principles and processes.[56] Thus, Ciceronian legal theory is utilised by Coke as the basis of and authority for his attempt to preserve the supremacy and independence of the common law.

## 3 Coke's Understanding and Use of Natural Law

In the previous section of this paper, I proposed that Coke's conception of the common law is directly and broadly influenced by Ciceronian natural law jurisprudence and rhetorical theory. In this section, I examine Coke's understanding and use of this Ciceronian jurisprudence. I begin with Coke's understanding of the place of natural law in the laws of England, and the use he makes of natural law in his theoretical and judicial writings. This is followed by case studies of Coke's reasoning in *Calvin's Case* and *Bonham's Case*. I argue that Coke placed classical natural law firmly within the fabric of English law, and on several occasions relied on natural law principles in a manner which resulted in their determining the direction of common law evolution.

### 3.1 *The Place of Natural Law in the Laws of England*

Coke states in the First Volume of his *Institutes*:[57]

---

54 *Ibidem*, 63–64.

55 *Ibidem*, 64–65.

56 See further Postema, "Classical Common Law Jurisprudence (Part II)," 2.

57 Co. Litt. 115 b.

> The Law of England is divided [...] into three parts; the Common Law, which is the most generall and ancient Law of the realme; of part whereof, Littleton wrote; 2. Statutes or Acts of Parliament; and 3. particular Customes (whereof Littleton also maketh some mention). I say particular, for if it be the generall Custome of the realme, it is part of the Common Law.

Coke repeats this tripartite division of English law into common law (encompassing general unwritten custom), written statute, and particular unwritten custom on several occasions in various contexts.[58] It is clear that Coke's formulation here is influenced by *Bracton*, which asserts that England alone uses unwritten law and custom, as well as written law,[59] and by Fortescue, who states that "all human laws are either law of nature, customs, or statutes."[60] However, this separation of law into written and unwritten sources also features prominently in Cicero's thought, particularly in relation to the distinctions he perceives between natural law and manmade 'positive' law.[61]

Coke also states in the first Volume of his *Institutes* that there are 'divers Lawes' in the realm of England.[62] He lists a total of fifteen. These include, first, the law of the Crown; second, the law and custom of parliament; third, the law of nature; fourth, the common law; fifth, statute law; and sixth, reasonable customs. The list also includes ecclesiastical or Canon law, civil law (in ecclesiastical and other courts), the law of the forest, and the law merchant. Although it is far from clear, it would appear that he is here listing what he considers to be the types of law in use *in* England, rather than the broad parts into which English law itself is divided. It is possible that in dividing the law of England into only three of his fifteen listed types of law, he is referring to those types which were usually applied in the English common law courts, in which he practised. However, as I discuss below, the law of nature explicitly features in both his theoretical and judicial writing, suggesting that he did at least understand natural law principles to work alongside the common law, or

58 See, e.g., Coke's Preface in Edward Coke, *Le quart part des reportes del Edward Coke* (London: In ædibus Thomæ Wight, 1604), unpaginated; Case de Modo Decimandi (1609) 77 Eng. Rep. 1448, 1451; 13 Co. Rep. 37, 40.

59 Henry de Bracton, "Introductio," in *On the Laws and Customs of England*, trans. Samuel E. Thorne, vol. II (Cambridge, MA: Harvard University Press, 1968), 19.

60 Fortescue, *De Laudibus Legum Anglie*, ch. xv, 37.

61 See, e.g., Cicero, *On the Laws*, I.18–19, I.42, II.10, II.11.

62 Co. Litt. 11 b.

indeed to form part of the common law itself.[63] He most frequently employs natural law principles in cases which he determines pertain specifically to the law of nature, and in cases in which common law principles or precedents are lacking.

### 3.2 *Coke's Use of Natural Law*

The majority of Coke's references to the law of nature in his theoretical writing are in relation to familial obligations.[64] In this context, natural law principles appear to function where no conflicting statute has been enacted which supersedes them. He acknowledges that statute is able to displace particular natural law principles, at least in certain circumstances.[65]

Coke also refers to natural law in several other contexts. His attempt to reconcile the law of villeinage with natural law principles in the First Volume of his *Institutes* is particularly interesting. He examines the origins of servitude, questioning how "[v]illeinage or servitude began, and for what cause," given that it is said "*libertas a Deo hominis est indita naturae*."[66] We may discern two distinct arguments attempting to explain and justify the existence of villeinage, a common law principle which would appear to be clearly in violation of the natural law principle preserving the freedom of the individual. Firstly, Coke asserts, following *Bracton* and *Fleta*, that free men were placed into captivity by the law of nations, not by the law of nature, upon the establishment of private property rights, which led to violence and conflict. In consequence of such violence, it was "ordained by constitution of nations" under penalty of law that men should not kill one another, but should rather take those they have defeated in battle into servitude. These prisoners of war held in bondage are called 'servants' or 'slaves' (*servi*) not because they serve their masters, but rather because they were protected (*servabantur*) by the masters who did not kill them in battle. Further, slaves actually retain their natural freedom, as they are permitted by their masters to exercise their own agency, unless a particular action is forbidden by law or force.[67]

---

63 See R.H. Helmholz, "Bonham's Case, Judicial Review, and the Law of Nature," *Journal of Legal Analysis* 1, no. 1 (2009): 332–333.

64 R.H. Helmholz, *Natural Law in Court: A History of Legal Theory in Practice* (Cambridge, Massachusetts: Harvard University Press, 2015) notes at 103 that principles governing relations between family members were "fundamental parts of the law of nature as it was [...] understood" in the early modern period.

65 See, e.g., Co. Litt. 78 a.

66 Co. Litt. 116 b. This maxim originates in Fortescue, *De Laudibus Legum Anglie*, ch. XLII, 104.

67 Co. Litt. 116 b.

Secondly, Coke introduces a traditional Christian argument in proposing that servitude was 'first inflicted' as a result of human vice, in particular the dishonouring of one's parents, and the invention of wine and drunkenness. In relation to the latter, Coke states: "And herewith agreeth the divine: *Ante vini inventionem inconcussa libertas. Non esset hodie servitus, si ebrietas non fuisset.*"[68]

Coke's efforts to reconcile the coexistence of the seemingly contradictory principles of natural law and servitude, and his attempts to convince the reader that they are, in fact, perfectly compatible, indicate the significance he placed on the law of nature: if natural law principles were not important, it would not matter that common law principles appeared to conflict with them. These attempts also suggest his adherence to the understanding that it was not possible for the common law, as the artificial perfection of reason of the learned, to be in conflict with principles of natural law, which were themselves the command of the rational Divine, discovered and shared through the reason of humankind.

Coke again refers to natural law principles during a discussion on usury. He states:[69]

> By the statutes of 3. H. 7. and 11. H. 7. all Usury is damned and prohibited, and there it is called Dry exchange. So as usury is not only against the law of God, & the laws of the Realm, but against the law of nature. *Usura contra naturam est, quia usura sua natura est sterilis, nec fructum habet.*

We can see the origins of his objections to usury as being against the law of nature, and as being 'sterile' and 'fruitless', in the writings of Aristotle.[70] Cicero, of course, also discusses it, comparing it in wickedness to homicide.[71] In the above example, Coke acknowledges that an action forbidden by natural law has been expressly prohibited by English statutes. In the same work, during a discussion of single combat, duels, and other forms of private revenge, Coke states that these are forbidden as:[72]

---

68 *Ibidem*. A marginal note asserts that the Latin is that of St Ambrose, but does not provide an exact reference. It appears to originate in his *De Elia et Ieiunio*, 1.5.10–11.

69 Co. Inst. 3, 152.

70 Aristotle, *Politics*, trans. H. Rackham. Loeb Classical Library 264 (Cambridge, MA: Harvard University Press, 1932), 1258 b.

71 Cicero, *On Duties*, II.89.

72 Co. Inst. 3, 157. See the discussion of *Bonham's Case*, below.

> It is also against the law of nature and of nations, for a man to be judge in his own proper cause, *judex in propria causa*, especially *in duello*, where fury, wrath, malice, and revenge are the rulers of the judgement [...] But it is objected, that this single combat may be undertaken for revenge, and preservation of the honour of the party grieved. 1. The honour or estimation of the party may more justly and notoriously be revenged, and repaired by the magistrate in publique, than by the party in private. 2. There is nothing honourable, that is against the laws of his country, and the law of nature and nations.

Once again, these examples evidence Coke's apparent assumption that common and natural law principles must align. In his discussion on usury, he emphasises that an action prohibited by natural law has been considered so heinous by English lawmakers that it has been forbidden not only by the common law but also by statute. In his explanations on the reasons for the prohibition on private vengeance, he is at pains to clarify that being a judge in one's own cause is not only in violation of natural law and the law of nations, but also of the law of one's country, that is, the common law. We see the manifestation of this understanding in Coke's judgment in *Bonham's Case,* below.

## 3.3 *Case Studies*

### 3.3.1 Calvin's Case

*Calvin's Case*,[73] decided in 1608, is arguably the most well-known and clearest example of Coke's use of natural law in his judgments. What has not been examined in as much detail is Coke's use of distinctly Ciceronian jurisprudence. This is one of two reported cases I have, to date, identified in which Coke refers expressly to Cicero in his judgments as an authority for principles of law central to the disposition of the suit.[74]

The case concerned the question of whether persons born in Scotland following the union of the English and Scottish crowns by the accession of James I in 1603 (the *postnati*) were English subjects able to hold property. The matter was ultimately heard in the Exchequer Chamber before all the judges of England, including Coke, then Chief Justice of the Common Pleas. It was determined that allegiance to the king was a personal obligation, and that, there-

73 (1608) 77 Eng. Rep. 377; 7 Co. Rep. 1 a.

74 Dr Foster's Case (1615) 77 Eng. Rep. 1222; 11 Co. Rep. 56 b is the other. In this case, at 60 a, Coke cites particular sections of Cicero's Verrine and Catalinarian Orations as authority for the proposition that one who is convicted is not necessarily attainted and adjudged, whereas one who is attainted and adjudged is necessarily convicted.

fore, the *postnati* were English subjects who could legally hold land under the law of England.[75]

In his report of the case, Coke outlines the history of proceedings, and summarises the arguments for the defendants, who were asserting that Calvin, an infant born in Scotland after the accession of James I, was an alien and therefore could not hold land in England. He then turns to the arguments of the plaintiff, and his own arguments in agreement. He firstly refers to the antiquity of the common law, refined by successions of learned lawmen.[76] As we have seen, this notion has close links to Cicero's own learned men, endowed with the reason of the law. Here, Coke ties the Ciceronian notion of law as reason attained by learned men with the legal maxim that no man should be wiser than the laws. Coke reports that it was held by the judges (including himself) as part of the disposition of the case:[77]

> For the lawes: 1. That ligeance, or obedience of the subject to the soveraigne, is due by the law of nature: 2. That this law of nature is part of the laws of England: 3. That the law of nature was before any judiciall or municipall law in the world: 4. That the law of nature is immutable and cannot be changed.

Coke's subsequent definition of natural law is aligned with the classical natural law tradition, and is strongly reminiscent of Cicero's own definition.[78] Coke states:[79]

> The Law of Nature is that which God at the time of creation of the nature of man infused into his heart, for his preservation and direction; and this is *Lex aeterna*, the morall Law, called also the Law of Nature: and by this Law, written with the finger of God in the heart of man, were the people of God a long time governed.

---

75 For a detailed discussion of the background circumstances and facts of the case, see David Ibbetson, "The Arguments in Calvin's Case (1608)," in *Studies in Canon Law and Common Law in Honor of R.H. Helmholz*, ed. Troy L. Harris, Studies in Comparative Legal History (Berkeley: The Robbins Collection, 2015), 213–230; Polly J. Price, "Natural Law and Birthright Citizenship in Calvin's Case (1608)," *Yale Journal of Law & the Humanities* 9, no. 1 (1997): 73–146.

76 (1608) 77 Eng. Rep. 377, 381; 7 Co. Rep. 1 a, 3 b.

77 *Ibidem*, 4 b.

78 Cicero, *On the Laws*, II.10.

79 (1608) 77 Eng. Rep. 377, 392; 7 Co. Rep. 1 a, 12 b.

Coke expressly associates this understanding of natural law with Cicero. He quotes Biblical passages, and cites Aristotle, *Bracton*, Fortescue, and St German as authorities for the principle that allegiance is due to one's sovereign under natural law. He then quotes from Book III of Cicero's *De Legibus*.[80] This quote also features on the title page of Coke's Second Volume of *Reports*.[81] The Latin Coke uses here is slightly different. He states:[82]

> And herewith accordeth Tully, lib. 3. *de Legibus, Sine imperio nec domus ulla, nec civitas, nec gens, nec hominum universum genus stare, nec ipse denique mundus potest.* This law of nature, which indeed is the eternall law of the Creator, infused into the heart of the creature at the time of his creation, was two thousand years before any law written, and before any judiciall or municipall lawes.

Coke also refers to Cicero, in addition to Fortescue, as providing "the reason wherefore lawes were made and published."[83] He states: "Tully, *lib. 2. officiorum: at cum jus aequabile ab uno viro homines non consequerentur, inventae sunt leges.*"[84] This appears to be a pithier adaptation of Cicero's Latin.[85] Coke continues: "Now it appeareth by demonstrative reason, that ligeance, faith, and obedience of the subject to the Soveraigne, was before any municipall or judiciall lawes."[86] He thus employs Ciceronian jurisprudence as an authority for establishing a principle of natural law, which is central to the disposition of the case.

Shortly thereafter, he again emphasises the immutability of natural law principles in arguing, with references to *Bracton* and St German, that the bond between sovereign and subject cannot be removed by statute or judge-made law:[87]

> Seeing then that faith, obedience, and ligeance are due by the law of nature, it followeth that the same cannot be changed or taken away;

80 *Ibidem*, 13 a.
81 Coke, *Le second part des reportes del Edvvard Coke*, unpaginated.
82 (1608) 77 Eng. Rep. 377, 392; 7 Co. Rep. 1 a, 13 a.
83 *Ibidem*.
84 *Ibidem*.
85 Cicero, *On Duties*, II.42: "*Id si ab uno iusto et bono viro consequebantur, erant eo contenti; cum id minus contingent, leges sunt inventae, quae cum omnibus semper una atque eadem voce loquerentur.*"
86 (1608) 77 Eng. Rep. 377, 392; 7 Co. Rep. 1 a, 13 a.
87 *Ibidem*, 392, 13 b. See also *ibidem*, 407, 25 a.

> for albeit judicial or municipal laws have inflicted and imposed in several places, or at several times, divers and several punishments and penalties, for breach or not observance of the law of nature, (for that law only consisted in commanding or prohibiting, without any certain punishment or penalty); yet the very law of nature itself never was nor could be altered or changed. And therefore it is certainly true, that *jura naturalia sunt immutabilia.* And herewith agreeth Bracton, lib. 1. cap. 5. and Doctor and Student, cap. 5 and 6. And this appeareth plainly and plentifully in our books.

The statement in *Bracton* to which Coke refers is "*Iura enim naturalia sunt immutabilia.*"[88] *Bracton's* Latin is again taken verbatim from Azo's *Summa Institutionum.*[89] St German states in cap. 2 of *Doctor and Student*: "*Nam iura naturalia immutabilia sunt.*"[90] Chapters 5 and 6, which Coke cites here, do not repeat this language, but expound the first two of St German's six grounds of the law of England, namely, the law of reason and the law of God, respectively. The initial paragraphs of cap. 5 include the following statement by the student of English law, in answer to the Doctor of Divinity's asking what the law of nature is called in the laws of England:[91]

> It is not vsed amonge them that be lernyd in the lawes of Englande to reason what thynge is commaundyd or prohybyt by the lawe of nature and what not: but all the resonynge in that behalfe is vnder this maner: as when anythyng is groundyd vpon the lawe of nature: they say that reason wyll that suche a thyng be don/ and yf if be prohybyte by the lawe of nature. They say it is agaynst reason or that reason wyll not suffre that it be don.

Prior to Azo, *Bracton* and St German, the immutable quality of the law of nature was articulated by Cicero, following the Aristotelian natural law tradition, in similar terms:[92]

88 *Bracton* 1.5.s.8, in Maitland, *Select Passages from the Works of Bracton and Azo*, 37.

89 Azo on Inst.1.2, in Maitland, *Select Passages from the Works of Bracton and Azo*, 38.

90 T.F.T. Plucknett and John L. Barton, eds., *St. German's Doctor and Student*, Publications of the Selden Society 91 (London: Selden Society, 1974), 14.

91 *Ibidem*, 31, 33.

92 The Latin is as follows: "*Est quidem vera lex recta ratio naturae congruens, diffusa in omnes, constans, sempiterna, quae vocet ad officium iubendo, vetando a fraude deterreat; quae tamen neque probos frustra iubet aut vetat nec improbos iubendo aut vetando movet. huic legi nec obrogari fas est neque derogari ex hac aliquid licet neque tota abrogari potest,*

> Indeed true law is right reason agreeing with nature, extending to all, unchanging, everlasting, which summons to duty through its commands, and deters from wrong action through its prohibitions; which nevertheless neither commands or prohibits honest men in vain, nor moves wicked men through its commands or prohibitions. It is lawful neither to weaken this law nor is it permitted to repeal any part of it, nor is it possible to abolish it wholly, nor truly are we able to be released from this law either by the senate or by the people, and nor is another explainer or interpreter of it to be sought, nor will there be another law at Rome, another at Athens, another now, another in the future, *but one law both everlasting and immutable shall endure both for all peoples and for all time*, and there shall be one common master and commander as it were of all people, God, who is the inventor, arbitrator, proposer of this law.

In this context, Coke provides examples of immutable natural law principles remaining operative despite the enactment of statutes which would appear to provide otherwise:[93]

> By the statute of 25 Ed. 3. cap. 22. a man attainted in a *Praemunire*, is by expresse words out of the king's protection generally: & yet this extendeth only to legall protection, as it appeareth by Littl. fol. 43. for the Parliament could not take away that protection which the law of nature giveth unto him: and therfore notwithstanding that statute, the king may protect and pardon him.

In determining how he should decide the matter, Coke is emphatic in his assertions that were there to be found an absence of common law principles or precedents, the case must be determined according to the artificial reason of the law possessed by learned lawmen, and not by natural reason, even if that

---

*nec vero aut per senatum aut per populum solvi hac lege possumus, neque est quaerendus explanator aut interpres eius alius, nec erit alia lex Romae, alia Athenis, alia nunc, alia posthac, sed et omnes gentes et omni tempore una lex et sempiterna et immutabilis continebit, unusque erit communis quasi magister et imperator omnium deus, ille legis huius inventor, disceptator, lator.*" Cicero, *On the Republic*, trans. Clinton W. Keyes. Loeb Classical Library 213 (Cambridge, MA: Harvard University Press, 1928), III.33, emphasis added.

93 (1608) 77 Eng. Rep. 377, 393; 7 Co. Rep. 1 a, 14 a.

reason is "of the wisest man," if he "professeth not the Lawes of England."[94] Here, Coke is again referring to the Ciceronian notion that only learned and wise men of the law, possessing the law's artificial perfected reason may adequately determine legal questions. Natural reason is not sufficient.

There are several other extant reports of the arguments in *Calvin's Case*.[95] Interestingly, these do not include Coke's references to Ciceronian sources. For example, Hawarde's notes of the arguments in the case do not mention Coke citing either Cicero or Aristotle.[96] A State Papers manuscript summarising the arguments presented in the matter has Coke quoting Aristotle, but there is no mention of Cicero.[97] It is therefore possible that Coke did not in fact refer to Cicero at all during his arguments in court, but rather added the references subsequently when he prepared his case report for publication. What might this indicate? Perhaps Coke's arguments in court were restricted to the practical disposition of the question at issue, that is, the status of the *postnati*, whereas his published version of the case allowed him the opportunity to further explore the jurisprudential principles behind his reasoning, enabling him to better fulfil one of his express purposes in publishing his reports, namely, to provide instruction to his readers "in the right rule and reason of the case in question."[98] Cicero's writings are clearly important to Coke's theoretical conception of law, and were considered to be of sufficient importance to include in his published version of the case intended for the instruction and education of others.

A further interesting variance in the Hawarde and State Papers reports is that both include Coke referring expressly to the law of nature, rather than to the common law, as the first part of his threefold division of the law of England, and so following Fortescue's tripartite division of human laws into the law of nature, customs, and statutes.[99] This division does not appear in Coke's own report of *Calvin's Case*. Hawarde's version of Coke's judgment reports that he stated: "The law of England consists of the laws of 1. nature, the gift of God, which cannot be changed, 2. customs, 3. statutes. Nature writes the law of

94 *Ibidem*, 400, 19 a.

95 See Ibbetson "The Arguments in Calvin's Case". Baker, "Coke's Note-Books," 73 posits that Coke's original notes of the case were contained in a part of his collection of manuscript notebooks which is now lost.

96 W.P. Baildon, *Les Reportes Del Cases in Camera Stellata 1593 to 1609, from the Original MS of John Hawarde* (Privately Printed, 1894), 349–366..

97 The National Archives, SP 14/34, fols 11–23 v.

98 Coke's Preface in Edward Coke, *La sept part des reports Sr. Edvv. Coke* (London: Printed for the Societie of Stationers, 1608), unpaginated.

99 Fortescue, *De Laudibus Legum Anglie*, ch. XV.

government in the heart of man for his preservation, by government and in obedience."[100] The State Papers manuscript records that Coke asserted:

> Common law is compounded of 3 things: the law of nature; customs; statutes. Aristotle in his polit: Government and obedience are of nature. Obedience before law [...] *Jus naturae nullo jure civili deleri potest.* The king's natural prerogative can not be limited as no Act of Parliament can take away a non obstante.[101]

As noted above, in his report of the case, Coke simply states that "this law of nature is part of the laws of England,"[102] which is no more than he asserts in his theoretical writing (taking his use of 'of' here to be equivalent to laws 'in' England). It is possible that the disparity indicates an evolution of Coke's thought on this issue, given the time period between his judgment in 1608, and the publication of the First Volume of his *Institutes* in 1628. It is also possible that it indicates some confusion, or at least a lack of clarity, in Coke's understanding of the precise relationship between the common law and the law of nature. Did he view natural law as a type of law in England which existed alongside and in harmony with the common law, or did he conceive of it as an inherent part of the common law itself?[103]

### 3.3.2 Bonham's Case

The facts and circumstances surrounding *Bonham's Case*,[104] decided in 1610, have been expounded at length elsewhere,[105] and shall not be repeated in detail here. In brief, Dr Bonham brought a suit of false imprisonment against the London College of Physicians, which had caused him to be arrested and detained. The College, by the authority of Letters Patent and two subsequent

---

100 Baildon, *Les Reportes Del Cases in Camera Stellata*, 357–358.

101 The National Archives, SP 14/34, fol. 21 v. The manuscript's assertion that Coke stated the common law (rather than the law of England) to be composed of natural law, custom and statute creates additional confusion.

102 (1608) 77 Eng. Rep. 377, 382; 7 Co. Rep. 1 a, 4 b.

103 Allen D. Boyer, "Understanding, Authority, and Will: Sir Edward Coke and the Elizabethan Origins of Judicial Review," *Boston College Law Review* 39, no. 1 (1997) asserts at 45–6 that lawyers in Coke's day conflated theories of law as reason, custom and nature, and that Coke did the same.

104 (1610) 77 Eng. Rep. 646; 8 Co. Rep. 113 b.

105 See, e.g., Theodore F.T. Plucknett, "Bonham's Case and Judicial Review," *Harvard Law Review* 40, no. 1 (1926): 30–70; S.E. Thorne, "Dr. Bonham's Case," *Law Quarterly Review* 54, no. 4 (1938): 543–552.

statutes, held powers including to admit doctors to practise medicine in the City of London, to penalise those who practised without the College's permission, and to penalise and imprison those who committed malpractice. The penalty for unlicensed practice consisted of fines, half of which would go to the king, and half to the College. The College pleaded that Dr Bonham had practised medicine in London in violation of its rules, and that his amercement and subsequent imprisonment were within its authority. Dr Bonham argued, inter alia, that as a graduate of the University of Cambridge, he was outside the ambit of the Letters Patent and statutes. Following extended arguments by both parties and the Judges of the Common Pleas, judgment was given in favour of Dr Bonham.

In his report of the case, Coke sets out his own argument, in favour of Dr Bonham, at length. His reasoning is firmly based on principles of statutory construction. In the course of setting out his reasons, he makes the following statement in relation to the powers of the College:[106]

> The censors cannot be judges, ministers, and parties, judges to give sentence or judgment, ministers to make summons, and parties to have the moiety of the forfeiture, *quia aliquis non debet esse iudex in propria causa; imo iniquum est aliquem sui rei esse iudicem:* and one cannot be Judge and attorney for any of the parties [...] And it appears in our books, that in many cases, the common law will control acts of parliament and sometimes adjudge them to be utterly void, for when an act of parliament is against common right and reason [*est encounter common droit & reason*], or repugnant or impossible to be performed, the common law will control it and adjudge such act to be void.

Two primary interpretative traditions have arisen in the wake of Coke's pronouncement. The first, pioneered by Plucknett in 1926, argues that, in stating the common law is able to 'control' statutes and judge them 'void', Coke is appealing to some form of higher, 'fundamental' law to impose limits on the powers of the Crown and Parliament, and is, in effect, carrying out the first

106 (1610) 77 Eng. Rep. 646, 652; 8 Co. Rep. 113 b, 118 a. Baker has examined the manuscript containing Coke's original notes of *Bonham's Case*. See Baker "Coke's Note-Books," 77 n. 96: "Anyone who wishes to find the original of the renowned statement on judicial review in *Dr. Bonham's Case* [...] will be disappointed. Being printed posthumously, no alterations were made except translation." The italic phrase in square brackets in this extract is Coke's original law French.

instance of what would evolve into the principle of judicial review.[107] The other interpretative tradition, comprehensively articulated by Thorne in 1938, asserts that Coke is appealing to no such law, and is not undertaking any form of judicial review (which would be anachronistic), but is simply making a determination based on ordinary principles of statutory construction, which he applies strictly to the relevant instruments.[108]

Arguing in support of the latter approach, Williams undertakes a thoughtful analysis of contemporary meanings of 'void', and is persuasive in his contention that its lack of a consistent or narrow technical meaning should induce caution in those asserting the involvement of strong principles of judicial review.[109] However, I do not find his arguments that natural law has no place in Coke's judgment to be convincing. Williams states that a natural law interpretation is based entirely on external judgments and texts, is not considered by any of Coke's contemporaries, and does not consider the cases referred to by Coke in his judgment, which are determinative in their own right.[110]

I propose that Coke is indeed undertaking an exercise of statutory construction, but that this exercise relies in part on natural law principles of the Cice-

107 Plucknett, "Bonham's Case and Judicial Review". See also Raoul Berger, "Doctor Bonham's Case: Statutory Construction or Constitutional Theory?," *University of Pennsylvania Law Review* 117, no. 4 (1968): 521–545; Boyer, "Understanding, Authority, and Will"; Lawrence Joseph Perrone, "The Fundamental and Natural Law "Repugnant Review" Origins of Judicial Review: A Synergy of Early English Corporate Law with Notions of Fundamental and Natural Law", *BYU Journal of Public Law* 23, no. 1 (2008): 61–82. Charles M. Gray, "Bonham's Case Reviewed," *Proceedings of the American Philosophical Society* 116, no. 1 (1972): 35–58, has undertaken a thorough and thoughtful analysis of several additional manuscript reports of the case, which do not include Coke's famous statement. He therefore argues that Coke appears not to have considered this aspect in his ex tempore judgment, but added it subsequently, prior to the publication of his report, at which point he did intend to make a claim of something like judicial review.

108 Thorne, "Dr. Bonham's Case". See also R.A. MacKay, "Coke – Parliamentary Sovereignty or the Supremacy of the Law?", *Michigan Law Review* 22, no. 3 (1923): 215–247; L. B. Boudin, "Lord Coke and the American Doctrine of Judicial Power," *New York University Law Review* 6, no. 3 (1929): 223–246; Michael Lobban, "A History of the Philosophy of Law in the Common Law World, 1600–1900," in *A Treatise of Legal Philosophy and General Jurisprudence*, ed. Enrico Pattaro, vol. 8 (Dordrecht; New York: Springer, 2005); Ian Williams, "Dr. Bonham's Case and Void Statutes," *Journal of Legal History* 27, no. 2 (2006): 111–128.

109 Williams, "Dr. Bonham's Case and Void Statutes".

110 *Ibidem*, 121. The cases cited by Coke may indeed be determinative in their own right, but Coke's inclusion of natural law principles in his judgment indicates that he did not consider them sufficient and, at least in his published report, was concerned to incorporate broader jurisprudential points.

ronian tradition, their interaction with the common law, and their effect on statutes. Coke's use of natural law principles may not be obviously apparent if *Bonham's Case* is examined in isolation; however, a nuanced analysis of the precise terms employed in his judgment, in the context of his other writings, reveals the centrality of the law of nature in his statement extracted above. I also suggest that this interpretation of his judgment was implicitly followed on at least one occasion by his contemporaries.

Furthermore, if Coke's conception of natural law is understood as previously suggested, that is, as a type of law operating in England alongside or within the common law,[111] on my interpretation of his judgment in *Bonham's Case*, his subsequent statements in the *Institutes* on the power of Parliament to control the common law may be viewed as entirely consistent. There, Coke states: "The *Common Law* hath no controller in any part of it, but the high Court of Parliament, and if it be not abrogated or altered by parliament, it remaynes still."[112] On an initial reading, this statement may appear to contradict that made by Coke in *Bonham's Case* that the common law may control Acts of Parliament. The circumstances in which he asserts that the common law may so control statutes must be carefully examined, however. There should be no controversy in his statements that a statute will be pronounced void if "repugnant" (which Thorne explains is a contradiction within the statute)[113] or "impossible to be performed". It is his assertion that the common law may adjudge a statute void if it is "against common right and reason" which has caused interpretative difficulties.

I suggest that 'common right' refers to the common law, and that 'reason' in this particular instance refers to natural law. I further suggest that Coke's use of 'and' here is cumulative. Thus, the common law may not control a statute simply because the statute is against the common law in and of itself – that would indeed contradict Coke's later statements in his *Institutes*. It is in circumstances where a statute is against a principle of natural law, which has also been incorporated as an express principle of common law, that the com-

111 Helmholz, "Bonham's Case, Judicial Review, and the Law of Nature," makes this argument at 334, and asserts that many of the modern problems of interpretation of *Bonham's Case* arise from the assumption that Coke must have been relying on *either* the common law or on natural law. This assumption is incorrect. Coke and his contemporaries regarded the common law and natural law as normally being in agreement, and as working alongside and in harmony with each other. See also R.H. Helmholz, "Natural Law and Human Rights in English Law: From Bracton to Blackstone," *Ave Maria Law Review* 3, no. 1 (2005): 21.

112 Co. Litt. 115 b, emphasis added.

113 Thorne, "Dr. Bonham's Case," 549.

mon law may declare it void. In other words, Coke's statement is applicable when a principle of natural law has been expressly incorporated into the common law and is identified as a common law, as well as a natural law, principle. Despite Coke's statement in *Calvin's Case* regarding the immutability of natural law, it is possible, based on statements made in the *Institutes* and referred to above,[114] he may have considered that a principle of natural law which had not been expressly adopted as a common law rule (and thereby 'reinforced') was able to be displaced by statute, hence his emphasis on the principle in this case being identified by both the natural and common law.

Coke uses the phrase 'common right' as synonymous with 'common law' in several instances in his theoretical writing. For example, in his commentary on Littleton, explaining Littleton's own use of the term, he states:[115]

> *'De common droit'.* Of common right [...] that is, by the common law, so called [...] And it is to be observed, that the common law of England sometimes is called right, sometimes common right, and sometimes *communis justitia* [...] And in this sense being largely taken, as well the statutes and customes of the realme, as that which is properly the common law, is included within *common droit.* Littleton in this his treatise nameth *common droit* sixe times.

The phrase 'encounter reason' appears frequently in *Littleton on Tenures*. For example, Littleton states that manorial customs which are not 'encounter reason' are to be permitted. Coke comments that 'enconter reason' is here "not to be understood of every unlearned man's reason, but of artificiall and legal reason warranted by authority of law: *Lex est summa ratio.*"[116] This indicates no more than that Coke took Littleton's use of 'reason' to mean that Ciceronian artificial perfection of reason acquired by learned lawmen, which has already been discussed. However, an examination of Coke's discussions of the principle that a man cannot be a judge in his own cause reveals not only that he identified this as a principle of natural law, but also that he employed the term 'reason' as meaning the equivalent to 'natural law' in this particular context.[117] As noted above, St German expressly refers to natural law as 'rea-

114 See, e.g., Co. Litt. 78 a.

115 Co. Litt. 142 a–b. See also, e.g., Co. Inst. 2, 56.

116 Co. Litt. 62 a.

117 See Berger, "Doctor Bonham's Case," 529; Peter Glenn Burgess, "Custom, Reason and the Common Law: English Jurisprudence 1600–1650" (Ph.D. thesis, University of Cambridge, 1988), 57; Perrone, "The Fundamental and Natural Law "Repugnant Review" Origins of

son' in his treatise *Doctor and Student*, and Coke makes explicit reference to St German's use of 'reason' as meaning the law of nature in 1608 in the *Case of Modus Decimandi*.[118]

Coke states in the First Volume of his *Institutes*, repeating Littleton's own words: "'*Est encounter reason, que si tort soit fait a un home, que il de ceo serra son judge demesne.*' For it is a Maxime in Law, *Aliquis non debet esse iudex in propria causa*."[119] He states, in the Third Volume of his *Institutes*: "It is also *against the law of nature* and of nations, for a man to be Judge in his own proper cause, *Judex in propria causa*."[120] These pronouncements appear to indicate that Coke viewed the common law as not only aligning with this natural law principle (which it inevitably must), but as also having expressly adopted the principle as a 'common law' principle.

Brownlow and Goldesborough's report of Coke's arguments in *Bonham's Case* provides a clearer indication than his own report that it was specifically the rule that a man cannot be a judge in his own cause which formed the basis of his pronouncement that statutes may, in certain circumstances, be declared void:[121]

> and also [Coke] said that the said President and College cannot commit any Physician, which exerciseth the said faculty without admission, for the space of a Month, nor bring their Action before themselves, nor levy that by any other way or meanes: But ought to have their Action or exhibit an Information upon the Statute [...] for they ought to pursue their power which is given to them by the Statute, for otherwise the penalty being given, the one Moytie to them, and the other to the King, they shall be Judges in *Propria causa*, and shall be Summoners, Sheriffs, Judges and parties also; which is absurd, for if the King grant to one by his Letters Patents under the great Seale, that he may hold Plea, although he be party, and if the King doth not appoint another Judge, than the Grantee which is party, the Grant is void, though that it be confirmed by Parliament.

---

Judicial Review," 65–66; J.W. Gough, "Fundamental Law in the Seventeenth Century," *Political Studies* 1, no. 2 (1953): 162–174 more generally.

118 (1608) 77 Eng. Rep. 1424, 1428; 13 Co. Rep. 12, 16.

119 Co. Litt. 141 a.

120 Co. Inst. 3, 157, emphasis added.

121 (1609) 123 Eng. Rep. 928, 933; 2 Brownl. & Golds. 255, 265.

My argument here proposes that Coke's intended meaning of 'against common right and reason' is unique. His use of the phrase itself, however, is not. It is possible that the phrase originated with Littleton, in a fifteenth century case in the Common Pleas.[122] This was an action on trespass. Littleton, at that time a Sergeant-at-Law, appeared for the plaintiff. In the course of his arguments, he states: "*Et si un veut prescriber de chose que est encontre le Ley, en reason le Court ne sufrira my* [...] *ceo est enconter reason, & enconter reason, & enconter commen droit: purque le Court ne suffrira tiel prescription.*"[123] Hassall records that Coke owned a copy of the Year Book containing this report in his private library,[124] and given his vast knowledge of case law, I suggest it is highly probable that he was familiar with it.

'Common right and reason' appears again ten years later, in a case in the Common Pleas concerning a debt on an obligation. The arguments for the plaintiff include the statement: "*Et pur ceo que il voile estre sure del issue a estre trie la lou ceo de comen droit & reason doit estre trie il pria son proces la.*"[125] Almost 20 years after this, in 1484, during an action on trespass in the King's Bench, Serjeant Vavasour applies the descriptor 'common' to both 'right' and 'reason' in his declaration that "*cest custome est void: car il est enconter comon droit, & auxy enconter comon reason.*"[126] This may indicate a shift in the understanding of the terms, which is taken even further in 1499, in a case concerning a *scire facias* in the Common Pleas. Here Danvers JCP says of a 1485 statute: "*Adire que il est enconter comon droit, ceo n'est issint: car comon droit est comon reason.*"[127] Coke was also in possession of the printed Year Book containing this last report,[128] and was likely familiar with it, but, as we have seen, was emphatic in his insistence that the common law was in no way

---

122 I base this statement on a search of the fully indexed and paraphrased section of *Seipp's Index*, covering the printed Year Book reports from 1399 to 1535: see https://www.bu.edu/law/faculty-research/legal-history-the-year-books/. Three of the four examples discussed here have been identified by Barbara A. Singer, "The Reason of the Common Law," *University of Miami Law Review* 37, no. 3 (1982): 812–813 n. 84.

123 YB 34 Hen. 6, fol. 15, Mich, pl. 28 (1455).

124 Hassall, *A Catalogue of the Library of Sir Edward Coke*, 32, item 386, STC 9740 (Beale R 192).

125 YB 5 Edw. 4, fol. 55, Trin, pl. Long Quinto [14] (1465). This quinto volume is not included in Hassall's edition of Coke's library catalogue.

126 YB 2 Rich. 3, fol. 15, Mich, pl. 42 at fol. 16 (1484). This volume is not included in Hassall's edition of Coke's library catalogue.

127 YB 14 Hen. 7, fol. 17, Hil, pl. 7 at fol. 19 (1499).

128 Hassall, *A Catalogue of the Library of Sir Edward Coke*, 33, item 388, STC 9922 (Beale R 409).

synonymous with common reason, taking the latter to mean the reason of the populace at large.

It is unfortunate that, "as with so many of the complex conceptions that populate the Year Books, the lawyers who so often used 'reason' never defined it."[129] We may only speculate as to what Littleton intended when he employed the term, and as to the reasons, if indeed there were any, for the apparent shift in meaning of 'reason' to 'common reason' to 'common right'. Relevantly for our present purposes, however, Coke was careful and deliberate in his use of Littleton's version of 'against common right and reason', and clear in his identification of 'reason' with the classical natural law tradition.

In support of his conclusion that Coke's judgment in *Bonham's Case* is a matter of simple statutory construction with "little role for fundamental law,"[130] Williams argues that in Coke's "only reported explicit judicial reliance on the relevant passage in *Bonham's Case*," namely in *Rowles v Mason*,[131] Coke asserts that the common law 'disallows' statutes, but clarifies that this is only in cases where there is 'repugnancy' in the statute in question.[132] The relevant passage in *Rowles v Mason* is as follows:[133]

> Coke Chief Justice [...] said [...] that the Common Law consists of three parts. First Common Law. Secondly Statute Law, which corrects, abridges, and explaines the Common Law: The third Custome which takes away the Common Law: but the Common Law Corrects, Allows, and Disallows, both Statute Law, and Custome, for if there be repugnancy in Statute; or unreasonablenesse in Custome, the Common Law Disallowes and rejects it, as it appeares by *Doctor Bonham's case*.

In this passage, it is not only "against common right and reason" which Coke omits as a basis for declaring a statute void: he also omits "impossible to be performed." Coke's statement is made in the context of a discussion of whether a custom "warrants the cutting of [...] Trees by the Copy-holder."[134] He explains that common law can correct both custom and statute. Relevantly to the case at hand, the common law may disallow an unreasonable custom and, in the parallel case of a repugnant statute, it may do the same. Common

129 Singer, "The Reason of the Common Law," 798.
130 Williams, "Dr. Bonham's Case and Void Statutes," 125.
131 (1612) 123 Eng. Rep. 892; 2 Brownl. & Golds. 192.
132 Williams, "Dr. Bonham's Case and Void Statutes," 125.
133 (1612) 123 Eng. Rep. 892, 895; 2 Brownl. & Golds. 192, 197–198.
134 *Ibidem*, 895, 197.

right and reason, or impossibility, are not mentioned because they do not pertain to the legal issue under determination. In a case involving no principles of natural law, it would be irrelevant for Coke to refer to that part of *Bonham's Case* dealing with such.[135] His omissions in this case can say nothing helpful about his use, or otherwise, of natural law in *Bonham's Case.*

Although there may not be any contemporary cases expressly citing Coke's statement in *Bonham's Case* as authority for the common law's power of control over statutes in violation of common and natural law principles, Hobart CJ appears to implicitly follow, or at least reach the same determination as, this aspect of Coke's judgment in *Day v Savadge.*[136] This case was an action for trespass, in which the plaintiff alleged that the defendant had unlawfully taken away a bag of nutmegs. The defendant pleaded that he was entitled to distrain the bag according to a custom of the City of London, which he prayed be determined by the certification of the mayor and aldermen of the City. In holding for the plaintiff that the case should be tried by jury and not determined by certificate, Hobart CJ asserts that "it was against right and Justice, and against natural equity to allow them their Certificate, wherein they are to try, and judge their own Cause."[137] Further, he states:[138]

> By that that hath been said it appeares, that though in pleading it were confessed, that the custome of Certificate of the customes of London is confirmed by Parliament, yet it made no change in this case, both because it is none of the customes intended, and because even an Act of Parliament, made against naturall equitie, as to make a man Judge in his owne case, is void in it self, for *Jura naturae sunt immutabilia,* And they are *leges legum.*

135 MacKay, "Coke – Parliamentary Sovereignty or the Supremacy of the Law?" acknowledges as much in his statement at 226 that "the grounds of disallowance are here much narrower" than in *Bonham's Case.*

136 (1614) 80 Eng. Rep. 235; Hob. 85. See Berger, "Doctor Bonham's Case," 541; Mark D. Walters, "St. German on Reason and Parliamentary Sovereignty," *The Cambridge Law Journal* 62, no. 2 (2003): 362 n. 156. Gray, "Bonham's Case Reviewed," argues at 51 that Hobart CJ's judgment in this case supports the 'stronger judicial review' interpretation of Coke's judgment in *Bonham's Case.*

137 (1614) 80 Eng. Rep. 235, 235; Hob. 85, 86.

138 *Ibidem*, 237, 87. Plucknett, "Bonham's Case and Judicial Review," identifies Hobart's Latin at 49 n. 53 as "a rather serious misquotation of Bracton," and suggests at 50 that the omission of any reference to Coke's judgment in *Bonham's Case* was due to Hobart CJ's 'natural caution', which "warned him against too open a tribute to one whose fortunes had already begun to decline."

Here, once again, a statute is declared void on the basis that it is in violation of a principle of natural law (Hobart CJ uses the phrase 'natural equity', but the Latin indicates that this is synonymous with natural law) which is also understood as an express rule of the common law (in Hobart CJ's words, "against right and justice"). Further, although not concerning the validity of a statute, Bridgman's report of *Samborne v Harilo*, a case concerning trespass, cites Coke's judgment in *Bonham's Case* as one of the authorities for the same natural law principle, namely, that a man acting as judge in his own cause is 'against reason'.[139]

I propose that Coke's pronouncement in *Bonham's Case* was an exercise in statutory construction which incorporated natural law theory to declare that a statute in violation (whether intentionally or otherwise) of a principle recognised as an express rule of *both* natural law and the common law may be adjudged 'void' by the courts. I agree with the scholars who argue for a narrow interpretation of this case, that Coke would not have conceptualised his statement as some sort of principle of judicial review or as reflecting any notion of separation of powers, which may indeed be anachronistic[140] (although Baker does suggest that the concept of judicial review, if not the term itself, was in place by the late sixteenth century, and extended "to the exercise of prerogative jurisdiction and to the validity of commissions and letters patent which granted authority over, or infringed the property interests of, subjects"[141]). However, I suggest that on those rare occasions when a statute was clearly contrary to a principle which was recognised as an express rule of both natural law and common law in a manner which could not be corrected by strict construction, it does not go too far to say that Coke would have placed limitations on the power of Parliament, perhaps not so much in terms of what was permissible as in terms of what was possible.[142] Such a view allows Coke's judgment to be consistent with his subsequent pronouncements in the *Institutes* that statutes may control the common law.

139 (1621) 123 Eng. Rep. 1162, 1164; Bridgman, J. 9, 12.

140 See, e.g., Gough, "Fundamental Law in the Seventeenth Century".

141 J.H. Baker, "Introduction," in *Reports from the Notebooks of Edward Coke*, ed. John Baker, vol. 1. Publications of the Selden Society 136 (London: Selden Society, 2022), cxlvii.

142 Michael Lobban, "The Common Law Mind in the Age of Sir Edward Coke," *Amicus Curiae*, no. 33 (2001), suggests at 21 that Coke may have had in mind "constitutional boundaries which parliament could not cross."

## 4 Conclusion

In this paper, I have set out to demonstrate that aspects of Coke's legal theory are, to a significant degree, Ciceronian in origin. I have examined Coke's understanding and use of classical natural law principles in his theoretical and judicial writings. I have also argued that Coke's judgments in *Calvin's Case* and *Bonham's Case* utilise Ciceronian natural law to an extent greater than previously identified.

The Ciceronian origins of Coke's jurisprudence and his use of classical natural law principles suggest ties between the common law, natural law, and classical scholarship, which are closer and more extensive than previously acknowledged. The identification and analysis of the influence of classical natural law jurisprudence on late sixteenth and early seventeenth century English legal theory has the potential to reorient our understanding of the development of the early modern common law.

# PART 3

## *After 1650*

CHAPTER 8

# The Concept of Natural Law in Thomas Hobbes's Theory of Sovereignty

*Carlos Pérez-Crespo*

## 1 Introduction

The conceptualization of natural law in Thomas Hobbes's theory of sovereignty concerns the discussion in Hobbes scholarship about the nature of the moral precepts that bind the prince. It refers above all to the moral limitations on exercising sovereign power. In historiography this discussion has become relevant in the context of political power being increasingly arbitrarily exercised in contemporary politics. This essay, then, primarily analyzes the intellectual history of the ways in which Hobbes scholars have understood that natural law expresses a conceptualization of how the sovereign power is morally limited. It stresses the importance of the concept of natural law in understanding Hobbes's theory of sovereignty on the moral principles to which the prince is subject. My analysis is presented in three parts. First, I explain the passages in Hobbes's work relating to this discussion. Second I give an overview of the literature seeking a concept for understanding Hobbes's theory of natural law, and finally I give the current state of this discussion in the literature. The paper concludes that Bobbio's conceptualization of Hobbes's theory of natural law as a kind of 'basic norm' (*Grundnorm*) is still a relevant project for understanding the moral foundations of exercising sovereign power.

## 2 Natural Law in Hobbes's Theory of Sovereignty

The discussion on the concept of natural law in Hobbes scholarship has centered on a conceptualization of the moral duties that limit the prince's exercise of sovereign power. Various studies have summarized the main passages in Hobbes's theory of sovereignty in which natural law plays a fundamental role. In fact, we find Hobbes's references to natural law in his most important works, such as *The Elements* (1640/1650), *De Cive* (1642), and *Leviathan*

 | DOI:10.1163/9789004748712_010

(1651).[1] The relationship between Hobbes's writings and natural law has been analyzed from various perspectives, such as religious studies, or conceptualizing positive law, morality, and international law.[2] Here I focus only on the relationship Hobbes posits between the theory of sovereignty and natural law. He mainly introduced the concept of natural law in Chapters 14 and 15 of *Leviathan*, in Chapter 15 of *The Elements of Law*, and in Chapter 2 of *De Cive*. Following here, I briefly explain the concept of natural law in some important passages of this work.

Chapter 14 of *Leviathan* begins with a statement that "the right of nature, which writers commonly call *Jus Naturale*, is the liberty each man hath, to use his own power, as he will himselfe, for the preservation of his own Nature."[3] Hobbes elaborates, saying that this refers to the *right* to preserve life, determining that individuals may use whatever means necessary to achieve this end. Richard Tuck's classic 1979 work refers to an intense debate here, going back to Taylor's thesis[4] and continued by Warrender's reading,[5] as to whether self-preservation is a *right* or a *duty* arising from natural law. Beyond this debate, Hobbes clearly defines this natural law with the term 'precept,' i.e., as a "general rule found by Reason," according to which everything that harms a human's life is forbidden. Hobbes thus distinguishes between *Jus* and *Lex*, i.e., between *Right* and *Law*, understanding the first term as *obligation* and the second as *liberty*. Since in a state of nature individuals are practically in a state of war, Hobbes points out that the first fundamental law of nature is "to seek peace, and follow it."[6] Hobbes's definition further call it "the summe of the Right of Nature," which for him is also related to the idea of self-preservation, but with seeking peace as part of the goal: "By all means we can, to defend our selves."[7] In *The Elements*, Hobbes points out that "the law

1 See: Thomas Hobbes, *Three-Text Edition of Thomas Hobbes's Political Theory: The Elements of Law, De Cive and Leviathan*, ed. Deborah Baumgold (Cambridge: Cambridge University Press, 2017).

2 S.A. Lloyd, "Natural Law," in *The Oxford Handbook of Hobbes*, eds. Al P. Martinich and Kinch Hoekstra (New York: Oxford University Press, 2013).

3 Thomas Hobbes, *Leviathan. Revised Student Edition*, ed. Richard Tuck (New York: Cambridge University Press, 2003), 91.

4 Alfred Edward Taylor, "The Ethical Doctrine of Hobbes," *Philosophy* 13, no. 52 (1938): 406–424.

5 Howard Warrender, *The Political Philosophy of Hobbes: His Theory of Obligation* (New York: Oxford University Press, 1957).

6 Ibid., 92.

7 Ibid.

of nature consisteth not in consent of men, but reason."[8] In *De Cive*, he repeats the same, pointing out that "the law of nature is not an agreement of men, but the dictate of reason."[9] In *The Elements*, Hobbes conceptualizes natural law as the 'dictates of reason':

> Reason is no less of the nature of man than passion, and is the same in all men, because all men agree in the will to be directed and governed in the way to that which they desire to attain, namely their own good, which is the work of reason. There can therefore be no other law of nature than reason, nor no other precepts of natural law, than those which declare unto us the ways of peace, where the same may be obtained, and of defense where it may not.[10]

For my analysis, it is important to explain the relationship between this definition of natural law and Hobbes's theory of sovereignty. Hobbes is well-known for his statement on the right of nature that "every man has a Right to every thing; even to one another's body."[11] In *The Elements*, *De Cive*, and *Leviathan*, Hobbes explains that in this situation that is life threatening the individual transfers his right to everything in order to protect his life and liberty. For Hobbes "the mutuall transferring of Right, is that which men call Contract."[12] He defines the "contract" with the terms "covenant" and "pact." In *De Cive* he also defines establishing contracts as a natural law: "Another of the laws of nature is, to perform contracts, or to keep trust."[13] In *The Elements* and *Leviathan*, Hobbes defines the breach of this contract as "unjust" or an "injury." The contract is thus related to natural law and also to the concept of *justice*: "But when a Covenant is made, then to break it is Unjust: And the definition of Injustice, is no other than the not Performance of Covenant. And whatsoever is not Unjust, is Just."[14] In Chapters 16 and 17 of *The Elements*, Chapter 3 of *De Cive*, and Chapter 15 of *Leviathan*, Hobbes lists and explains all the other natural laws. Further, in Chapter 18 of *The Elements* and Chapter 4 of *De Cive*, Hobbes develops the argument that natural law is "divine law." I

8 Thomas Hobbes, *Three-Text Edition of Thomas Hobbes's Political Theory: The Elements of Law, De Cive and Leviathan*, ed. Deborah Baumgold (Cambridge: Cambridge University Press, 2017), 141.

9 Ibid.

10 Ibid., 144.

11 Ibid., 145.

12 Ibid., 149.

13 Ibid., 163.

14 Ibid., 164.

will not list the various natural laws individually, although we can group them all together as moral imperatives and constraints. Hobbes explains how they operate in the *forum internum* ("inner forum") and then summarizes natural laws as "eternal" and "immutable":

> The laws of nature are immutable and eternal: what they forbid, can never be lawful; what they command, can never be unlawful. For pride, ingratitude, breach of contracts (or injury), inhumanity, contumely, will never be lawful, nor the contrary virtues to these ever unlawful, as we take them for dispositions of the mind, that is, as they are considered in the court of conscience, where only they oblige and are laws.[15]

The concept of natural law in Hobbes's theory of sovereignty relates specifically to the extent to which it limits the prince's exercising of sovereign power. It refers to the sovereign's duty regarding the 'safety of the people' as a natural law. Hobbes does not explicitly mention this *salus populi* principle in his list of natural laws but it is, of course, a political-moral maxim derived from the first fundamental law, i.e., the pursuit of peace. Turning to the relationship between exercising sovereign power and the people's safety, these chapters discuss issues that are common knowledge to the Hobbes scholars: as an English philosopher he primarily developed his theory of sovereignty in *Leviathan* (Chapter 18), *The Elements* (Chapter 20), and *De Cive* (Chapter 6). Hobbes's concept of sovereignty is expressed in the sovereign's unlimited power, his power to command, and his right to legislate. He refers to the concept of sovereignty as "supreme command" and "supreme power" and always highlights the power to legislate, as in stating "Now the notes of supreme command are these: to make and abrogate laws, to determine war and peace, to know and judge of all controversies, either by himself, or by judges appointed by him."[16]

The question is whether there is a natural law that limits the exercising of this sovereign power. In other words, what is the fundamental *duty* of the sovereign? We find answers in Chapter 28 of *The Elements*, Chapter 13 of *De Cive*, and Chapter 30 of *Leviathan*. *The Elements* explains that there is a *law* on the sovereign's exercise of power, identified as the *salus populi*, while *De Cive* defines this concept as the "safety of the people," and *Leviathan* defines it as

15 Ibid., 184.

16 Thomas Hobbes, *De Cive*, Ibid., 230.

"the procuration of the Good of the people."[17] Especially in *De Cive*, Hobbes defines most clearly that the sovereign's exercise of power is subject to the moral-political constraint of the "safety of the people":

> Now all the duties of rulers are contained in this one sentence, the safety of the people is the supreme law. For although they who among men obtain the chiefest dominion, cannot be subject to laws properly so called, that is to say, to the will of men, because to be chief and subject, are contradictories; yet is it their duty in all things, as much as possibly they can, to yield obedience unto right reason, which is the natural, moral, and divine law. But because dominions were constituted for peace's sake, and peace was sought after for safety's sake; he, who being placed in authority, shall use his power otherwise than to the safety of the people, will act against the reasons of peace, that is to say, against the laws of nature. Now as the safety of the people dictates a law by which princes know their duty, so doth it also teach them an art how to procure themselves a benefit; for the power of the citizens is the power of the city, that is to say, his that bears the chief rule in any state.[18]

Recent literature on the concept of natural law in Hobbes's theory of sovereignty has also emphasized that the goal of sovereignty is the "safety of the people." This is, for example, the interpretation of Philip Pettit's[19] important work on the concept of the state and Hobbes's theory of sovereignty. Pettit regards Hobbes's political-moral maxim of *salus populi* as a 'goal' of sovereign power, although Hobbes's description refers to a moral duty based on natural law.[20] More precisely, in *De Cive*, Hobbes adds that the "happiness" of the people is also at stake.[21] Since the sovereign has a moral duty to his subjects here, Lloyd's essay on Hobbes[22] interpreted the concept of natural law in Hobbes's work as a "law of reciprocity" in which the sovereign and subjects

17 Ibid., 336.

18 Thomas Hobbes, *De Cive*, Ibid., 339–340.

19 Philip Pettit, *The State* (Princeton/Oxford: Princeton University Press, 2023).

20 Ibid., 65, 125.

21 Thomas Hobbes, *Three-Text Edition of Thomas Hobbes's Political Theory: The Elements of Law, De Cive and Leviathan*, ed. Deborah Baumgold (Cambridge: Cambridge University Press, 2017), 340.

22 S.A. Lloyd, "Natural Law," in *The Oxford Handbook of Hobbes*, eds. Al P. Martinich and Kinch Hoekstra (New York: Oxford University Press, 2013), 265–270.

are primarily bound together by the sovereign's moral duty to protect and safeguard the people. Further, Zagorin[23] also reads these passages from *Leviathan* and *De Cive* as a moral or normative theory in Hobbes's work rather than as a theory of unlimited sovereignty, as does, for example, the influential reading of Schmitt.[24] However, in addition, there is an important and skeptical interpretation of these passages.

Notably, Hobbes's maxim of *salus populi* is a key concept featuring in the Roman republicanism that appears in Cicero's speeches. Although Hobbes refers to this maxim as a law on the sovereign's power and it therefore represents a moral constraint on his exercising absolute and unlimited power, there is also important literature that rejects this reading of Hobbes in normative and republican terms. The latter position seriously doubts that Hobbes intended to establish a normative theory rather than an egoistic and mechanistic political theory. For Herbert,[25] the theological character of natural law in Hobbes's work does not deny that Hobbes's view that subjects must obey the sovereign. Hobbes believes that one is obliged to uphold covenants not because of a moral imperative but because "it is a logical implication of one's natural inclination to act with regard to one's own interests and not disregard threats to 'the benefit of life'."[26] The aim of this essay is not to simply repeat ideas given in the established literature which show that Hobbes's work accepts precepts limiting the prince's exercise of sovereign power. Nor is the aim to resolve this discussion among scholars who doubt that Hobbes's theory of natural law contains a normative political theory. The objective is to explain how Hobbes scholars have conceptualized natural law by drawing on a range of legal, political, and moral theories. They have arrived at this natural law definition by drawing analogies with concepts introduced by other authors of political and constitutional theory. To understand this conceptualization, I now give a brief historical overview of the concept of natural law in the Hobbes scholarship.

---

23 Perez Zagorin, "Hobbes as a Theorist of Natural Law," *Intellectual History Review* 17, no. 3 (2007): 239–255.

24 Carl Schmitt, *The Leviathan in the State Theory of Thomas Hobbes: Meaning and Failure of a Political Symbol* (Chicago: University of Chicago Press, 2008).

25 Gary Herbert, "The Non-Normative Nature of Hobbesian Natural Law," *Hobbes Studies* 22, no. 1 (2009): 3–28.

26 Ibid., 26.

## 3 The Conceptualization of Natural Law in Hobbes's Theory of Sovereignty

The literature on the concept of natural law in Thomas Hobbes's work continues to develop. A recent article by Mansell[27] in the *Intellectual History Review* on Hobbes's theory of the right to resist has revived the discussion on how natural law forms the basis for the English philosopher's theory of sovereignty. Mansell argues that in Hobbes's political theory to protect oneself from death threats and physical danger is not only *natural* for individuals, but above all else, he finds, they have the *right* to self-protection. Mansell's central thesis is that there is an irreconcilable paradox between the theory of the individual right to resist and the concept of sovereignty in Hobbes's work. For Hobbes, natural law prescribes the individual's right to decide on the means necessary for self-preservation. However, according to Mansell,[28] Hobbes simultaneously assumes that this right to decide on self-preservation measures cannot be transferred to the sovereign, since every individual retains this right as a natural law. For Mansell, this reveals a point of tension between the natural law of individuals and the theory of sovereignty in Hobbes's work. Mansell finds that in spite of this contradiction having been discussed in the Hobbes literature for many years, it has not been resolved:

> Familiar discussion in Hobbes scholarship, though seldom with reference to natural law theory, concerns the apparent tension between the transfer of private judgment to the sovereign and the residual possibility for resistance to preserve one's life. For example, Steinberger observes "that […] the sovereign is owed absolute obedience and that the sovereign may be disobeyed in certain cases." He describes it as "an apparent contradiction so substantial as to raise serious doubts about the cogency of Hobbesian political thought in general." And Sreedhar contends there is a "genuine puzzle about how to understand the relationship between the conditional nature of Hobbes's account of political obligation and the unconditional, or absolute, nature of the Hobbesian sovereign."[29]

The discussion Mansell took up shows the topicality of the concept of natural law and the challenge it still represents for Hobbes scholarship. Although a

27 Samuel Mansell, "Hobbesian Resistance and the Law of Nature," *Intellectual History Review* (2023).

28 Ibid., 14–16.

29 Ibid., 1–2.

detailed analysis of the relationship between the concepts of natural law and sovereignty in Hobbes's work developed in the 1930s, its origins date from the end of the nineteenth century[30] when Hobbes's work experienced a remarkable reception and intellectual development in Germany through the sociologist and philosopher Ferdinand Tönnies.[31] Tönnies's famous work[32] influenced the interpretation of Hobbes's work in German-speaking countries quite remarkably. Notably, it was Tönnies who discovered Hobbes's *The Elements of Law*, a manuscript written in 1640. Tönnies's central thesis is that Hobbes brought together the classical tradition of natural law and the seventeenth century's new theory of the sovereign state. For him, Hobbes's concept of natural law is the basis of his theory of sovereignty, which explains why Tönnies associates it with authors such as Hugo Grotius and Samuel Pufendorf. Thus, according to Tönnies, in order to understand Hobbes's concept of natural law, one must examine the meaning this concept had in Hobbes's context and among his interlocutors at the time. In this sense, Tönnies had already anticipated Quentin Skinner's contextualist reading of Hobbes.[33]

The interpretation Tönnies introduced, which resulted from his discovery and reading of *The Elements of Law*, received an important impetus at the beginning of the twentieth century when, toward the mid-1930s, an intellectual discussion developed in England and Germany about the concept of natural law in Hobbes's theory of sovereignty. Of course, Europe was then experiencing a period of political crisis with the rise of fascism in Italy and Germany. Important texts were published during the 1930s, which discussed the concept of natural law in Hobbes's theory of sovereignty. In 1935 Leo Strauss published his book on Hobbes,[34] in German, positioning the English philosopher as the heir to the Aristotelian tradition of natural law.[35] Shortly

30 See: Tomaž Mastnak, "Hobbes in Kiel, 1938: From Ferdinand Tönnies to Carl Schmitt," *History of European Ideas* 41, no. 7 (2015): 966–991.

31 Ferdinand Tönnies, *Schriften Zu Thomas Hobbes*, ed. Arno Bammé (München/Wien: Profil Verlag, 2015).

32 Ferdinand Tönnies, *Hobbes: Leben Und Lehre* (1880/1896; repr., Hamburg/Frankfurt: Severus Verlag, 2019).

33 Quentin Skinner, "Thomas Hobbes and His Disciples in France and England," *Comparative Studies in Society and History* 8, no. 2 (1966): 153–167; Quentin Skinner, "The Ideological Context of Hobbes's Political Thought," *The Historical Journal* IX, no. 3 (1966): 286–317.

34 Leo Strauss, *The Political Philosophy of Hobbes: Its Basis and Its Genesis* (1936; repr., University of Chicago Press, 1963).

35 Leo Strauss, *Leo Strauss: Gesammelte Schriften: Band 3: Hobbes' politische Wissenschaft und zugehörige Schriften – Briefe*, ed. Heinrich Meier (Hamburg: Springer-Verlag, 2022), 257–258.

afterward, in 1938, the National Socialist jurist, Carl Schmitt, published a response to Strauss' reading, denying that Hobbes's theory of sovereignty was based on his theory of natural law. Schmitt[36] understood Hobbes as having rather a coherent egoistic understanding of human nature. Interestingly, simultaneous to Schmitt's claim, Alfred Edward Taylor, professor emeritus at Edinburgh University, published a seminal essay in which he conceptualized Hobbes's theory of sovereignty as a moral theory of power.[37] Taylor accepts that Hobbes's theory of sovereignty contains a psychological understanding of human egoism, but treats this as separate to Hobbes's concept of natural law as a moral theory of political power. This thesis became so influential among scholars of the time that, since the 1960s, it became known as 'the Taylor thesis.'[38] Virtually all subsequent studies of Hobbes's concept of natural law have been directly or indirectly influenced by Taylor's essay.

Due to the importance of Taylor's thesis to the study of the natural law concept in Hobbes's work, it is worth briefly summarizing his argument. Taylor's article, titled "The Ethical Doctrine of Thomas Hobbes," claims that Hobbes's scholarship mistakenly focuses overly on the content of *Leviathan*, which he defines as a *Streitschrift*, i.e., as a polemical work written in the context of a civil war. *De Cive*, on the other hand, is a less combative manuscript in which Hobbes develops his moral theory of political power. For Taylor, the question from which Hobbes departs, asks: "What is it that a good man *ought* to do?" To which Hobbes answers: "Obey the sovereign."[39] This obedience, however, is motivated by the moral duty to seek good for oneself in order to avoid anarchy. For Taylor, this indicates that Hobbes's psychological theory of the passions and egoism is separate from his moral theory of obedience. For Taylor, the duty to fulfill a contract in Hobbes's political theory refers to a deontology, an obligation to which the individual is bound in order to be a "good citizen." Taylor thus claims that there is a parallelism between the moral theory of Hobbes and the moral theory of Kant.[40] Although historically anachronistic, Taylor's treatment of Hobbes's theory of sovereignty as a proto-Kantian moral theory represents the first major attempt to understand natural law as a nor-

36 Carl Schmitt, *The Leviathan in the State Theory of Thomas Hobbes: Meaning and Failure of a Political Symbol* (Chicago: University of Chicago Press, 2008).

37 Alfred Edward Taylor, "The Ethical Doctrine of Hobbes," *Philosophy* 13, no. 52 (1938): 406–424.

38 Stuart M. Brown, "Hobbes: The Taylor Thesis," *The Philosophical Review* 68, no. 3 (1959): 303–323; C. Tarlton, "Rehabilitating Hobbes: Obligation, Anti-Fascism and the Myth of a 'Taylor Thesis.'" *History of Political Thought* 19 (1998): 407–438.

39 Ibid., 406.

40 Ibid., 409.

mative concept in Hobbes's work. For Taylor, Hobbes's moral theory focuses on the moral imperative of authority and it entails that the sovereign is not bound by civil law, but is subject to the moral imperative of natural law. Natural law is an "imperative of reason" that limits the sovereign's power to command because it requires him to exercise his power with benevolence, mercy, humanity, and good judgment. Taylor concludes that the concept of natural law in Hobbes's theory of sovereignty is to limit the power of the sovereign in a moral sense.

Taylor's thesis has had a lasting influence on the historiography of Hobbes's concept of natural law. Virtually every discussion on this concept is an extension or refutation of Taylor's interpretation. In 1957, Howard Warrender,[41] professor at the University of Sheffield, published one of the most important texts on this topic. Although he disagrees with Taylor's reading, he too recognizes it as valid, thus continuing the reading of Hobbes's concept of natural law as a theory of moral obligation. He concludes, similarly to Taylor, Hobbes, that the concept of natural law is a theory of moral constraint on the sovereign exercising power. This view is still framed by Taylor's anachronistic view that Hobbes's concept of natural law is comparable to Kant's deontological ethics. The idea remains that natural law theory is a moral theory because it provides precepts for human behavior, while it is also a legal theory because it offers a means of checking the legitimacy and validity of legal norms. The discussion about the concept of natural law in Hobbes's theory of sovereignty reached its climax in Keith Brown's book entitled *Hobbes Studies*,[42] which dealt mainly with Taylor's thesis. In the following decades, the debate continued among important Hobbes scholars. Gauthier[43] gives a moral theory of Hobbes's concepts of obedience and duty, while Tuck's classic book on natural law theories[44] contains an important chapter on Hobbes in which he again discusses the concept of natural law in relation to the concept of the sovereign's duty. Norberto Bobbio, an eminent Italian political scientist, published an English edition of his study on natural law according to Hobbes.[45] This was followed in

41 Howard Warrender, *The Political Philosophy of Hobbes: His Theory of Obligation* (New York: Oxford University Press, 1957).

42 Keith C. Brown, *Hobbes Studies* (Cambridge: Harvard University Press, 1965).

43 David P. Gauthier, *The Logic of Leviathan: The Moral and Political Theory of Thomas Hobbes* (Clarendon P., 1969).

44 Richard Tuck, *Natural Rights Theories: Their Origin and Development* (Cambridge University Press, 1979).

45 Norberto Bobbio, *Thomas Hobbes and the Natural Law Tradition* (1989; repr., Chicago: University of Chicago Press, 1993).

the 1990s by the studies of Burgess[46] and in the 2000s by Zagorin.[47] Finally, Stephen State[48] summarizes the entire intellectual development of this historiography on Hobbes's concept of natural law as no other has done before.

However, Hobbes research since the 1960s has strongly criticized the examination of Hobbes's concept of natural law using Taylor's analogies to other authors such as Kant. Notably, Skinner's contextualist approach criticizes the natural law approach Taylor initiated. As mentioned earlier, Taylor's thesis had an impact on the Hobbes historiography of the 1960s. Skinner[49] criticizes the fact that Hobbes is analyzed from a philosophical perspective related to natural law theory rather than from a historical context. Skinner's articles[50] of the mid-1960s are a reaction to this philosophical tendency to interpret Hobbes largely from his texts without due consideration of his context. Skinner specifically criticizes the interpretation initiated by Taylor and developed by Warrender: "It becomes clear, in short, that to accept a deontological interpretation of Hobbes's views is to remove any meaningful points of contact between Hobbes and his own intellectual milieu."[51] Skinner's critique emphasizes that rather than interpreting Hobbes's work within a normative and philosophical framework, there is a need to present historical evidence. Still, Skinner's critique does not clarify the concept of natural law in Hobbes's theory of sovereignty either. Although it is important to know the historical context of Hobbes's work, it is nevertheless important to explain how the concept of natural law as a normative concept in Hobbes's theory of sovereignty was developed. Skinner's contextualist approach is limited because it cannot explain, from a normative point of view, how natural law is related to the nature of the principles that bind the sovereign power of the prince.

Scholars examining the relationship between natural law and Hobbes's theory of sovereignty have emphasized its problematic nature. For Zagorin, mod-

46 Glenn Burgess, "On Hobbesian Resistance Theory," *Political Studies* 42, no. 1 (1994): 62–83.

47 Perez Zagorin, *Hobbes and the Law of Nature* (Princeton: Princeton University Press, 2009).

48 S.A. State, *Thomas Hobbes and the Debate over Natural Law and Religion* (New York/London: Garland Publishing, 1991).

49 Quentin Skinner, "The Ideological Context of Hobbes's Political Thought," *The Historical Journal* IX, no. 3 (1966): 286–317.

50 Quentin Skinner, "Thomas Hobbes and His Disciples in France and England," *Comparative Studies in Society and History* 8, no. 2 (1966): 153–167; Quentin Skinner, "The Ideological Context of Hobbes's Political Thought," *The Historical Journal* IX, no. 3 (1966): 286–317.

51 Ibid., 316–317.

ern natural law theory began not with Grotius but with Hobbes, which would mean that Hobbes's concept of natural law should be examined as the starting point of natural law theory. This discussion is in dialogue with Tuck's analysis of the historical origins of Hobbes's concept of natural law. In the constitutional theory literature dealing with the relationship between natural law and the theory of sovereignty, Hobbes has been portrayed as advocating a purely mechanistic theory of the state, divorced from natural law. This is, for example, Schmitt's now influential thesis on Hobbes, which excludes any moral limitation of the sovereign's power. For Schmitt, the sovereign creates law and is subject to nothing but his own will, so that there is no moral limitation of natural law on the sovereign.[52] For this reason, Schmitt sees Hobbes's theory of sovereignty as a precursor to his concept of *decisionism*. Schmitt's conceptualization of Hobbes's theory of sovereignty is precisely what leads us to the following discussion. Since Taylor's thesis, attempts have been made to conceptualize Hobbes's idea of natural law through analogies with other authors, such as Kant, and through theories of political and constitutional law. An important conceptualization in this respect is Bobbio's approach of comparing Hobbes's concept of natural law to Kelsen's concept of the basic norm. The next section explains how Bobbio uses this concept to explain Hobbes's theory of sovereignty and why this analogy, although historically anachronistic, is nevertheless an important contribution to Hobbes studies.

## 4 Bobbio's Conceptualization of Hobbes's Natural Law as Kelsen's *Grundnorm*

Hobbes's description of natural law envisages moral limits to the exercise of sovereign power, but the problem now is how to *conceptualize* this in his theory of sovereignty. Bobbio's book on natural law in Hobbes's work[53] gives an important position in this discussion, presenting the concept of natural law as similar to Kelsen's concept of basic norm (*Grundnorm*), which represents an important constitutional and political theory approach for understanding Hobbes's theory of sovereignty. This Kelsenian reading should be seen as a

52 See, for example, Schmitt's reading of Hobbes in *The Leviathan in the State Theory of Thomas Hobbes: Meaning and Failure of a Political Symbol.*

53 Norberto Bobbio, *Thomas Hobbes and the Natural Law Tradition* (1989; repr., Chicago: University of Chicago Press, 1993).

response to Schmitt's reading of Hobbes as a precursor of *decisionism*. In the 1930s, Schmitt published his influential interpretation of *Leviathan*,[54] where in chapter 4, he presents Hobbes as a political thinker entirely in the tradition of legal positivism. For Schmitt, it is nonsense to speak of a theory of natural law in Hobbes in order to justify, for example, a right of resistance: "The endeavor to resist the Leviathan, the all-powerful, resistance-destroying, and technically perfect mechanism of command, is practically impossible."[55] Schmitt finds no real starting point in Hobbesian theory for exercising a right to resist, because to assume a right to resist would, in his view, mean that Hobbes recognizes a right to civil war or a return to the state of nature. Since the state is already established in Hobbes's theory of sovereignty, Schmitt finds the right of resistance in Hobbes's work not only inconsistent, but even utopian.[56] Schmitt's interpretation is clearly a critique of the reading that emphasizes the importance of natural law. For him, natural law has no relevant place in Hobbes's theory of sovereignty because it does not limit sovereign power at all.

Bobbio's reading of Hobbes's concept of natural law is in dialogue with constitutional theorists such as Schmitt, discussing the relationship between natural law and positive law. Bobbio's early writing on Hobbes's work appeared exactly in the heyday of Taylor's thesis, in the 1960s.[57] Chapters 4 and 5 of the English edition of his book set out how natural law shapes Hobbes's theory of sovereignty. Bobbio points out that "Thomas Hobbes belongs, *de facto*, to the history of the natural law tradition," but "*de jure* to the tradition of legal positivism."[58] The Italian's central thesis is that Hobbes is the initiator of what is known in the nineteenth century as *legal positivism*.[59] This perspective of Bobbio is now widely accepted in constitutional theory literature. However, in contrast to Schmitt's reading of Hobbes as a legal positivist, he finds that Hobbes simultaneously belongs to the natural law tradition. Bobbio wonders how it is possible that the two schools of legal thought, which are portrayed as antagonistic in the twentieth century, could coexist in Hobbes's work. He finds an answer in the close relationship between the concepts of natural law and civil law in Hobbes's work. It is true the Hobbesian conception

54 Carl Schmitt, *The Leviathan in the State Theory of Thomas Hobbes: Meaning and Failure of a Political Symbol* (Chicago: University of Chicago Press, 2008).

55 Ibid., 46.

56 Ibid., 46–47.

57 Norberto Bobbio, "Hobbes E Il Giusnaturalismo," *Rivista Critica Di Storia Della Filosofia* 17, no. 4 (1962): 470–485.

58 Norberto Bobbio, *Thomas Hobbes and the Natural Law Tradition* (1989; repr., Chicago: University of Chicago Press, 1993), 114.

59 Ibid., 115.

of what is just or unjust in the state of nature offers no criterion. Bobbio points out that when the will of the sovereign creates positive law, the criterion of what is just and unjust appears with it. Yet, in contrast to Schmitt's decisionist reading, Bobbio finds no totalitarian conception of the state in Hobbes's theory of sovereignty, since it never says that only the sovereign can determine what is just and unjust.[60]

Bobbio questions why Hobbes's theory of sovereignty appeals to a theory of natural law. Indeed, Hobbes allows for natural law in his theory of sovereignty in that his legal positivism coexists with his conception of natural law. Bobbio acknowledges that legal positivists' appropriation of Hobbes's theory of sovereignty is coherent.[61] However, he thinks that the English philosopher started from natural law and arrived at legal positivism. Hobbes's conception of natural law differs from his contemporaries' approach. For Hobbes, argues Bobbio, there is no distinction between good and evil in natural law; what counts is the goal, i.e., the pursuit of peace.[62] Thus, Hobbes defines natural law as a "dictate of reason." Bobbio points out that the laws of nature in Hobbes's description of the list of natural laws, refer primarily to moral imperatives. Bobbio therefore argues that the laws of nature in Hobbes not only prescribe good and evil, but also have an end, which is established by the first fundamental law of nature, namely to seek peace and preserve life. For Bobbio, this explains how Hobbes starts from a conception of natural law but arrives at a conception of legal positivism, because the end is peace. To this end, individuals renounce their right to everything and establish a civil society. In other words, in contrast to Taylor's description of natural law being analogous to Kant's deontological ethics, Bobbio finds Hobbes has a teleological rather than a deontic ethics.

Although Bobbio acknowledges the legal positivism of Hobbes's theory of sovereignty, he also emphasizes how Hobbes constrains the sovereign through natural law.[63] The sovereign stands between the laws of nature and the citizens. The citizens are subject to the positive law, but the sovereign is not, for he is *legibus solutus*. The law Hobbes applies to the sovereign comes from natural law: "The sovereign is bound to observe natural laws. The laws of nature are thus silent for citizens, but they hold for the sovereign."[64] Thus, although it appears that Hobbes glorifies positive law, he ultimately establishes the limits and corrections of sovereign power. However, Bobbio points

60 Ibid., 117.
61 Ibid., 118.
62 Ibid., 119.
63 Ibid., 136.
64 Ibid., 137.

out that if the sovereign were to violate natural law, the subject is still not empowered to disobey the sovereign.[65] In this regard, Bobbio notes that Hobbes saves his absolutist theory of the state by pointing out that when the sovereign commits an unjust act, he is accountable to God, even if not to his subjects.[66] The sovereign can also make a mistake in his pursuit of peace. But the sovereign's error in his decisions does not give the subjects the right to resist. According to Bobbio, there is only one exception to this approach: the order of the sovereign that endangers the life of the subject.[67] This approach, of course, agrees with the first fundamental law of nature, which enshrines the right to self-defense in order to preserve peace. Bobbio thus asserts that natural law becomes the fundamental principle of Hobbes's theory of sovereignty:

> Hobbes [...] is a legal positivist by inclination and way of reasoning, but is by necessity a natural law theorist. He thus considers the supreme norm that supports the positive legal system to be a law of nature. Although he eliminates all interference from the law of nature as soon as the positive legal system has been instituted, he cannot avoid positing the law of nature at the basis of that system. That is, he falls into the arms of natural law theory when he seems to have definitely escaped from it.[68]

Bobbio has provided a groundbreaking interpretation from a constitutional and political theory perspective by conceptualizing natural law in Hobbes's theory of sovereignty in a similar way to Kelsen's concept of the basic norm in his classic book.[69] Bobbio here extended Taylor's neo-Kantian reading, which understood natural law in Hobbes as a political-moral imperative.[70] Bobbio

65 Ibid., 139.

66 Ibid.

67 Ibid., 140.

68 Ibid.

69 Hans Kelsen, *Pure Theory of Law* (1934; repr., Berkeley, CA: University of California Press, 1967); Andrei Marmor, "The Pure Theory of Law," in *The Stanford Encyclopedia of Philosophy*, ed. Edward N. Zalta (Metaphysics Research Lab, Stanford University, 2021), https://plato.stanford.edu/archives/fall2021/entries/lawphil-theory/.

70 Alfred Edward Taylor, "The Ethical Doctrine of Hobbes," *Philosophy* 13, no. 52 (1938): 406–424; Stuart M. Brown, "Hobbes: The Taylor Thesis," *The Philosophical Review* 68, no. 3 (1959): 303–323; C. Tarlton, "Rehabilitating Hobbes: Obligation, Anti-Fascism and the Myth of a 'Taylor Thesis.'" *History of Political Thought* 19 (1998): 407–438.

argues that natural law has the function of a basic norm (*Grundnorm*)[71] in the language of Kelsen's theory of law,[72] so that natural laws are not really laws, but rather "theorems" or "scientific principles," meaning: "They do not command but rather demonstrate. They do not oblique (or coerce), but rather aim to persuade."[73] In other words, the laws of nature are not binding legal norms but they demonstrate the validity of a system of legal norms. For Bobbio, Hobbes's theory of sovereignty, like Kelsen's theory of law, reduces everything to a *Grundnorm*.[74] The difference, however, is that the English philosopher conceives of this basic norm not as a normative hypothesis but as natural law. In Hobbes's theory of sovereignty, natural law is not binding, since only positive law is binding on citizens. However, Hobbes's concept of natural law has the function of giving force to the totality of the positive order. Bobbio's point is that natural law has the function of justifying positive law. For this reason, he sees no contradiction between natural law and the conception of legal positivism in Hobbes's theory of sovereignty. Bobbio argues that natural law strengthens positive law in Hobbes's theory of sovereignty.[75] Once the state has been established, natural law is no longer binding. Therefore, Hobbes accepts natural law only as a means or 'device' to justify the absolute validity of positive law.

Using this analogy to Kelsen's concept of *Grundnorm*, Bobbio argues that Hobbes, on the basis of natural law, gives a space, albeit very small, to the possibility of being disobedient to the sovereign.[76] We are dealing here with a form of the right to resist or to express civil disobedience, which Schmitt ruled out in his reading. Burgess,[77] Steinberger,[78] and Sreedhar[79] have dealt with this side of Hobbesian political thought, emphasizing the importance of natural law. However, Bobbio takes a different approach. He refers to the beginning

---

71 Norberto Bobbio, *Thomas Hobbes and the Natural Law Tradition* (1989; repr., Chicago: University of Chicago Press, 1993), 145.

72 Uta Bindreiter, *Why Grundnorm?: A Treatise on the Implications of Kelsen's Doctrine* (Berlin: Springer Science & Business Media, 2002).

73 Norberto Bobbio, *Thomas Hobbes and the Natural Law Tradition* (1989; repr., Chicago: University of Chicago Press, 1993), 145.

74 Ibid.

75 Ibid., 147–148.

76 Ibid., 168–170.

77 Glenn Burgess, "On Hobbesian Resistance Theory," *Political Studies* 42, no. 1 (1994): 62–83.

78 Peter J. Steinberger, "Hobbesian Resistance," *American Journal of Political Science* 46, no. 4 (2002): 856–865.

79 Susanne Sreedhar, *Hobbes on Resistance: Defying the Leviathan* (Cambridge University Press, 2010).

of chapter 3 in *De Cive*, where Hobbes points out that the sovereign must always be obeyed unless his commands conflict with the commands of God. However, Bobbio then explains how Hobbes rules out the possibility of subject disobedience to the sovereign due to the sovereign ultimately deciding what is good or bad, what is just or unjust. For Bobbio, the duty to obey the ruler has only two exceptions.[80] The first is if the ruler's commands offend God, and the second is if the ruler commands his subjects to honor him as if he were God himself. Yet, it is not clear to what extent these exceptional situations would really constitute a reason for disobedience to the sovereign. For Bobbio, the only natural law that survived after positive laws were introduced, is the law of obedience to civil laws.[81] Although Bobbio ends up concluding, like Schmitt, that Hobbes's theory of sovereignty is related to positive law, his great contribution is to conceptualize natural law as a "basic norm" (*Grundnorm*) that validates and legitimizes the system of positive laws.

## 5 The Contemporary Approach to Hobbes's Natural Law

Contemporary literature has recognized the importance of natural law in Hobbes's theory of sovereignty, but has not conceptualized it as Bobbio attempted to do with his analogy to Kelsen's theory of the basic norm.[82] Importantly, Hobbes's concept of natural law as something else because of its importance for constitutional and political theory. Bobbio's analogy not only explains the meaning of natural law, but also extends Taylor's proposal to understand natural law as a moral duty binding on the sovereign in his exercise of power. His proposal of natural law as a basic norm is not a description, but an attempt at a constitutional theory of sovereignty, which is precisely a legal-philosophical understanding that goes beyond the description of the context, in keeping with Skinner's criticism of the 1960s.[83] Although Mansell explains the tensions and difficulties of linking the theory of sovereignty to natural law, he does not propose a *concept* to define this relationship, as Bob-

80 Norberto Bobbio, *Thomas Hobbes and the Natural Law Tradition* (1989; repr., Chicago: University of Chicago Press, 1993), 169.

81 Ibid., 171.

82 Norberto Bobbio, *Thomas Hobbes and the Natural Law Tradition* (1989; repr., Chicago: University of Chicago Press, 1993).

83 Quentin Skinner, "Thomas Hobbes and His Disciples in France and England," *Comparative Studies in Society and History* 8, no. 2 (1966): 153–167; Quentin Skinner, "The Ideological Context of Hobbes's Political Thought," *The Historical Journal* IX, no. 3 (1966): 316–317.

bio did. The concept of natural law remains controversial in Hobbes scholarship, but it also emerges as a very important construct for contemporary state theory. In a sense Pettit presupposes it in his proposal to include the political-moral maxim of the *Salus populi suprema lex esto* as a moral duty in Hobbes's theory of the state.[84] Although Pettit defines this maxim as a 'goal,' he is in fact referring to the classic deontological discussion of the Taylor thesis about the moral imperative in exercising sovereignty to provide for the safety of the people. This idea envisages Hobbes's concept of natural law in the theory of sovereignty.

In contemporary literature, there seems to be two antagonistic positions: either Hobbes was a natural law theorist or a positive law theorist. Bobbio's analogous comparison of the natural law concept in Hobbes's theory of sovereignty and Kelsen's basic norm concept was an important attempt to find a synthesis of these two schools in Hobbes's theory of sovereignty. However, Bobbio's reading of Hobbes on the relationship between natural law and the theory of sovereignty is truly eclectic compared to the current literature. For Bobbio, Hobbes creates a synthesis between the first fundamental law of nature, based on natural law, and his positivist approach to constitutional law. Recent work on the concept of natural law in Hobbes's work is not as eclectic as Bobbio's suggestions. Cooper's book,[85] for example, locates Hobbes almost entirely in the natural law tradition, which is why he even attributes him to scholastic philosophy. In this perspective, Hobbes's natural law focuses primarily on morality and religion and their influence on the theory of sovereignty. This approach emphasizes natural law as a matter related to Hobbes's philosophy of religion, which makes evident the influence of Leo Strauss's reading.[86] Gary Herbert,[87] in contrast, gives a reading which denies the possibility of a normative character in Hobbes's theory of natural law. Since this debate about whether Hobbes was a natural law theorist or a legal positivist is immense, I will now focus exclusively on the current state of how the concept of natural law is understood in Hobbes's theory of sovereignty.

---

84 Philip Pettit, *The State* (Princeton/Oxford: Princeton University Press, 2023), 65, 125.

85 Kody W. Cooper, *Thomas Hobbes and the Natural Law* (University of Notre Dame Press, 2018).

86 Leo Strauss, *Leo Strauss: Gesammelte Schriften: Band 3: Hobbes' politische Wissenschaft und zugehörige Schriften – Briefe*, ed. Heinrich Meier (Hamburg: Springer-Verlag, 2022), 263–278.

87 Gary Herbert, "The Non-Normative Nature of Hobbesian Natural Law," *Hobbes Studies* 22, no. 1 (2009): 3–28.

Mansell's essay best exemplifies how puzzling the conceptualization of natural law in Hobbes's theory of sovereignty still is.[88] The central question he analyzes is whether the debate on the natural law concept in Hobbes's theory of sovereignty indicates whether there are laws that constrain sovereign power. In other words, the problem is whether natural law is superior to positive law. In referring to the important work of Burgess,[89] Steinberger,[90] Zagorin,[91] and Sreedhar.[92] Mansell highlights that the debate as to whether Hobbes is moving away from or closer to the natural law tradition has primarily been analyzed in Zagorin's work. The classic works of Warrender[93] and Burgess[94] tend to acknowledge that Hobbes was a natural law theorist. The importance of the laws of nature to Hobbes's theory of sovereignty is ascribed to his view these laws are prescriptive rather than descriptive. Hobbes's enumeration of natural laws in *The Elements, De Cive*, and *Leviathan* shows the importance of these laws for his conception of politics. He relates the concept of natural law to his idea of the "dictates of reason." More important in discussing the limits of sovereignty, however, is that natural law imposes some limitation on sovereign power if it is seen to act against God. Since natural laws are "eternal" and "immutable," they are higher than the power of the sovereign. However, extent to which violating the laws of nature invalidates the legitimacy of sovereignty, remains controversial: "Burgess adds that Hobbes, unlike Aquinas, does not believe that a sovereign command in conflict with natural law cannot be a valid law."[95]

When Mansell analyzes Hobbes's concept of natural law, he assumes that it leads to internal tensions and contradictions. To show this, he analyzes the case of the right to resist. Mansell points out that natural law in Hobbes's work

88 Samuel Mansell, "Hobbesian Resistance and the Law of Nature," *Intellectual History Review* (2023).

89 Glenn Burgess, "On Hobbesian Resistance Theory," *Political Studies* 42, no. 1 (1994): 62–83.

90 Peter J. Steinberger, "Hobbesian Resistance," *American Journal of Political Science* 46, no. 4 (2002): 856–865.

91 Perez Zagorin, *Hobbes and the Law of Nature* (Princeton: Princeton University Press, 2009).

92 Susanne Sreedhar, *Hobbes on Resistance: Defying the Leviathan* (Cambridge University Press, 2010).

93 Howard Warrender, "Hobbes' Conception of Morality," *Rivista Critica Di Storia Della Filosofia* 17, no. 4 (1962): 434–449.

94 Glenn Burgess, "On Hobbesian Resistance Theory," *Political Studies* 42, no. 1 (1994): 62–83.

95 Samuel Mansell, "Hobbesian Resistance and the Law of Nature," *Intellectual History Review* (2023): 6.

"generates the tension between the right to resist and the duty to obey."[96] For Mansell, Hobbes, unlike the natural law theorists who preceded him, holds that sovereign command is independent of its moral content. In Hobbes's theory of sovereignty, therefore, the sovereign's actions are the only authoritative way to interpret natural law in civil society. Yet, Mansell emphasizes that the only way to disobey the sovereign would be if he were to issue a command that violates natural law, pointing to the first fundamental law of nature that establishes the duty to preserve life. Mansell thinks that this could open a space for legitimate disobedience, the subject being disobedient because he rightfully should disobey, Hobbes's theory of sovereignty. As can be seen, these positions contradict each other, which would prove the contradictions of Hobbes's theory of natural law. Mansell echoes Slomp's reading that an individual can decide whether to (dis)obey a sovereign's command if it violates natural law: "The laws of nature are moral laws and, as sources of moral obligation, are superior to the civil laws of the commonwealth."[97] Mansell, however, returning to the issue Bobbio first raised, sees another contradiction here, since Hobbes on the one hand recognizes the right to disobey a command that violates natural law, but at the same time claims that it is a natural law not to break the contract. Mansell concludes that Hobbes's theory of sovereignty poses an insoluble problem because sovereignty, while limited by natural law, is at the same time limited to nothing other than the sovereign's own will.

The question of how to conceptualize natural law in Hobbes's theory of sovereignty seems to be a puzzling issue in contemporary literature. Mansell affirms that the interpretation of the right to resist in Hobbes's theory of sovereignty should at least be nuanced. Indeed, it would be necessary to analyze case by case the description of the exceptional cases in which Hobbes recognizes the possibility of disobedience to the sovereign. In disobedience to the sovereign, a space opens up, albeit in a very extraordinary way, for recognizing the importance of natural law in Hobbes's theory of sovereignty. Mansell's argument continues to revolve around Bobbio's claim regarding the tension in Hobbes's work between natural law and legal positivism. The fundamental question in interpreting the concept of natural law remains whether there is a limit to the power of the sovereign once the state has been established. A possible answer lies in the forgotten work of the German Hobbes expert, Ferdinand Tönnies. For him, natural law in Hobbes's work belongs in the realm of moral philosophy. The role it plays in the theory of sovereignty thus amounts

96 Ibid., 7.

97 Ibid., 11.

to an "abstract doctrine of law."[98] In this sense, the sovereign realizes natural law through positive laws. For Tönnies, however, natural law is so merged with positive law in Hobbes's theory of sovereignty that the real theoretical problem is the almost impossibility of distinguishing between the two.[99] This leads to the problem that while natural law is recognized as a moral imperative, it is not yet clear when and under what circumstances natural law actually limits the power of the sovereign. In other words, for Tönnies it is clear that Hobbes's theory of sovereign power implies a moral duty to limit power, but it is not clear what consequences this has for the theory of sovereignty.

## 6 Conclusion

This essay has given an overview of the various attempts to conceptualize natural law in Hobbes's theory of sovereignty. These attempts began in the 1930s and contained an important proposal in the Taylor thesis by drawing an analogy between Hobbes's concept of natural law and Kant's deontological ethics. The aim of these analogies was not only to describe, but also to explain the concept of natural law as a normative theory of politics. However, these kinds of analogies, viewing Hobbes as proto-Kant, were considered anachronistic and beyond contextual analysis. For this reason, the question of Hobbes's natural law has been a puzzle for decades. Various passages in Hobbes's work seem to contradict his own postulates when he assumes that the will of the sovereign determines what is good and bad, just and unjust. Since the 1960s, the debate has revolved around the question of whether Hobbes was a natural law theorist or rather the founder of what became known in the nineteenth century as legal positivism. Essentially, the debate still centers on the significance of Hobbes's use of natural law in defining the sovereign's moral duties. Although Hobbes recognized the importance of natural law in setting boundaries for the sovereign, contemporary literature still debates the internal contradictions this statement raises for the theory of sovereignty. The problem with the current literature is that it focuses on description, but not on finding a concept or an analogy by which to understand Hobbes's concept of natural law. This explains the importance of Bobbio's attempt to draw a parallel between natural law and Kelsen's concept of the "basic norm" (*Grundnorm*).

98 Ferdinand Tönnies, *Thomas Hobbes: Leben Und Lehre* (1896; repr., Stuttgart: Frommann Verlag,1925), 198.

99 Ibid., 230.

Bobbio's project of conceptualizing Hobbes's natural law as the equivalent of Kelsen's basic norm remains relevant for properly understanding Hobbes's theory of sovereignty. The main reason for this lies in the proposal presupposing that in Hobbes one can find a constitutional theory that presupposes a teleological ethics. The validity of positive laws is justified by the goal of striving for the first fundamental law of nature: the pursuit of peace and self-preservation. Bobbio's postulate is in line with the forgotten distinction Tönnies made about the concept of natural law in Hobbes's work. Natural law would be located within the horizon of moral philosophy, while in the theory of sovereignty it plays the role of an "abstract legal doctrine." It is precisely the latter definition that indicates Bobbio's analogy between natural law and Kelsen's basic norm as still relevant.

Although Bobbio's work was responded to the reading of Hobbes's theory of sovereignty as a pure theory of legal positivism, the implications of his project can be extended to the present day. If we accept the anachronism of the analogy, but embrace the theoretical implications of this reading of Hobbes, we can understand that natural law consists not only of precepts that regulate human behavior, but also validates the totality of positive norms. This contradicts the readings that affirm Hobbes's natural law as an object that must be regarded as nonsensical. It is precisely this last postulate that Schmitt expresses in his decisionist reading of Hobbes. Against the decisionist reading, Bobbio discovers an interesting horizon that pits Kelsen's reading of Hobbes against Schmitt's reading. Intellectual historians may find this reading of Hobbes anachronistic, but constitutional and political theorists find it very provocative and intriguing. This essay has sought above all to emphasize its importance for Hobbes's scholarship.

CHAPTER 9

# 'A Title to Another's Plenty': Rights of Charity in Locke's Political Thought

*Signy Gutnick Allen*

## 1 Introduction

This paper proposes to set John Locke's theoretical claims about property and labour alongside comments made in his written policy proposals. I suggest that doing so can help us to understand an apparent tension between two elements of his theory: on the one hand, the injustice of appropriating the legitimately held property of another and, on the other, the statements throughout his corpus outlining not merely an obligation to engage in charitable action when we are able but also the suggestion that the needy have a legitimate *claim* to others' goods. As Locke repeatedly notes, the origin of the state is the creation of a 'Power' to 'preserve the Property' of its members.[1] Respecting this property right is framed as an issue of justice, against which the demands of charity might be understood as either a contradictory feature of the theory, or as a limitation upon that right. Recent attempts to place these elements of the theory in their proper relation to each other have led to arguments that we should read Locke as giving a 'particularly firm basis' for 'traditional' (Thomistic) practices of charity.[2] Locke is thus presented as something very different from the theorist of rapacious proto-capitalism sometimes identified by earlier twentieth-century readers.[3]

I want to suggest here that while the *Two Treatises of Government* contains the clearest account of Locke's understanding of property rights, both in the state and prior to its creation, examining his concrete proposals for poor relief

1 John Locke, *Two Treatises of Government*, ed. Peter Laslett (Cambridge University Press, 2010 [1689]), 324. See also the statement that individuals in the state of nature put "*on the bonds of Civil Society* […] by agreeing with other Men to joyn and unite into a Community, for their comfortable, safe, and peaceable living one amongst another, in a secure Enjoyment of their Properties." Locke, *Two Treatises*, 331.

2 James Tully, *A Discourse on Property: John Locke and his adversaries* (Cambridge University Press, 2006), 132.

3 For a classic statement of this position, see C.B. Macpherson, *The Political Theory of Possessive Individualism: Hobbes to Locke* (Oxford University Press, 2011 [1962]).

 DOI:10.1163/9789004748712_011

helps to illustrate his analysis of the nature and source of most actual, rather than theoretical, poverty in seventeenth-century England. Reading the two texts together may indicate that in fact the Lockean right of charity, even in its most demanding form, is one which can be accommodated relatively easily into a society characterised by deep inequality.[4] While one right may act, in theory, as a limitation on the other, I will conclude by speculating that Locke's reliance on a simplified distinction between the truly needy and the 'begging drones' who illegitimately live on the labour of others is itself the outcome of his presentation of the origins and nature of private property.[5] As a result, his tangible views on how to distribute poor relief cannot be set aside as a mere product of his time but instead need to be taken seriously in any discussion of his understanding of the potential for economic redistribution. While it may be going too far to suggest that the policies which will be explored below are a necessary entailment of Locke's views on property, they may well be quite natural ones.

I will begin by outlining Locke's account of the origins of property and his comments about the claims the genuinely needy have on the property of more prosperous members of society. Turning to two prominent schools of thought in Locke scholarship, we will see that this apparent tension, between the rights of owners to dispose of their property as they wish and their obligation to use their surpluses for the maintenance of others, has been resolved in at least two ways. One approach argues that the obligation to provide charity is an 'imperfect duty': it does not originate in a *claim* made by the needy but is instead best understood as required by a 'Law of *Reputation*' which has its origins in our desire for the esteem of other.[6] In this account, we have an obligation to cultivate a charitable disposition within ourselves towards others but this cannot be understood as an enforceable call to radically reorganise economic distribution within society. A second school argues that the needy do indeed have a genuine claim to the goods of others: a 'title to another's plenty.' According to readers including James Tully and A. John Simmons this claim itself represents

4 My argument thus departs from the claim made by John Marshall, that the *imperfect* duty Locke "celebrated was a very limited sharing of resources by those who possessed the vast majority in a society of massive inequality, and it served to perpetuate that broad distribution of resources." John Marshall, *John Locke: Resistance, Religion and Responsibility* (Cambridge University Press, 1994), 325.

5 John Locke, "An Essay on the Poor Law," in *Locke: Political Essays*, ed. Mark Goldie (Cambridge University Press, 2002), 184.

6 For discussion of the role of the 'Law of *Reputation*' in Locke's *Essay Concerning Human Understanding* (1689) see Tim Stuart-Buttle, *From Moral Theology to Moral Philosophy: Cicero and Visions of Humanity from Locke to Hume* (Oxford University Press, 2019), 54–67.

a genuine and enforceable limitation on property accumulation, justifying both state intervention, such as taxation for the purpose of poor relief, and the argument that some especially large amounts of property ownership might be illegitimate in the first place.

Following a summary of these two approaches, I turn to a document which has been labelled by one of the proponents of the second school as simply evidence of Locke's 'personal feelings' regarding poor relief rather than his philosophically considered position: the 1697 *Draft of a Representation, Containing a Scheme of Methods for the Employment of the Poor*, written at the behest of the Board of Trade (published in Mark Goldie's 1997 collection of Locke's *Political Essays* as the *Essay on the Poor Law* and referred to henceforth as the *Essay*).[7] This work has frequently been used by scholars to articulate Locke's views on class.[8] Such readings, often set alongside his comments in the essay *On the Reasonableness of Christianity* (1695) about those whose "hand[s are] used to the plough and the spade" have led to the argument that Locke regarded the labouring and propertyless as less rational than those who had demonstrated their reason through appropriation; the former were therefore to be excluded from the political community. In the hands of readers such as C.B. Macpherson Locke's political system was thus tainted from the outset by overt bigotry towards the working classes.[9]

However, we need not share this view in order to find the *Essay* illuminating. Readings of Locke since Macpherson have emphasised the extent to which his work uses natural law theory to prioritise labour and was in fact intended as a criticism of the wastefulness of the idle aristocracy.[10] A wholesale denigration of the role of the worker in his political theory is therefore tenuous, and indeed some of Locke's other policy writings, such as his 1693 *For a General Naturalisation*, demonstrate the extent to which he saw labour as not merely the foundation of a nation's wealth but also of a just immigration policy encouraging the migration and settlement of skilled workers into England.[11] Nonetheless, while the *Essay* may not illustrate Locke's theory of the rationality of the *worker*, there is more evidence that he intended to tell us

7 A. John Simmons, *The Lockean Theory of Rights* (Princeton University Press, 1992), 335.

8 See Richard Ashcraft, *Revolutionary Politics & Locke's* Two Treatises of Government (Princeton University Press, 1986), Chapter 6 for a discussion of various interpretations of Locke on class and work.

9 Macpherson, *Possessive Individualism*, 221–229.

10 Ashcraft, *Revolutionary Politics*, 273–274.

11 John Locke, "For a General Naturalisation," in *Locke: Political Essays*, ed. Mark Goldie (Cambridge University Press, 2002). For discussion of this essay, see David Resnick, "John Locke and the Problem of Naturalization," *The Review of Politics* 49, no. 3 (1987): 368–388.

something about the rationality and moral attitudes of the *poor*. This in turn raises questions not only about the place of charity in his system, but also about the boundaries of political belonging and the extent to which state interference in the lives of its citizens is appropriate. As a result, while the material from the *Essay* has occasionally been treated as something of an embarrassment or sideshow, I argue that placing it alongside his theoretical work helps us to understand Locke's own understanding of the interplay between the demands of natural law and the internal purpose and workings of the modern state.

## 2 Property Rights and Charity Obligations

Locke's presentation of the origins of private property, and in particular the way in which the earth, given to 'Mankind in common,' came to be legitimately divided among individuals, is well known.[12] In contrast to the Patriarchalist Robert Filmer, the target of much of the first of the *Two Treatises*, Locke argued that God had not given the world and its resources directly to Adam to bequeath to his heirs, a reading of Genesis which, in Filmer's hands, had become a justification of absolute rule and the conflation of political and patriarchal power and thus anathema to political thinkers arguing for basic pre-political freedom and equality. However, unlike theorists including Hugo Grotius and Samuel Pufendorf, who had also emphasised the world's initially being held in common, Locke rejected the assertion that taking more from the common stock than what was required for one's direct use required others' consent.[13]

Making this theoretical move required that Locke be able to demonstrate that this kind of unilateral appropriation did not harm the rights of others, thus obviating the need for permission. This he achieved through what Robert Nozick would label the 'Lockean proviso,' according to which the initial accumulation of resources from the commons is limited by ensuring that there is still "enough, and as good" left behind. As a result, our own accumulation does not represent "any prejudice to any other Man."[14] This limitation is, at first, a

12 Locke, *Two Treatises*, 286.

13 For a good discussion of Locke's aims here see Tom Pye, "Property, Space and Sacred History in John Locke's Two Treatises of Government," *Modern Intellectual History* 15, no. 2 (2018): 327–352.

14 Locke, *Two Treatises*, 291. Robert Nozick, *Anarchy, State, and Utopia* (Blackwell Publishing, 2017 [1974]); 175–182.

natural one acting on our own ability to gather and use the goods of the earth. Locke argues that the process of appropriation involves the mixing of our labour, over which we have absolute earthly dominion, with natural resources, as when we gather apples from the "Trees in the Wood."[15] There is only so much labour we can engage in, and so at this initial stage of human development "considering the plenty of natural Provisions there was a long time in the World, and the few spenders, and [...] how small a part of that provision the industry of one Man could extend it self [...] there could be then little room for Quarrels or Contentions."[16] Even if we find ourselves to be remarkably efficient, gathering and hoarding too many of these apples will simply result in the excess rotting rather than being eaten, a further breach of the natural laws which Locke argues govern this form of property acquisition: "As much as any one can make use of to any advantage of life *before it spoils*; so much he may by his labour fix a Property in. Whatever is beyond this, is more than his share, and belongs to others. Nothing was made by God for Man to spoil or destroy."[17]

However with the invention of money, and thus both the means to trade goods and hire workers, both of these natural limitations on acquisition are overcome: trade means that we are no longer limited to acquiring the goods we will directly consume ourselves, and the ability to employ others means that we can be vastly more ambitious in our plans of appropriation. This is especially important when we consider that for Locke, labour mixing does not simply result in ownership over the goods of the earth we have collected, such as the crop of an orchard we have planted, but also of the land we have thus transformed.

As a result, large-scale inequality in landholdings becomes a theoretical possibility. In Locke's initial discussion of this process of unilateral acquisition he presents this as something of a 'zero-sum' game.[18] In a series of lectures he gave in 1663–1664 at Christ Church, Oxford, now known as the *Essays on the Law of Nature*, he argued that natural law cannot be reduced to mere self-interest because "if the private interest of each person is the basis of that law, the law will inevitably be broken, because it is impossible to have regard

15 Locke, *Two Treatises*, 288.
16 Locke, *Two Treatises*, 290.
17 Locke, *Two Treatises*, 290 (emphasis mine).
18 Heikki Haara and Tim Stuart-Buttle, "Beyond Justice: Pufendorf and Locke on the Desire for Esteem," *Political Theory* 47, no. 5 (2019), 722.

for the interests of all at one and the same time."[19] The case of natural resources is cited as a prime example:

> The inheritance of the whole of mankind is always one and the same, and it does not grow in proportion to the number of people born. Nature has provided a certain profusion of goods for the use and convenience of men, and the things provided have been bestowed in a definite way and in a predetermined quantity; they have not been fortuitously produced nor are they increasing in proportion with what men need or covet. Clothes are not born with us, nor do men, like tortoises, possess and carry about shelters that have originated with them and are growing up together with them. Whenever either the desire or the need of property increases among men, there is no extension, then and there, of the world's limits. Victuals, clothes, adornments, riches, and all other good things of this life are provided for common use. And so, when any man snatches for himself as much as he can, he takes away from another man's heap the amount he adds to his own, and it is impossible for anyone to grow rich except at the expense of someone else.[20]

By the time he turned to the *Two Treatises* more than three decades later, however, Locke had come up with a means of explaining how, especially following the creation of money, unilateral acquisition did not come at the "expense of someone else": the productive capacity of labour. According to this model, labour is not only a means of identifying which elements of the common stock we as individuals can lay legitimate personal claims upon, but the process of labouring itself, and therefore appropriation, is the mechanism by which the Lockean proviso is satisfied. The more intensive this labour, then, the better off we all are, even if we do not directly benefit ourselves:

> He who appropriates land to himself by his labour, does not lessen but increase the common stock of mankind. For the provisions serving to the support of humane life, produced by one acre of inclosed and cultivated land, are [...] ten times more, than those, which are yielded by an acre of Land, of an equal richnessee, lyeing wast in common. And therefor he, that incloses Land and has a greater plenty of the conveniencys of life

19 John Locke, "Essays on the Law of Nature," in *Locke: Political Essays*, ed. Mark Goldie (Cambridge University Press, 2002), 131.

20 Ibid.

> from ten acres, than he could have from an hundred left to Nature, may truly be said, to give ninety acres to Mankind.[21]

We thus see a nexus of ideas begin to form: self-ownership, including therefore of our own labour; labour as a means of appropriation; and labour as increasing the production of the earth, thus not only leaving behind enough and as good, but indeed of leaving behind more than when the appropriation began. On this account, it is not obvious that it is privatisation which is responsible for this immense gain in productivity, rather than simply labour itself, but it is clear that for Locke these ideas cannot be separated and so the development of private, productive land is presented as the only alternative to waste land held in common.

This process of property acquisition occurs in the pre-political state of nature, and Locke emphasises that it is largely due to our need to protect this property that we agree to set up government. This aim being at the heart of why individuals agree to engage in a commonwealth-creating social contract also helps to set the limits of state power:

> But *Government* into whatsoever hands it is put, being as I have before shew'd, instrusted with this condition, and *for this end*, that Men might have and secure *their Properties*, the Prince or Senate, however it may have power to make Laws, for the regulating of *Property* between the Subjects one amongst another, yet can never have a Power to take themselves the whole or any part of the Subjects *Property*, without their own consent. For this would be in effect to leave them no *Property* at all.[22]

While consent was therefore unnecessary in the initial process of acquisition, *appropriating* property which has been claimed already does indeed involve the breaching of rights and thus the spectre is raised of not merely absolute but arbitrary power. This is something which Locke also emphasises in his explanation of government functions such as legitimate taxation:

> 'Tis true, Governments cannot be supported without great Charge, and 'tis fit every one who enjoys his share of the Protection, should pay out of his Estate his proportion for the maintenance of it. But still it must be with his own Consent, *i.e.* the Consent of the Majority, giving it either by themselves, or their Representatives chosen by them. For if any one

21 Locke, *Two Treatises*, 294.
22 Locke, *Two Treatises*, 361.

> shall claim a *Power to lay* and levy *Taxes* on the People, by his own Authority, and without such consent of the People, he thereby invades the *Fundamental Law of Property,* and subverts the end of Government. For what property have I in that which another may by right take, when he pleases to himself?[23]

Once property has been correctly appropriated, it is largely the right of its owner to determine its use; even the case of taxation is framed by the need to pay for the protection afforded by the state, and hence via an appeal to the interest of the propertied in the systems put in place to protect their rights.

As a result of these structuring elements of the theory, it may therefore seem strange to see Locke emphasise the importance of charity. Nevertheless, remarks to this effect are found across his works. He is clear in a number of places, particularly in the first of the *Two Treatises* and in the *Essays on Natural Law,* that those with property are under an obligation to use it to assist the needy. Thus we see the claim that even were a single man (Adam) the sole proprietor of the world, it would not be permitted to him to "deny all the rest of Mankind Food, and so at his pleasure starve them."[24] In Essay VII of the *Essays on Natural Law* he argues that one of the "things of which the outward performance is commanded" is "the relief of one in trouble, the feeding the hungry" so long as "our property supplies means for charity."[25] Moreover, Locke's framing of charitable giving opens up the possibility that the needy have claim rights on the prosperous, just as those with property have a right to resist the state when it comes to arbitrarily expropriate them. Thus he not only makes the argument in moral terms, writing that it is a "Sin in any Man of Estate, to let his Brother perish for want of affording him Relief out of his Plenty" but also frames charity as itself a form of property rights, stating that it 'gives every Man a Title to so much out of another's Plenty, as will keep him from extream want, where he has no means to subsist otherwise."[26]

This raises a series of questions. What form would a claim to one's title in another's plenty take? Is there a tension between the property owner's right to dispose of their property as they wish and their obligation to assist the truly needy? The following section will examine ways in which various approaches to the texts have sought to reconcile these different rights claims.

23 Locke, *Two Treatises,* 362.
24 Locke, *Two Treatises,* 169.
25 Locke, "Essays on the Law of Nature," 123.
26 Locke, *Two Treatises,* 188.

## 3 Reconciling Rights

Among scholars who suggest that there need not be a tension between property rights and charitable obligations, the turn towards understanding Locke's project in its religious context has been particularly important.[27] In contrast with earlier, Marxist-influenced readings which saw him as laying the groundwork for individualistic and acquisitive liberal capitalism, readers including James Tully, John Dunn and Tim Stanton have emphasised the extent to which we need to recognise Locke's comments about property as being related to his account of God's plan for humanity. As Locke wrote in Chapter IV of the first *Treatise*, it is a consequence of God's "bid" to "Mankind [to] increase and multiply" that all have a "Right to make use of the Food and Rayment, and other Conveniences of Life, the Materials whereof he had so plentifully provided for them."[28] As we saw in the discussion of property rights above, Locke explicitly links labour, and the initial limits on appropriation due to the danger of spoilage, to God's purpose understood in this way. This purpose should not simply be seen as a source of limitations on appropriation but also, unsurprisingly given the account of productive labour, an impetus for it:

> God, when he gave the World in common to all Mankind, commanded Man also to labour, and the penuary of his Condition required it of him. God and his Reason commanded him to subdue the Earth, *i.e.* improve it for the benefit of Life, and therein lay out something upon it that was his own, his labour. He that in Obedience to this Command of God, subdued, tilled and sowed any part of it, thereby annexed to it something that was his *Property*, which another had no Title to, nor could without injury take from him.[29]

While the passage does emphasise the potential for injury in taking another's goods, this focus on God's plan for humankind, and the ways in which labour and appropriation function to fulfil this plan, have led some readers to emphasise this broader purpose as a way to understand potential obligations on the

---

27 This has been flagged both by scholars who argue for an imperfect duty of charity and by those arguing for a perfect duty. See, for an example of the former, Robert Lamb and Benjamin Thompson, "The Meaning of Charity in Locke's Political Thought," *European Journal of Political Theory* 8, no. 2 (2009): 229–230 and for an example of the latter, Juliana Udi, "Locke and the Fundamental Right to Preservation: On the Convergence of Charity and Property Rights," *The Review of Politics* 77, no. 2 (2015), 191–192.

28 Locke, *Two Treatises*, 169.

29 Locke, *Two Treatises*, 291.

propertied and, possibly, limitations on absolute rights of ownership. However, Locke's own double-pronged description of the nature of the charitable obligation, as both moral and legal, has meant that in turn the nature of this limitation remains contested.

The first of the two schools of thought, stressing charity as a *moral* limitation, understands property itself as but one mechanism within a holistic system. Steven Forde, for instance, emphasises that according to natural law, the individual property right "is not an absolutely fundamental or foundational right" but is rather a "necessary means to something else [...] not the preservation of individuals per se, but the common good of mankind."[30] For Forde, this reading is intimately bound up with reading Locke as a deeply Christian thinker: he points out that while we may have an absolute right over our own bodies and labour with respect to other humans, we are nonetheless God's creation and therefore our very labour can be understood as undertaken in line with the divine purpose.[31] According to this reading charity must be understood as operating on a different moral plane to justice rather than being an aspect of it: charity is, as he puts it, a "duty" but while it is a "more exacting moral standard" it is one "to which people cannot strictly be held" because, unlike the domain of justice, it is not a matter of "respecting the possessions of others."[32] While both property and charity can be understood as means of satisfying the common good, ultimately any tension between the two is presented as requiring a utilitarian calculation regarding how this common good will be best and most consistently satisfied. According to Forde's reading of Locke, this calculation suggests that it is best met through a political system which defends and respects the property rights of individuals rather than one which permits the poor to enforce a claim on the wealthy.

Echoing this strict division between the demands of justice and of charity, Robert Lamb and Benjamin Thompson have argued that the latter can best be understood as an *imperfect* duty: we have an obligation to cultivate a charitable disposition towards others, rather than a duty to redistribute wealth in specific ways.[33] They emphasise that the ways in which this disposition might manifest itself may not be in positive acts but rather through restraint, including from legal yet self-interested behaviours. In making this case, Lamb and Thompson analyse a text unpublished in Locke's lifetime, the '*Venditio*' (1695), which discusses the rights of merchants to determine prices. In that

30 Steven Forde, "The Charitable John Locke," *The Review of Politics* 71, no. 3 (2009), 432.
31 Forde, "Charitable John Locke," 436.
32 Forde, "Charitable John Locke," 451–452.
33 Lamb and Thompson, "The Meaning of Charity."

work, Locke writes that if a grain dealer opts to sell his wares to the poor at under the market rate this choice is "indeed charity but not what strict justice requires."[34] By contextualising Locke's discussion of charity through his writing on toleration, the argument is pushed further and we see that charitableness is not simply a question of acts of charity (as we might consider the choice to sell grain cheaply) but of a more general attitude. It could, for instance, involve modelling Christian love, by interpreting others' actions with generosity. Crucially, this is indeed an obligation, but it is a religious rather than a legally enforceable one which could be used to generate interventionist political structures.

This trend in Locke scholarship in many ways developed in opposition to an earlier set of studies which argued that, by contrast, we can indeed see charity as a duty which is of equal standing to those of justice and which emerges from rights held by the needy. James Tully, for instance, argues that a "proprietor who has more than enough to sustain himself is under a *positive* duty to sustain those who do not." Similarly, John Dunn describes the "duties of justice and charity" which all individuals "owe to one another as jural equals."[35] A. John Simmons, while carving out the narrower conditions under which this duty might apply, also emphasises that charity should not be understood as an imperfect duty. Instead, he turns to a passage from the *Essays on the Law of Nature* to make the case that charitable obligations should be understood as "conditional (perfect) positive duties":

> There are things of which the outward performance is commanded, for example [...] the relief of one in trouble, the feeding the hungry: in these matters we are not under obligation continuously, but only at a particular time and in a particular manner. For we are not obliged to provide with shelter and to refresh with food any and every man, or at any time whatsoever, but only when a poor man's misfortune calls for our alms and our property supplies means for charity.[36]

Simmons argues that accordingly "I am bound to give to others not always, but only when their needs and my means require it. But when these conditions are

34 John Locke, "Venditio," in *Locke: Political Essays*, ed. Mark Goldie (Cambridge: Cambridge University Press, 2002), 340.

35 John Dunn, *The Political Thought of John Locke: An Historical Account of the Argument of the 'Two Treatises of Government'* (Cambridge: Cambridge University Press, 1995), 169. Emphasis mine.

36 Locke, "Essays on the Law of Nature," 123.

satisfied, charity is absolutely required"; the obligation and right are each activated at the moment when the conditions are satisfied, regardless of other considerations emphasised in the 'moral' reading, such as whether one's esteem will be burnished by this particular interaction, or whether it is legal to avoid giving alms.[37]

One possible response to this second approach is that it does not adequately address the problem of a potential clash between the *rights* of justice and charity: might not the claim of the needy undermine the title of the proprietor? Tully's solution to this is neat and economical. Where the first set of thinkers examined above argued that any clash could be avoided by rendering charitable obligations imperfect and hence bolstering property rights (even as owners both should and are likely to give alms) he suggests that the surplus goods held by proprietors are simply already in the position of property owned by the poor. As he explains, the way Locke sets up the purpose and origins of the right to property *in* things means that when it comes to the destitute, "man's need creates a title *in* the goods of another, thus individuating his natural right not to be excluded from the means of preservation."[38] True charity and property do not contradict each other, in other words, because charity is itself a kind of legitimate property, even when it is in the possession of another.[39] However, while this appears to solve the problem at the theoretical level, two challenges remain: first, how could this natural law model which located ownership rights in the poor be practically implemented and, second, did Locke approach the claims of his own society's actually existing needy along the lines of this model?

## 4 Lockean Charity in Practice

It is undeniable that Locke believed in a moral duty to develop charitable attitudes towards others. Nonetheless, given his rights-based language of titles, it is also too hasty to dismiss the Lockean case for a genuine claim of some kind on the part of the needy. In this section I suggest that it was possible for Locke to adopt the second, more stringent account of charity while nonetheless avoiding the kinds of political challenges to existing property distribution which such an account may seem to entail. If the Lockean right of the

37 Simmons, *Lockean Theory*, 339–340.

38 James Tully, *An approach to political philosophy: Locke in contexts* (Cambridge: Cambridge University Press, 1993), 113.

39 See also Udi, "Locke and the Fundamental Right to Preservation," 194.

needy is indeed an encroachment on property rights, it may well turn out not only to be a fairly minor and easily accommodated one, but also one which was intended to be understood in this way.

This is, I argue, the message of the *Essay* which outlines Locke's proposed changes to the system of poor relief in England and which he presented to the Board of Trade in October 1697, following the Board's 1696 survey to measure the actual costs of the parish relief system. Established that year as an advisory body to the Royal Council, the Board was not a legislative body, but was rather tasked with providing expert guidance on both domestic financial policy and colonial administration; Locke was a founding member.[40] While the text was rejected, possibly for being seen as broadly too harsh, some changes were subsequently made to the Poor Law which echo Locke's suggestions, such as the introduction in 1697 of the 'shame sanction' requiring that recipients of poor relief and their offspring be identifiable through compulsory badging.[41]

The Board's intervention on this topic was not accidental. The 1690s were a decade in which the question of poor relief was widely understood to be pressing. It witnessed rising rates paid out due to historically bad harvests and economic depression, the result of which was increased expenditure, especially on exceptional or discretionary payments to working-age men who would, under normal conditions, be expected to support themselves from labour alone.[42] Locke clearly thought that this moment was an opportunity to consider the topic from its foundations, writing that the question of relief is "a matter that requires every Englishman's best thoughts; for there is not any one thing that I know upon the right regulation whereof the prosperity of his country more depends."[43] This 'matter' involved both philosophical questions regarding issues of morality and justice, discussed above, and practical implementation.

40 See Peter Laslett, "John Locke, the Great Recoinage, and the Origins of the Board of Trade: 1695–1698," *The William and Mary Quarterly* 14.3 (1957): 370–402.

41 See Mark Goldie's editorial notes to Locke, "Essay on the Poor Law," 182. Paul Slack, *The English Poor Law 1531–1782* (Macmillan, 1990), 40. On badging, see Steve Hindle, "Dependency, Shame and Belonging: Badging the Deserving Poor, C.1550–1750," *Cultural and Social History* 1.1 (2004): 6–35. For Locke's suggestion regarding badging (which does not in fact emphasise the shaming aspect of the practice), see Locke, "Essay on the Poor Law," 197–198. This response suggests that while scholars including Richard Ashcraft and Juliana Udi have argued that the document can ultimately be seen as motivated by an egalitarian and even compassionate approach to the poor, this was not the immediate response of Locke's contemporaries. Udi, "Fundamental Right to Preservation"; Ashcroft, *Revolutionary Politics*, 273.

42 Slack, *English Poor Law*, 27–28, 32.

43 See Mark Goldie's editorial notes to Locke, "Essay on the Poor Law," 182, quoting Letter 2398.

The *Essay* is characterised by a consistent distinction between the truly needy and those who are illegitimately claiming support, a demarcation which we have already seen referenced in his more theoretical comments above. Strikingly, as we will explore below, this bifurcation leaves little space for the category of the working or underemployed poor, a group which was nonetheless taking up increasing space in public discussion at the time when Locke was writing.[44] Locke's own understanding of the genuine/idle distinction helps to shed light on what Locke thought the 'matter' requiring consideration actually was, and how it related to the 'prosperity' of the nation. It indicates that for him the question was not simply provoked by the specific context of the 1690s but was rather a more fundamental point about the legitimacy of private property itself in the context of widespread need. In other words, issues of poor relief needed consideration because to understand the issue badly would place at risk the broader system of property which underpinned his account of productivity, and hence of national prosperity.

This is not simply a claim that too much poor relief would result in unjustifiable or unsustainable appropriation from private property owners, thus threatening individual rights. Locke does present this as the occasion for his comments, writing that "the multiplying of the poor, and the increase of the tax for their maintenance, is so general an observation and complaint that it cannot be doubted of," noting that this "has been a growing burden on the kingdom these many years."[45] Indeed, he is clearly concerned about this contextual or situated fact, writing that "the streets everywhere swarm with beggars [...] that [number] of beggards swarming in the street is manifestly very great."[46]

However, setting his various writings alongside each other shows that Locke's theory of poverty itself is based on a specific conception of the productive capacity of privatised land. He recognised that if the category of the needy was not defined in a very particular way, an idea hinted at in the *Two Treatises* and fleshed out in the 1697 *Essay*, then the very foundations of the justification of the private property regime, which he believed to be at the heart of English prosperity, would be at risk. Moving from the philosophical question of whether the right to charity undermines the property right towards his account of the practical considerations surrounding a system of poor relief thus allows us to ask a different question: what understanding of charity, and of the

44 See the discussion, for example, in Alexandra Shepard, "Poverty, Labour and the Language of Social Description in Early Modern England," *Past & Present* 201 (2008): 51–95.

45 Locke, "Essay on the Poor Law," 183.

46 Locke, "Essay on the Poor Law," 190.

population which is eligible for it, is required for Locke's theory of property to be successful and therefore legitimate on its own terms?

The distinction between the genuinely needy and the 'sturdy beggar' who refused to work was a long-standing one in English society, alongside the idea that those in the latter category needed to be put to work, as we can see in the development of the Elizabethan 'work houses.'[47] Locke, in replicating it, might therefore be seen as a product of his time. But simply reducing Locke's views on poverty and its nature and origins to seventeenth-century artefacts risks obscuring the extent to which these ideas are entwined with his broader political theory. If they are likely entailments of his account of the justification of property itself, then it becomes difficult not only to set aside the distinction between the genuinely and the illegitimately needy, but also to expand the category of the legitimately poor beyond the very narrow scope he offers in the *Essay*.

Turning to the content of the *Essay* itself, we can see how Locke goes about defining the 'matter' under consideration. In it, he argues that the reason for the increased tax burden is not "from scarcity of provisions, nor from want of employment for the poor, since the goodness of God has blessed these times with plenty."[48] The only reason Locke can conceive of for the increase in those calling upon poor relief is moral depravity. Men have both chosen not to work and have chosen to live beyond their means, especially by having more children than they can support. It is thus crucial for Locke to distinguish between the truly needy and the merely workshy or profligate, and this distinction drives his policy proposals. As he writes:

> Could all the able hands in England be brought to work, the greatest part of the burden that lies upon the industrious for maintaining the poor would immediately cease. For, upon a very moderate computation, it may be concluded that above one half of those who receive relief from the parishes are able to get their livelihood.[49]

The major concern of systems of poor relief is therefore not the distribution of genuine charity as such, but rather pushing those who "pretend they cannot get work" and who live off the "stock of the kingdom," a figure he places at

47 Marjorie K. McIntosh, "Poverty, Charity, and Coercion in Elizabethan England," *The Journal of Interdisciplinary History* 35. 3 (2005): 457–479.

48 Locke, "Essay on the Poor Law," 184.

49 Ibid.

100,000, into productive employment.[50] Among these "idle vagabonds" Locke counts all men between 14 and 50 years of age found begging, who are to be set to hard labour; this will apply to any found begging without a pass, regardless of their known capacity to work, suggesting that for Locke, the threshold for this capacity is set fairly low.[51] This, he claims, will solve most of the problem immediately: such individuals "being thus suppressed, there will not, we suppose, in most country parishes, be many men who will have the pretence that they want work."[52]

This focus on providing employment permeates Locke's policies; the text is therefore more about the question of poverty than it is about the moral or rights-based problem of charity, at least explicitly. As a result, most of the proposals involve not a loss of property, in the form of compulsory contributions towards poor relief, but rather policies which reinforce the relationship between labour and self-sufficiency. We can see this in Locke's account of how parishes should approach those who claim to lack work. He writes that:

> In order to the taking away of that pretence [of a want of employment], whenever it happens [...] the guardian of the poor of the parish [shall] acquaint the parish that such a person complains he wants work, and shall then ask whether anyone is willing to employ him at a lower rate than is usually given, which rate it shall then be in the power of the said guardian to set; for it is not to be supposed that anyone should be refused to be employed by his neighbours, whilst others are set to work, but for some defect in his ability or honesty, for which it is reasonable he should suffer.[53]

As he puts it, "he that cannot be set on work for 12d per diem, must be content with 9d or 10d rather than live idly."[54] The closest that Locke does come to suggesting that this kind of policy involves what we might consider to be charitable action involving a loss to the giver is when he notes that if no one in the community volunteers to employ such individuals, then all individual rate-

50 Locke, "Essay on the Poor Law," 184, 189.

51 Locke, "Essay on the Poor Law," 185.

52 Locke, "Essay on the Poor Law," 187.

53 Locke, "Essay on the Poor Law," 187–188. Alongside frequent references to the possibilities for moral reform, discussions of poor relief often emphasised the need to *punish* the idle poor. M.J. Rozbicki, "To Save Them from Themselves: Proposals to Enslave the British Poor, 1698–1755," *Slavery & Abolition* 22. 2 (2001): 33; 38.

54 Locke, "Essay on the Poor Law," 188.

payers in the parish can be forced to employ them on a rotating basis and again at the (lower) rate set by the guardian of the poor.

While both Locke's analysis of the idle worker, and his proposed solution of hiring such individuals to perform already-existing work, indicate a highly moralised and individualised account, he does occasionally recognise that there are structural limits to the work which some individuals can carry out. Some of his suggestions are for what could be seen as the removal of systemic barriers to labour, such as his account of labourers' wives who are unable to work due to childcaring duties. His proposed solution is that children as young as three years old should be taken from poor families during the day and placed in working schools, in order that both parents can obtain paid employment: "by this means the mother will be eased of a great part of her trouble in looking after and providing for them at home, and so be at more liberty to work."[55]

The case of poor families reminds us of Locke's framing of the topic around his concern for national prosperity; perhaps unsurprisingly the idle poor are presented as being not merely a drain on resources but also as an untapped source of further wealth. Once children have entered working schools, they work for the community rather than for their family: of such schools we read that "though at first setting [them] up may cost the parish a little, yet [...] [they] will quickly pay [their] own charges, with an overplus' which will be returned to the parish."[56] A parallel claim is made regarding the case of the man sent to work at sea, whose wages are then sent not only to support his wife and children but also the poor of the parish.[57] We might find here a connection to the argument that those who can work but do not until forced by the parish are to be paid at lower rates. The lack of rationality which is assumed among the idle poor is used to sever their economic identity from that of the wage labourer who is able to make contracts on his own terms and who, Locke argues, should not be pressured into exploitative employment due to his

55 Locke, "Essay on the Poor Law," 190.

56 Locke, "Essay on the Poor Law," 192. While this paper emphasises the role of working schools as generators of income for parishes, it is worth noting that from Locke's perspective, there were further benefits: the schools were an opportunity for moral and religious instruction and would also be a means of ensuring that children had daily meals (albeit frugal ones). One question this raises is of the role of the parish in assuming parental authority, which Locke connects elsewhere in his work to the ability to support one's children. Locke, *Two Treatises*, 210. On this dynamic in practice see Tim Wales, "'Living at Their Own Hands': Policing Poor Households and the Young in Early Modern Rural England," *Agricultural History Review* 61, no. 1 (2013): 28.

57 Locke, "Essay on the Poor Law," 188.

need for work.[58] Locke's position is thus neatly summarised: "This, rightly considered, shows us what is the true and proper relief of the poor. It consists in finding work for them, and taking care that they do not live like drones upon the labour of others." As a result, the vast majority of poor relief will not involve charity understood as a limitation on the use rights associated with private property; indeed, the opposite is true, with most policies designed to reduce the relief paid out to the community's indigent.

Turning to the genuinely needy recipients of relief, Locke is careful here too to limit the extent to which claims upon the community can be made. While he does note that "if any person die for want of *due* relief in any parish in which he *ought* to be relieved, the said parish should be fined according to the circumstances of the fact and the heinousness of the crime,"[59] quite a lot rides on the question of what is indeed due to the person in question. In his description of how the elderly and disabled poor should live, he writes that "those who are not able to work at all, in corporations where there are no hospitals to receive them, [should] be lodged three or four or more in one room, and yet more in one house, where one fire may serve, and one attendant may provide for many of them, with less charge than where they live at their own choice scatteringly."[60] This account seems to be perfectly consistent with his presentation of the charity right outlined above, according to which it is only those who have no other means to support themselves who have a title in the surplus property of others, and in which this title is only to that which will keep the poor from 'extream want.' This subsistence level of relief is thus presented as provided on the terms of the giver rather than as a self-preservation right determined and claimed by the needy, albeit with an external measure found in the danger of actual death.[61] While, as we saw, Locke abandoned the

58 Locke, *Two Treatises,* 170: "a Man can no more justly make use of another's necessity, to force him to become his Vassal, by with-holding that Relief, God requires him to afford to the wants of his Brother, than he that has more strength can seize upon a weaker, master him to his Obedience, and with a Dagger at his Throat offer him death or slavery." Some readers have suggested that such passages should be read as Locke's rejection of capitalist employment contracts based on necessity. See Tully, *Discourse on Property,* 136–137.

59 Locke, "Essay on the Poor Law," 198 (emphasis mine).

60 Locke, "Essay on the Poor Law," 197.

61 The question of 'titles' raises a further complication, which this paper does not have space to adequately address: the extent to which it makes sense to think about a perfect obligation to help those in need as a form of 'charity' at all. In contemporary discussions there is certainly suspicion of this move. One solution might be to frame this title not as a right to *charity* but as a right to the means of preservation. This answer might help clarify some matters while muddying others, however. While it might explain Lockean limits to the right, to what is needed to keep body and soul together, it's not clear why, once

zero-sum story about property accumulation he outlined in the *Essays on the Law of Nature*, the suggestion that those who are the recipients of genuine charity are indeed living at the expense of others, no matter how legitimate this is, may help to justify this fairly limited assistance.

## 5 Reading the Essay Alongside Locke's Theory of Property

A question that this summary of the *Essay* raises is the extent to which a modern Lockean theory might be able to adopt the broad principles outlined, while rejecting his specific recommendations or framing, such as the systemic removal of children from poorer families or the setting to work of the unemployed at artificially low rates. Might the Lockean charity right, in other words, be retained as a limitation on the private property right without these concrete elements of its seventeenth-century application?

In this section, I conclude by arguing that Locke is unable to escape not only a moralised account of poverty, according to which it is generally caused by an irrational refusal to work rather by circumstance, but also that this inability is linked to the account of labour and property appropriation which he developed long before considering the details of poor relief.

As mentioned above, there were a number of reasons outside of individual control for rising poor rates in the 1690s, such as a series of poor harvests. This indicates that Locke's claim regarding the widespread availability of work, and hence the source of poverty, was a misdiagnosis. My suggestion is that by previously arguing that the almost universal appropriation of land through its cultivation had led to vastly more resources, and therefore vastly more

self-preservation is invoked, the right is limited to the *surplus* of others. Moreover, self-preservation evokes the possibility of the needy themselves determining what they require and how to obtain it, something which Jeremy Waldron accepts in his account of the right: Locke "seems to be committed not to a view about *giving* but to the view that neither the rich nor civil society on their behalf is entitled to *resist* the poor when the poor attempt to seize their surplus goods for themselves. It is not a question of forcing the rich to do anything: it is enough that they be compelled to simply stand back and let the poor take what (on account of their 'pressing Needs') is rightfully theirs." Jeremy Waldron, *God, Locke, and Equality: Christian Foundations in Locke's Political Thought* (Cambridge: Cambridge University Press, 2002), 185. This vision seems at odds with both the account outlined in the 1697 *Essay* and with the presentation of taxation based on consent rather than legitimate appropriation, cited above. For discussion of the history of the idea of rights of self-preservation see S.G. Swanson, "The Medieval Foundations of John Locke's Theory of Natural Rights: Rights of Subsistence and the Principle of Extreme Necessity," *History of Political Thought* 18.3 (1997): 399–459.

opportunities for labour, Locke was unable to accommodate the possibility that this form of property acquisition would not adequately distribute opportunities for self-preservation through available paid work. In the *Two Treatises* he wrote, of the power of enclosing land, that:

> There cannot be a clearer demonstration of any thing, than several Nations of the *Americans* are of this, who are rich in Land, and poor in all the Comforts of Life; whom Nature having furnished as liberally as any other people, with the materials of Plenty, *i.e.* a fruitful Soil, apt to produce in abundance, what might serve for food, rayment, and delight; yet for want of improving it by labour, have not one hundredth part of the Conveniences we enjoy: And a King of a large and fruitful Territory there feeds, lodges, and is clad worse than a day Labourer in *England*.[62]

Locke's staking his theory of unilateral acquisition not only on this productivity, but also on this productivity benefiting the 'day Labourer' as well as the landowner raises the question of the impact on his theory if these labourers found themselves in increasingly precarious economic circumstances, as was arguably the case when he wrote the *Essay*. If the majority of those put in a position of claiming poor relief were not lazy or vicious, but merely unable to access the kinds of work which might constitute "enough and as good" being left behind at the moment of initial appropriation, then it is possible that Locke's theoretical edifice was more vulnerable than it initially seemed.

The analysis I have provided here is speculative, but it might lead to a view of what Locke was *doing* in his policy writing which is somewhat at odds with recent philosophical approaches to his theory more broadly. When Joshua Cohen, for instance, presented his analysis of how Locke was able to reconcile an account of natural equality with what Cohen termed "the legitimacy of a class state" he went on to argue, using a range of Lockean texts (though not the *Essay*), that while Locke's *preferred* outcome is a landowner's state, and the propertyless would plausibly have good reasons to consent to this, this is not a necessary entailment of Locke's commitments.[63] The views of the actual poor

62 Locke, *Two* Treatises, 296–297.

63 Joshua Cohen, "Structure, Choice, and Legitimacy: Locke's Theory of the State," *Philosophy & Public Affairs* 15, no. 4 (1986): 301–324. For an account which suggests that the philosophical Locke (in contrast to the historical Locke) might be read as providing the resources for 'welfare-state capitalism' partly due to the self-preservation right see Kristin Shrader-Frechette, "Locke and Limits on Land Ownership," *Journal of the History of Ideas* 54.2 (1993): 201–219.

Locke wrote about in actual England could thus be hived off as essentially irrelevant, and the radical potential, at least, of the theory was thus maintained. Lockean principles could well be used to design a much more egalitarian, distributive commonwealth.[64] What I have suggested in this chapter, in contrast, is that once Locke committed himself to the view that labour not only rendered land productive but also legitimated private ownership, he was backed into a corner: a lack of available work might threaten claims both about productivity and about the linked legitimacy of ownership, as the Lockean proviso arguably ceases to be fulfilled. The answer, then, was to suggest that there was no shortage of opportunity after all. Not only are the categories of genuinely needy and idle among the poor thus a natural outcome of his prior commitments, but so too is the argument that the latter will always outnumber the former, leading to a focus on policies, however harsh or misguided, designed to push the supposedly irrational and malicious individuals placed in this category into underpaid and coercive labour.

## Acknowledgement

This chapter was written while Signy Gutnick Allen was a fellow of the 'Just City' project at the University of Zurich, led by Professor Benjamin Straumann and funded by the European Research Council (ERC) under the European Union's Horizon 2020 research and innovation programme (grant agreement No. 864309).

64 See Waldron for an analysis which cautions against the danger of extrapolating from Locke's concern for universal preservation to a 'social democrat' Locke who might well recognise that it is in the best interests of humanity for property rights to be deployed in a generous welfare state. Waldron, *God, Locke, and Equality*, 185.

CHAPTER 10

# New World, Immemorial Possession: Commons and Private *dominium* in Portuguese America (Camamu, Seventeenth to Eighteenth Centuries)

*Sarah Limão Papa*

## 1 Introduction

On October 17, 1779, in Portuguese America, in a village called Camamu, a Catholic Priest submitted a petition to the Queen of Portugal. The petition sought royal grace to permit Father Marcelino Francisco de Mello and his brother, the sergeant major Antonio Jozé de Mello, to continue jointly erecting and fabricating a watermill for processing sugar cane in a portion of land of which he was *senhor* and *possuidor* – lord and possessor – for more than fifteen years. The watermill had been demolished by order of the governor general of Brazil, who claimed that the construction encroached upon land held in common use by the people of Camamu since time immemorial, dating to the period when the Jesuits owned the property. This dispute uncovered a complex web of social and legal interactions within this land that can be traced centuries back until the beginning of colonization.

Before the foundation of the village of Camamu, in 1563, the governor of Brazil, Mem de Sá, made a testamentary disposition, including the portion of land in question, to the Society of Jesus. For centuries, the Jesuits promoted the occupation of the region with indigenous and colonists' settlement, by managing their estate and conducting evangelical missions. In the lands of Camamu, the Society of Jesus traded in timber, held watermills, farms, and pastures of their own, but they also transferred part of their lands to settlers through tenancy agreements, such as ground rents and emphyteusis. With the suppression of the Society of Jesus from the Portuguese Empire, in 1759, their dominions in Camamu where confiscated. The lands, then, went to public auction, being acquired in partnership by three men in 1763. Later, a Catholic priest purchased the land from the partners and, around fifteen years after the acquisition, he began constructing a watermill for processing sugarcane, known as an *engenho de açúcar* in Portuguese, or simply *engenho*. However, while the *engenho* was still under construction in 1779, colonial authorities demolished it to clear the area surrounding the village of Camamu for the

 | DOI:10.1163/9789004748712_012

common use of the people. After this, we arrive at the case, when Father Marcelino asked the Queen of Portugal for royal grace to continue the construction of his sugar mill and to receive reparation for the damage he had suffered.

At first glance, the village of Camamu seems to be an interesting case to trace a chain of *dominia* – titles for acquiring ownership – that can be followed for centuries. However, this diversity of juridical relations that people formed around this land reveals not only the ways in which land was distributed and acquired in the colony, but also the legal meaning of accessing the land, namely, which set of rights and obligations were attached to land usage in Portuguese America. Under Jesuit domain, the lands of Camamu were colonized, and a village was formed. After their expulsion, changes in ownership reflected a tension typical of the transition from the eighteenth to the nineteenth centuries: how to accommodate communal and private rights in the age of enclosure?[1]

The end of the eighteenth century is often considered a landmark in the birth of juridical modernity, characterized by the empowerment of the individual, the rise of the national state, and the consolidation of an idea of absolute property. The case of the *engenho* of Camamu illustrates the clash between communal legal practices and the evolving notions of property and governance, highlighting the complexities of this transitional period. Considering this scenario, the aim of this paper is to analyze how a specific parcel of land has been legitimately used in different ways by different subjects – individuals, community, the Crown, and the Society of Jesus – and how royal and local authorities mediated the conflicts that arose, by identifying which legal arguments and instruments were used to justify the different uses of the land.

## 2 The Society of Jesus and the Village of Camamu

To enable the governance of the colony, the Portuguese Crown divided their possessions in America into jurisdictional spaces named captaincies, which could be donatary or royal. Based on the late medieval institute of lordship, the donatary captaincies were hereditary, and they were attributed to a subject by means of a donation charter (*carta de doação*), which described the

1 Enclosure refers to the process during the eighteenth and early nineteenth centuries where commons and wastelands were consolidated into individually owned farms, leading to the displacement of peasants and altering agricultural practices and land rights. See: E.P. Thompson, *Customs in common* (London: Penguin Books, 1991).

rights and obligations of the donatary captain over that space.[2] The extent of the donatary captain's jurisdiction over a certain territory could vary a lot depending on the terms of the donation chart, but it usually involved matters of civil and criminal justice, as the power to nominate special magistrates (*ouvidores*),[3] as well as the power to grant land – through *sesmarias*. When expressly stated by the donation chart, the donatary captain could also have the privilege of *non appellando*, which meant that the decisions of its magistrates could not be appealed within royal courts. In theory, the donatary captain could have more temporal jurisdiction than a royal captain.[4]

The scope of the jurisdiction of the Brazilian captains, particularly their capability of granting lands, was described by a Jesuit from Bahia, who wrote a letter to the Father General Claudio Acquaviva, in 1586, in order to provide him with information on the lands in Camamu. According to this document, these captains were not lords of the land "in the same way that a man in Europe is of his entailed property or household" because, in Brazil, the captains could only acquire personal property up to ten leagues of land, out of which they could not hold more than two leagues continuously in the same territory. In these ten leagues of land, the captains were lords and, as these lands belonged to their entailed property, they could "lease and sell them as they wish." As the captain had the duty to promote the settlement of the captaincy, he was entitled to grant the remaining land "freely to whoever asks for them without imposing any rent or tribute, but only with a tithe to God, and this is what they call here giving *sesmaria*." Once lands were granted in *sesmarias*, neither the captain or his successors could take them back or impose tributes or obligations, and "those to whom *sesmarias* are given are so much the owners that they can sell, donate, and lease them as they do every day."[5]

2 Graça Salgado, *Fiscais e meirinhos: a administração no Brasil colonial* (Rio de Janeiro: Nova Fronteira, 1990), 46.

3 The office of *ouvidor* was an important position within the judicial administration. According to the eighteenth-century jurist, Mello Freire, the *ouvidores*, in Brazil, were like the *corregedores*, in Portugal, who "*regiam jurisdictionem spirant.*" *Ouvidores* were responsible for criminal and civil cases within their jurisdiction, as well as to judge appeals from decisions of ordinary judges. See: Yamê Paiva, *Os regimentos dos ouvidores de comarca na América portuguesa, séculos XVII e XVIII: esboço de análise* (Nuevo Mundo Mundos Nuevos, 2017).

4 Gustavo César Machado Cabral, "Os senhorios na América Portuguesa: o sistema de capitanias hereditárias e a prática da jurisdição senhorial (séculos XVI a XVIII)," *Jahrbuch für Geschichte Lateinamerikas 52.1* (2015): 75.

5 The original document was written in Spanish, and transcribed by Coelho Filho, who translated and published a Portuguese version in: Luiz Walter Coelho Filho, "Informação das

This system of land grants played a crucial role in colonization by transferring the responsibility of occupying and cultivating land to the vassals. This incentivized the vassals to make the land productive through agriculture, primarily relying on the labor of peasants and enslaved people, driving the expansion and economic exploitation of the colonies.[6] By analyzing conflicts between major landlords and peasants, Alveal observed that, in practice, *sesmarias* grants enabled for the accumulation of large amount of land under the *dominium* of a few families. These families would then transfer the duty of cultivation of the land to peasants and small farmers who would become their tenants, contributing to the creation of a colonial signorial regime. In many cases, as explained by Alveal, after smallholders' exercise possession over wasteland, these families would force them to pay fees without previous contract of rents or emphyteusis, claiming that they were the owners of the land by title of *sesmarias*, even though they were absent or did not previously comply with the duties of demarcation or cultivation.[7]

The history of the village of Camamu is inseparably linked to the history of a *sesmaria* grant. Initially, the region was part of the captaincy of Ilhéus, which was donated by King Dom João III to the clerk Jorge de Figueiredo, in 1534. Through a donation chart (*carta de doação*), Jorge de Figueiredo became the first donatary captain of Ilhéus, where he granted great parcels of land, in *sesmaria*, to the Governor of Brazil, Mem de Sá, who donated part of these lands to the Society of Jesus by testamentary disposition.[8] These lands, known as *fundo das doze léguas*,[9] were populated by the Aimorés, an indigenous nation accused of barbarianism and anthropophagy by one of the most prominent Jesuits of the Brazilian mission, José de Anchieta.[10] These accusations

Terras do Camamu no ano de 1586. Manuscrito sobre a Sesmaria dos Jesuítas," *Revista do Instituto Histórico e Geográfico Brasileiro* v. 182, no. 487 (2021): 291–310.

6 Nelson Nozoe, "Sesmarias e apossamento de terras no Brasil colônia," *Revista EconomiA* v. 7, no. 3 (2006): 587–605.

7 Carmen Alveal, *Senhorios Coloniais: direitos e chicanas forenses na formação da propriedade na América Portuguesa* (Niterói: Proprietas, 2022).

8 Marcelo Henrique Dias, *Economia, sociedade e paisagens da capitania e comarca de Ilhéus no período colonial* (Niterói: Universidade Federal Fluminense, 2007), 43.

9 *Fundo das doze léguas* can be translated as land of twelve leagues, since the name serves as to make a reference to the size of the donation, estimated in 79,2km. In: Luiz Walter Coelho Filho, "Informação das Terras do Camamu no ano de 1586. Manuscrito sobre a Sesmaria dos Jesuítas," *Revista do Instituto Histórico e Geográfico Brasileiro* v. 182, no. 487 (2021): 291–310.

10 Filipe Eduardo Moreau, *Os índios nas cartas de Nóbrega e Anchieta* (Annablume, 2003), 304.

served to justify the subduing of the natives and the seizure of their lands through just war and conversion.[11]

Despite being within the jurisdiction of a donatary captain, social historians attribute to the Jesuits a primary role in colonizing the lands of Camamu.[12] Until the end of the sixteenth century, the Jesuits could only make use of a small fraction of the land, located on an island, in which they cultivated small crops and raised cattle, an activity that did not require much labor force, and that, according to Father Manuel da Nóbrega, was better suited for the Jesuits, especially in lands inhabited by indigenous peoples, since "people did not make use of it out of fear of the Indians, but for the priests, it was permitted to move among the Indians."[13] This capability of "moving among the Indians," which was related to the Jesuits' evangelical mission and knowledge of local languages, enabled the missionaries to expand the frontiers of the empire, by promoting both indigenous and colonist settlements, while acting as mediators between them.[14] The means by which the Jesuits were able to promote both indigenous and colonists' settlements in the region were their double role as tutors for the converted natives and landlords to the free peasants.[15]

11 See: Anthony Pagden, *The fall of natural man: the American Indian and the origins of comparative ethnology* (Cambridge University Press, 1986).

12 Marcelo Henrique Dias, *Economia, sociedade e paisagens da capitania e comarca de Ilhéus no período colonial* (Niterói: Universidade Federal Fluminense, 2007), 111. For more, see: Rafael dos Santos Barros, *Da letra da lei às práticas coloniais: arranjos e conflitos na sesmaria dos jesuítas, 1700–1750* (Salvador, 2016).

13 Letter to Father Francisco Aragonese, requesting permission to seek land from the Governor of Brazil, Martim Afonso. June 11, 1561. ARSI, Bras 15, 114.

14 In Portuguese America, the missionaries had a prominent role in forging the Empire, using conversion to turn indigenous people into vassals of the Christian King while also asserting the political influence of the Church on both sides of the Atlantic. See: Giuseppe Marcocci, *Pentirsi ai Tropici: casi di coscienza e sacramenti nelle missioni portoghesi del'500* (Bologna: Edizioni Dehoniane, 2014), 15; And, Tamar Herzog, *Frontiers of possession* (Cambridge: Harvard University Press, 2015), 70.

15 As part of their role in the conversion of indigenous peoples, the Jesuits established educational institutions. The *Colégios* served various purposes, including the education and care of orphans, as well as the instruction of both indigenous and non-indigenous populations in matters of faith and academics. The first *Colégio* of Brazil was founded in Bahia, in 1549. The reasons for its foundation are deeply intertwined with the expansion of the Portuguese Empire, as elucidated in a document written in 1598: "The occasion for this was the desire of King Dom João of Portugal of good memory to populate this land of Brazil, which was under his conquest: and seeing on one hand the great fruit that Father Master Francisco was producing in India, both in the conversion of the Gentiles and in the spiritual benefit of the Portuguese, and on the other hand the obligation to convert the natives of this land, as it belonged to the mastery of Christ, whose perpetual administrator he is, and for whose sake he takes its *dízimos*; it seemed to him that the members

Due to the long-lasting resistance of the Aimorés, alongside with ecclesiastical limitations for land leases, it was only in the beginning of the seventeenth century that the Jesuits were able to attract colonists to their lands and promote the occupation of Camamu.[16] Hence, Camamu had not been colonized by Portuguese descendants when the missionaries began their efforts to settle there, as can be observed in the History of the Foundation of the College of Bahia, written in 1589:

> [...] these lands are hindered by a cruel and fierce people who do not allow the Portuguese to settle there. Once this impediment is lifted, which will happen when God sees fit to remove that plague, the lands will be very profitable because they are very good and have plenty of water for sugar mills.[17]

The resistance of the Aimorés was not the only obstacle faced by the Jesuits in promoting settlements in Camamu. Their religious vows also restricted their economic activities. Unlike other major landlords and religious orders, the Jesuits were bound by apostolic poverty, which meant they could not freely dispose of their lands nor engage in every agricultural activity without proper authorization. For example, before engaging in the extraction of *pau-brasil* (Brazilwood), they needed an explicit permission, which arrived in 1573, under the conditions that "it is done out of necessity to sustain our members, without scandalizing the locals or making it appear as a commercial enterprise, and ensuring that it is not used for superfluous things."[18]

The Jesuits also had several limitations on how they could rent their lands. To cope with the principle of inalienability of Church property, they were not allowed to grant lands *in perpetuum*. According to the missionaries of Bahia, differently from European soil, with each harvest, the Brazilian lands would be worth less, and fewer people would be interested in acquiring the right to

---

of the Company were suitable to relieve his conscience in the conversion of its natives. And so, at his request, our Father Ignacio of good memory ordered that some of ours should come to begin what the King intended, and they came in the year 1549 with Governor Tomé de Souza, who was the first whom the King sent to populate and govern this state of Brazil." In: Fundação dos Collegios e Residencias do Brasil, 1598, ARSI, BRAS 11.II, fl. 497.

16 Rafael dos Santos Barros, *Da letra da lei às práticas coloniais: arranjos e conflitos na sesmaria dos jesuítas, 1700–1750* (Salvador, 2016), 48.

17 ARSI, Bras. 11 I–II, *fundatio collegii bahiens*, 497.

18 Letter from Father General Guevardo Mercuriano to Provincial Ignatio Tholosa dated December 12, 1573. In: ARSI, Bras 2, 43.

cultivate it. Consequently, tenants would seek long-term contracts, especially perpetual ones. After intense negotiation with Rome, the Society of Jesus obtained authorization to lease their lands without restrictions, in 1601, being able to establish long-term rents and emphyteutic leases.[19] Although the Pope had given his license *in absolute*, the license should not be used if the land could be rented for certain years or leased for lives "because it is always considered that either of these two means is better than the emphyteusis *in perpetuum*."[20]

During the medieval period in Europe, ground rents and emphyteutic leases were broadly used by landlords who possessed great extensions of land.[21] In Portugal, emphyteutic leases were widely used by manorial estates, municipal councils, and religious orders to promote cultivation of wasteland. Although granting lands *in perpetuum* was not compatible with the inalienability of Church property, it was not uncommon to find ecclesiastical land granted in emphyteusis.[22] In the transition to early modern age, the Church in the Peninsula started to limit land leases for the duration of lives (*aforamentos em vidas*), a policy that was incorporated by the constitutions of the bishoprics published in the sixteenth century.[23] Following this tradition, land leases for the duration of lives was also a common form of granting rights to the land in Portuguese America. The terms of the contracts could include various obligations and restrictions on the lessee's use of the land and its resources which allowed landlords to exercise significant control over the territory and its tenants.[24]

Finally, by renting great portions of land in long-term leases, while also pacifying indigenous people through their missionary activities, the Society of Jesus promoted the settlements and formation of villages, attracting to

---

19 Serafim Leite, *História da companhia de Jesus no Brasil. Vol. I* (Rio de Janeiro: Civilização Brasileira, 1938), 161.

20 ARSI, Bras. 3, 173.

21 Rosa Congost and Pablo F. Luna, eds., *Agrarian Change and Imperfect Property: Emphyteusis in Europe (16th to 19th centuries)* (*Rural History in Europe, vol. 15*) (Turnhout: Brepols, 2018).

22 Cassiano Malacarne, "A regulação da enfiteuse ou aforamento pelo direito romanocanônico e monárquico em Portugal em fins do século XIII e começo do XIV: predecessores da enfiteuse no Brasil," *Sæculum–Revista de História*, no. 26 (2012): 13.

23 Margarida Sobral Neto, "Formas de acesso à posse da terra e à fruição de rendimentos fundiários em Portugal na Época Moderna: o caso da enfiteuse," in *XIV Congresso Internacional de Historia Agrária* (Badajoz, 2013), 16.

24 Manoela Pedroza, "Padres-senhores, enfiteutas, foreiros e partidistas: práticas proprietárias e conflitos sobre direitos de propriedade na América portuguesa (séculos XVI, XVII e XVIII)," in *XII Congresso Brasileiro de História Econômica* (Niterói. 2017).

Camamu several families that were at the margins of the land grant system – peasants who dedicated themselves to subsistence agriculture.[25] Since the lease could include a wide range of obligations and restrictions, the missionaries not only led the occupation of the region but also regulated how the people of Camamu could use the land and its natural resources, for instance, by determining the kind of crops that could be planted, how improvements could be done, which kind of animals could be raised, in which *engenho* the tenants could benefit their sugarcane, and so on.[26] As illustrated by Pedroza, in occasions, the tenants of the Jesuits were forbidden to commercialize wood, some were obliged to provide two thirds of their sugar production to the Priests,[27] and others were only allowed to plant cassava.[28] Some of these restrictions were related to their rental agreements, others could be part of a broader colonial policy, as in the case of cassava.[29] In any case, the way that the Jesuits managed their estates and the relations that they forged with local communities continued to resonate long after they were suppressed from the Portuguese Empire, as illustrated by the dispute between Father Marcelino and

25 Rafael dos Santos Barros, *Da letra da lei às práticas coloniais: arranjos e conflitos na sesmaria dos jesuítas, 1700–1750* (Salvador, 2016), 48.

26 Marcelo Henrique Dias, *Economia, sociedade e paisagens da capitania e comarca de Ilhéus no período colonial* (Niterói: Universidade Federal Fluminense, 2007), 331.

27 The practice of sharecropping of sugar cane, known in Brazilian historiography as *cana obrigada*, was largely practiced in the context of the colonial sugar economy. It describes a rural partnership in which the landlord – who also owned the sugar mill – allocated portions of the land to free men, farmers, and peasants through legal agreements. These peasants cultivated sugar cane at their own expense, bringing the harvested cane to be processed in the mill. As part of the agreement, they shared a portion of the production with the landlord. Although it describes a legal agreement between two free individuals, these contracts were deeply marked by power imbalance. For more, see: Stuart B. Schwartz, *Sugar plantations in the formation of Brazilian society: Bahia, 1550–1835* (Cambridge University Press, 1985); Vera Lúcia Amaral Ferlini, *Terra, trabalho e poder: o mundo dos engenhos no Nordeste colonial*, 1988.

28 Manoela Pedroza, "Padres-senhores, enfiteutas, foreiros e partidistas: práticas proprietárias e conflitos sobre direitos de propriedade na América portuguesa (séculos XVI, XVII e XVIII)," in *XII Congresso Brasileiro de História Econômica* (Niterói, 2017), 22.

29 It was not uncommon that the Crown would edit a norm ordering, indistinctly, the cultivation of a specific kind of plant in a certain territory. In February of 1688, the Portuguese Crown determined that the inhabitants of different regions in Bahia were obliged to plant mandioca (cassava) in order to prevent food shortage, without distinguishing between the types of *dominium*. The order was reinforced later, in 1701. According to the document, this norm should be observed by whoever did not own at least six slaves. In: *Alvará régio sucitando a observância da lei de 15 de fevereiro de 1688 obrigando os habitantes da capitania da Bahia à plantação de mandioca.* In: AHU, Bahia, Cx. 8, Doc. 1351–1355.

the People of Camamu over the common lands of the village. Before delve into this case-study, the next topic is dedicated to contextualizing the ownership regime, in Portuguese America, in the broader framework of the early modern age and the *ius commune* tradition.

## 3 As Many *dominia* as People and Things: An Overview of *iura in re* in Portuguese America

Current trends in legal historiography, led by authors such as Hespanha, Clavero, and Grossi, have been representing the juridical culture of early modern societies as plural and diverse, maintaining some level of continuity with the juridical and political fragmentation inherited from medieval traditions. For these authors, before the emergence of the modern state, law and governance were not under a monopoly of the central political power. As a consequence, instead of a major rupture from the medieval period, the juridical culture of early modernity can be better characterized by a growing tension between the maintenance of the *ius proprium* of local communities and the expansion of the legislative power of the Monarch.[30]

Considering this scenario, royal normative acts were just one form of expression of the law, among various others with distinct legitimacy, such as Roman law, Canon law, feudal law, and local customs.[31] Since there was no ultimate rule on solving normative conflicts, the application of law was casuistic, which means that all these different norms functioned as *topoi*[32] or knowledge of normativity[33] in solving concrete cases. Overall, the local juridical culture also depended on several factors related to the social fabric of the different communities, such as their centrality within the broader scope of the Kingdom, the role of local landlords and religious authorities, the ethnicity of the population, and the level of literacy of local judges and other authorities. Fur-

30 See: António Manuel Hespanha, *A Cultura Jurídica Europeia: Síntese de um Milénio* (Almedina, 2003); Bartolomé Clavero, *Antidora: Antropología católica de la economía moderna* (Giuffrè, 1991); Paolo Grossi, *L'Europa del diritto* (Laterza & Figli Spa, 2016).

31 Gustavo César Machado Cabral, *Ius commune: uma introdução à história do direito comum do Medievo à Idade Moderna* (Editora Lumen Juris, 2019).

32 António Manuel Hespanha, "Porque è que existe e em que è que consiste um direito colonial brasileiro," *Quaderni Fiorentini per la storia del pensiero giuridico moderno* v. 35, no. 1 (2006): 59–81.

33 Thomas Duve, "Legal History as a History of the Translation of Knowledge of Normativity," *Max Planck Institute for Legal History and Legal Theory Research Paper Series*, no. 2022–2016 (2022).

thermore, as part of the tradition of the *ius commune*, specific rules had the power to derogate general rules, which increased the flexibility of the law.[34] A similar phenomenon can be observed in Portuguese America – but in a greater degree due to local circumstances – which led Hespanha to defend the existence of an autonomous colonial law in Brazil, beyond the occasional enactment of specific rules by the Portuguese Crown. For Hespanha, in this legal framework, juridical autonomy was less a product of specific legislative enactments than of "the local capacity to address the juridical gaps or indeterminacies inherent in the very structure of the *ius commune*."[35] Moreover, this legal autonomy does not set the Brazilian juridical experience apart from the European juridical background. On the contrary, the very structure of the *ius commune* enabled the particularism of peripheral legal orders such as the Brazilian colony, by providing a series of principles and norms that adapted well to casuistic legal cultures.[36] Consequently, the occasional rules enacted by the Portuguese Crown were not the sole determinants of legal practice. Instead, they coexisted with and were often mediated by the flexible, context-specific application of a broader and more complex legal tradition.[37]

It is important to note that, despite this normative diversity typical of premodern state societies, the second half of the eighteenth century, in Portugal, was marked by numerous enlightenment-inspired reforms, primarily led by the Marquis of Pombal, the Secretary of State for King José I (1750–1777). Unlike liberal movements typical of this period, the aim of these reforms was to modernize the Empire, while also increasing the monarch's political control

---

34 For a broader perspective on local law, see: Alejandro Aguero, "Local Law and Localization of Law," in *Spatial and temporal dimensions for legal history: research experiences and itineraries, v. 6 (2016)*, 101; and, António Manuel Hespanha, "As fronteiras do poder: O mundo dos rústicos," *Seqüência: estudos jurídicos e políticos* v. 26, no. 51 (2005), 47–106. For the Brazilian case, see: Gustavo César Machado Cabral, Delmiro Ximenes de Farias and Sarah Kelly Limão Papa, *Fontes do direito na América Portuguesa: estudos sobre o fenômeno jurídico no período colonial (séculos XVI–XVIII)* (Fi, 2021).

35 António Manuel Hespanha, "Porque è que existe e em que è que consiste um direito colonial brasileiro," *Quaderni Fiorentini per la storia del pensiero giuridico moderno*, v. 35, no. 1, 59–81 (2006): 59–60.

36 Hespanha, "Porque è que existe e em que è que consiste um direito colonial brasileiro", 80.

37 For the Spanish colonies, see: Víctor Tau Anzoátegui, *Casuismo y sistema: indagación histórica sobre el espíritu del derecho indiano* (Universidad Carlos III de Madrid, 2021); and: Alejandro Agüero, "Local Law and Localization of Law," in *Spatial and temporal dimensions for legal history: research experiences and itineraries* v. 6 (2016), 101.

over the metropole and overseas.[38] Although a large number of reforms were carried out, there was no major rupture in the Portuguese governance until the second half of the nineteenth century. One major reason was that these moves toward centralization of power faced significant resistance from other social bodies in preserve their self-governance.[39] In matters of justice, there was an attempt of juridical reformation with the enactment of the *Lei da Boa Razão*, which aimed to promote the primacy of royal norms.[40] For Garriga and Slemian, the Lei da Boa Razão ultimately contributed to increase the importance and relevance of jurisprudence – both doctrinal and judicial – due to the attempt of replacing established rules of interpretation with vague guidelines.[41] Hence, even in the second half of the eighteenth century, despite being positioned as the head of political authority, the monarch did not exercise total control over social and juridical affairs. Rather, the fragmented political structure inherited from medieval societies persisted, with the king's role seen as maintaining harmony among various social bodies.

As the ultimate arbiter of order, a major virtue associated with monarchs was their power-duty to dispense justice.[42] This concept of justice, encompassed within a broader idea of *iurisdictio*, included not only judicial functions, but also what are now considered political competencies, such as legislative and administrative duties.[43] These functions were inseparable from one another and were not systematized into public and private spheres, as seen in modern conceptions of governance, until the nineteenth century.[44] Hence, political power and governance were part of a broader conception of author-

---

38 Kenneth Maxwell, *Pombal, paradox of the Enlightenment* (Cambridge University Press, 1995), 160.

39 Pedro Cardim, "Centralização política e Estado na recente historiografia sobre o Portugal do Antigo Regime," *Revista Nação e defesa*, no. 87 (1998), 150.

40 Gustavo César Machado Cabral, "A lei da boa razão e as fontes do direito: Investigações sobre as mudanças no direito português do final do antigo regime," *Anais do XIX Encontro Nacional do CONPEDI* (2010), 6117.

41 Carlos Garriga and Andréa Slemian, "Em trajes brasileiros: justiça e constituição na América ibérica (c. 1750–1850)," *Revista de História* (2013), 200.

42 António Manuel Hespanha, *Cultura Jurídica Europeia: Síntese de um milénio* (Coimbra: Almedina, 2012), 115. For more, see: Jesus Vallejo, *Ruda equidade, ley consumada: concepción de la potesdad normativa (1250–1350)* (Madrid: Centro de Estudios Constitucionales, 1992).

43 Carlos Garriga, "Orden jurídico y poder político en el Antiguo Régimen," *Istor: Revista de Historia Internacional* 4, no. 16 (2004), 11.

44 Luca Mannori and Bernardo Sordi, "Science of administration and administrative law," in *A treatise of legal philosophy and general jurisprudence*, eds. Enrico Pattaro et al. (Dordrecht: Springer, 2009), 225–261.

ity, which, in catholic monarchies, included the duty to declare the law, based on a preexisting divine order.[45] This divine aspect not only reinforced the authority of the monarch, but also allowed him to perform acts of grace. As the holder of grace, the king had the power of casuistic normative creation, alteration, or revocation of existing rules in specific cases, thus, establishing particular norms valid only among the concerned parties.[46] The domain of grace was a primary manifestation of royal generosity, as a form of recognition for services and favors rendered by vassals. However, like any other institutional act of the monarch, it also had its limitations. Acts of grace, Garriga observes, were intended to perfect and not to destroy the established order. As a consequence, any act that sought to modify inalienable rights required a just cause, except in cases of supreme public utility.[47] According to Hespanha, acts of grace could not infringe upon the rights of third parties, could not be subject to payment, and should observe principles of good faith and equity.[48]

Perhaps one of the most requested acts of royal grace, in the Portuguese colony, was the *sesmarias*, an instrument of land grants from medieval roots. As the effectiveness of the *dominium* granted by a *sesmaria* was subordinated to the fulfillment of some conditions, such as cultivation of crops on the land, Varela and Alveal classified *sesmarias* as conditional property in opposition to a modern idea of absolute property, typical of the nineteenth century.[49] Nevertheless, it was not uncommon that the Crown would edit a norm ordering the cultivation of a specific kind of crop in a certain territory, without distinguishing between the types of *dominium*, as exemplified in a normative act determining the cultivation of cassava.[50] For Mateus, the consistent argument that the donation was due to services that the vassals had done or would do for

45 Alejandro Agüero, "Las categorías básicas de la cultura jurisdiccional," in *De justicia de jueces a justicia de Leyes: hacia la España de 1870*, ed. Maria Llorente (Cuadernos de Derecho Judicial, 2006), 31–32.

46 António Manuel Hespanha, "Direito comum e direito colonial," *Panóptica* 1 (2006): 111–115.

47 Garriga Carlos, "Orden jurídico y poder político en el Antiguo Régimen," *Istor: revista de historia internacional* año IV, no. 16(2004): 17.

48 António Manuel Hespanha, "Direito comum e direito colonial," *Panóptica, Vitória* ano v. 1 (2006), 107–108.

49 See: Laura Beck Varela, *Das sesmarias à propriedade moderna: um estudo de história do Direito brasileiro* (Rio de Janeiro: Renovar,, 2005), 193. Carmen Margarida Oliveira Alveal, *Converting land into property in the Portuguese Atlantic World: 16th–18th century* (The Johns Hopkins University, 2008).

50 *Alvará régio sucitando a observância da lei de 15 de fevereiro de 1688 obrigando os habitantes da capitania da Bahia à plantação de mandioca.* In: AHU, Bahia, Cx. 8, Doc. 1351–1355.

the king is evidence that the *oikonomia* of grace is the primary political and legal foundation of the donation of *sesmarias*.[51] Hence, cultivation was not a duty that would apply only to land grants, rather, it was a form of materialization of acts of possession.

According to Hespanha, the idea that the owner could do what he wanted with the owned thing was already present in the juridical culture of early modernity. Nevertheless, this idea coexisted with a perception of *ius in re* based on a plurality of rights, each derived from the different uses that could be attributed to things. Furthermore, these different uses could be divided between different individuals or groups.[52] Consequently, the relationships between individuals and the land encompassed a variety of forms, allowing for multiple rightful claims over the same parcel of land, which often led to disputes being mediated by local authorities and Crown officials, as illustrated by the case involving a dispute over land usage between a Catholic priest and the people of the village of Camamu.

Toward the end of the eighteenth century, when Father Marcelino Francisco de Mello asked the Queen of Portugal for royal grace to continue the construction of a sugar mill in partnership with his brother in a parcel of land that he owned and possessed – as *senhor* and *possuidor* – for more than sixteen years, significant shifts were occurring within the Western legal framework. These changes were influenced by the Enlightenment movement, which advocated for a sharper distinction between humans and things based on rationality and self-determination of the will, leading to the consolidation of subjective rights and the systematization of norms between real and personal rights.[53] This period, known as the Age of Revolutions, is also considered to be

51 Rafael Cronje Mateus, "O débito de gratidão do rei como fundamento político jurídico das doações de sesmaria: o caso da capitania do Ceará (1679–1682)," *Fortaleza* (2023), 15.

52 António Manuel Hespanha, "Como os juristas viam o mundo, 1550–1750: direitos, estados, pessoas, coisas, contratos, ações e crimes," in CreateSpace Independent Publishing Platform (2015), 182.

53 In early modern Europe, following a medieval tradition, humans and non-human entities were legally categorized according to their position within the natural order. Considering that this natural order encompassed all things, it was not possible to draw a rigorous line between persons and non-human entities, resulting that even things, like colors or animals, could have their set of rights and obligations, as well as some degree of legal agency and *dominium*. In: António Manuel Hespanha, "Como os juristas viam o mundo, 1550–1750: direitos, estados, pessoas, coisas, contratos, ações e crimes," in CreateSpace Independent Publishing Platform (2015), 206–208. Although, for the *ius commune* tradition, the frontiers between humans and things seemed blurred, that was not the case for the Salmantine scholars, an intellectual movement known as Second scholastic

a milestone for the emergence of the modern concept of private property, with the French Revolution serving as the most emblematic example of how an idea of individual ownership was beginning to solidify in European law. This process was intensified by the movements of codification, yet, it did not completely obfuscate the various forms of *ius in re* from the ancien régime.[54]

In Brazil, legislative efforts to modernize land acquisition and transmission would come later, in the second half of the nineteenth century, with the first civil code only being published in the early twentieth century.[55] Hence, despite these major transformations, ownership continued to operate within the *ius commune* framework, at least until the end of the nineteenth century, with possession serving as an important argument in solving judicial disputes over lands and enslaved people.[56] Besides possession, *dominium* was another concept widely used in agrarian disputes, with petitioners often claiming to be *senhores* and *possuidores* of the contested land – lords and possessor – which indicates that possession was a central argument for ownership, but being recognized as the rightful *dominus* was also significant.

Following the *ius civile* tradition, Bartolus described ownership in terms of *dominium*, as "the right of complete disposal over a corporeal thing, as long as it is not prohibited by law."[57] Nevertheless, by feudal law, *dominium rerum* could be divided between *utile* and *directum*: between who had *dominium* over the totality of the thing for being the direct owner, and who had *dominium* over the usage of the thing. In this scenario, neither the lord or the

due to the influence of Aquinas's Scholasticism. In the thirteenth century, Thomas de Aquinas' concept of personhood was already associated with human *ratio*, and, according to the Franciscan philosophy, humans were subjects who love and will. By the fifteenth century, it was a consensus among theologians from Salamanca that rationality was a human quality, resulting that "as God had created the world for man, only man had genuine dominion." In: Francisco C. Urbano, "The Salamanca School on Slavery: From Naturalism to Culture and Awareness," in Max Planck Institute for European Legal History Research Paper Series no. 2020–02 (2019).

54 Paolo Grossi, *Il dominio e le cose: percezioni medievali e moderne dei diritti reali* (Giuffrè, 1992), 662; See also: Bartolomé Clavero, "Les domaines de la propriété, 1789–1814: propiedades y propiedad en el laboratorio revolucionario," in *Quaderni fiorentini per la storia del pensiero giuridico moderno* 27 (1) (1998).

55 Ricardo Marcelo Fonseca, "A Lei de Terras e o advento da propriedade moderna no Brasil," *Anuario mexicano de historia del derecho* v. 17 (2005), 97–112.

56 Mariana Armond Dias Paes, *Esclavos y tierras entre posesión y títulos: la construcción social del derecho de propiedad en Brasil* (*siglo XIX*). *Global Perspectives on Legal History, 17* (Max Planck Institute for Legal History and Legal Theory, 2021).

57 Thomas Rüfner, "The Roman concept of ownership and the medieval Doctrine of Dominium Utile," in *The Creation of the Ius Commune*, eds. (Edinburgh University Press, 2010), 128.

tenant could dispose freely of the land.[58] Nevertheless, although the *communis opinion* may have been that the owner could dispose of the owned thing according to his will, Hespanha – drawing on Meccarelli's lessons on *arbitrium* – observes that this will was limited by several factors related to prudence and moderation.[59]

Besides moderation and *duplex dominium*, these limits were also related to other rightful uses that different people could have over the same thing.[60] In the course of the nineteenth century, as a broader movement toward codification was unfolding, many of these different rights and their legal instruments, such as *dominium utile* and *emphyteusis*, were considered, by jurists, as feudal burdens to be overcome – obstacles, defects, imperfections – to the consolidation of a perfect model of ownership.[61] One important legal institute also deemed by nineteenth-century jurists as incompatible with private ownership – but that was central in the case-study of Camamu – is the institute of *ius in re aliena*,[62] which encompassed servitudes or encumbrances, such as the right of passage and pasture. Some servitudes are personal, which means that they cannot be transferred. Others, such as the right of passage, oblige the land itself in such a way that whoever comes in the possession of the land, acquires also the servitude.[63] Moreover, the legal consequences of servitudes can vary depending on the perspective: for the beneficiary, it is a right, but for the one who must endure it, it is a burden. In Portuguese America, some disputes over access of things of common usage were described in terms of servitudes of the people (*servidões* or *serventia dos povos*), which leads us to another question: were commons a form of servitudes or were servitudes an essential legal instrument of accessing the commons? Although a single case-study does not

58 Thomas Rüfner, "The Roman concept of ownership and the medieval Doctrine of Dominium Utile," (2010).

59 António Manuel Hespanha, "Como os juristas viam o mundo, 1550–1750: direitos, estados, pessoas, coisas, contratos, ações e crimes," in CreateSpace Independent Publishing Platform (2015), 182.

60 António Manuel Hespanha, "Como os juristas viam o mundo, 1550–1750: direitos, estados, pessoas, coisas, contratos, ações e crimes," (2015), 178.

61 See: Rosa Congost and Pablo F. Luna, eds., *Agrarian Change and Imperfect Property: Emphyteusis in Europe (16th to 19th centuries). Rural History in Europe, vol. 15* (Turnhout: Brepols,, 2018); Giacomo Pace Gravina, *La terra e il codice: l'enfiteusi. Per la storia pensiero giuridico moderno* (Milano: Giuffrè, 2023).

62 Paolo Grossi, *Il dominio e le cose: percezioni medievali e moderne dei diritti reali* (Giuffrè, 1992), 662.

63 António Manuel Hespanha, "Como os juristas viam o mundo, 1550–1750: direitos, estados, pessoas, coisas, contratos, ações e crimes," in CreateSpace Independent Publishing Platform (2015), 201.

have the potential to answer this question, it can offer good insights on the legal nature of the commons in Portuguese America, as will be explained in the next topic, alongside the main question that motivated the analyzes of this case-study: If Father Marcelino was the rightful *dominus* as *senhor* and *possuidor* – lord and possessor – of the land by title of purchase, why did he need to seek royal grace to build a sugar mill in his own land?

## 4 On Watermills and Commons: Mediating Public and Private Rights in the Village of Camamu

The importance of sugar mills as agents of colonization – and distribution of land – was evident from the earliest days of colonization, as demonstrated in the normative directives of the first General Governor of Brazil Tomé de Souza, in 1548. The document gives instructions on how to set boundaries and secure possession over the lands of Brazil for the Portuguese Crown, after which Tomé de Souza should grant lands within these boundaries. If the land to be granted was suitable for *engenhos de açúcar*, the waters within the designated area were also to be granted.[64] When analyzing the formation of the landed patrimony of the Municipality in the captaincy of Bahia, Fonseca claimed that Tomé de Souza prioritized these private concessions, neglecting the demands of the emerging municipality, and consequently, the necessity of the local population for accessing commons within the city of Salvador.[65]

This prominence attributed to sugar mills within the colonial enterprise would not be significantly diminished in the years to come, but it would certainly face some obstacles, such as changes in the economic, social, and natural landscape of the colony.[66] During the next two centuries of colonization,

64 For the transcription, see: Marcos Carneiro de Mendonça, *Raízes da Formação Administrativa do Brasil* (IHGB, 1972)

65 Cláudia Damasceno Fonseca, "Posse da terra, patrimônio municipal e bem comum: notas para uma história fundiária de Salvador e seu recôncavo1," in *Salvador da Bahia: escravidão, economia, poderes e representações (séculos XVI–XIX)*, eds. Evergton Sales Souza, Medicci Ana Paula and Pedro Cardim (Editora da Universidade Federal da Bahia, 2022), 174.

66 It is important to note that sugar mills are not a brand-new invention of early modern colonialism, but rather the unfolding of a technology that has been evolving in agrarian societies for centuries. Reflecting on advancements in milling, Marc Bloch noted that the widespread adoption of watermills in medieval Europe catalyzed profound legal innovations. These innovations encompassed ownership and contracts, labor customs, and commercial practices. Moreover, according to Bloch, mills were predominantly of seignorial origin, with lords of mills exercising their authority through bans and monopo-

royal authorities, local officials, lords of sugar mills, and planters of sugar cane have engaged in multiple disputes regarding the necessity of allowing or forbidding the construction of sugar mills, motivated by different phases of the sugar economy and the availability of natural resources.[67] For the chief administrator of the Royal Treasury, Antônio Lopes de Ulhôa, "the sugar mills are the settlements and villages that make this captaincy, and, state habitable, and where they do not exist, it is almost uninhabited."[68] On the other hand, the proper function of a sugar mill usually involved access to water and extensive use of wood. At the beginning of colonization, this was not a problem, but, as villages and sugar plantations advanced over the Atlantic Forest, the industry faced environmental and logistical constraints. An example of this is reflected in the *regimento* from 1677 addressed to Roque da Costa Barreto, appointed as governor of Brazil. Chapter 27 of this directive stipulated that sugar mills should not be constructed too close to each other. The aim was not to promote the conservation of the forests in the sense we understand today, but rather to guarantee that each *engenho* would have sufficient access to fuelwood to function properly, since "it would be much more important to have fewer mills with plenty of firewood, than to have more mills with a shortage of it, and to consume it in such a way that everyone would run out and everything would be lost."[69] In 1681, a royal decree prohibited the inland con-

---

lies, such as the use of the baking-oven and wine-press. These monopolies allowed landlords to control production and trade within their domains. Similarly in Brazil, to own a sugar mill was not only economical advantageous, but it could also improve social status and jurisdictional power within the scope of the household and vicinity. As observed in 1701 by the Jesuit João Antonil, "to be the master of a sugar mill is a title that many aspire to, because it brings with it being served, obeyed, and respected by many." See: Marc Bloch, *Land and Work in Medieval Europe*, trans. JE Anderson (Routledge & Kegan Paul, 1967), 152–153; André João Antonil, *Cultura e opulencia do Brasil: por suas drogas, e minas, com varias noticias curiosas do modo de fazer o assucar, plantar, & beneficiar o tabaco; tirar ouro das minas; & descubrir as da prata; e dos grandes emolumentos, que esta conquista da America meridional dá ao Reyno de Portugal com estes, & outros generos, & contratos reaes* (Deslandesiana, 1711).

67 Marcelo Lunardi do Carmo, "Novas unidades produtivas e a crise do setor açucareiro baiano no século XVII: a visão econômica dos senhores de engenho," *45º Encontro Nacional de Economia-ANPEC* (2017), 7.

68 Antônio Lopes de Ulhôa, *provedor-mor da Fazenda* (chief administrator of the Royal Treasury). In: AHU, Bahia, Cx 16, doc. 1894.

69 Regimento dado ao Governador e Capitão-General do Estado do Brasil Roque da Costa Barreto, passado em 23 de janeiro de 1677, pelo Príncipe D. Pedro, regente de Portugal. In Documentos históricos. VI. 5: 1663–1677 (Correspondencia dos Governadores Geraes e Regimento dado ao Governador Roque da Costa Barreto) (Rio de Janeiro: Augusto Porto & C, 1928), 374.

struction of sugar mills within half a league of distance from each other under the same argument of availability of firewood.[70] For the Overseas Council in Lisbon "it seemed fair that the sugar mills which were first established by clearing roads and woods through inland should be preserved, and that others should not be allowed to be built if they harmed their wood supply."[71]

In the case of Father Marcelino, the existence of other watermills or the absence of licenses was not among the central arguments used by the colonial authorities in order to demolish his construction. Instead of competing with another *engenho* over the access of natural resources, the sugar mill of the vicar of Camamu was deemed as a threat for the local population in accessing the commons. For the Governor of Brazil, although Father Marcelino had a legal title and exercised possession cultivating the land, the purchase should be considered void for the construction of the *engenho* was infringing upon the "public and acquired right" of the people of Camamu over the uses of a port, a road, wood, water, and pastures.[72]

The place where the Priest intended to build his *engenho* was located in a parcel of the *fundo das doze léguas* that were claimed to be in the possession of the people of the village of Camamu since time immemorial – since the Jesuits were the owners of the land. In 1767, a similar argument was present in a case involving common access to water. In the city of Salvador, locals claimed continuous possession of a water fountain, a tradition upheld by their ancestors since the period when the Jesuits owned the property. The access to the water fountain was enabled by a servitude of passage, which, according to them, should remain free regardless of changes in ownership.[73] For Damasceno, the use of the word "possession" is to be interpreted as a form of usufruct

70 Alvará de 3 de Novembro de 1681. Não se fabriquem engenhos de açúcar no Brasil a menor distância que mil e quinhentas braças de uns a outros. Liv. XXXIV, Chancellaria, fl. 122 v. In: Collecção Chronologica da Legislação Portugueza, 1675–1683 e Suplemento à Segunda Série 1641–1683. Available in: www.governodosoutros.ics.ul.pt, accessed April 8, 2024.

71 The decree was a response from the Crown to a petition of the officials of the municipality of Bahia regarding the inconveniences of constructing additional sugar mills. AHU, Bahia, Cx 25, doc. 3031.

72 For this case-study, I have consulted mainly three sets of primary sources from the Overseas' Archive: AHU, Bahia, Cx. 58, Doc. 11070–11087; AHU, Bahia, Cx. 58, Doc. 11090–11122; AHU, Bahia, Cx. 177, Doc. 13294.

73 DHAM-Atas da Câmara, v. 11, 95–96. Ata da câmara, 31 de outubro de 1767. In: Cláudia Damasceno Fonseca, "Posse da terra, patrimônio municipal e bem comum: notas para uma história fundiária de Salvador e seu recôncavo1," in *Salvador da Bahia: escravidão, economia, poderes e representações (séculos XVI–XIX)*, eds. Evergton Sales Souza, Medicci Ana Paula and Pedro Cardim (Editora da Universidade Federal da Bahia, 2022), 191.

based on customary law. It is important to note, however, that usufruct, when considered as a personal right, does not hold transgenerational power, since the personal right of usufruct was terminated upon the death of the usufructuary.[74] On the other hand, real rights had the potential to secure the access to the common thing for the generations to come, making the beneficiary not an individual, rather, a collective body.[75] In fact, according to Conte, the interpretation adopted by the humanist tradition on rights of usage during the sixteenth century was to conceive them not in terms of personal rights, but rather, as iura in re aliena. As a consequence, the residents of a village could access the things that were essential for their subsistence, such as collecting firewood or grazing livestock, which could be exercised on "lands belonging to private persons (usually lords owning very large parcels of land), and public subjects, such as the administrative commune of a city."[76] In the Portuguese legal tradition, certain things, such as navigable waters or the seashore, could not be entirely appropriated by private owners, even when parts of such goods fell within private domains. The Crown, as the ultimate holder of jurisdiction, could regulate how such uses were exercised.[77]

Considering this legal framework, it seems to be no coincidence the use of words such as *posse* and *servidão* or *serventia* to refer to the access to things held in common in the village of Camamu. The use of the word "servitude" was also observed in a similar case in São Luís do Maranhão. In 1739, the governor of Pará wrote a letter to the King of Portugal, explaining how he proceeded after a monastery had obstructed the access of the people to common things by enlarging their fences with the construction of a wall, which included within their boundaries "the fountains, with a well of stones constructed at the expense of the Municipality, and the paths that the people have served themselves of (*se servia*) since time immemorial, for accessing water, going to the beach, and for fetching firewood and other necessities." According to the

74 António Manuel Hespanha, "Como os juristas viam o mundo, 1550–1750: direitos, estados, pessoas, coisas, contratos, ações e crimes," in CreateSpace Independent Publishing Platform (2015), 203.

75 Monica Chiantini and Emanuele Conte, "Qualificazioni giuridiche dei beni collettivi: una breve rassegna storica," in *Il bosco: biodiversità, diritti e culture dal Medioevo al nostro tempo,* ed. Alessandra Dattero (Roma: Viella, 2022), 169–189.

76 Emanuele Conte, "The Many Legal Faces of the Commons. A Short Historical Survey," *Quaderni storici* v. 56, no. 3 (2021), 631.

77 António Manuel Hespanha, "Como os juristas viam o mundo, 1550–1750: direitos, estados, pessoas, coisas, contratos, ações e crimes," in CreateSpace Independent Publishing Platform (2015), 169.

governor, he had issued an order upon the locals' request – making a special mention to poor people and women[78] – demanding the construction to be demolished and instructing the town officials to return the fountains and servitudes to the people. Moreover, he also wrote a letter to the Guardian Father of the same convent, asking him to refrain from such violence.[79]

The convenience of the pathway that granted access to a port of salty waters and that enabled the people of Camamu to make use of the natural resources of the land was corroborated by different neighbors who were called to testify over the petition of Father Marcelino. According to several testimonies, the Jesuits, who were the first possessors of the land, had never created any impediments for the access to roads, wood, water, and pastures in this parcel of their lands that encompassed the surrounding area of the village, which were seen by these witnesses as uncultivated lands – *realengos* and *baldios*. According to the Portuguese *ius proprium*, *realengos* were under the patrimony of the prince,[80] while *baldios* were under the governance of the Municipal Council. Since these things were not *res nullius*, they could not be acquired for private domain without consent of the king or the municipality.[81]

The magistrate (*ouvidor*) of Camamu, Francisco Nunes da Costa, gave his opinion on the case in a letter written in May of 1782 to the successor governor, Marquez de Valença, in which he gives complete information about the representation of the vicar of Camamu and the investigations he carried out about the facts mentioned in it. In this letter, Costa supports the right of the People of Camamu to their possession over *baldios* and *realengos*, since "this was the possession and the right of the people at the time of the general sequestration of the assets of the former Jesuits, and in this state, the said twelve leagues of land were auctioned off to three partners, residents of this town of Camamu." For the *ouvidor*, although the common land was encompassed by the *fundo*

---

78 In the case of the village of Camamu, women, enslaved, and poor people are also often mentioned by the Governor who ordered the demolition, as well as by many witnesses.

79 "And there they made the same requests to me, not only in writing, but also through the pleas of a considerable number of women who, on several occasions, came together to complain that the men did not come to do so out of fear of the *capitão-mor* and the *ouvidor geral*" in: AHU, Belém do Pará, Cx. 7, Doc. 667.

80 In 1780, the same governor that ordered the demolition of the *engenho* in this case-study, Manuel da Cunha Meneses, complained to the Royal Secretary Martinho de Melo e Castro that, in the captaincy of Ilhéus, the municipalities were charging the collection of wood from mangroves, which, according to the Governor, were *realengos* of the King, who granted the rights of usage to the poor by royal grace. In: AHU, Bahia, Cx. 55, Doc. 10653.

81 António Manuel Hespanha, "Como os juristas viam o mundo, 1550–1750: direitos, estados, pessoas, coisas, contratos, ações e crimes," in CreateSpace Independent Publishing Platform (2015), 177.

*das doze léguas*, the Jesuits "never extended their property to the surroundings and suburbs of this village," since they recognized them as *realengos* "belonging to the convenience of the people." The reason for that, observed the magistrate, was that these lands were originally under the sovereign domain of the king by the right of conquest, and the primary objective of this conquest was to promote settlements. The magistrate also recurs to legal analogy by mentioning a royal decree regarding religious missions and indigenous settlements (*aldeias*). In the law of November 23, 1700, it is stated that one league of land around the *vila dos índios* – native settlements – should be reserved for their subsistence.[82] For the magistrate, the Monarch could not grant more privilege to *vilas dos índios* than to *vila dos brancos e Europeos* – white and European settlements. The magistrate concludes by advising the current governor to represent this to the king "to whom all the natural and acquired Rights of the Vassals are subject to," asking for the purchase to be considered void and the Priest get compensated by the Municipal Council, so that the People can be reintegrated in their ancient possession and liberty, for even if the vicar of Camamu was considered to have a just right of possession and dominion over the purchased property, "here arises another superior right to his, which is that of public utility that absorbs the right of individuals whenever it is necessary for the good and interest of all."[83]

This document reveals a significant attempt of the magistrate on identifying the different uses of the land from both the Priest and the community, and to confront these different uses in terms of public and private rights. This perception on the dynamics between public and private domain represents a major difference between the testimony from the neighbors – who were mainly illiterate farmers and other local officials – and the reports of colonial authorities – such as the General Governor and the Magistrate. For the first group, there seems to be no incompatibility between the private domain of the Priest and their public rights of usage, as long as the Priest did not create any impediments for the access of the people to the commons, as has been practiced since the period in which the Jesuits owned the lands.[84] For the

82 Alvará sobre a medição da legoa de terra as aldeas. Lisboa, 23 de novembro de 1700. In: Annaes da Bibliotheca Nacional do Rio de Janeiro, 1906, volume XXVIII (Rio de Janeiro: Officinas de Artes Graphicas da Bibliotheca Nacional, 1908), 393.

83 AHU, Bahia, Cx. 58, n. 11070–11087.

84 According to different witnesses, the Priest would allow only selected people to collect wood in his lands. In one testimony, the planter of sugar cane, Captain José Ramos da Silva, said that the Priest had physically assaulted slaves that attempted to collect wood in his lands, including a woman. This testimony was also corroborated by the planter of cassava, Francisco Gonçalves Ferreira, who claimed that the Priest "forbids the majority

magistrate, who was sent to investigate the facts that motivated the petition of Father Marcelino, it was not possible to conciliate this private domain with "the common use and freedom of the people," since the proper function of an *engenho* required extensive use of firewood, and large amount of land dedicated to pastures, cultivation of sugarcane, and habitation of the slaves. This could, in the future, exhaust the utility of the land for the community. A similar opinion was demonstrated by the Municipal Council. For the officials who accompanied the magistrate on the inspection of the area in which the demolition took place, the people of the village could not survive if the land did not remain vacant. Nevertheless, it is noteworthy that, in July of 1782, Father Marcelino was granted authorization to continue the construction of his *engenho* as there was no other more convenient place, due to the necessity of accessing water, as long as he did not create any impediments for the people of the village to access water, wood, and pasture.

Yet, the arguments of the magistrate raise another question: if there is an incompatibility between the private *dominium* of Father Marcelino and the public *dominium* of the village due to necessities of common good and public utility, then why not expropriate the land? As already mentioned, following the opinion of the magistrate, the conclusion of the Governor was that the purchase made by the Priest should be considered void, and the Municipal Council should compensate Father Marcelino for his loss, so that the neighbors should be reinstated in their "ancient possession, just like the times in which the lands were from the denominated Jesuits and, after that, from the Majesty."[85] Could the argument for the voidness of the purchase with due compensation be considered a form of expropriation for the common good? Or perhaps the avoidance on treating the case of Father Marcelino as a case of expropriation may have been due to the fact that the demolition took place without due compensation?

To answer the first question, it is necessary to start with another one: was expropriation of land for the common good an available legal instrument of governance of the land in this period? For Reynolds, the answer is positive, as "rights in land are never absolute, but their limitations differ in different societies."[86] In the Portuguese juridical culture, following the *ius commune* tradition, expropriation of the land for the common good was founded in yet

of the people to collect woods, beating up the slaves that go there to cut (wood)" In: AHU, Bahia, Cx. 58, n. 11090–11122.

85 AHU_ACL_CU_005, Cx. 177, D. 13294, 11.

86 Susan Reynolds, *Before eminent domain: Toward a history of expropriation of land for the common good* (Univ of North Carolina Press, 2010), 4.

another form of dominion, related to the exercise of sovereign power – *dominium eminens*.[87] In another case, in which the municipality of Bahia requested Royal permission to use the senate's revenue in order to demolish a building in private domain, the act of expropriation is referred to as "sale made against the will of the *senhorios* (owners), case in which the law favored them." One justification for the demolition was that "by night, (the building) was filled with blacks, mulattos, and vagrant women."[88] In the sixteenth-century Spanish colony of Peru, the reference to forced sales in cases of expropriation was also identified by González Escudero as a tool of dispossession of indigenous peoples.[89]

As for the second question, the lack of due procedure before the acts of demolition was one of the majors complains of Father Marcelino. On his petition to the Queen, he claimed that he tried to plead with the Judge in charge of executing the Governor orders, so that he could have time to present a proper defense. According to him, not only was he ignored by the Judge, but also by the Governor who, instead of offering him the opportunity to defend his case, sent a second order to demolish the fences that protected his crops from animals, acting as to punish the Priest for protesting against his decision.[90] In order to persuade the Queen on granting him the required grace of building his *engenho*, Father Marcelino claims that God, in the verge of punishing Adam, "did not rely on the knowledge that He, as the infinite God, already had of Adam's guilt, but still called him and heard him out due to His innate mercy."

87 António Manuel Hespanha, "Como os juristas viam o mundo, 1550–1750: direitos, estados, pessoas, coisas, contratos, ações e crimes," in CreateSpace Independent Publishing Platform (2015), 182.

88 AHU_ACL_CU_005, Cx. 173, D. 13022, 5. Regarding limitations on *dominium*, Hespanha observed that "the enjoyment (of the thing) was limited by the concept of honest use" In: António Manuel Hespanha, "Como os juristas viam o mundo, 1550–1750: direitos, estados, pessoas, coisas, contratos, ações e crimes," in CreateSpace Independent Publishing Platform (2015), 182.

89 Damian A Gonzales Escudero, "Expropiar para reducir: una herramienta jurídica para la formación de una reducción de indios en Lima durante el siglo XVI," in *Poder, sociedad y administración de justicia en la América Hispánica (siglos XVI–XIX)* (2021), 641–647.

90 It is important to note that, according to some witnesses, the existence of fences was not considered an impediment for the common access to the land, since the fences had open gates. What occasionally disturbed the access of people was the behavior of the priest, who would not allow everyone to collect wood. Moreover, Father Marcelino argued in more than one occasion that the construction of fences was a common practice in Brazil, for "there could be no farm without fences, and in the entries gates, for the defense and conservation of the cattle necessary for the production." In: AHU_ACL_CU_005, Cx. 58 \Doc. 11067.

According to the opinion of the *ouvidor*, the procedure for the demolition of the *engenho* should be considered a legitimate reintegration of possession. For the magistrate, if, by the laws of the kingdom and the *ius commune* (*Direito Comum*) any of the particulars of the village could, by themselves, resort to self-help to remove by force the violence and disturbance caused in their ancient possession, "with even more justice and reason" could the recovery of possession be ordered by their representative, the Governor, who had the "superior right to conservate and maintain the People of his Government in Peace, and in the free use of public things."

Regardless of the real intentions of the parties involved, the demolition of the *engenho* of the vicar of Camamu was not considered a case of expropriation. Rather, as pointed out by the magistrate, the Governor's orders were an act to recover possession for the benefit of the People, thus, a possessory remedy. In accordance with the Portuguese law and the *ius commune* tradition, these proceedings "were summary, without publication of evidence or witnesses."[91] This approach exemplifies how this legal tradition not only safeguarded property rights but also protected diverse land uses.

## 5 Conclusion

This paper aimed to explore the relationship between public and private rights in the village of Camamu, focusing on the legal nature of commons and the interplay between communal and private domains. The demolition of the *engenho* de Camamu, initially perceived as a case of expropriation for the common good, revealed a deeper conflict over the possession of things held in common, which led to further investigation into the legal nature of common lands in Portuguese America. In this case study, different actors instrumentalized legal categories such as *ius publicum*, *ius privatum*, *ius in re*, *ius in re aliena*, *servitudes*, *dominium*, and *possessio*, which, despite dating back to Roman Law, have undergone numerous transformations throughout Western legal history. The historical context of Camamu is crucial to understanding how these categories were actually perceived by different people.

The formation of the village was significantly influenced by the private domain of the Jesuits, who were granted an extensive parcel of land known as *fundo das doze léguas*, where Camamu was later founded. The dynamics of

91 António Manuel Hespanha, "Como os juristas viam o mundo, 1550–1750: direitos, estados, pessoas, coisas, contratos, ações e crimes," in CreateSpace Independent Publishing Platform (2015),181.

land usage under the Jesuits' ownership allowed for communal use of certain areas, which became a legal practice deeply rooted in the community. Following the expulsion of the Jesuits and the subsequent public auction of their lands, ownership dynamics shifted, leading to disputes such as the one involving Father Marcelino. His attempt to assert private *dominium* over land historically used by the community for accessing water, wood, a road, a port, and pasture, sparked significant opposition. Moreover, what should be a dispute between common and private domains gained another dimension: the public rights of the people.

As an instrument of mediation, law functions as a cultural artifact, unveiling not only agreements but also disputes on the legitimate framework of certain practices. In the case study of the village of Camamu, the diversity of uses of the land and its natural resources was perceived by different actors in different ways. The magistrate's use of formulas typical of expropriation for the common good and public utility coexisted with efforts to accommodate both communal and private interests through a servitude, reflecting the tension between lingering traditional practices and emerging modern legal frameworks. When Father Marcelino acquired a parcel of land in the village of Camamu, he did not acquire unrestricted use of the land, since the dynamics between the previous owners and the locals had instituted a servitude for the benefit of the community, allowing the people to access commons. Therefore, the people of the village of Camamu not only had a right of usage of the land but were also in possession of these commons since time immemorial – an *ius in re* or *ius in re aliena* that was by no means inferior to the private *dominium* of the vicar of Camamu.

## Acknowledgement

This paper has been written as part of my ongoing doctoral research within the IberLAND project. This project has received funding from the European Research Council (ERC) under the European Union's Horizon 2020 research and innovation program (grant agreement No. 101000991).

POSTFACE

# When God Went AWOL – Natural Law in Early-Modern Discussions on Domestic Governance

*Alain Wijffels*

## 1 Introduction

Natural law: for centuries, lawyers' favourite oxymoron. Nature stands for chaos, law for order. And as lawyers do not shy away from pleonasms, one might even say: irrational chaos *v.* rational order. Of course, identifying nature with chaos, and law with order, will instantly raise forceful objections: to some, because they believe that the universe is organised and functions according to some divine project or immanent logos; to others, because they regard all law as instruments of inequality and exploitation, which inevitably ends up in tensions and upheaval.

## 2 Natural Law in the Belgian Curriculum, Half a Century Ago

Half a century ago, when I was an undergraduate in Belgium, a course on natural law was still part, nationwide, of the statutory compulsory curriculum. While the statutory provisions made natural law a compulsory subject, they fell short of detailing the contents of the course. The result was that, within the relatively rigid order of the national curriculum, the natural law course offered an opening to an unregulated state of nature, where every lecturer was practically entirely free to decide what they (at the time, still almost always a he) would teach. In my university, the course included a conventional outline of natural law throughout history (one of the most useful topics for a student who was to become a legal historian), followed by *capita selecta* which I suppose were meant to justify the relevance of natural law at the time. When I attended the course in my second year, these special topics discussed by the lecturer included readings of Herbert Marcuse and an outline of workers' organisations in the then Socialist Federal Republic of Yugoslavia. A time capsule, indeed. Some brief mention was made of a modest 'renaissance' of natural law by the end of the nineteenth century and towards the beginning of the twentieth century in France. That renaissance was presented as a reaction

 | DOI:10.1163/9789004748712_013

against the excessive destitution of the working classes generated by the Industrial Revolution and the inability of a positivistic legal culture to prevent or redress the social injustices of the era. The renaissance of natural law identified during the years after the second world war in German legal scholarship, on the other hand, was not discussed during my student time.

In other universities, the same statutory course could follow completely different lines, as even the historical part was not prescribed by law. Natural law was barely mentioned in any other course on the curriculum. The legal courses bathed in an ocean of complacent positivism, so self-conscious of its supremacy that it could generously allow other legal authorities – case law, legal scholarship, even, to a lesser degree, forms of custom – to thrive in the margins of codes and statutes, like minor green areas in the shade of the high-rising blocks which were the analogous defining architectural features of the era.

Occasional references to natural law in the positive law (the vast majority of articles of the original 1804 French civil code, for example, were still in force) were usually subsumed under different categories, such as equity or judicial policy considerations. Most jurisprudential subjects focused on approaches which consciously or unconsciously avoided the phrase natural law, as the latter, like legal history, increasingly looked like something from the past, an exotic foreign country, where lawyers did things differently. Or perhaps the labelling changed – never a neutral operation – such as in the case of the *Wertungsjurisprudenz,* which proved much more than a method of construction.

That impression did not change during the following decades, when I taught at different law faculties. In my own research on late-medieval and early-modern legal history, I inevitably came regularly across references to natural law, both in scholarly works of the period and in legal practice, but those encounters only confirmed my impression that, indeed, scholars and practitioners mentioning natural law then were doing things differently from my positive law colleagues in my own time.

Devolution in Belgium put an end to the national curriculum, course requirements belonged henceforth to the jurisdiction of the devolved Communities, and the configuration of legal education became to some extent determined through a common framework worked out by the deans of the law faculties within a Community. Natural law vanished from the curriculum, though when I was asked in 2023 to write a report on the teaching of constitutional history in the Benelux countries, I was surprised to come across one surviving course named Natural Law at a French-speaking university. Otherwise, by now, I expect that most fellow academics of younger generations, unless they have retained some historical awareness (for which a few courses giving historical surveys of political thought may prove helpful), would be at a loss when asked to define natural law. Even in my student days, any student could get a pass by merely stating that natural law had had a multitude of meanings over the ages – that was the commonplace everyone seemed to agree upon, the only meaningful thing to remember about natural law. At the same time, it was a truism which further contributed to undermine natural law's claims to provide norms transcending historical epochs and particular jurisdictions.

## 3 *Chassez le Naturel ...*: New Forms of Natural Law?

As the years went by, however, and no doubt because I also had a course on comparative law in my brief, the ghost of the undergraduate natural law course, kept alive through my legal-historical readings, came back to haunt me and I started to recognise – perhaps simply a delusion resulting from growing older – patterns which could at least be interpreted as velleities of an emergence of what resembled in all but name the apparently defunct natural law. When I was a law student, human rights were still a very marginal topic, but within years after my graduation, they started permeating all areas of the law. Before the end of the twentieth century, human rights law had risen to such strengths (in some continental European countries, it was understood to overrule national law, including Acts of Parliament) that it triggered reactions and opposition. The ensuing debate – still ongoing – has raised anew old questions, such as: what is the foundation of human rights, beyond the formal enacting by the lawmaker? Are such enactments merely positive law, that can be changed at will by the lawmaker (or possibly by a constitutional assembly, or by the people in a referendum)? Or are the foundations of human rights such that these rights express legal norms beyond the power of the human will? In any case, who controls in a polity the prerogative to express the substance and scope of human rights? Some of these questions are uncannily reminiscent of those raised by the reference to natural law in pre-modern (and, critically, pre-democratic) societies.

Another example that comes to mind is the development, also since the last quarter of the twentieth century, of environmental law. In this area, too, the growing business of environmental law, first at a national level, and soon taken up by international environmental law, clashed with more mundane economic (and social) interests. Nevertheless, from one climate change conference to the next, the demands nurturing environmental law have resulted in a wide-scale indictment of the 'Anthropocene,' and reversed the conventional roles attributed in the relationship between humankind and the natural world. Sustained interest by comparative lawyers for the cosmology of 'chthonic people' (in my undergraduate days still referred to in scholarly textbooks as 'primitive populations') and attempts to recognise 'rights,' or even a degree of legal personality, to natural entities such as rivers or mountains, although still shackled by traditional legal categories, are indicative of how some deep-rooted conventional approaches in the (Western) mind have been challenged in recent decades. During the same period, Western societies have also witnessed a sustained challenge to multi-secular anthropological postulates, often expressed alongside presumed antinomies such as woman/man, rural/urban, alien/native, poor/rich, common/noble, unfree/free, disabled/able, dead/alive ... dichotomies which were often presented as part of the natural order, entailing discriminating normativities. The challenge to such dichotomies has been strongly countered by various social groups, to such extent that new cultural divides have been wrought in Western societies, which appear to prevent the emergence of a wide consensus on any natural order of our societies. The lack of consensus may to some extent explain why natural law no longer fulfils the role of reference it played in former centuries, or why it seems to have been replaced by other references. In the course of that process, it often tends to be absorbed by positive law, the contours of which have become more blurred in current legal theory. In jurisprudential literature, natural law has retained some appeal.

## 4 Necessary and Contingent Norms

In past and present, the consensus on the foundations and essential features of what was referred to as natural law has always been relative. The identification of natural law norms in the perception and theoretical construct of the universe (with a helping of experimentation) may provide some clues about the structure and functioning of the physical world which are necessary, in the sense of: that cannot be avoided or disabled.[1] Long before Newton's formulation of the law of gravity, people realised that an unrestrained body over a

1 Sarah Limão Papa's case study of litigation in Portuguese America towards the end of the eighteenth century offers a detailed analysis of how different private and public actors instrumentalised different notions and principles of the civil law tradition in order to argue which interests in land, translated in different (and, over the long term, evolving) real property rights, would prevail. The central issue opposed the owner of a watermill used

drop will fall. Such physical 'laws' do not have as such any moral or legal significance. The ancient Greeks have nonetheless been credited with an aptitude for combining such physical normativity with precepts of morality based on what was supposed to be common experience. One example is that of the so-called Pythagorean cup, better known to visitors of modern Greek tourist sites as *ἡ δίκαιη κούπα,* which has in its (underneath, open) stem and a central column a cavity, linked to an open pipe in the part of the cup where a liquid (say, wine) is poured. The effect is that, when the cup is filled beyond a certain limit, its contents will be siphoned away through the pipe and escape under the stem. The device can be seen as an application of scientific findings, but its form as a wine cup entails a popular moral caveat against greed. Whereas no one will argue that every person who accumulates 'excessive' assets or power will end up with losing all of it, as surely as the 'cup of justice' dries up, the application is not just a caveat. It suggests that there is a common causal link between greed and loss, though perhaps not as inevitable as the disappearance of the wine in the cup. Needless to say, the transposition of the physical mechanism to a social normativity rests on shaky grounds: few societies in history have been able to exclude huge differences in wealth and power among its population,[2] and sufficient numbers of inordinately wealthy people

for sugar production and the local (partly native) population. Underneath the legal claims, Limão Papa's analysis shows that the conflicting interests were affected by both natural and economic necessities which were largely beyond the control of the private and public actors intervening in this case. The sugar production relied on an adequate and constant water supply for the working of the mill, and of a long-term sustainable supply of firewood from surrounding forests, in addition to other natural and human resources which all had to be accommodated in the mill's environment. Traditionally, the local population had relied on the same natural resources within the same area. The colonial public governance had to anticipate the management of sufficient natural resources and take into account the economic viability of the enterprises in supervising the sugar industry. The local population, in accordance with an essentially chthonic approach, also had to access those resources in order to survive and maintain its traditional ('customary') lifestyle. Everyone involved, in other words, faced natural and social environmental constraints, which, even though they were not referred to as 'natural law,' imposed on all actors to adjust their conduct to necessary forces, not less binding than the rules usually ascribed to natural law. The civil law tradition provided a flexible framework for creating a forum where each of the interests at stake could qualify as a real property right (whether individual or common), all subject to the supreme test of the public interest. In a broader context, Sarah Limão Papa's contribution may also be linked to the way international law has been instrumentalised by capitalist interests and discourses for justifying land governance in the European powers' overseas territories, already during early-modern times at the expense of chthonic approaches to natural resources (e.g. E. Tourme-Jouannet, *Le droit international, le capitalisme et la terre d'hier à aujourd'hui*, Brussels, Bruylant, 2021).

or powerful autocrats have disproved that there is any necessity in greed bringing about one's downfall. The morality of the cup of justice is therefore no more than what any moral principles can achieve: a critical assessment of human behaviour against standards of good and evil, or (bringing the terms closer to natural law discussions), of what is right and wrong, but without any in-built 'correcting' mechanism.

Complexity is introduced when the principle of entelechy is attributed to organisms of the physical world (by virtue of the biases of the Western classical and Christian traditions, the principle has usually not been extended to inorganic matter), which, even at a pre-moral stage, instils a tension between *Sein* and *Sollen* in living organisms. At this morally indifferent stage, however, the *Sollen* element remains part of the predefined natural reality, so that the potential of a living organism remains subjected to a necessary (i.e., unavoidable, except for external factors) normativity. From ancient Greece until recent times (except for end-of-the-world narratives) the universe was (in theoretical or practical terms) assumed to be everlasting. Medieval scholars referred to Aristoteles for claiming "*mundus non moritur*" (a principle that played a part in the formation of the misguided doctrine of everlasting *corpora mystica*), and although important features (*dispositiones*) could change and even die out, the universe itself was supposed to survive forever. In Christian times, entelechy was retrieved and redefined according to what was attributed to a divine project. Some ancient thought – notably the Stoa – had already given a strong ethical sense to (human) natural vocation. At least two major features of natural law thinking in later times were already firmly established by the authors of the Greek-Roman Antiquity. First, a human being's sociabil-

2 That may even be an understatement for portraying late seventeenth-century English society, when John Locke developed his theory on the foundations of civil society and state, centered – already at the stage of the state of nature – around (landed) property. Signy Gutnick Allen's chapter discusses how Locke's acknowledgement of charity as either a duty towards the indigents or a claim of those indigents can be reconciled with the inviolable right of property. The issue was highly topical in Locke's own days, with regard to poor relief measures, and it remains of course a vexed issue until the present day. Locke's statements on charity and poor relief may express (putting it mildly) an over-optimistic view on how the increase of productivity of property through labour may increase the available means to all, including the propertyless. In Locke's arguments, not least because of his morally biased social-economic policy considerations, charity appears both in minimalist terms and discriminatory. Even in the historical context of his days, it is not obvious whether his proposals would pass the test of a social and economic analysis. The enduring success of Lockean thought in historiography and political theory suggests that founding a natural theory on the interests of the ruling classes offers a yardstick for historical social-economic studies which transcends the contingencies of any particular era.

ity as part of their natural finality.[3] In order to fulfil their development, human beings are said to need a community – a family, a clan, a city – which, although viewed as a necessary requirement, can be organised according to dissimilar forms of governance. Since natural law discussions, as any mental constructs on social order in general, emerge at a stage where communities have already developed established forms of governance, the elites who conceive those constructs tend to select those features which appear most apt at reinforcing the power structures within their communities, giving them a legitimation in the 'natural order of things,' and if possible also a religious foundation. Understandably, this works out more easily for legitimising the domestic governance than the foreign governance vis-à-vis other polities. In the domestic order, depending on the form of government, divine law, natural law and ethical codes may even play a critical role in the overall legitimising process, as when their purpose is to restrain what is perceived to be an arbitrary and unjust exercise of power.[4] At all these stages where a normativity is founded on the postulate of sociability (which can also be expressed as a natural law

3 Inevitably, the natural leaning to sociability was understood in various ways by different early-modern authors. Jeffrey Dymond recalls how during the sixteenth century, some key arguments by Cicero on the subject, already well known in medieval learning, were given more prominence in legal scholarship. In his analysis of François Connan, Hugues Donneau and Johannes Althusius, Dymond analyses the reception – at times almost verbatim – of Cicero's ideas on the 'natural' emergence and development of civil society through the need of socialisation, but also how the fabric of social groups and ensuing polities required both a ruling authority and civil laws – natural law being applicable to a primeval state of nature, but inadequate to govern the more organised social communities and polities which subsequently developed. The latter required a *ius gentium*, differentiated from the natural law. In terms of governance, the Ciceronian influence was particularly striking in the emphasis by those early-modern jurists on the foundational role of law in the polity, but also for its functioning as a distinct entity (or 'personality'), and the need to have offices ensuring the rule of law and justice in society. In Connan's and Althusius' works, that scheme can even be recognised, albeit realised in different degrees, at various levels of a multi-layered polity.

4 Such a restraining function may even be recognised in a 'minimalist' concept of natural law, as in Henning Arnisaeus' philosophy set out by Paolo Astorri and Lars Cyril Nørgaard. Against the backdrop of contrasting Lutheran traditions and a backlash of some Lutheran theologians against what they perceived to be excessive encroachments of philosophy on the proper area of theology – a rivalry which entailed implications with regard to political governance – Arnisaeus sought to give a Ciceronian twist to human nature compatible with Paul's statement in his Epistle to the Romans that all humans have the law derived from God "written in their hearts" to define natural law as the "just reason and foundation of virtues." That capacity of rational beings to make judgements did not provide, in Arimaeus' argument, precise guidelines, and was not even foundational for the emergence of the polity. However, the authors point out, although Arimaeus did not specify the obligations

norm), natural law acquires a quality of *Sollen* increasingly distinct from the *Sein* of a (notional) pre-political natural state.[5]

The second feature which is associated with developing the social dimension of human beings as a result of their natural finality has consisted in linking the natural law to some notion of rationality. The rationality can be immanent (for example, it can include the very postulate of a living organism's natural finality), or it can be provided by an external actor – conveniently elaborated as a divinity which may be regarded as the author of the universe's creation, to which it assigns its finality, down to the finality of every living creature. Whereas the *ratio naturalis* of most creatures may appear unreflective, more like the particular instinct of a species, a human being's rational capacity may extend to self-reflection – and thus to a reflection on what the creation's or a human's natural finality is supposed to be – and even developed beyond the instinctive natural reason to more autonomous mental processes – possibly in quite specialised forms, such as for example the artificial reason

which may be derived from natural law, "it seems more important *that* natural law constrains the exercise of political power than the ways these constrains are implemented."

5 Moreover, apart from the more theoretical constructs of a 'natural order of things' referring to divine and natural law, that natural order has sometimes been recognised in apparently immemorial, but in fact historically contingent, institutions. As Pedro R.S. Santos points out in his chapter on Petrus Gudelinus' doctrines on feudal law (and, in its continuation, of the law of public peace), feudal institutions may at one stage have been regarded as part of the natural social and political order, but that perception was lost in early-modern times. Gudelinus remarked that no traces of feudal law could be found in the ancient Roman law, and he accepted the idea that it was a system that had been introduced after the Roman Empire's disintegration. However, because of its incorporation in the late-medieval corpus of civil law (and no doubt also because of its crucial role in the social, economic and political life of his time, and in legal practice), he fully accepted its place – witness his own commentaries – in the learned legal culture alongside the civil law. If the system of feudal law could therefore not be held to express a natural social order, but an 'organically' grown body of institutions and law, it relied nonetheless on a fundamental principle of public faith, which was recognised as a principle of natural law necessary for securing public peace, whether in the domestic political order or in relation with foreign polities. Gudelinus, in his attempts to systematise the law, appeared to be a pragmatic lawyer (an early *usus modernus* lawyer) rather than a 'rationalist' jurist: Santos highlights Gudelinus' "organic understanding of law and politics," opposed to "the frame of the feudal order as a geometrical body." This may be seen as a good indication that Gudelinus' understanding of natural law remained anchored in the late-medieval tradition: for in the later early-modern rationalist conception, a structure *more geometrico* conveyed precisely the 'real' structure of nature and the universe. In the eighteenth century, an English garden devised by Capability Brown brings to mind the artificial reason of the common lawyers, while the French garden laid out by André Le Nôtre, because of its strict geometrical outline, was supposed to express the true structure of nature, as grasped by a scientific reason.

early-modern common lawyers pretended to have acquired through long study and practice of English law.

## 5 Between the Devil of Positive Law and the Deep Blue Sea of *ius divinum*

The introduction of reason in presentations of natural law not only made it possible (or so authors claimed) to uncover and specify the already existing norms attributed to that law, it offered an opportunity to elaborate creatively theories of natural law. From the sixteenth century onwards, the theorisation of natural law, which during previous centuries had been held on a tight leash by the theorisation of divine law, emancipated (to some extent) from the theological discourse. This trend towards a secularised doctrine of natural law (as it is conventionally characterised in historiography) remained nonetheless, depending on the authors, more or less rooted in theological and religious groundwork, but it acquired greater autonomy as the institutional religious constraints lost their former grip on social life. At the same time, natural law thinking had to accommodate new political realities.[6] The deepening fault-line between Roman Catholicism and Protestant doctrines made it much more difficult to agree on common grounds with respect to religious issues: while some early-modern scholars devised natural law doctrines which fitted rather well their own political and religious environment, others, more ambitiously, recognised in natural law a potential for devising doctrines which, in their mind, might assert a greater validity by transcend-

---

6 Marie Seong-Hak Kim's chapter (which will whet the reader's appetite for her monograph *Custom, Law, and the Monarchy. A Legal History of Early Modern France* (Oxford: Oxford University Press, 2021)) analyses a prime example, through the prism of Bodin's understanding of the political mechanisms in France on which the increasing ascendancy of the monarchy rested, of how political reality could impose (and, in a way, 'sanction') principles of governance which acted as constraints that were not less strict than the authority often ascribed to natural or divine law. The monarchy's ever-expanding need for income through credit was met by devices such as *rentes* or the selling of public offices. In the long term, the system only worked if the monarchy honoured its debts and obligations, a duty it was forced to fulfil by virtue of natural law. However, it is clear that as regards creditworthiness, market forces were at play, and those could arguably even be less tampered with than natural law principles. Even so, in the context of sixteenth-century French politics, the monarchy could find some leeway for tapping resources normally unavailable, such as the Church's sources of income. The established legal concepts of emergency, public necessity and common interest could be harnessed to tamper with ordinary rules, and 'natural reason' could be called to the rescue for legitimising policies on behalf of the realm's superior interest.

ing the political-religious divide. It was no doubt a successful recipe for working out a natural law that might approach a blue-print for a law of nations (and later on in early-modern times, *ius naturale* and *ius gentium* became closely associated in scholarship on international law), but it also proved useful for legitimising sovereignty in domestic governance, at a time when the typical late-medieval pattern of concurrent sovereignty was giving way, both in theory and in practice, to a model of exclusive sovereignty. The *raison d'état* appeared prominently in writings on international relations, but it also pervaded domestic governance. *Potestas absoluta* had been a well-established feature of governance in late-medieval legal scholarship, but once concurrent political actors had been marginalised or neutralised in the internal political system, the potential and temptation to exercise that power more routinely led to a power culture which would later be decried as arbitrary or absolutist rule. Concomitantly, early-modern political theories reinforced their understanding of the formation of civil society and state from the perspective of the individual human being. Ultimately, it was through their individual reason that human beings came to create a polity. In contrast to Western European tradition and political reality, the various forms of covenant or social contract leading to the establishment of the polity were mostly hypothetically envisaged by natural law theorists to have been made by individuals, not by social groups – yet another reminder of a tendency among early-modern scholars to discount autonomous ephoral authorities between the supreme sovereign and the citizens.[7]

---

7 But no more than a tendency, and Geert Sluijs gives a striking counter-example in analysing (in contrast to Justus Lipsius' political writings) the work and teaching of Diodorus Tuldenus, who was writing at a time when the emphasis on the exercise of absolute power was gaining ground. In many ways, Tuldenus remained faithful to the original concept of legal studies developed in late-medieval universities, i.e. as the science of the art of good government, where justice as a central virtue and the rule of law played an essential role. In that approach to public governance, jurists, because of the expertise they had acquired in determining justice in conflicts of interests (whether in litigation or in deciding public policies) and because of their ability to deal with such conflicts within the boundaries of the law, had a call to take a significant part in the polity's governance. Sluijs' analysis establishes that Tuldenus, perhaps (looking at it with the benefit of hindsight) in what was in his lifetime a rearguard battle, resisted the brave new model of the exclusive sovereign and championed instead the benefits of concurrent political actors. In the long-term tradition of the Low Countries, but also against the backdrop of the Spanish rulers' will to neutralise those concurrent actors in his own day, Tuldenus appears to have favoured the key requirement of granting the Estates assemblies a control position on the levying of taxes, and thus also at least indirectly on the rulers' policies. The Joyous Entry of Brabant, despite its historical

In any case, a matrix of multi-layered governance would have faced the additional difficulty of accommodating the diversity of such forms of governance. In order to retain the strength of what had been the divine underpinning of natural law, the natural law of the rational individual had to stand the test of universal validity without being directly buttressed by the Creator's purpose. That test of universal validity would come to full fruition from the late seventeenth century onwards, strongly influenced by the successes of rationalist *more geometrico* thinking in the natural sciences. Before that time, however, emphasis on generally valid principles and processes are recognisable in the secularising literature on natural law. The emphasis was linked with already previously held views on the immutable character of natural law in time and space.[8] That emphasis was necessary in order to give natural law some weight against the historically and territorially contingent human-made positive law. As long as natural law enjoyed a niche between divine law and positive law, it had perhaps been easier to grant it a degree of flexibility. As now, one of the purposes of natural law theories consisted in overcoming the pre-national and ideological rifts within the (Western) Christian world – and in pretending to include in one's theories non-Christian populations and polities as well – the requirement of a quasi-independent natural law's claims to universal validity in time and space became more pressing.

While the religious pillar on which Western culture had rested was showing signs of material fatigue, the other pillar, the ancient classical Greek-Roman

contingency, to which every sovereign pledged their oath at the beginning of their reign, had become a fundamental law to which the sovereign had bound herself or himself: through that solemn commitment, there was an obligation from which natural law would not allow sovereigns to exempt themselves.

8 The issue of natural law's immutability is at the centre of Rafael Cronje Mateus' chapter. On that issue, the author offers a detailed illustration of Aristoteles' medieval reception by Thomas Aquinas, and, at the beginning of early-modern times, further elaboration of the latter by Domingo de Soto. The chapter shows how Aquinas' and de Soto's political thinking articulated around concepts of nature and reason were rooted in theology. Divine power was presented as a paradigm for the political ruler's power, though a modern reader may be tempted to see in that presentation a *trompe l'œil*, whereby theologians projected into the divine sphere the characteristics they wished to attribute to the Christian world's political rulers. Their theories rested on an anthropology supposed to recognise natural law's 'first principles,' beyond change, but its more particular and specific articulation ('conclusions') appeared to be more open to change. Since God's Justice was fundamental, and also the ideal model for the ruler's justice, de Soto worked out a theory which envisaged that God could change the specific application of (divinely based) natural law, by changing the nature of things, which he could as his own creation's *dominus*, without changing his Justice. This faculty, transposed (with some qualifications) to the ruler as *dominus* of his polity, could underpin a broad field of applications for the ruler's absolute power or Prerogative.

heritage, seemed more resistant and could further be strengthened by an enhanced historical understanding of the ancient world. Moreover, scholars enjoyed more freedom in their interpretations and handling of those classical sources. Although their reading and handling of 'pagan' works was often ideologically motivated, ancient Greek-Roman sources offered a less factional *res communis* for scholarly discussions. The revived interest in ancient classical culture during the sixteenth century is reflected in the more sustained references in many legal scholarly works of the time to a wide range of authors. The preference for certain authors and the way they were incorporated in arguments by early-modern scholars differed as they expressed various intellectual and political biases, yet, at the surface, there was a broad common pool of works from which scholars could net the formulas and ideas they specifically wanted for their own use. In that early-modern literature, references to Cicero were ubiquitous – to such extent that one may be tempted to wonder: since they had Cicero, why bother about natural law? If ever someone had thought of drafting a *lex citandi* of natural law authorities, Cicero may easily have topped the list.[9]

Divine law implied its own enforcement, if not in this life, then in one's after-life. The God of the Old Testament– constructed, one is tempted to say, in its often ruthless authors' image – revealed his at times inscrutable justice.

9 References to Cicero's statements on natural law and natural reason appear in most of the early-modern works discussed in the chapters of this volume, only occasionally with a critical note (as in the case of Tuldenus). Dymond gives a convincing analysis of Cicero's reception in Connan's work. Rosalind Acland's chapter discusses specifically Sir Edward Coke's use of Cicero in his theoretical and practical works. Coke appears to have incorporated partly reformulated key statements by Cicero in his own references to natural law throughout his work and reasoning. A comparative reading of some of his reports raises the possibility that such references may have been omitted in his forensic arguments, but that he integrated them when reporting the cases so as to give the reasoning a stronger theoretical underpinning, and perhaps also to enhance their educational value for students of the common law. (One may wonder whether it may also have served a strategy for making clear that this was a register of reasoning common lawyers were just as well familiar with as their civil law rivals). Even so, one is left with the impression that Coke was only satisfied to refer to (Ciceronian inspired) natural law by securing that it had been duly incorporated in the common lawyers' artificial reason. *Nulla salus extra ius commune anglicanum* is the constant unspoken undercurrent in Coke's work. Acland's analysis of some of Coke's most famous reported cases show that duly fortified by a dose of natural law, the common law could not only act as a justification for determining an issue, but also as a device for construing statute law, and as such as a control mechanism. Acland's reading of Coke's use of natural law may thus even provide an argument for the more general tendency in early-modern times towards a degree of 'positivising' natural law (here in the specific context of the English common law).

When early-modern natural law became less a derivation of divine law, immanent justice could still be claimed, but its enforcement was less evident. The professed universal validity of natural law required a strong ethical support in the communities where it was asserted, which in turn required a degree of specification. Specification resulted mostly in human positive law, sanctioned by human justice. In the hierarchy of authorities, natural law may have been positioned clearly above positive law, beyond the reach of any human lawmaker, who could neither change it nor depart from it, but early-modern legal culture grew increasingly proto-positivistic, with a growing chasm between the natural law's non-enforceable justice and the positive law's enforceability, even if it contradicted natural law. By the end of the *Ancien Régime*, the concept of a 'European Public Law' (*droit public de l'Europe*) in international relations (a concept which included elements of internal public law) tried to conceive the international community as a system similar to that of the physical world, the mechanisms of which were apparently being unlocked by the new natural sciences. The underlying idea was that, somewhat as the presumed equilibrium which natural laws preserve or restore in the physical universe, the international system was auto-regulatory, in the sense that if one element of the system disrupted the system's natural state of balance, such as a country starting a war, or verging towards hegemony, the other elements of the system would 'naturally' react so as to restore the balance and peace. Both the phrase and the concept of 'public law' applied to European inter-state relations are remarkable: because without adhering to some notional *civitas maxima* theory, it suggested nevertheless that the relations between states had solidified in a state-like system (in German, one comes in the eighteenth century occasionally across the translation: *Europäisches Staatsrecht*), with a corpus of treaties similar to codified law (as in the *codex iuris gentium*). References to a state and to codification in the context of a European system of sovereign states could at least imply that, contrary to conventional wisdom, these sovereign states were perhaps no longer in a primeval state of nature.

The *droit public de l'Europe* was a remarkable attempt to envisage a joint effect of natural reaction (such as an entity's sense of self-preservation) and rational considerations. In the era when *ius naturale* and *Vernunftrecht* were largely equiparated, other areas relied on a similar congruence between natural and rational behaviour: provided one's anthropology assumed a rational subject who would – barring aberrant circumstances – raise above its passions and act according to its natural sense of survival, self-preservation (and possibly self-improvement), the paradigm of a self-regulatory system could also be applied to individuals in conceiving a rational criminal law, or a rational law of contracts. However, even when rationalism had reached its zenith, the most die-hard rationalists would refrain from intimating that a human being's behaviour was consistently auto-regulated by reason. For all the superior status granted to natural law, its enforceability depended on the instruments of state governance, which inevitably brought it within the sphere of positive law. Throughout history, natural law has found it difficult to avoid being either overshadowed by divine law, or absorbed by positive law.

## 6 Natural Law Beyond the State of Nature?

Although omnipresent in early-modern jurisprudence, natural law was never an unambivalent notion – and the same can be said with regard to the human reason with which it was closely associated. Perhaps the best-known ambivalence can be related to those arguments which differentiated between a 'state of nature' and an organised 'civil society'. The features of the (hypothetical) state of nature depended on an author's anthropology, which could greatly vary. Similarly, opinions varied as to whether a principle governing the state of nature remained valid or not in the civil society.[10] For example, if one assumes that in the state of nature, the strong prevail over the weak, whether strong refers to brutish physical superiority, or the capacity of a weaker party to achieve physical superiority, does such a (*ex hypothesi*) 'natural law' principle remain valid in the established civil society ("Might is right" in a literal

10 Carlos Pérez-Crespo gives a critical survey of modern scholarship on Hobbes, specifically focused on the categorisation of Hobbes as a 'naturalist' or 'positivist,' whereby the issue at stake is whether the sovereign's power is limited by natural law or not. The discussion shows that much depends on what scholars have read in Hobbes' natural law (and in which of his books). From the abundant literature he refers to, Pérez-Crespo highlights in particular the 'anachronistic' (one may also say: diachronic) readings by A.E. Taylor who gave Hobbes' natural law a moral purpose of Kantian inspiration, and by N. Bobbio, who is credited with 'conceptualising' Hobbes' natural law as a *Grundnorm* not unlike Kelsen's. Do any of these readings answer the question, whether natural law, either as a moral obligation or as a foundational norm legitimising the sovereign, could in any way restrict the Hobbesian sovereign's powers? The question leads to a Catch 22 dilemma when it is raised with regard to the citizens' problematic right of resistance, as natural law may be seen to oblige the citizens to obey the sovereign's law absolutely, but there may be exceptional circumstances where the sovereign's command is to such extent incompatible with the very purpose of the state (and perhaps the very first commandment of God) that citizens would be entitled to resist and disobey such a command. The problem for Hobbesian scholars is therefore not so much how one constructs the legitimacy of the sovereign's power, but whether and how that power can ever be delegitimised.

sense – for in the state of nature where physical force prevails, there is not much point in differentiating between right or wrong, legal rights do not exist, and behaviour cannot be ascertained according to a standard of justice)? The theme does not pertain to scholarly discussions only: for centuries, it has grasped the popular imagination, not least through the many adaptations of Aesop's fable of the wolf and the lamb, which itself had many close equivalents in non-Western cultures. But does the dialogue between the wolf and the lamb take place in a state of nature? Aesop's purpose is to illustrate the point that the wolf first tried – through several accusations which were as many 'fake stories' – to justify his intention to kill the lamb by claiming that the latter had wronged him. The story therefore may suggest that there was some kind of norm which could justify avenging a wrong. Regardless, the wolf ends up killing the lamb with total impunity. The French version by Jean de la Fontaine, first published in 1668 (the same year when Hobbes published a revised version of *Leviathan* in Latin, and when the treaty of Aix-la-Chapelle rewarded Louis XIV's invasion of the Spanish Netherlands with substantial territorial gains), provides even more elements for reflection: the opening sentence refers explicitly to reason (in the sense of justification, but reason expresses itself through reasoning: "*La raison du plus fort est toujours la meilleure*"), and the fable ends in its final sentence with the killing without any due process of law or justice ("*sans autre forme de procès*"). In-between, the lamb has at first proved the wolf's accusations to be factually incorrect because impossible, but finally, the wolf comes up with a more plausible argument: the lamb enjoys the protection of those who wage a constant and merciless war against wolves (shepherds and their dogs). The moralising character of fables inevitably implies that even in the state of nature, dos and don'ts apply, but without being enforced. Of course, the whole tone of La Fontaine's version may betray a critical note with regard to the superiority of the wolf's reason – but the criticism does not go beyond describing (hardly even deploring) a sorry state of affairs. If any such criticism was intended, ironically, it would have been aimed at the persistence of the "might is right" norm in a context where the stage of civil society had been reached, where it should no longer have been applicable.

The issue of identifying any norms in the state of nature, and determining whether they still applied – legitimately or not – in the civil society divided some of the most influential natural law writers. In 1674, Spinoza wrote to an acquaintance: "As far as Politics is concerned, the difference you ask about, between Hobbes and me, is this: I always preserve natural Right unimpaired, and I maintain that in each State the Supreme Magistrate has no more right over its subjects than it has greater power over them. This is always the case in the state of Nature."[11] From that passage, one may infer that Spinoza held that there was continuity between the state of nature and the state of the civil society, at least with regard to the foundation and extent of state power in domestic governance. At the same time, his answer suggests that such a continuity was not upheld in Hobbes' political theory.

Despite a widely shared terminology and the disposition to emulate methodological features of mathematical and scientific models, early-modern 'rationalist' natural law scholarship was not monolithic. Diverging strands led to distinct and recurrently conflicting orientations. One rationalist tradition, sometimes dubbed as a form of rationalist monism, considered that the human reason provided the deductive method allowing to work out natural law from 'evident' premises, but also principles of action, and was therefore self-sufficient as the foundational human capacity to construct natural law. Another tradition considered that, besides the deductive rational capacity, a degree of empirical observation and analysis was required in order to establish principles of natural law. To some extent, the first tradition reflected the endeavours of some scholars to retain the recognition and construct of natural law as an exclusively human prerogative, whereby action was inferred from rational necessity. The second tradition emphasised the obligations in natural law (in particular, inherited from the Creator's will), which required more space for the human will and freedom. The parameters of these traditions could be further complicated as the notion of sociability could be articulated in varying degrees. In the second, non-monistic tradition, the understanding of obligations could differ depending on whether one was referring rather to an external ('personal') God or to some immanent divinity. With some simplification, one may draw a fault-line by testing an author's thought on the issue whether the ethical sphere is part of the natural world or not.

On such a infinite spectrum natural reason could be called to encompass, it became possible to lose sight of God and divine law. Although some natural law authors preferred to steer within close range of the shoreline of divine governance, arguing that the natural order reflected after all God's own creative spirit, for others, that very argument was precisely an encouragement to venture on the high seas, where the divine ordering became invisible behind the horizon. Early-modern authors, however bold their theories, could rarely be caught red-handed on an offence of atheism. Secular tendencies of natural law maintained in the end at least a tenuous link with a religious (Christian) foundation, but their itinerance could be mostly autonomous from any sus-

11 Benedictus de Spinoza, *The Collected Works of Spinoza vol. 2*, ed. and trans. Edwin Curley (Princeton: Princeton University Press, 2016), Letter 50 (2 June 1674), 406.

tained reference to God and his law. Christian rulers could still refer to be sovereigns by the grace of God, and even polities beyond the Christian world could be said to have legitimacy because they existed according to (the Christian) God's design, but the challenge an increasing number of political theorists referring to natural law sought to meet was to explain the foundation of polities within the natural order – which various forms of rationalist self-confidence claimed to be possible without relying, except for a minimal acknowledgement of deference, on the divine. Early-modern natural law scholars did not give leave to God in order to elaborate by themselves their theories, but admitted that his presence was no longer required as it had been in a previous age where political theory was dominated by theology. Early-modern scholars would not declare that God was dead. Even if they had admitted that he had died (*quod sine summo scelere &c.*), or even if one were to follow the most radically secular reading of their works, divine law, to borrow a formula from a different context and age, was still seen to rule natural law from his grave.

And although several chapters in the present volume have highlighted how early-modern authors writing on natural law reflected the particular political environment and circumstances of their age – de Soto in early Habsburg Spain, Bodin in late-Valois France, Goudelin and van Tulden in the Spanish-controlled Netherlands under the Archdukes, Locke and Hobbes in Commonwealth, Restoration and post-Stuart England... – the circulation of their works beyond the fault-lines of Catholic and Protestant jurisdictions is at least some indication to what extent their natural law theories could operate as common ground, if only for maintaining the polemical debates within the boundaries of a shared scholarly culture.

The real fault-lines between early-modern discourses on natural law before the paradigm of exclusive sovereignty was also worked out to some extent in European political reality need to be looked for elsewhere. In the continental civil law tradition, as it started with the study of Roman law texts in universities and the production of canon law scholarship and legislation, the purpose of that late-medieval jurisprudence had been to promote a science of the art of good government. Meta-juristic concepts of Justice, the Common Good (or Public Interest), Peace... were fundamental in developing the methods and reasoning (starting from the statements and cases in the *corpora iuris*) for dealing with issues of policy and conflicts of interests at different levels of public governance. Jurisprudence provided a framework, which was perhaps first and foremost a political and legal culture, ensuring that public governance was exercised within a rule of law, in the sense that from policy decisions down to their implementation in specific cases, legal principles and rules directed the decision-making process, but always with the purpose of the fundamental concepts in mind. The so-called *ius commune* expressed as a form of a positive legal system was no more than the outer crust of that legal culture of governance. As several chapters in the present volume show, even when that crust started disintegrating and was partly recycled as *ratio scripta*, the ideals of the fundamental concepts required by good, i.e. legitimate, governance remained powerful references in the writings of sixteenth- and early seventeenth-century authors. At the same time, power relations and their theorisation in several polities underwent profound transformations, and these were reflected in political theories. Although the terminology of the old ideals of governance was upheld, the ideals themselves were affected by these transformations, and so was the natural law that was supposed to underpin the new political theories.

While God remained *in absentia*, early-modern natural law, as it became more secular and autonomous, could be channelled in different, at times opposite directions. Whatever their take on natural and positive law, i.e. wherever and however they recognised reason and order, or chaos and passions, early-modern scholars were all the more challenged to bridge or reconcile the growing chasm of natural law's oxymoron. That challenge and its ensuing polemics were some of the most fruitful effects of early-modern natural law theories. In that sense – and bearing in mind that some of the most formidable minds of the epoch contributed to the debate, as documented in the essays of this volume – one may conclude (notwithstanding the dreadfully bad pun) that in the continuous scholarly efforts trying to make sense of public governance, both domestic and international, early-modern natural law proved a most useful moron.

# Index


Albert and Isabella, Archdukes and Sovereigns of the Netherlands 112–114, 140–141
Althusius, Johannes 75–79
Ammirato, Scipione 122
Andreae, Jacob 149
Aristotle 43–47, 49, 52, 144–148, 150, 152, 154, 156, 163, 175, 178–179, 181–182, 202
Arnisaeus, Henning 146–150, 153–160
Aquinas, Thomas 41–51, 118, 157, 161, 163–164, 213, 251
Azo, of Bologna 164, 179

Bartolus, de Saxoferrato 59, 251
Besoldus, Christopher 116
Bodin, Jean 13–27, 31–39, 84, 153
Botero, Giovanni 119
Bracton, Henry of 163–165, 173–174, 178–179

Cardano, Gerolamo 122
Cato the Elder, Marcus Porcius 124
Cato the Younger, Marcus Porcius 139
Caselius, Johannes 145–146, 155
Charles IX, King of France 28
Charles V, Holy Roman Emperor 42
Charles, Prince of Asturias 53
Chemnitz, Martin 145, 149
Chyträus, David 145, 149
Cicero, Marcus Tullius 61, 64–65, 67–69, 71–73, 75–79, 93, 106–107, 122, 129, 139, 156–157, 161–167, 169–173, 175–181, 186, 192
Connan, François 61–67, 70–75, 77, 79
Contzen, Adam 157
Coke, Edward 161–192
Coornhert, Dirck Volkertszoon 112
Cujas, Jacques 87, 103

da Costa Barreto, Roque 254
da Costa Nunes, Francisco 257
de Covarrubias y Leyva, Diego 157
de l'Hôpital, Michel 27–28, 31–32
de Malestroit, Jean 15–16
de Mariana, Juan 157
de Vitória, Francisco 42, 84, 132
de Ribadeneira, Pedro 119
de Robespierre, Maximilien 86
de Soto, Domingo 40–41, 47–49, 52, 54–56
de Souza, Tomé 253
de Ulhôa, Antônio Lopes 254
Destrée, Pierre 44
de Ubaldis, Baldus 59–60, 90
Doddridge, John 169
Donellus, Hugo 61, 63, 65–67, 70–73, 75, 77, 79
Duarenus, Franciscus 87, 101
Dumoulin, Charles 99
Duns Scotus, John 50

Fleta (author of) 174
Fortescue, John 164, 173, 178, 181
Francis I, King of France 17, 21
Francisco de Mello, Marcelino 238–239, 245, 250, 253, 255, 257, 259–260, 262
Frederik I Barbarossa, Holy Roman Emperor 104

Gaius (Roman Jurist) 92
Gentili, Alberico 132, 158
Gerson, Jean 163
Gratian 59, 155
Grotius, Hugo 19, 90, 116, 144, 160, 163, 202, 206
Gudelinus, Petrus 83–86, 88–89, 92–109
Günther, Owen 145–146, 152

Hesenhus, Tilemann 149
Hobart, Henry 190–191
Hobbes, Thomas 19, 132, 134, 144, 195–216
Hofmann, Daniel 151–152
Hooker, Richard 163
Hotman, François 37, 87, 103, 139
Huber, Samuel 151
Hunnius, Ägidius 151

Innocent IV 58

Justinian I, Roman Emperor 34, 84, 98, 107, 124, 131, 164

Kant, Immanuel 203–206, 208–209, 215
Kelsen, Hans 206, 209–212, 215–216
Kirchner, Timotheus 145

Littleton, Thomas de 170, 173, 186–189
Lipsius, Justus 19, 111–131, 133, 135, 137–141, 143
Locke, John 90, 217–237

Machiavelli, Niccolò 111–112, 114–117, 119, 122, 123, 125
Maitland, Frederic William 57–58
Matthiae, Christian 154–155, 157
Martini, Cornelius 146, 150, 152, 154
Melanchthon, Philipp 144–146, 157
Moore, Francis 166

Ockham, William of 50

Panormitanus (Niccolò Tedeschi) 59
Pasquier, Étienne 22
Plato 117, 157
Pfaffrad, Caspar 151
Pufendorf, Samuel 144, 163, 202, 220
Puteanus, Erycius 113, 126, 128–129

Quintilian 169

Schmitt, Carl 200, 203, 206–207, 210–211, 216
Selnecker, Nicolaus 149
Seneca the Younger, Lucius Annaeus 100, 111, 115–116, 121–122, 126–127, 130, 157
St. German, Christopher 161, 178–179, 186
Strauss, Leo 44, 202–203, 212
Suárez, Francisco 19, 157, 163

Tacitus, Publius Cornelius 111, 137
Taylor, Edward Alfred 196, 203–209, 211–212, 215
Thomas, John Henry 163–165
Tönnies, Ferdinand 202, 214–216
Tuldenus, Diodorus 113–116, 123, 126–143

Ulner, Peter 149

Vásquez, Gabriel (Vasquius) 105, 157
Vindiciae, Contra Tyrannos (author of) 139
Voegelin, Eric 44
Von Gierke, Otto 57–58

Whitaker, John 89

www.ingramcontent.com/pod-product-compliance
Lightning Source LLC
Chambersburg PA
CBHW051401240926
51852CB00002B/80
*9789004748705*